IN THE RING
WITH
JAMES J. CORBETT

Adam J. Pollack

Win By KO Publications
Iowa City

In the Ring With James J. Corbett

Adam J. Pollack

(ISBN-13): 978-0-9799822-5-5

(hardcover: 55# acid-free alkaline paper)

Includes footnotes, appensix, bibliography and index.

Manufactured in the United States of America.

Win By KO Publications

Iowa City, Iowa

winbykopublications.com

Contents

Preface: A Unique Approach

For those of you who have read *John L. Sullivan: The Career of the First Gloved Heavyweight Champion*, you already know my style. This is volume 2 of my series on the heavyweight champions of the gloved era, which I like to call *Reigns of Fame and Shame*. It is the most thorough, detailed, well-researched and cited biography of James J. Corbett's rise and championship career ever written.

This book is for the avid boxing enthusiast who wants greater detail and accuracy than boxing books typically provide. Corbett's own autobiography omits many fights and exhibitions and contains multiple glaring inaccuracies. Unlike most Corbett biographies, this book contains extreme detail based on local primary source accounts, cites its sources, corrects past inaccuracies and omissions, and focuses more on Corbett's boxing life rather than personal life. I rely on multiple local stories and analyses to give a broader and more accurate perspective on Corbett's career. This book:

1. Presents facts and analysis that no other book has presented, revealing previously unknown historic knowledge to address many unsolved mysteries.
2. Provides and cites multiple local and national primary source fight accountings to highlight differences in what was said at the time, rather than to simply put forth one version of truth.
3. Analyzes opponents' careers so that the significance of Corbett's bouts against them can be put into perspective.
4. Discusses Corbett's skill development and presents critiques of his style and skill over the course of his career, offering a broad perspective of viewpoints, and noting how opinions changed over time.
5. Provides social, legal, and historic context and analysis to explain how events outside the ring impacted what was or was not allowed to take place inside the ring. This includes a discussion of the impact of anti-prize fight laws and the color line.

As with the Sullivan book, I tell the story of Corbett's fight career up to and including his championship reign. Extensive details of his loss of the crown and post-championship fights will be provided in subsequent books, focusing on how those bouts related to other champions' careers.

I bring to life an era's boxing scene, to assist you in experiencing the period and to understand these fighters' relative merits. I analyze fighters, who they fought, and why those bouts were important. Providing fighter backgrounds and context for what others were doing at the time brings to life what the bouts meant and creates a better framework to assess a champion's career.

Without the benefit of film, it is difficult to determine the accuracy of mere written accounts. The reality is that many observers can witness the same event and have many different perspectives regarding what occurred. We cannot see the bouts and develop our own opinions, and therefore must rely on these written accounts. Whenever attempting to reconstruct historic events, analysts must consider such issues as sight, memory, ability to comprehend what is being seen without the benefit of replay, whether the reporter actually saw the bout or is relying on others, and the particular selection of facts to report. Also to be considered is the objectivity, honesty, and motivation of sources recounting events, including the extent to which a reporter embellishes or adds facts, desire to boost sales, impact of bribes, personal feelings towards a fighter based on his race, personality or style, historic judging perspective and criteria, and local allegiances. This is why it is so important that more boxing books provide multiple fight accountings and citations to sources, as this book does.

By presenting multiple viewpoints, this book provides you with an overall feel for what was said about what occurred so that you may draw your own conclusions. The book also meticulously cites sources so that you can cross-check them yourself, instead of having to rely on unsupported and often inaccurate assertions so typical of boxing books.

When not utilizing multiple sources, I usually try to rely on a local source, because local writers are usually the most accurate and thorough, and the author most likely actually viewed the bout. That said, local accounts are not always the final word, because sometimes non-local reporters were more interested in a fight than were the locals, though they may or may not have been more objective.

Ultimately, by combining factual results, well researched analysis of sources, and history, sociology, and law with critical views of the bouts, I have told the story of this champion in a unique way so that you may obtain a new perspective about James J. Corbett.

CHAPTER 1

Corbett and the Transition

Since the early 1700s, bareknuckle boxing had been the norm. Rounds ended only when or as soon as an opponent was wrestled, thrown, or knocked down. Unless a fighter went down, the round continued indefinitely, but a round could also end very quickly if a fighter was dropped within the first few seconds. A downed boxer had 30-38 seconds to again continue. There were no limits to the number of rounds. Holding and hitting was legal. Fights were often lengthy wars of attrition. This was how boxing was conducted for well over a century.

In America and England, the law clamped down hard on bareknuckle pugilists, often sentencing them to lengthy terms of imprisonment and imposing hefty fines if they were caught. In the late 1800s, gloved boxing under the Marquis of Queensberry rules gradually rose to prominence, primarily because of the slightly less stringent legal stance towards such bouts. These bouts had fixed three-minute rounds with one-minute rests. If knocked down, boxers had to rise and continue after only ten seconds. Wrestling, and holding and hitting were made illegal. Depending on the agreement, points decisions could be rendered. Such bouts were perceived as less brutal and more civilized, and were often tolerated if they were sold as limited-rounds exhibitions of skill. Nevertheless, gloved boxing certainly had its own legal hurdles to overcome.

In the early 1880s, the phenomenal heavyweight champion John L. Sullivan made gloved bouts popular across the United States, and began gloved boxing's path towards acceptance as a legitimate sport which could determine a man of championship merit. During the mid- to late-1880s, the shift to gloved bouts as the norm was perceptible. Still, because of its lengthy history and prestige amongst fight purists, bareknuckle bouts under the traditional London Prize Ring Rules occasionally continued being practiced during that decade, even sometimes by champion Sullivan.

James J. Corbett is the first heavyweight champion that fought his entire official career only in gloved Marquis of Queensberry rules bouts. As such, he represents the completion of the transition from the bareknuckle era to the gloved era of boxing. He is also the first boxing champion to have some of his bouts recorded on film.

Despite the increased acceptability of gloved boxing, the law and boxing continued doing battle, and would continue doing so during Jim Corbett's career. By the mid- to late-1880s, Corbett's hometown of San Francisco was often allowing gloved fights to the finish as long as they were held in athletic clubs. Still, there remained a certain political, social, and legal uncertainty about the sport. Most states, including California, would oscillate back and forth between legalizing boxing, then banning it, and then reversing themselves. Political opposition was a constant impediment that the sport confronted, and the courts often got involved.

Like John L. Sullivan, Jim Corbett dealt with many legal obstacles. In Sullivan's time, laws made "prizefights" illegal. One of the ways boxers eluded these statutes was by arguing that only bareknuckle boxing under the London rules were prizefights, that those laws did not cover gloved boxing. During Corbett's rise, many states shored up the legal loopholes and passed laws specifically banning gloved boxing as well. Still, California was one of the few places in the country that occasionally perceived professional gloved fights to the finish as legal.

Regardless of the legal and political opposition, boxing was increasing in popularity and participation throughout the 1880s. This was mostly thanks to Sullivan, who made boxing a popular money-making national and international sport. More and more athletes were taking up the sport and capitalizing on its appeal. Short, typically 4-round gloved exhibition bouts in athletic clubs were commonplace activities throughout the country.

During his career, Corbett capitalized on the popularity that Sullivan had gained the sport, often performing in plays and friendly exhibitions. At that time, there was no television or movies to keep the populace entertained. Thus, people were more than willing to pay to see theatrical performances and athletic exhibitions, both of which often included boxing. Like Sullivan, Corbett made plenty of money both as an actor and as a gloved exhibitionist.

Jim Corbett stood anywhere from 6'0" to 6'1 ½", and usually weighed in the 180-pound range. He was known as "Pompadour Jim" (because of his hair style) or the "California Wonder," and only much later became known as "Gentleman Jim," as a result of a play that he performed in called *Gentleman Jack*.

Stylistically, Corbett was in many ways the antithesis of Sullivan. The ferocious Sullivan attacked with speed and power to knock out his opponents quickly. Corbett had a speedy but more cautious, defensive, and less powerful style. He was renowned for his crafty boxing skills, utilizing slick footwork and good head movement, as well as clinches and other defensive techniques. He had excellent timing and was a superior judge of distance. Ring intelligence was necessary given that he was not a big puncher or risk taker. He threw quick punches to the body and head and had a complete offensive arsenal, but did not have the huge power of a rare devastating puncher like Sullivan. Corbett was a precursor to the styles of boxers like Gene Tunney and Muhammad Ali, and as such, was gloved boxing's first masterful stylist. A fancy boxer such as Corbett was perfect for the type of skilled exhibitions that were generally allowed by the law under the gloved system, even in some of the strictest jurisdictions.

John L. Sullivan, 1882

Also unlike Sullivan, Corbett learned to box through instruction at a boxing club, having an amateur career before turning pro and gradually gaining national notoriety. Sullivan learned boxing from observation and experience, and was so amazingly talented that he almost immediately rose to the top of the sport as a professional, taking on the best the world could offer, generally scoring knockouts.

Corbett made a calculated ascent, slowly gaining valuable experience and knowledge before tackling the world's best. During his years at the local San Francisco Olympic Club, Jim boxed in a number of amateur exhibitions. These were generally short limited-rounds gloved exhibitions, sometimes to a decision. He boxed fellow amateurs, but also exhibited against top professionals. He often utilized his speed, footwork, and defensive skill to defeat stronger and more experienced opponents in bouts for points. Boxing with professionals in short bouts gave Jim the experience and knowledge he needed in order to later take on the world's best in lengthy fights to the finish in the pro game. Corbett also had a number of informal semi-secret or private fights in places like his father's stable or outside of town. Such experiences enabled Corbett to hone his skills carefully over time and made him the craftiest boxer in the world.

During the 19th century, being an amateur brought greater social prestige amongst the upper and middle classes than did being a professional. Amateurs, who boxed for love of sport and glory, were considered gentlemen to be revered, while professionals, who boxed in fights to the finish for money, were often referred to as "pugs," a derisive term. Being an amateur was seen as an end in and of itself, rather than merely a stepping stone to the pro game. Many athletes remained amateurs for their entire careers, and were part of a prestigious subculture. This is the world of which Corbett became a part. To earn a living, Corbett was a bank teller by day, and boxed in the evenings. He was also eventually hired by athletic clubs to be a salaried boxing coach, or "professor," as they were venerably called at that time.

Being a professor at an athletic club brought with it respect, prestige, and some money. Having a talented professor and exhibitor such as Corbett increased the popularity of the athletic club with which he was associated. Jim was a popular boxing coach and had a number of pupils under his tutelage. It is often said that teaching helps the teacher learn and reinforce his own skills. Professor Corbett sparred often with his students, and occasionally gave exhibitions with them and professionals before club members. At his best, Corbett could give both boxers and punchers fits. He truly was a learned artist.

Corbett could have quite easily remained an amateur and boxing professor for the rest of his life, but he was good enough and ambitious enough to be something more. When he later engaged in professional matches, Jim could subsequently return home to continue his occupation as a boxing professor in between fights, or he could travel around making money by giving exhibitions, all of which kept him in sharp form. Thus, whether as a boxing amateur, a professor, a professional, or a traveling exhibitor, Corbett always had a place and a way to work constantly on his skill, making him a formidable world class boxer and eventually heavyweight champion of the world.

CHAPTER 2

The Experienced Amateur

James John Corbett was born on September 1, 1866 (eight years after John L. Sullivan) and grew up in the San Francisco area. Like Sullivan, Corbett was of Irish descent. As of 1880, the United States contained 38 states and 49.3 million people, but over the next decade would grow to 44 states and over 62 million people. Corbett's home state of California had a total population of less than one million.[1]

Much of what historians know about Corbett's early career has come from his own recollections. Unfortunately, Corbett's autobiography omitted a number of bouts, did not provide dates for most of the bouts he discussed, and he sometimes mixed up the order of the ones that are known. It has been difficult to discover exactly when some of Corbett's fights occurred. He also had a tendency to exaggerate or alter stories in order to make them more interesting, and as we all know, with time, memory fades. His accounts will sometimes be reproduced herein, but will be counterpointed against primary source research revealed here for the first time, solving many of the mysteries of his career and providing a more accurate picture of events.

Corbett said that as a youngster, he was not shy about engaging in street fights with fellow grade school students. Corbett told of what was perhaps his first fight, one with a larger boy who was six years older (possibly an exaggeration), named Fatty Carney. An approximately 14-year-old Corbett knew nothing of boxing other than what he had once observed from one fellow (years later Jim said that he had watched his older brother box). Still, instinctively he was able to utilize head movement and footwork to avoid blows. He also used a trick he had observed, of looking at the stomach but striking at his opponent's face, which was somewhat of a feint. Because Jim was doing better in the fight, Carney eventually wrestled him to the ground to use his superior brute strength. However, the wrestling was stopped by an older man who told Carney to fight fair or he'd cane him. They resumed and Corbett eventually licked him. The next day, Jim was expelled from school for having had this fight.[2]

---

[1] The 1890 U.S. Census reflected that there were 62,116,811 total people in the U.S. The three states with the largest populations were New York (5,997,853), Pennsylvania (5,258,014), and Illinois (3,826,351). California only had 1,128,179 persons. The total U.S. black population was listed as 7,388,182. Compare this with the year 2000 U.S. Census, which shows the total U.S. population to be 281,421,906, California to have 33,871,648 people, and the total black population to be 34,658,190.

[2] Richard K. Fox, *The Life and Battles of James J. Corbett, The Champion Pugilist of the World* (New York: Richard Fox, 1892, 1895), 7-9; James J. Corbett, *The Roar of the Crowd* (New York: G.P. Putnam's Sons, 1925), 5-7.

Jim was enrolled in a different school, but his extracurricular fighting continued. He kept gloves in the family stable, and occasionally fought there, as well as around town in places like the fire engine house and a blacksmith shop.[3] Jim eventually gained a bit of a local reputation.

Corbett said that even before having any formal training, one of his early boxing experiences was against Billy 'Forty' Kenealy in Jim's father's stable. It was an even match for a while until Jim ducked and came up with his head, striking and dazing Bill by accidentally landing his head on Kenealy's chin. Bill was almost out when it was stopped.[4] Corbett and Kenealy would eventually become sparring partners at the Olympic Club, where they were fellow pupils. Some secondary sources indicate that while there, Corbett defeated Kenealy in a 4-round bout. Bill later became a Corbett pupil.

Corbett's fighting and disciplinary problems eventually got him expelled from school once again, this time at age 14 or 15. When disciplining Jim for his behavior, a teacher whacked his hand with a stick, but Jim refused to give him the other hand. After being chased about by the school's teachers, Jim rammed his head into the stomach of one of them, knocking that teacher down. His school days were over.

Subsequently, Corbett took a position as a bank clerk at the local branch of the Nevada Bank in San Francisco. According to Jim, he held that job for about six years, keeping it throughout his early boxing career. Corbett was the boxing banker.[5]

Corbett has also said that although he had no training, he began boxing frequently in informal bouts as a young boy as early as 1879, when he was about 12 or 13 years old. "During this period from 1879 to 1886 – I used to box frequently."[6] Corbett likely began fighting a bit later than he recalled.

A little known story Corbett told in 1895 was that local neighborhood gang rivalries often lead to fights. A young 12-year-old Corbett was assigned the task of fighting a smaller boy named Joe Robinson. However, the unschooled Corbett got pounded in the eyes, nose and mouth, drawing blood, causing swelling and raising lumps on his forehead. His followers stopped the fight and led him away.

> That was an awful blow to my vanity. It set me to thinking and later on I made friends with that boy. He told me that his big brother was a clever boxer and that he had taught him how to fight. I resolved as soon as I could to learn how to fight, a resolve which I subsequently

[3] Corbett at 9-12.
[4] Fox, *Life and Battles* at 9.
[5] *New York Clipper*, September 10, 1892; Corbett at 9; Armond Fields, *James J. Corbett: A Biography of the Heavyweight Boxing Champion and Popular Theater Headliner* (Jefferson, North Carolina: McFarland & Co., 2001), 11-12. Fields focuses more on Corbett's personal and theatrical life, at 1 saying, "Until now, his personal life and extensive theatrical career have never been researched or revealed." Fields called Corbett's autobiography "revisionist history." See also, Patrick Myler, *Gentleman Jim Corbett: The Truth Behind a Boxing Legend* (Great Britain: Robson Books Ltd., 1998), 10-13.
[6] Corbett at 9-12.

made good. That fight taught me the worth of science in fighting and indirectly put me where I am today.[7]

An 1889 newspaper account of Jim's early career said that Corbett began boxing in his father's livery stable in Hayes valley at age 15 (around 1882). Before he was 16 years old, he "managed to get away with all the youths of pugilistic propensities in that quarter of the town." After becoming a bookkeeper at the bank, he "used to practice boxing every evening in the stable on any one that might turn up." Clearly, Corbett gained a bit of a local reputation as a fighter even before he had any formal training.[8]

Heretofore unknown by historians is the fact that eventually, an Olympic Club middleweight named Denny Dillon gave Corbett boxing lessons at the stable. "After having given him lessons for six months he asked Corbett to join the Olympic Club, as he thought he could beat any one there. Corbett accepted the invitation, joined the Olympic Club and from this time may be dated his first recognition as a pugilist."[9] Thus, Corbett did have some boxing experience and a bit of schooling even before he was taught at the Olympic.

According to Jim, at about the time he entered the Olympic Club (probably late 1884 or early 1885); he had an informal street fight with "Jewish" Joe Choynski and knocked him out cold in the 1st round.[10] Nearly a year later, the two met again. This time, Choynski had been taking boxing lessons at the local Golden Gate Club. Choynski staggered Corbett with a right, but a few seconds later, Corbett dropped him. That same day, Corbett fought Choynski's brother and put him out for the count.[11]

There is semi-primary source evidence that Corbett defeated Choynski at least twice as youths, likely somewhere between 1884 and 1885. They would fight twice more, in 1887 and 1889.[12] Richard K. Fox's 1892 Corbett biography claimed that Jim scored a KO1 over Choynski in his father's barn, a later KO2 with bare knuckles, and still a year later, a KO1 (this third bout is unconfirmed). These were not formally sanctioned bouts but simply private meetings between two local toughs.[13]

An 1889 account of Corbett's career provided this story of his early meetings with Choynski:

> The first time Corbett ever met Choynski was in the Hayes Valley Livery Stable. [Choynski] came out one evening with seven friends to

---

[7] *Cleveland Plain Dealer*, February 24, 1895.
[8] *San Francisco Evening Post*, May 30, 1889.
[9] *San Francisco Evening Post*, May 30, 1889.
[10] Corbett at 38; *Daily Picayune*, January 26, 1894; Myler at 27 claimed Choynski quit. The first Corbett-Choynski fight likely occurred before Jim joined the Olympic Club, but this is unclear.
[11] Corbett at 40.
[12] *National Police Gazette*, March 8, 1890; *New York Clipper*, September 10, 1892. Corbett and Choynski likely fought twice as youngsters, then again in 1887, and for the fourth time in 1889. In late 1889, Corbett said that he had defeated Choynski four times. *Portland Evening Telegram*, December 27, 28, 1889.
[13] Fox, *Life and Battles* at 10-11.

do up the terror of the valley. He put on the gloves, but after the first round was glad to quit, as Corbett had given him a most unmerciful drubbing. After this Choynski took lessons for six months, and he arranged a fight with bare knuckles between himself and Corbett. The fight took place on the sand hills at the head of California street. Corbett stopped him in the first round. Choynski's next appearance was at the Olympic Club when he fought a four-round contest with Corbett, in which he was considerably worsted.[14]

Their bout at the Olympic took place in early 1887 (to be later discussed). Little did young Jim and Joe realize that they would both eventually become well respected world-class contenders. As professionals, they would meet again.

During the 1880s, while Corbett was a young lad, John L. Sullivan was the world heavyweight champion, and future champion Bob Fitzsimmons was a 154-pound middleweight boxing in New Zealand and Australia. At the time they were boxing, a heavyweight was anything above middleweight, which was a mere 154 pounds (11 stones by English standards).

As of March 6, 1884, George Robinson was the Olympic Club's heavyweight champion, and on that date, Corbett was amongst a huge crowd that watched Robinson disgrace himself against a prime John L. Sullivan, incessantly dropping to the floor in order to avoid Sullivan's blows, until he was disqualified in the 4th round. An estimated 12,000-15,000 observers attended the bout, generating around $20,000.[15] Back then; this was huge money, especially given that most people didn't make much more than $1,000 in a year. This likely demonstrated to Corbett the financial gain to be had from status as the heavyweight champion. Boxing could mean big bucks.[16]

---

14 *San Francisco Evening Post*, May 30, 1889.

15 Mike Donovan, *The Roosevelt That I Know* (New York: B.W. Dodge & Co., 1909), 138; *New York Clipper*, March 15, 1884; *San Francisco Daily Examiner*, March 7, 1884; *Daily Picayune*, April 12, 1884, citing a San Francisco newspaper report.

16 According to one source, adjusting for inflation (most likely using the consumer price index), the $20,000 the Sullivan-Robinson fight earned John L. in 1884 was the equivalent of $395,723.64 in 2005. What costs $20,000 today would only cost $1,010.81 in 1884. According to another source, based on nominal GDP per capita, $20,000 in 1884 was the equivalent of $3,963,159 in 2005. Using the unskilled wage rate, $20,000 was the equivalent of $2,418,461.54 in 2005. The Inflation Calculator, http://www.westegg.com/inflation; Samuel H. Williamson, "What is the Relative Value?" Economic History Services, June 2005, http://www.eh.net/hmit/compare. "The CPI is most often used to make comparisons partly because it is the series with which people are most familiar. This series tries to compare the cost of things the average household buys such as food, housing, transportation, medical services, etc. For earlier years, it is the most useful series for comparing the cost of consumer goods and services. It can be interpreted as how much money would you need today to buy an item in the year in question if it had changed in price the same as the average price change. The GDP per capita is an index of the economy's average output per person and is closely correlated with the average income. It can be useful in comparing different incomes over time. The unskilled wage rate is good way to determine the relative cost of something in terms of the amount of work it would take to produce, or the relative time it would take to earn its cost. It can also be useful in comparing different wages over time. The unskilled wage is a more consistent measure than the average wage for making comparisons over time."

George Robinson, 1884

In his 1925 autobiography, Corbett recalled his first observations of a 26-year-old Sullivan. He said that a young Sullivan was much different from an old Sullivan. The aged Sullivan was thought of as sluggish, heavy of foot, standing in one place, and only having a right. However, Corbett said that a prime Sullivan was a terrific hitter with both hands and was pretty quick with both his feet and hands, as fast as heavyweight champion Jack Dempsey of the 1920s. Still, Corbett also felt that Sullivan was not a highly skilled fighter, calling him a member of the "slugger class."[17]

According to some later sources, in about 1884, Corbett was an athlete at San Francisco's Olympic Athletic Club, the preeminent and oldest athletic club in America, where amateur athletic training, exhibitions and tournaments in a myriad of sports took place.[18]

Corbett in his autobiography was not specific as to when he joined the Olympic Club. He said that he entered the club during the time that a substitute gym was being used, while a new one was being built. A fire had burned down the club's first gymnasium on June 20, 1883, so it was obviously sometime after that, and the new club was not finalized until 1885.[19] *The History of the Olympic Club*, published in 1893, said that Corbett joined the club in 1884, but did not say when during that year he joined.[20]

According to Corbett's autobiography, like Sullivan, his first love was baseball, and he initially played that sport at the Olympic. Training in many sports took place there, such as baseball, gymnastics, wrestling, fencing, track and field, and boxing.

Eventually, Corbett tried his hand at boxing. According to his autobiography, he told the German club boxing instructor that he had boxed hundreds of times, and wanted to box with him. The two sparred and the instructor showed him up.

---

[17] Corbett at 115-116.
[18] Cyberboxingzone.com; Corbett at 21; *National Police Gazette*, June 17, 1905. The Olympic was founded in May 1860. Fields at 15.
[19] Corbett at 12-13; Fields at 16; *The History of the Olympic Club* (Art Publishing Co.: San Francisco, 1893), 25.
[20] *Olympic Club* at 81.

The next day, although only middleweight sized (according to him), Jim sparred the 215-pound club heavyweight champion, who Corbett called "Blackbeard" because of his big beard. The unschooled Corbett was knocked out. Jim said that he did not take up boxing there again until about a year later.

Whether or not this is a true story is unknown. Corbett was not beyond telling interesting stories in order to increase book sales. This story was not told in the 1892 Fox biography.[21] However, it makes a certain amount of sense: A cocky young and talented fighter with some successful informal experience gets badly shown up by knowledgeable trained fighters, and does not really take up the sport again until he later receives proper coaching.

Jim said that he really started to learn boxing after the new club opened and the Olympic hired Professor Walter Watson to be its boxing instructor.[22] The approximately 30-year-old Walter Watson was born in London, England in 1854 and he began boxing when he was 18 years old. He won several boxing tournaments and began giving instructions at age 20, being hired by several prominent London boxing clubs. In 1883, Watson came to New York to teach boxing, working at Wood's Gymnasium and the New York Athletic Club. During that time, on August 2, 1884 in Philadelphia, Watson sparred with Jack Dempsey.[23]

The lease for the new Olympic Club was signed on March 10, 1885. On March 30, 1885, Walter Watson, "a celebrated exponent of the manly art," arrived in San Francisco from the east coast to teach boxing at the Olympic Club. "Watson recently knocked out the famous pugilist, Professor McClellan, in New York City."[24] Thus, Watson could not have given an 18-year-old Corbett formal boxing instruction any sooner than April 1885, because he did not teach at the Olympic until this time. It might have been even later than that when Jim first started taking lessons from Watson.[25]

Things really got going at the newly opened Olympic in April 1885. An April 21 issue of the *San Francisco Chronicle* said, "The gymnasium of the Olympic Club is now open to members, and already the spacious rooms, replete with the most novel and expensive apparatus, are well patronized by members of the club, who are very proud of their gymnasium." The evening classes were set for Monday, Wednesday, and Friday from 8 to 10 p.m., while the afternoon classes were Tuesday, Thursday, and Saturday from 4 to 6 p.m.[26]

---

[21] Corbett at 12-14; Fields at 14, 16; *Olympic Club* at 25. The German instructor may have been Lamartine Fulda (a.k.a. Lem Fulda), who was of German ancestry.

[22] Corbett at 12-14.

[23] *San Francisco Morning Call*, December 3, 1896; *New York Clipper*, August 9, 1884.

[24] *Daily Alta California*, March 31, 1885.

[25] Although before now, every Corbett biography has claimed that he began publicly exhibiting in 1884, they are incorrect, likely relying on Corbett's inaccurate memory. See Fox, *Life and Battles* at 10; Fields at 14-16.

[26] *San Francisco Chronicle*, April 21, 1885, December 12, 1886.

Professor Walter Watson, 1883

The Olympic Club held the grand opening of its new gymnasium on May 5, 1885, celebrating its 25th anniversary. It was called the most popular club in the Western metropolis, containing luxurious parlors with expensive furniture, reception-rooms, billiard-rooms, a club house, and a gymnasium hall with machines "to set every muscle of the body in motion." Members and their lady escorts, totaling about 1,200 to 1,500 persons, enjoyed a program of music and dancing.[27] The club was destined to be the area's most popular social and sporting hub.

The following is the earliest account of a Corbett bout, revealing for the first time when Corbett first publicly boxed. A month and a half after Walter Watson arrived in San Francisco, on May 19, 1885; an athletic tournament of the Pacific Coast Amateur Association was held at San Francisco's Mechanics' Pavilion. It featured track events, bicycle races, wrestling, a tug of war, gymnastics exercises, weightlifting, and "sparring," meaning boxing. Six athletic clubs participated. After some running and bicycle races, fellow lightweight Olympians T. McCord and De Witt Van Court gave a boxing exhibition. Corbett had likely sparred with these men during their training at the Olympic.

The second boxing exhibition was between the Pythian Athletic Club's William T. Welch and 18-year-old J.J. Corbett. The local press listed both Corbett and Welch as heavyweights. Corbett was actually a heavyweight much sooner than most realize, even from the beginning of his training at the Olympic. The belief that he was a middleweight during these years was likely formed in reliance upon Corbett's later incorrect claims that he was only a middleweight.

The *San Francisco Chronicle* merely said of their exhibition, "Welch showed superior hitting powers." The local *Daily Alta California* said that all

[27] *San Francisco Chronicle*, May 6, 1885.

of the sparring exhibitions were enjoyable to the spectators and creditable to the boxers. However, it also said that Welch was "particularly worthy of mention." The *San Francisco Call* was more direct in stating that Welch was better. "Welch was altogether too quick, and won without an effort." Thus, it appears that Welch caught the eye of the press more so than Corbett did.

Weightlifting and an exhibition on the horizontal bars followed. Welch was then defeated in a spirited middleweight Greco-Roman wrestling match against Gus Ungerman. Welch's being listed as a heavyweight boxer but middleweight wrestler may have been due to the fact that the two sports had different weight classifications. This is unclear. Fellow Olympians Joseph Benjamin and Eugene Van Court, both of whom were likely also Corbett sparring partners, then gave a lightweight wrestling exhibition. Other events followed.[28]

It is not known exactly when, but some months later, Corbett boxed Welch again and apparently stopped him or made him quit in the 1st round. An 1890 source reporting Corbett's early meetings with Welch said that before Watson took Jim in hand, "he knew so little of the fistic art" that William Welch "defeated him easily in a scientific four-round contest for a gold medal." However, "After Jim had the benefit of Watson's instruction for a few months he made extraordinary progress, and on meeting Welsh again in a sparring bout in the Acme Club nearly knocked him out in one round."[29] Thus, it is possible that even as of mid-May 1885 that Corbett had not yet taken lessons from Watson. However, at some point in 1885, Corbett benefited from Watson's teachings and quickly improved.

Corbett said that he sparred often with Professor Watson, who showed him the sport's finer points. Soon thereafter, to their amazement, Jim was able to defeat his older brothers in sparring.[30]

Without mentioning the Welch bout, an 1889 account of Corbett's early career said that Jim's first set-to at the Olympic was against Lem Fulda, who later became president of the prestigious California Athletic Club, where mostly professional bouts took place. "The first to feel the weight of Corbett's blows was L. Fulda, now President of the California Athletic Club. At that time he was the leading middleweight of the Olympic. Corbett, however, went at him pretty heavily, and made him stop in about

---

[28] *San Francisco Chronicle*, April 28, May 19, May 20, 1885; *Daily Alta California, San Francisco Call*, May 18, 20, 1885. In the days prior to the exhibition, William was called either Welch or Welsh, but the post-exhibition reports listed him as Welch.

[29] *San Francisco Chronicle*, February 24, 1890. The Acme Club was located in Oakland. See also *Brooklyn Daily Eagle*, June 9, 1895; Michael T. Isenberg, *John L. Sullivan and His America* (Chicago: University of Illinois Press, 1988), 304. Corbett does not report these fights in his autobiography and no dates are listed in these and other sources. Most early accounts of Corbett's record do not mention the Welch bouts at all, and Corbett was generally said to have been undefeated as an amateur. However, they did in fact box.

[30] Corbett at 16-17.

four minutes."[31] Fulda later denied that they had boxed, but Corbett confirmed that they had:

> Do you blame him for denying it? Why, I was only a kid when that happened. Now, if a kid should lick me, I don't think I would like to have it known, either. But, just the same, that statement in the Post was true to a letter. Fulda won't deny it in my presence. This is just how it happened: Walter Watson, who was then instructor at the Olympic Club, was somewhat vexed at the manner in which Fulda used to criticize his pupils. Fulda would frequently put on the gloves with one of Watson's pupils, and "give him points," which he said Watson was not capable of teaching. So one day when Fulda made one of these propositions to me, Watson took me aside and told me to punch Fulda as hard as I could. Well, we had it, and I thumped him until he quit.[32]

However, Professor Watson contradicted the assertion that Corbett had bested Fulda:

> Professor Watson says that when he became instructor at the club Fulda was the best boxer there. Fulda was most gentlemanly in his conduct toward his pupils and never acted as described in the published statement referred to. He always assisted beginners with his advice, and the only set-to he had with Corbett was a spar in the attic, which was a mere friendly affair on which no question of respective merit could be settled. Fulda was about retiring from active membership with the club when Corbett came on the scene so that there never was any rivalry between them.[33]

Given that Watson was present, this sparring session obviously took place after March 30, 1885, and likely after May 19, if Corbett did not become a Watson student until after the first Welch bout. Corbett's boxing with Fulda has never before been mentioned by secondary sources.

Two months after the first Corbett-Welch bout, on July 24, 1885, the Olympic Club held the first of what would be a future series of events in which its members were entertained by various athletic contests. It was largely attended, and the first part of the program was what the *Alta* called "a lively four-round set-to between Messrs. Corbett and Grosenberg, in which the former displayed science and hitting powers that made his antagonist bear considerable resemblance to a shuttle-cock." This bout has never before been mentioned by any secondary source. Clearly, even then, an 18-year-old Corbett demonstrated some ability. The *Chronicle* said that on

---

[31] *San Francisco Evening Post*, May 30, 1889.
[32] *San Francisco Evening Post*, May 31, 1889.
[33] *San Francisco Chronicle*, June 3, 1889. In 1890, Lamartine Fulda was described as standing 5'10", weighing about 200 pounds, and being born of German parents. *San Francisco Morning Call*, May 11, 1890.

future tournament nights boxing would be made a principal feature, for Professor Watson had a number of students prepared to contest in that sport.

That evening's entertainment also featured a Greco-Roman wrestling match between Dave Eiseman and Joseph Benjamin. Eiseman would one month later box Corbett. The *Chronicle* listed Eiseman as weighing 137 pounds to Benjamin's 127 pounds. At this point, Eiseman was said to be better known as a boxer than wrestler. Benjamin pinned him and won the wrestling match.[34] Eiseman was mentioned in a March 1884 issue of the *National Police Gazette* as being from the Golden Gate Club and having won an amateur walking race against a member of the Olympic Club.[35] A late April 1885 issue of the *San Francisco Chronicle* called Eiseman a middleweight wrestler and boxer.[36] Clearly, Eiseman was an all-around athlete.

For the first time, primary source evidence of Corbett's exhibitions with both Dave Eiseman and Mike Cleary has been located and revealed herein, clearing up a century's worth of prior uncertainty and confusion regarding when these bouts actually took place and what happened.

On August 28, 1885, the Olympic Club held another one of its exhibition nights before a crowd of 1,500 to 2,000 spectators. Professional Mike Cleary was the featured guest, and he sparred with two amateurs: Jim Corbett and Dave Eiseman, who later in the evening sparred with each other. Boxing Cleary was significant for Corbett because the 5'8 ½" 175-pound Cleary was well respected and world renowned, considered both powerful and skillful.

Mitchell defeats Cleary, San Francisco, 1885

---

[34] *Daily Alta California, San Francisco Chronicle*, July 25, 1885.
[35] *National Police Gazette*, March 22, 1884.
[36] *San Francisco Chronicle*, April 28, 1885.

Mike Cleary

Mike Cleary had fought the who's who of boxing, having many recorded fights going all the way back to 1875. Amongst his more notable early bouts, he defeated Jimmie Weeden in an 1876 70-round bareknuckle fight that lasted 1 hour and 38 minutes. The powerful Cleary had won quite a few of his numerous fights via early knockout, usually as a result of his famed right hand. He had an 1882 KO3 over former John L. Sullivan foe George Rooke. In 1883, Cleary engaged in a 3-round exhibition bout with Sullivan. Mike was reported to have had a 5-round draw with Dominick McCaffrey. In 1883, Cleary was dropped and being pounded on by Charley Mitchell until the police stopped the bout in the 3rd round. In 1884, Cleary fought Jake Kilrain to a 4-round draw and "lost" a 4-round official draw decision to Jack Burke.

In February 1885, Cleary knocked out former Sullivan opponent Captain James Dalton in the 1st round. The police stopped a May 1885 Cleary-Mitchell rematch in the 4th round, with Mitchell being the superior fighter. One report said of Cleary that "[h]e has a right half-arm jolt that is simply terrible."[37]

According to the local *Daily Alta California*,

> Mike Cleary was the star of the evening, and his appearance with the club members gave many of the onlookers valuable points and hints as to the defects of amateurs generally, which do not become conspicuous until shown off by comparison with a graceful professional.

Cleary boxed 2 rounds with Corbett, who was called the "coming heavyweight of the Club."

---

[37] Boxrec.com; *Daily Alta California*, March 2, April 27, 1885. Cleary would much later help spar with and prepare John L. Sullivan for his 1889 bout with Jake Kilrain.

Corbett and Cleary opened, and gave a very clever exhibition. Corbett's reach and strength were tremendous, but not equal to Cleary's science and quickness, and the latter was easily able to secure the best of it, especially as Corbett did all the leading. Mike was very gentlemanly, however, and did not attempt to make a show of his opponent, who has only been taking lessons something over three months. In the second round Corbett wisely let Mike do the leading, and contented himself with solid returns without making much of an attempt to guard.[38]

This account, by saying that Corbett had only been taking lessons for "something over three months," supports the position that Corbett began taking lessons from Walter Watson in around May 1885. It also once again indicates that Corbett was a heavyweight, even at that point. Also, although well thought of, the much less experienced Corbett was not seen as being quite on Cleary's level. Other local accounts agreed.

According to Corbett, after they boxed, Cleary told him that he was a comer and would be a great boxer one day, that Corbett got away from his right better than anyone he had ever fought.[39] There is later evidence that Cleary was in fact quite high in his regard for Corbett.

After Cleary and Corbett sparred, Tom McCord and Jimmy Smith boxed 2 rounds. Cleary then sparred 2 rounds with Dave Eiseman. Eiseman was vigorous with his onslaughts, but Cleary eventually took control of matters. Eiseman gave a very creditable showing in both rounds and was applauded. McCord and Smith then boxed 2 more rounds while Eiseman rested.

The final bout of the evening was between Corbett and Eiseman.

Corbett was considerably the larger, but Eiseman was confident that his experience and science would carry him through, and he began fighting. The adherents of both were doubtful of the result, but it was not long in abeyance, for a most complete transformation took place. Corbett, who made a comparatively poor showing with Cleary, went at once to the front, and Eiseman, who had done very well, retrograded until he was but a child in the heavyweight's hands. The hitting was hard and rapid, and Corbett punched the unfortunate all over the ring, fighting him to a standstill just as time was called at the end of two minutes. The second round opened vigorously, but Eiseman was too distressed at the end of a few seconds to continue it, and appealed to the referee to know whether the contest was a setto or a fight to a finish. The official admonished Corbett, but a heavy left-hander from Eiseman set the ball rolling again, and before two

---

[38] *Daily Alta California*, August 29, 1885. Corbett and others have incorrectly claimed that these exhibitions took place in 1884, and on different dates.
[39] Corbett at 28.

minutes was up Eiseman quit, partly through the intervention of friends and partly through desire.[40]

The *Chronicle* also confirmed that Corbett and Cleary sparred, though without providing details, and gave its description of the Corbett vs. "Eisman" exhibition.

> The final bout was between the two club men, Eisman and Corbett. The latter was fresh and outweighed his opponent, who had not wholly recovered the wind which Cleary knocked out of him. In the first round there was some hard hitting, in which Corbett got the better of it. In the second round Corbett went in for a knock-out, and Eisman's condition by that time was so much impaired that he was quickly fought to a standstill and a knock-out would have followed, had not Professor Watson, the boxing teacher, stopped the contest.[41]

The *San Francisco Call* confirmed that Cleary boxed 2 rounds each with Corbett and Eisman, "in which the superiority of professional over amateur boxing was only too apparent." It said that the event of the evening was the wind-up between Corbett and Eisman, "each claiming superiority as a boxer and representing different factions in the club."

> Eisman appeared to poor advantage from the first, being no match for his antagonist, who is a much heavier man than he and consequently forced him around the circle, tapping him hard or light as he felt inclined and showing a decided preference for fairly hard amateur hitting from the shoulder. In the second round the referee reminded Corbett that the boxing was only for fun, while Eisman showed an inclination to quit. Corbett in the middle of the round good naturedly poked his glove under the nose of his mortified antagonist several times and Eisman, concluding that he had had enough, retired from the circle amid the whoops and yells of Corbett's delighted friends. Neither men displayed any science in the encounter and Corbett's victory was purely the result of superior weight, strength and good nature.

Another less detailed local source, the *San Francisco Evening Post*, said that Cleary showed that he knew much more about boxing than Eisman and Corbett, and that the set-to between Corbett and Eisman was a slugging match until the referee interfered. "The club experts say that Corbett was all over Eisman."[42]

These accounts alter the previous historic understanding of Corbett and Eiseman's meeting. Clearly, this was part of an exhibition show in which both had previously boxed Mike Cleary, Corbett was a heavyweight and was

---

[40] *Daily Alta California*, August 29, 1885.
[41] *San Francisco Chronicle*, August 29, 1885.
[42] *San Francisco Evening Post*, August 29, 1885.

much larger than Eiseman (who one month earlier had been listed at 137 pounds), the rounds were only two minutes long, and in the 2nd round, Eiseman either voluntarily retired or it was stopped by Professor Watson, not wanting to see him absorb further punishment and be completely knocked out. This was not Jim's first bout at the Olympic, nor was it a bout for the club middleweight championship as some have reported. The press generally referred to Corbett as a heavyweight and Eiseman as a middleweight.[43]

An 1889 account of his career said that the Eiseman bout took place three months after Corbett entered the Olympic Club, after his bout with Fulda. If true, it would put Corbett's entry into the Olympic in 1885. The Welch bout was not mentioned by this source.[44]

The day after the Corbett-Cleary/Eisman exhibition, on August 29, 1885 in Cincinnati, Ohio, heavyweight champion John L. Sullivan dropped Dominick McCaffrey several times en route to a 7-round decision victory. Later that year it was said that Sullivan had earned at least $157,000 in his career, but his spendthrift attitude and tours of bar rooms calling for wine had left him $16,000 in debt.[45]

Corbett also discussed the fact that he had the opportunity to spar privately with world middleweight champion Jack Dempsey, who was then considered the best overall boxer in the world, other than Sullivan. Dempsey was undefeated in at least 25 fights.

According to Jim, in their sparring, Dempsey began with multiple feints, but Corbett was good at maintaining himself just out of range and did not react to the feints. Eventually, the two exchanged blows, and the better Corbett did, the harder Dempsey fought, until it became a ferocious battle. Dempsey ended it after 30 minutes, impressed with Corbett. The two weighed themselves afterwards, with Dempsey scaling in at a mere 144 pounds. Corbett claimed to have weighed 160 pounds (though his claimed weights for himself tend to be much lower than what was usually the case). Corbett said that he gained a bit of a local reputation for doing so well against a world champion.[46]

Dempsey was staying in the San Francisco area, having bouts in Northern and Southern California from May to September 1885, so their sparring likely took place during that time. There is evidence that Dempsey later highly touted Corbett. An 1889 source said that Dempsey recognized Corbett as perhaps the most scientific sparrer in the country.[47]

---

[43] *Daily Alta California, San Francisco Chronicle*, July 25, 1885; *San Francisco Call*, August 29, 1885.
[44] *San Francisco Evening Post*, May 30, 1889.
[45] *Daily Alta California*, October 5, 1885.
[46] Corbett at 28-33; *Daily Alta California*, January 21, 1889.
[47] *Morning Oregonian*, December 10, 1889, December 12, 1889.

Corbett could have possibly sparred with Mike Cleary on other occasions in private as well, because in early October 1885 it was reported that Cleary was "taking daily work at the Olympic Club."[48]

Corbett knew how to learn and improve from every sparring encounter, and he had plenty of sparring opportunities at the Olympic. Jim realized the importance of boxing skill and strategy:

> A boxer to be successful must study his man as an artist studies the subject for a picture. "Feel him out" if possible without giving your own points away. Study two or three different counters for every blow, so that your opponent will not know which one to expect. Keep any plan you have formed well in mind and wait for an opportunity to use it.... Early in my experience I found that a sure judgment of distance and a quick eye were absolutely necessary to make the good boxer.... I used to allow the boys to swing for me to see how nearly I could estimate their reach. Practice enabled me to gauge the blows so closely that I could feel the wind of their gloves on my face. ...

> I think I have learned a point or two from every man I ever put up my hands against. They would have a few things with which I was not familiar, then after the bout I would go to my room or the gymnasium and practice them until I got them down fine. ...

> Early in my experience I used to be fond of parrying blows. I found that they would sometimes get through my guard in spite of everything. Then I began to rely upon my legs and my eyesight. I found it a great deal better plan. If I was not sure of what a man intended to do I found it the best plan to step to my right and keep away until I sized up my opponent's intentions. ... About the only time I ever parry a blow is when I am cornered and the rope will not allow me to get back.[49]

On October 9, 1885, it was ladies' night at the Olympic Club, which meant that members could bring their female companions to the exhibitions. Women would eventually become part of the handsome Corbett's fan base.

After some Greco-Roman wrestling matches, Corbett boxed 3 rounds with E.G. Slossen or Slosson, one local source saying that Corbett won the bout. Other boxing bouts followed, including one between Professor Watson and a fellow named "Hare," who was likely James Hair.[50]

The ladies' night exhibitions were quite popular and successful, for the members were in full attendance. "Watson as professor of boxing is

---

[48] *Daily Alta California*, October 5, 1885.

[49] *Daily Picayune*, September 13, 1892.

[50] *Daily Alta California, San Francisco Evening Post*, October 10, 1885. Gymnastic athletic feats followed the boxing.

distinguishing himself through the achievements of his pupils." The Olympic Club was lauded. "No club in the world offers such advantages as does the Olympic. For $2 a month any one who is eligible can receive gymnastic, sparring, fencing and wrestling lessons from the best of instructors."[51] Corbett was receiving that instruction, sparring privately with fellow pupils, Watson, and sometimes pros, and then sparring again during special exhibition evenings.

On October 23, 1885, amongst the athletic exhibitions held at the packed Olympic Club gymnasium, Corbett and James Hair gave a "clever three-round exhibition with the gloves." This was likely the same Hare/Hair who sparred with Watson a couple weeks earlier. Another report said, "Corbett and Hair gave an excellent exhibition of fistic skill."[52]

A report of a November 6, 1885 Olympic Club tournament said that Corbett was supposed to box the winner of the Slosson-Hager (who might actually have been James Hair) heavyweight match, which took place that same night. That bout was so rough that the referee twice had to utilize the amateur rule which allowed him to end a round when either man had been fought to a stand-still, causing the rounds to be only one minute each. After his victory, Slosson was groggy and tired and could not go on. Therefore, Corbett "claimed the bout with Slosson by default, which the referee was obliged to give." Corbett was the Olympic Club's heavyweight champion.

Corbett was also supposed to box "Master Watson," but the Professor, who had earlier exhibited with another man, passed. "Mr. Corbett was to have boxed the Professor, but the latter being too much blown the rubber was decided in favor of Corbett." Thus, it appears that everyone was too tired to box Corbett that night.[53]

Later in the month it was said, "Complaint is made that there is too much 'slogging' and too little science about the sparring exhibitions at the Olympic clubrooms." Generally, the boxers were supposed to work with one another in these exhibition bouts and not try to take each others' heads off. At that point, the club was reported to have 726 members.

Around that time, local law enforcement officials began cracking down on professional boxing. "Boxing is dead here, and will be unless the present legal strictures are removed or pronounced unconstitutional." Naturally and thankfully, this did not affect Corbett. Being an amateur allowed him to continue boxing exhibitions unencumbered.[54]

On December 3, 1885, at another Olympic-sponsored exhibition show, there were "spirited boxing bouts by J. Corbett, J. Hair and E.P. Slosson."[55] It is unclear as to who boxed with whom, or whether all three boxed with

[51] *San Francisco Chronicle*, October 13, 1885.
[52] *Daily Alta California*, October 24, 1885; *San Francisco Chronicle*, October 27, 1885.
[53] *San Francisco Chronicle, Daily Alta California, San Francisco Evening Post*, November 7, 1885.
[54] *San Francisco Chronicle*, November 24, 1885; *Daily Alta California*, November 30, 1885.
[55] *San Francisco Evening Post*, December 4, 1885.

each other in round robin style, as was often the case. Another report said that amongst the usual myriad of sporting exhibitions and song, Walter Watson, Jim Corbett, J. Hair and E.P. Slosson engaged in sparring. It too lacked details regarding the pairings.[56]

Despite the attacks on professional boxing, amateur boxing was being praised.

> There is a very large and respectable element in San Francisco which takes an interest in sparring as an athletic exercise and a source of amusement. To be a spectator of a properly conducted pugilistic exhibition is not unworthy of a gentleman, and in England the upper classes have from time immemorial patronized the ring. Respectable patronage has everywhere succeeded in making the mere sport of boxing respectable.[57]

On January 1, 1886, a new San Francisco athletic club was organized, called the California Athletic Club. It had a hall capable of seating 800 people. Its teachers were brothers Sam and Richard Matthews. It opened February 1, and would eventually become a home to many top local and world class professionals, as well as some amateurs.

On January 22, 1886 at an Olympic Club exhibition, Corbett sparred with James McCarthy, who earlier that week was called an amateur pugilist of great promise, who had been developed in a very short period of time under Watson. Apparently McCarthy did quite well with Corbett. A subsequent report said,

> A newspaper reporter who witnessed the boxing of Corbett and McCarthy last Friday night at the Olympic Club seemed to have been led astray by ignorance of the technicalities of the manly art. McCarthy is the most promising of Mr. Watson's pupils, no doubt, but he has not, as yet, been put to a real test by Corbett. It is not unlikely the discussion caused by the recent exhibition may lead to a serious encounter between them. The following letter points somewhat in that direction:

> To the Editor of the Chronicle – Sir: It was stated in a morning paper that Corbett, heavyweight champion of the Olympic Club, was "bested" by a member of the club last Friday evening. Corbett claims that it was only an exhibition and therefore he only went in for a friendly set-to, and that he is still champion of the club and is ready at any time to defend that title. A FRIEND.[58]

A secondary source claims that in late May 1886, Corbett again exhibited with McCarthy, and this time Jim dominated. Unfortunately, no primary

[56] *Daily Alta California*, December 4, 1885.
[57] *San Francisco Chronicle*, December 15, 1885.
[58] *San Francisco Chronicle*, January 19, 26, 1886.

source citation was offered and this author has been unable to confirm it. A mid-February report said that McCarthy had not been heard from lately as a result of his being "constrained to relax his practice somewhat, as his father objects to his wearing any laurels that have been won in the ring."[59]

In early February 1886, the *Chronicle* wrote, "Pugilism...seems to be attracting considerably more than its fair share of attention. ... In spite of the law of the municipality several determined fights are likely soon to come off in this vicinity." The Olympic Club was doing so well that the initiation fee was set at $10, and it was up to the discretion of the board to raise it if the membership grew to over 750 members.[60]

During February, it was said that California Club Professor Richard/Dick Matthews and Corbett *might* give a boxing exhibition. Matthews was a 28-year-old 180-pound boxer who had begun his career in 1882 in Australia, and had quite a number of bareknuckle and gloved victories. It is unclear whether Jim and Dick actually ever exhibited. A secondary source claims that Corbett knocked him out in the 2nd round, but offers no primary source citation to prove the fight. Nothing has been found to support it, and the bout was not reported in any of Corbett's semi-primary source records.[61]

During January, it had been said that a strong effort would be made to bring about a glove contest between Corbett and Captain James Dailey/Daly while the latter was in the city. They were supposed to exhibit on February 12, 1886 before 200 members of the Olympic, but Daly failed to appear. Corbett instead boxed 3 rounds with Professor Watson.[62]

The Olympic saw the new California Club as a threat and in March issued an edict barring its members from participating there. "The Olympic Club is foolishly looking upon the California Club as a rival, judging from a resolution passed by the directors, which threatens all members participating in any of the California Club's contests with disbarment from the Olympic's amateur contests." Another paper lamented, "Many of the most valuable men of the Olympic have joined the California, and this action will tend to only further estrange them."[63]

On May 14, 1886, women turned out in such large numbers for the Olympic's ladies night exhibitions that it was crowded beyond its seating capacity. Two local papers said that Corbett gave a set-to with Robert

---

[59] Fields at 20-21; *San Francisco Chronicle*, February 16, 1886.

[60] *San Francisco Chronicle*, February 2, 9, 1886.

[61] *San Francisco Chronicle*, February 2, 16, 1886, November 3, 1885; Fields at 20-21.

[62] *San Francisco Chronicle*, January 19, 1886, February 13, 1886, March 9, 1886. A report as of early March said that Daly had left San Francisco. Daly and Corbett would eventually box, but it was not likely during this time. None of the weekly reports mentioned their boxing together. Captain James Dailey appears to be a different person than the later James Daly who became Corbett's sparring partner.

[63] *Daily Alta California*, January 26, 1886, March 15, 1886; *San Francisco Chronicle*, March 9, 1886. In late March 1886, Olympic Club Professors Sam Matthews and Captain Jennings left that institution to work at the California Club, receiving more money there, greater than the $50 per month they were receiving at the Olympic. *Daily Alta California*, March 29, 1886; *San Francisco Chronicle*, December 12, 1886.

McCord, who later reports listed as weighing 148 pounds. "McCord, though a much smaller man than Corbett, managed to hold his own against 'the crack of the club' with much credit."[64]

Oddly enough, another local paper said that Corbett boxed with William Welch, and did not mention McCord. "The sparrers amused the spectators but did no hard hitting."[65]

On the 28th, there was a large attendance at the Olympic's "gentlemen's night," which featured boxing and wrestling. Corbett was supposed to have exhibited with the California Athletic Club's Con Riordan, but one paper said that Riordan backed out at the last moment, "much to the disappointment of the audience and the disgust of Corbett, who declared: 'I am ready to spar anybody; I don't care who it is.'" Another paper said that the "outsider" had apparently failed to receive notice on time.[66]

Watson's skill as a teacher was being recognized, even on the east coast. In June, the *New York Clipper* noted that Watson was on vacation for a month and quoted a local San Francisco journal as saying, "Professor Watson in the short time he has been with the Olympic Club has made more and better boxers out of our California boys than we ever had before, and Corbett, McCarthy, Rhodes, O'Brien, McCord and others are young men that any athletic club in the world might be proud of." Jim probably sparred in the gym with all of those men.[67]

Corbett likely had many more bouts than what history has recorded. Some of his exhibitions and sparring matches were not officially recorded or extensively reported in the newspapers. It is therefore difficult to determine many of their dates or their exact order.

Regardless, it is clear that during his amateur career, Corbett gained consistent valuable experience against veteran professionals, Professor Watson, and other amateurs. Having short, limited rounds bouts also helped ensure that he could learn without the increased risk of being hurt in a lengthy professional finish fight. Corbett considered himself an amateur until about four years later, although as will be seen, his amateur status was questionable.[68]

---

[64] *Daily Alta California*, May 15, 1886; *San Francisco Chronicle*, May 15, 1886, November 8, 1890.
[65] *San Francisco Morning Call*, May 15, 1886. The evening's exhibitions also included wrestling, horizontal bars, lance exercises, acrobatics, and fencing.
[66] *San Francisco Morning Call, Daily Alta California*, May 29, 1886.
[67] *New York Clipper*, June 26, 1886.
[68] Corbett at 23-24.

CHAPTER 3

The Hippodromer

James J. Corbett became a professional boxer in July 1886. In late June, a 19-year-old Corbett traveled to Salt Lake City, Utah. After getting married there, wanting to make some money, Corbett signed to fight Frank Smith, Utah's heavyweight champion, for $100 a side, with the winner to take all of the gate money. The title of the local *Salt Lake Herald* article was "To a Finish," the stipulated length of the bout.[69] Thus, this was actually Corbett's first professional fight.

Corbett and Smith fought on July 3, 1886. Corbett hid his identity, giving his name as "Jim Dillon" so that he could make some money but continue to retain his amateur status. The Olympic Club only supported amateurs, and only those who boxed exclusively for it.

According to Corbett's autobiography, on the night of the fight, Smith thought that he had figured out that Dillon/Corbett was actually top world contender Charley Mitchell incognito. Mitchell was known as "the gentleman pugilist" because he dressed well. Since working for a bank, Corbett had dressed well, so Smith mistook him for Mitchell. Fearing that he would get his head taken off, Smith did not want to fight. Corbett did not correct this assumption, but promised not to hurt him if he went down in the 2nd or 3rd rounds. The fearful Smith agreed to go down and out in the 2nd round.

Corbett said that he actually hit Smith hard and often, hoping Smith would think he was really taking it easy on him and that he could do even more. He noted that he was not hurting Smith at all. Corbett also utilized some footwork and tried to demonstrate his skill to cover up "my real lack of hitting power." Although he was unable to hurt Smith, Frank was fooled, and in the 2nd round, after Corbett hit him about twenty times, as per their agreement, Smith took a dive.[70] This was the type of entertaining story that Corbett years later liked to tell in his vaudeville tours, but it was only partially true.

Revealed here for the first time, the local primary source reports from the *Salt Lake Daily Tribune* and *Salt Lake Herald* both confirm that there was a great delay before the Dillon (Corbett) of San Francisco versus Smith bout began. Initially, Smith did not appear. Dillon had to go talk with the

---

[69] *Salt Lake Herald,* July 2, 1886. A secondary source indicates that Corbett was married in Salt Lake on June 28, 1886 and that he fought in a professional bout in order to defray honeymoon expenses. Fields at 21. Actually, Jim fought two professional fights in Salt Lake.
[70] Corbett at 47-55. Corbett, writing many years later, has the date/timing of the bout, as well as the result, wrong.

200-pound Smith "for a long time before he could persuade him to enter the ring at all," bolstering Corbett's later claim that Smith was afraid that he was Charley Mitchell, and that Jim had to convince him to fight.

However, these reports gave a much different account of what happened than Corbett's version. They said that the fight was a "disappointment to all spectators" and a "farce." It was a succession of clinches and would have been a wrestling match had referee Duncan McDonald allowed it. "The men clinched continuously from beginning to end, and paid no attention to the referee's order to break, and several times had to be forced apart." Smith would grab around the neck at every opportunity and would not heed the calls to break. "The general impression was that Smith was to blame for most of the clinching, and the referee warned him twice that if he did not quit it he would give the fight to Dillon." It was merely "a series of clinches and breaks, and it was all the referee and seconds could do to get the men apart."

The two local sources disagreed on when the bout was terminated, but agreed upon how it was ended. The *Daily Tribune* said that in the 4th round, while clinched, the boxers fell down, with Smith on top. To that point, the few blows that were exchanged in the bout were landed about evenly. However, "The referee declared a foul for wrestling at the end of the fourth round, and gave the match to Dillon on that account." Thus, it was a disqualification win for Corbett, not a knockout as Jim claimed. The *Herald* said that Smith was disqualified in the 3rd round, when "the men began to wrestle, and both went to the floor, Smith on top. Time was called before the men were parted, and the referee awarded the fight to Dillon on a foul."

These local accounts correct the previous historic misinformation about this fight. Clearly, this was a 3rd or 4th round disqualification win for Jim, and not a KO2 or KO3 win as Corbett and later sources claimed.

Some called the fight a "hippodrome." A hippodrome was either a fraudulent contest with a predetermined winner or at least one in which the fighters were thought to be faking or just going through the motions, working with one another and not really genuinely competing. The *Tribune* said that although it was evidently not a hippodrome, it was a very poor exhibition.[71] Corbett's account lends some credence to the argument that it was a hippodrome. It could have been that Smith was so afraid that he merely held on for dear life to survive.

Another possible explanation for the bout's disappointing style is that Smith only knew how to wrestle, not punch, and that he simply wrestled in order to survive against a man he thought was a far superior boxer. The same day that the "powerfully built" Smith signed articles to meet Dillon/Corbett, he also signed to engage in a wrestling match against Nephi Howcroft, which took place two days after the Corbett-Smith boxing

---

[71] *Salt Lake Daily Tribune*, July 4, 1886; *Salt Lake Herald*, July 4, 1886.

match. Corbett seconded Howcroft, who wrestled against and defeated Smith, who was seconded by Duncan McDonald, the referee of the Corbett–Smith fight. Thus, within the span of three days, Frank Smith had been defeated in boxing and wrestling matches, and Corbett and referee McDonald had been involved both times, although in different capacities.[72]

Referee Duncan McDonald was a good fighter in his own right. The 6' approximately 160-174-pound McDonald was an experienced boxing veteran, having in 1884 lost to middleweight-sized Pete McCoy (a favorite Sullivan sparring partner) in a 31-round, two hour and fifteen minute battle. An August 1885 report of McDonald's 6-round decision win over Miles McNally said, "Both men are well known, and each has a reputation as a pugilist."[73]

Pete McCoy vs. Duncan McDonald, May 1884

Shortly after the Smith bout, according to Corbett, Duncan McDonald took Jim to Evanston, Wyoming to box a fighter they called "Danny Costigan," the name of a Jack Dempsey sparring partner, but who Corbett said was actually someone else. It was likely McDonald. Corbett this time impersonated and was billed as middleweight champion Jack Dempsey, and he said that he fought well enough to fool them.[74] Corbett and McDonald apparently claimed that they were Dempsey and Costigan as a marketing

[72] *Salt Lake Herald*, July 6, 1886.
[73] *New York Clipper*, May 24, 1884, August 8, 1885. Some say the McCoy loss was in the 34th round. *Denver Daily News*, December 29, 1886.
[74] Corbett at 55-58.

ploy to stimulate ticket sales. Whether or not they actually boxed in Wyoming is unknown.

Corbett likely boxed in at least one hippodrome with McDonald, but possibly more. Jim called McDonald a "bosom pal," and in his autobiography failed to mention their boxing together, but they did, possibly multiple times, although this has not been confirmed.[75] Given that they were friends, it is quite likely that they were working with each other and that any fight between them was at least semi-friendly, although this may or may not have been known to the paying public. The two may have traveled from town to town putting on entertaining sparring exhibitions to make money.

There is primary source evidence of at least two of their meetings, which could have been the only times that Corbett and McDonald boxed together. Five days after the Smith bout, and two days after Corbett and McDonald had acted as seconds in the Smith-Howcroft wrestling match, on July 8, 1886, while still in Salt Lake City, McDonald signed to box Dillon/Corbett. The fight was scheduled for 6 rounds with four-ounce gloves for $250 a side, the gate receipts to be split 75% to the winner and 25% to the loser after expenses, the bout to take place the following week.[76] Clearly, this was going to be the first time that they boxed against each other. It was Corbett's second professional bout.

Corbett was continuing to pose as Jim Dillon, fighting the referee who had just seen him in action and awarded him a fight. In fact, subsequent to their bout, a San Francisco newspaper expressly reported that Corbett had posed as "Jim Dillon" in a match with Duncan McDonald.[77]

The local *Salt Lake Daily Tribune* gave a description of the July 14, 1886 match between "Dillon" (Corbett) and McDonald. The caption said, "The General Opinion is That It Was a Hippodrome, but that it was a Good One." Even then, some suspected a fake. The *Salt Lake Herald* agreed, saying, "As an exhibition of boxing the affair was, perhaps, a success. As a fight, however, it was a failure. It is about time the public ceased to patronize hippodromes." It was believed that although they had put on an entertaining and interesting show, they had not really fought on the level, to win, but rather to simply put on a good and pleasing, but even exhibition. The *Salt Lake Democrat* said that a great number of spectators "declared freely that the affair was nothing more nor less than a hippodrome." It, however, also said that "some very pretty work was done by both men, and whether in earnest or not they were both certainly very much used up at the

[75] Corbett at 59.
[76] *Salt Lake Herald,* July 9, 1886.
[77] *San Francisco Daily Examiner,* July 19, 1886; See also *Daily Picayune,* September 2, 1892. The *Examiner* said that Corbett and McDonald had fought an 8-round draw, appearing evenly matched. It was incorrect regarding the number of rounds fought, as they only boxed 6 rounds, but it was a draw. Many secondary sources later relied on the incorrect San Francisco report regarding the number of rounds.

end of the last round and were barely able to reach their corners." Was it an act?

The boxers were reported to have worn 4- to 6-ounce gloves. One said that the gloves were a little thinner and lighter than those used by amateurs in friendly practice. The local sources all agreed that it was a 6-round contest, not the 8 rounds that most secondary sources have reported.

Both entered the ring wearing white tights up to the waist, but bare-chested. Dillon wore a blue belt and McDonald a patriotic one of stars and stripes. They wore low cut canvas shoes.

Called the Montana champion, McDonald was described as 31 or 34 years of age (the papers varied), 6' and 160 pounds. He was smaller than Corbett, but appeared "much more durable" than Jim. Corbett was listed as 6'1" and 26 years old, which was incorrect, because Corbett was only 19 years old. One local paper said that Jim weighed 178 pounds, while another said that he gave his weight as 187. Jim was introduced as the California champion, but they were not sure why.

DUNCAN McDONALD.

In the 1st round, Dillon/Corbett made a number of feints, and "jumped around the arena as nimbly and as spry as a cat." He was good at making clever dodges of McDonald's attacks. Neither man did much effective work, and some in the audience cried "Rats!"

They picked it up in the 2nd, with Dillon landing a "stunner" on Mac's chest, doing most of the work as Mac retreated. Mac then landed to the cheek, but Dillon made "pretty dodges" to elude the follow-up. It was give and take, and Dillon "placed a resounding blow on Dunc.'s back and the audience began to get enthused." McDonald landed a clean hit to the face and managed to secure the most points in this round of "neat sparring."

In the 3rd round, Dillon rushed in while the defensive McDonald avoided being hit, and Mac countered with some clean punches before they clinched.

In the 4th, Dillon landed a good left and the audience began cheering his name. Dillon landed a rib shot, one of the cleanest and hardest of the evening. They exchanged some "stunners," with Mac landing the "neatest blows." A "resounding blow" from Dillon landed on Duncan's chest, and they exchanged blows to the face. They fought on the inside a bit and the referee pulled them apart while they were hitting each other in the head.

In the 5th round, one paper said, "McDonald's body-blows seemed almost to knock Dillon off his pins. Finally Dillon fell, partly from the effect of a blow and partly from the slippery condition of the stage." Soon thereafter, they both slipped and fell down.

Another local report of the round disagreed just a bit, saying that while they were clinching, it was McDonald who fell to the floor, not Dillon. After he rose, they clinched again and both fell. Upon rising, Dillon seemed exhausted, while Mac seemed just a little better.

Both appeared tired in the 6th round, perhaps Dillon more so. However, they fought hard at close range with no let up. "It was just three minutes of continuous fighting, and it was very pretty work, even though it might have been a hippodrome, as many said it was." The audience went wild with cheering and enjoyed it, for they had put on a good show.

Another local paper agreed that the fighters and the audience were breathless in the 6th and final round.

> Dillon staggered about the stage like a baby learning to walk and pawed at Mac as fast as he could. Mac was on the defensive and, in his weak condition, had all he could do to ward off the patter of Dillon's fists. The round was very exciting, and though many clean blows were struck by both men, they were so light and in such quick succession that it would be difficult to say who got the worst of it.

All local reports agreed that the referee said that he could not decide in favor of either, so he declared it a 6-round draw. One report said that the audience seemed to think that McDonald got in the most points and clear blows and should have been awarded the contest. Another said, "From a seat on the stage it certainly appeared that McDonald got the better of it, but as there were many in the audience who will swear by Dillon to the end, they will not be denied that privilege."

Neither boxer objected to the referee's draw decision, which was taken as a sign that they had colluded to keep it even and that neither really had the desire to get over on the other. "[S]everal other facts point to the suspicion that the contest might have been a hippodrome." Responding to the allegation, "Both Dillon and McDonald pooh-poohed the idea of the entertainment being a hippodrome, and each praised the other's qualities as sparrers." Perhaps they really were just evenly matched, but there were strong suspicions otherwise.[78]

The *San Francisco Chronicle* had previously that month called Corbett an "invincible" "gentleman heavyweight." However, after it learned that he had engaged in this bout posing as Jim Dillon, the *Chronicle* said that Jim had dropped to the lower plane of the professional "pug." Apparently, amateurs were gentlemen; professionals were not. This also reveals recognition that Corbett was now a professional.[79]

A week after their bout, on July 22, 1886, still in Salt Lake posing as Dillon, Corbett participated in an exhibition show which was said to be for the benefit of the Olympic Club. He sparred in a 3-round set-to with Duncan McDonald. The crowd was pleased by their work, for both men displayed "wonderful science."[80] The date of this exhibition was previously unknown.

McDonald remained in Salt Lake City even after this, because on July 31, he refereed a wrestling match there, and he also fought there in late August.[81] Thus, it is possible that these were the only two times that Corbett and McDonald boxed, because according to a secondary source, Corbett returned to San Francisco, where, as a result of his being caught, the Olympic Club suspended him from club exhibitions for four months.[82] However, it is also possible that Corbett did not return to Frisco, but rather remained in the Salt Lake and surrounding areas for several months and occasionally exhibited with McDonald. The San Francisco newspapers did not mention Corbett's name until November.

On August 28, 1886 in Salt Lake City, Duncan McDonald fought former Sullivan title challenger and regular sparring partner Herbert Slade, dropping Slade in the 3rd round before going on to win an 8-round decision. In a September rematch, McDonald knocked out the 200–220 pound Slade in the 9th round.[83] Duncan McDonald was no slouch and was more than a fair fighter.

At year end, in late December 1886 and early January 1887, McDonald would become a member of John L. Sullivan's western tour sparring combination, and would exhibit several times with world champion Sullivan

[78] *Salt Lake Daily Tribune*, July 15, 1886; *Salt Lake Democrat*, July 15, 1886; *Salt Lake Herald*, July 15, 1886.
[79] *San Francisco Chronicle*, July 6, 1886, July 20, 1886.
[80] *Salt Lake Herald*, July 23, 1886.
[81] *Salt Lake Herald*, August 1, 1886.
[82] Fields at 22-23.
[83] *National Police Gazette*, November 15, 1884, October 16, 1886; *Salt Lake Daily Tribune*, August 29, 1886.

in 4-round bouts. McDonald was described as a brave, scientific and clever sparrer. One newspaper noted that McDonald did "excellent work both in stopping and leading considering the fact that Sullivan is in front of him, liable at any time to expend a portion of his surplus strength."[84] Another report of a Sullivan-McDonald exhibition said that "those who have any knowledge of the art could readily see the superiority of the 'big one,' yet the Butte City man is quite an adept."[85] Of yet another one of those exhibition shows, it was said that although the spectators were satisfied, those who knew something of the game realized that the sparrers had generally engaged in "make believe slugging matches" and "sham rough encounters."[86] This is likely what McDonald had done with Corbett. Regardless, the experience that Corbett had gained from sparring a highly skilled boxer such as McDonald was invaluable.

It is unclear whether the Olympic Club deemed that Corbett had forfeited his amateur status. Corbett did not give a public exhibition in San Francisco again until November. Perhaps this was his punishment for the Salt Lake bouts. The McDonald fight was a draw and not scheduled to the finish, so Jim might have gotten off on somewhat of a technicality, and the local San Franciscans might initially have been unaware of his bout with Smith, which was scheduled to the finish. It is also possible that the Olympic decided to somewhat overlook the compromising out-of-state transgression. Corbett had subsequently boxed an exhibition with McDonald for the Olympic's financial benefit, which may have had an influence.

Clearly though, despite the popular belief that Corbett did not become a professional until his 1889 bout with Joe Choynski, Jim Corbett had become a professional in Salt Lake City, and technically had or should have forfeited his amateur status. A late 1889 issue of the *San Francisco Chronicle* provided the definition of an amateur, which Jim had clearly violated:

> One who has never competed in an open competition, nor for either a stake money, gate money or entrance fee; one who has never competed under a fictitious name nor with a professional for any prize or where gate money has been charged; one who has never instructed, pursued or assisted in the pursuit of athletic exercises as a means of livelihood, nor for gain, nor any emolument.[87]

Despite the fact that he was actually a professional, over the next couple of years, Corbett's status was more ambiguous. Although he participated in sparring exhibitions, Corbett did not participate as a contestant in any amateur tournaments. The Olympic probably knew that he was no longer

---

[84] *Denver Daily News*, December 29, 1886.
[85] *Colorado Miner* (Georgetown), January 1, 1887.
[86] *Denver Tribune-Republican*, December 29, 1886.
[87] *San Francisco Chronicle*, September 23, 1889.

an amateur, but didn't want to completely lose its star either. Corbett was often still called an amateur, but clearly he was not.

Corbett likely realized that pursuing a professional career was not necessarily the best thing for him at this point anyway. In late July 1886 in Oakland, Tom Cleary (not Mike) scored a KO2 over Martin "Buffalo" Costello in a professional middleweight fight for the championship of the Pacific Coast and the gate money. Both were afterwards arrested and charged with a violation of the penal code which made engaging in a prize fight a felony punishable by up to two years of imprisonment. Merely being a spectator at such an event could lead to a sentence of six months in jail and a $500 fine. The two boxers went to trial, and in early November, a jury convicted them.

> Two years ago there were several trials for prize-fighting in the San Francisco courts, but the offenders escaped by technicality or perjury. The verdict of guilty in the Cases of Costello and Cleary proves that similar good luck cannot always be counted upon, and will most likely strike terror into the ranks of the professional bruisers.[88]

On November 8, 1886, the same day that the newspapers announced the felony convictions of Cleary and Costello, 8,000 people watched a number of athletic exhibitions at the Paper Carnival held at the local San Francisco pavilion. These exhibitions included boxing, for scientific exhibitions were legal. "The sparring was not very animated, but several scientific bouts were heartily applauded." Corbett and P.T. Goodloe, a fellow Olympian, "gave a rather pleasing exhibition." Corbett had returned to local exhibiting again.[89]

Before Duncan McDonald boxed with Sullivan on his tour, on November 13, 1886 in San Francisco, a then 20-year-old Corbett had the opportunity, along with a crowd of over 9,000, to watch 28-year-old John L. Sullivan stop Paddy Ryan in 3 rounds. Although this was a professional fight, Sullivan and Ryan had received a license from the Governor-elect of the State of California. Sullivan was special.[90]

According to his autobiography, Corbett watched the fight "getting points" because he believed, even then, that through agility and science; he could develop a system to one day defeat Sullivan.[91]

After the fight, Ryan said, "Well, Sullivan is the king of fighters, and whenever he hits a man the recipient of the blow is not very liable to soon forget its effects…. When Sullivan ever hits a man a full blow with his right, there is not much danger of the recipient coming up for another."[92]

---

[88] *Oakland Enquirer,* July 27, 1886, November 8, 1886.
[89] *San Francisco Chronicle,* November 9, 1886.
[90] *Oakland Daily Evening Tribune,* November 18, 1886.
[91] Corbett at 115-117.
[92] *Oakland Daily Evening Tribune,* November 15, 1886.

Speaking of Sullivan, respected fighter Billy Edwards observed that he lets one arm hang almost limp just in front of him, the other slightly bent, in order to stay relaxed and avoid muscle tension, which prevents "weariness to the muscles and leaves them free for action on the instant." He spoke of what it took to make a great fighter, noting that Sullivan had all of those qualities:

> Given pluck, and the science that comes of good training, and a light man may often clean out a big one. You know, as a rule, big men are slower than little ones. A quick man, of medium build, is really the most dangerous kind of a fighter. Sullivan is not only big and strong but wonderfully quick, and there lies his power; it is a very unusual combination. In fact, Sullivan has all the attributes of a great fighter. ... Yes, I think much of him as a fighter, for he is scientific as well as powerful.[93]

However, following the Ryan fight, one local paper criticized Sullivan's appearance, while still praising his superiority over every fighter:

> Sullivan is going down hill physically, and the first time he faces a really good man he is likely to be caught napping. Probably the really good man does not exist now, but he will be heard of before long. ... Age, ease and luxurious living have put a goodly paunch on Sullivan. ... [I]t was announced that he entered the ring at the moderate weight of 210 pounds. He looked to be at least 20 pounds heavier, and probably was. ... Sullivan is still a wonderful man, however, and Ryan has no more business with him than a club-armed savage has with a Gatling battery.[94]

Although Sullivan had been a Herculean physical specimen from 1880 to 1884, his alcohol habit began to take hold of him in those years, and he began slipping further and further in terms of how he took care of his body. Still, he was so immensely talented that he was able to overcome it all.

Four days after Sullivan defeated Ryan, on November 17, for their felony prize fighting convictions, Martin Costello was sentenced to six weeks in jail, while Tom Cleary received three months, the difference being that the judge felt that Costello had told the truth on the stand, while Cleary had perjured himself. Regardless, these were stiff sentences for men who had harmed no one but themselves.

For the moment, professional boxing was not the way to go for Corbett. The legal pendulum of boxing would continue swinging back and forth in California for quite some time. Eventually, as a result of the lobbying of the town's elite athletic clubs and some favorable jury and judicial decisions, professional boxing was essentially deemed to be legal if held in an athletic

---

[93] *San Francisco Evening Post*, November 6, 1886.
[94] *San Francisco Evening Post*, November 15, 1886.

club. This caused the California Club to flourish as the premier professional club. However, for the time being, professional boxers had to deal with the fear of legal repercussions.[95]

John L. Sullivan, 1885

[95] *Oakland Enquirer,* November 18, 1886; *New York Sun,* February 4, 1890.

CHAPTER 4

The Sparring Professor in Demand

Venturing out to nearby Oakland, on December 2, 1886, Jim Corbett took part in the first of the Acme Athletic Club's ladies' night exhibitions, which featured gymnastics, boxing, and wrestling, etc. Corbett of the Olympic Club exhibited with the Acme Club's heavyweight champion, Jack Kitchen. Their sparring "was very interesting, as both men displayed a great deal of science and training."[96]

In early January 1887 in Minneapolis, John L. Sullivan badly broke his left arm against Patsy Cardiff in a bout that was ruled a 6-round draw.

On January 25, 1887, again at Oakland's Acme Athletic Club, Corbett boxed a 3-round bout with Tom Johnson, "a well-known slogger." The date of this bout has previously been unknown. A couple years earlier, Johnson was reported to be a coming man who weighed about 185 pounds. The *Oakland Daily Evening Tribune* said, "J. Corbett, champion heavy weight of the Olympic Club, and Tom Johnson gave an exhibition in sparring in which the former proved himself to be the superior." The *San Francisco Chronicle* said, "Corbett's science asserted itself throughout the bout, and the Acme folks were enthusiastic in their appreciation of the fistic display."

Corbett had recently become a boxing professor and his skill as a coach was quickly noticed and appreciated.

> Jim has a few colts under his care and they are coming on wonderfully. He has been allowed the use of the California Athletic Club rooms for exercising his pupils, and they are to be congratulated on having so able a tutor. With unmistakable capability, he combines good temper and patience, and does not indulge in any of the rough work so disheartening to those receiving initiatory lessons in the noble art.[97]

The California Club supported both professionals and amateurs, and it had apparently either hired Corbett as an instructor or at least allowed him to work out there with his pupils. So, as of 1887, the 20-year-old Corbett was a banker, a teacher, and a boxer. His professorship was a testament to

---

[96] *Oakland Enquirer*, December 3, 1886; *Daily Alta California*, December 6, 1886; *Oakland Daily Evening Tribune*, January 26, 1887, April 20, 1887.
[97] *Oakland Daily Evening Tribune*, January 26, 1887; *San Francisco Chronicle*, January 27, 1887; *San Francisco Morning Call*, July 20, 1885.

Corbett's skills and talent, having boxed at the Olympic for just short of two years.

The fact that Corbett was teaching at the California Club and sparring at the Acme Club suggests that Corbett's relationship with the Olympic might have been a bit strained at that time, likely as a result of his Salt Lake bouts and the resulting discipline. However, it could also be consistent with the fact that many instructors and boxers often worked or sparred at other clubs. The same evening that Corbett sparred Tom Johnson at the Acme, Jack Kitchen sparred Professor Watson there also. As of early 1886, Watson had been teaching at the Acme Club as well as at the Olympic.

On February 2, 1887 at the Olympic Club, Corbett boxed an exhibition against professional heavyweight Mike Brennan, known as the "Port Costa Giant." The exact date has heretofore been unknown. The local *San Francisco Examiner* reported that they boxed as part of an exhibition show, so they likely sparred 3, possibly 4 rounds. It was said that the Olympic had departed from its previous policy, and was now allowing professional fighters into its periodic exhibitions.

> The Corbett and Mike Brennan battle was simply that of an accomplished boxer against a prize-ring fighter. Corbett knows how to box and Brennan knows how to fight. The result was some wild-rushes on the part of Brennan and some clever getting away on the part of Corbett. The former might probably have considerably the best of a battle should the two men ever come together for true business.[98]

At that time, Brennan was in training for a professional fight set to take place in four days, but his opponent pulled out due to illness. The following week's report said,

> Brennan is improving every day, with practice. Last week when he met Jim Corbett, the Olympic Club heavyweight, he showed that he had improved wonderfully in the past two months. It is safe to say that if Brennan can be made to understand the necessity of clever sparring instead of "bulling" he will make as clever a heavyweight as there is now in the ring.[99]

Although it was only a few rounds, this was very good sparring for Corbett, because Brennan was a respected fighter. Later in 1887, Brennan would be stopped in 44 rounds by 219-pound Joe McAuliffe, a then highly touted contender.

---

[98] *San Francisco Examiner*, February 4, 1887. Special thanks to Tom Welsh for assisting me in locating this bout.
[99] *San Francisco Examiner*, January 31, February 7, 1887.

MIKE BRENNAN, THE PORT COSTA GIANT.

An 1890 report of the Corbett-Brennan sparring said,

> Mike Brennan, the Port Costa giant, writes to the sporting editor of the *Chronicle*, taking exception to the statement of Professor Jim Corbett that he knocked Brennan out in three rounds. Mike says: "Corbett never stopped or knocked me out. I boxed him once three rounds in the Olympic Club, and I consider I had the best of it."

> No Mike; you did not have the "best of it." You certainly made some wicked swings, but the professor generally vacated the region you directed your blows at before your brawny fist got there.[100]

The exact dates and results of many of Corbett's early bouts remain uncertain. An 1889 account of Corbett's record to that point said that sometime in 1887, Corbett stopped Captain James Dailey or Daly of Philadelphia in 4 rounds.[101] Later reports of their contest said that Daly was stopped in 1 or 2 rounds. A March 1885 issue of the *National Police Gazette*

---

[100] *San Francisco Chronicle*, May 12, 1890.
[101] *San Francisco Evening Post*, May 30, 1889. This was likely a different Daly than the one who became his sparring partner years later.

had called Daly a "champion all-round athlete and more than promising phenomenon of the boxing world."[102]

Another bout noted by many sources but whose exact date is unknown was against the professional middleweight, Martin "Buffalo" Costello, whom Corbett bested "with ease." This has generally been listed as a 3-round match (or sometimes a 4-round "private affair"), though as is often the case with bouts unconfirmed by a primary source, this is not certain. It may have been part of one of the Olympic's periodic exhibitions.

The experienced Costello had or would have such results as: 1887 D34 and LKOby9 Frank Slavin, KO2 Bill Farnan - the only man to defeat Peter Jackson, and he also boxed in 1888 and 1890 4-round exhibitions with

Captain James Dailey

Peter Jackson. Both the Daly and Costello bouts allegedly took place sometime before Corbett's August 1887 bout with Jack Burke, but this is unclear.[103]

In early March 1887, there was some discussion of a potential professional bout between Corbett and Joe McAuliffe. "Corbett shows a little backwardness in coming forward and is squeamish about fighting for a stake!"[104] Although Corbett had become a professional with his Smith and McDonald bouts, he appeared to want to continue to maintain and assert his amateur status, or at least to resist moving forward as a professional. He specifically wrote to the *San Francisco Chronicle* in early March 1887, "I do not want to box any one, either amateur or professional, for a monetary consideration, and no inducement can make me alter my intention."

It was also reported that Corbett had joined the Alcazar Baseball Club. Jim was called a "heavy batter, good fielder and an excellent base runner."[105]

[102] *National Police Gazette*, March 7, 1885.
[103] *San Francisco Evening Post*, May 30, 1889.
[104] *Daily Alta California*, March 7, 1887.
[105] *San Francisco Chronicle*, March 10, 1887.

He, like Sullivan, enjoyed occasionally playing baseball throughout his career.

Joe Choynski

Heretofore unknown is the fact that on March 23, 1887 on gentlemen's night at the Olympic Club, 20-year-old James J. Corbett boxed 18-year-old Joe Choynski 5 rounds. Professor Watson had arranged a set-to between "his pupils of the Acme Club of Oakland and the Olympians." At that point, "Choynski" or "Choyinski" was listed as a professional boxer. After a number of exhibitions that night, the finale was between Joe and Jim.

> The evening's sport was brought to a close by a five-round contest between Mr. Choyinski (professional) and James Corbett, the heavyweight of the Olympics, and proved the most spirited contest of the evening, Corbett scoring a clean knockdown in the first round, and following it up by another in the second. In the third both administered some heavy hitting, and the round ended with Choyinski clinching to avoid punishment. In the fourth honors were easy, and in

the fifth and last round Choyinski led off and caught Corbett on the cheek, receiving a stinger in return on the forehead. Short-arm fighting followed, Choyinski going down several times to get away from his heavy opponent, and the round ended in some very hard-hitting, with the odds in favor of Corbett.[106]

Thus, it was quite clear that even at this point, Corbett was superior to Choyinski. Two years later, the two would meet again in a famous battle.

On May 11, 1887, the Olympic Club's ladies' night included set-tos by Professor Watson's juvenile class. During the evening, President Harrison, on behalf of the club members, presented Corbett with a "handsome medal, richly studded with jewels, as an emblem of the heavyweight championship of the club." Obviously, fences were indeed mended (if they were ever broken), and Corbett was still being recognized as the club's champion. Corbett clearly carried some prestige.[107]

Demand for Professor Corbett's teaching services was growing. It was reported at the end of May that Corbett had been engaged as an instructor by the Golden Gate Club, teaching on Tuesday and Thursday evenings, alternating instructional duties with Con Riordan and/or J.W. Geogan.[108]

A couple months later, a bout was announced that was then considered to be Corbett's first real test. It was to be held in late August 1887 against the far more experienced and famous professional, Jack Burke. The 25-year-old Burke was born in Ireland but raised in England, and may have been of Jewish descent. He began boxing as an amateur middleweight at age 15. In 1881, he fought Charley Mitchell to a 25-round bareknuckle draw lasting 1 hour and 17 minutes. They also boxed in gloved 1884 4- and 8-round draws. In December 1884, Burke fought Jake Kilrain to a 5-round draw. In February and March 1885, Burke won 5-round decisions over former Sullivan opponents Captain James Dalton and Alf Greenfield.[109] That year, Burke also defeated Greenfield in two other bouts, in 7 and 8 rounds.[110] The respected Greenfield had twice boxed Sullivan (1884 L2, 1885 L4).

More importantly, in June 1885, John L. Sullivan defeated a 23-year-old 5'8 ½" 170-pound Burke in a 5-round decision bout. Burke demonstrated his skill and pluck, but was dropped multiple times. A couple weeks later, Burke fought Mitchell to a 6-round draw, and they also fought to an 1886 10-round draw. In November 1886, the 162-pound Burke fought middleweight champion Jack Dempsey to a 10-round draw, although most thought that Dempsey had won.[111]

[106] *Daily Alta California*, March 24, 1887.
[107] *Daily Alta California*, May 12, 1887.
[108] *Daily Alta California*, May 30, 1887, June 6, 1887.
[109] Boxrec.com; *New York Clipper*, March 7, 1885.
[110] *San Francisco Daily Examiner*, July 25, 1887; *National Police Gazette*, December 4, 1886; Boxrec.com.
[111] *San Francisco Daily Examiner*, July 25, 1887; *National Police Gazette*, December 4, 1886; *San Francisco Chronicle*, November 23, 1886; See also the Sullivan volume – Adam J. Pollack, *John L. Sullivan: The Career of the First Gloved Heavyweight Champion* (North Carolina: McFarland & Co., 2006).

Jack Burke

When the scheduled 8-round Corbett-Burke match was arranged in early August 1887, the local *Daily Alta California* opined, "This is the first chance that Corbett has really had to meet any one capable of making him show all that there was in him, and will be a splendid opportunity for Jim to make a record for himself."[112] The *San Francisco Chronicle* said that the local sporting public would be very interested in the match, feeling that it would be a magnificent exhibition of science. It said that Corbett had been longing to stand before a professional of some repute, and that "in Burke he will find an opponent who is a thorough adept in the manly art and who has gained a name on the fistic roll of fame less by brute strength than by clever and effective sparring." Assessing the match up, it said,

---

[112] *Daily Alta California*, August 8, 1887.

Both Corbett and Burke are clever workers on their feet; both have had the advantage of tip-top condition, and although the former has a slight lead in the matter of weight and reach, it is probable that Burke's superior knowledge of ring tactics, and the fact of his being imbued with that feeling of confidence which long usage brings, will balance matters and make it hard to decide who will be the winner.[113]

As the bout approached, it was called "the all-absorbing topic." Many felt that Jim would more than hold his own with Burke, who was called "the Irish lad."[114]

A 20-year-old Corbett boxed the 25-year-old Burke on August 27, 1887 at San Francisco's Olympic Club. Many secondary source records list this as an 8-round draw[115], but Corbett claimed that Burke insisted prior to the match that it be a no decision bout.[116] Primary source reports support Corbett's assertion that there was no official decision. There was no referee (who usually rendered the decision) and Burke received a fixed price fee for the exhibition without any reference to the result of the contest, which was typical for no decision bouts and atypical for competitions where there would be a winner and loser. However, the newspapers rendered their own opinions.[117]

Corbett was listed as 6'1" and 180 pounds to Burke's 5'10" and 165 pounds. Wearing six-ounce gloves, their boxing began at 10:20 p.m. According to the *Examiner*, Corbett obviously had the superior height and reach, but seemed a bit nervous at first, mostly keeping away in the 1st round. They sparred, clinched and evaded, feeling each other out. In the 2nd round, they continued to exchange, clinch, and look for openings. The next 4 rounds were but repetitions of the first two.

> The sparring was very pretty, but Corbett with all his skill and grace can't hit very hard, and Burke didn't try to. The professional contented himself with thumping his gentlemanly adversary on the chest, and when he got punched with a little more pressure than was agreeable, retorted with a whack on the ribs. It was spar, exchange, clinch, more sparring…. Corbett showed much cleverness in keeping his head out of the way and letting Burke's arm slide along the side of his neck, and thus instead of getting blows enjoyed numerous hugs.

Corbett had the best of it in the 7th round, hitting Burke with a hard right to the ribs. There was an "animated" exchange and Corbett came out ahead. Corbett's right to the ribs was called the "one respectable blow of

---

[113] *San Francisco Chronicle*, August 8, 1887.
[114] *Daily Alta California*, August 15, 1887.
[115] Cyberboxingzone.com; Alexander Johnston, *Ten and Out!* (N.Y.: Ives Washburn, 1927), 71; Rex Lardner, *The Legendary Champions* (N.Y.: American Heritage Press, 1972), 73.
[116] Corbett at 24-28.
[117] *San Francisco Chronicle*, February 25, 1889.

the engagement." Corbett hit him with a "touch" to the right ear and a left "slap." Burke ended the round with two "smakers" on Corbett's chest.

The 8th round was more of the same, with each leading, blocking and clinching, until the round ended "a drawn fight." This was the newspaper's opinion, not a reflection of an official decision.

The *Examiner* called it a "light-hitting, scientific set-to at the Olympic Club" consisting of "eight animated but very mild rounds." With no money or decision on the line, it was not necessary for the pugilists to give it their all, which likely affected the way the men boxed.

Corbett was called a "clever amateur" and also described as "remarkably light on his feet, quick with his hands and altogether a first-rate amateur, but he lacks power. The Olympians cheered their champion after the wind-up, and he deserved their applause." Burke received his stipulated purse of $600 and Corbett gained glory (no pay), again perhaps indicating Jim's intention to continue his ambiguous amateur status.[118]

The *San Francisco Chronicle* also presented its version. Burke wore flesh colored tights and a green sash. Wearing dark-colored tights, Corbett was seconded by Walter Watson and Dennis Dillon. 800 people were in attendance to watch the bout, which began at 10:10 p.m.

This account was just a bit more critical of Corbett. It said that he seemed to lack confidence in the early part of the exhibition, but "brightened up" during the last two rounds. Both were cautious at first, with Burke a bit more of the aggressor. The men attempted blows to the body and head, both generally exhibiting solid defensive skills as they took turns leading and countering. Burke mostly landed to the chest. The 4th, 5th, and 6th rounds were "decidedly in Burke's favor." Jack mostly landed a left to the chest. Corbett attempted some inside work, but Burke was able to crowd and "body" Jim.

However, Corbett won the 7th round, becoming a bit more aggressive, and doing well in some exchanges. He was also more aggressive in the 8th round, although both were very much on guard. Corbett forced matters but Burke kept too close to him for anything significant to be done. "The round ended with honors easy." Corbett appeared to have gained confidence in the last two rounds.

The article's writer felt that Corbett should have lead more often and relied too much on counters, for Burke was good at elusive head movement. It also believed that he should have relied on his height and reach advantage on the outside more, to prevent Burke from hugging him.

The description of the bout though gave the impression that it was skillful, competitive and lively. "Taken as a whole the exhibition was, perhaps, the best, from a scientific point of view, that has taken place in San Francisco for years. That Corbett is a clever boxer no one for a moment

---

[118] *San Francisco Daily Examiner*, August 28, 1887.

can doubt." That said, it was the writer's opinion that Burke was the more scientific and had a "slight advantage" overall. "It must, however, have been patent to a disinterested spectator that Burke was by far the more scientific boxer of the two." Burke's blocking and head movement had been excellent. Still, this article bolstered Corbett's position that no official decision was given, because it was announced beforehand that there would be no referee, typical of a no decision exhibition bout. It did not mention an official decision being rendered.[119]

The local *Daily Alta California* said that only club members and the press were allowed to witness the match, which took place in a 20-foot ring. It confirmed that there was no referee. It said that Corbett weighed 172 pounds (as opposed to the *SFE* saying he was 180) to Burke's 165 pounds. Its assessment of the bout was as follows:

> Corbett acquitted himself well, but he was greatly overmatched, the professional seemingly playing with him. Burke struck his opponent with his open mitten several times on the chest during the contest, and once struck him a comparatively hard one on the nose. Corbett won the cheers of the crowd several times by getting in on Burke's neck and stomach. In the seventh round Burke appeared to be nettled for an instant, and let out savagely for Corbett's neck. By a clever dodge the blow was escaped by Corbett, who retaliated with a punch in Burke's wind. After the fifth round Burke paid the amateur boxer a compliment, by saying: "He's a very foxy boy with his dukes." Several members of the club stated that they had kept a record of points during the contest, and that Corbett was the winner by their record, having made 38 points to 28 points for Burke.... Neither of the men was scratched.... The contest was a clever sparring match, but bore little resemblance to a fight.[120]

A couple days after the bout, the *Chronicle* reported that some felt that although the Corbett-Burke bout was a "splendid display of fistic science," it was too tame. The *Chronicle* believed that the criticism was unfair.

> That [Burke] sparred lightly has to be considered in connection with the fact that there was no "roughing" for him to respond to. Corbett, on the other hand, neither flinched nor held back, and while many of his admirers seem a shade disappointed that he did not annihilate the much-traveled Irish lad...the fact remains that Corbett maintained his prestige as the leading amateur of the Pacific coast.[121]

The overall impression from these accounts is that the Corbett-Burke bout was really just a scientific exhibition, not a fight, wherein the men did

---

[119] *San Francisco Chronicle*, August 28, 1887.
[120] *Daily Alta California*, August 28, 1887.
[121] *San Francisco Chronicle*, August 29, 1887.

little hard hitting, just exhibiting their wonderful skills and working with each other in a fairly friendly but somewhat competitive fashion, keeping it relatively even, yet still interesting.

An early September 1887 *Alta* report said that Corbett had retired from the ring, owing to the fact that he was employed in a prominent mercantile house which objected to his boxing. *The Alta* lamented that fact, because it felt that Jim was the best ring representative on the coast, who could "do up any and all of the local fighters just as fast as they come up." A *Chronicle* report provided a different reason that Corbett would not be engaging in future public or private sparring contests. "This is in accordance with a promise made to his relatives prior to his contest with Jack Burke." Corbett was not mentioned in the local press for the rest of 1887, so he may well have taken some time off. However, his "retirement" was not permanent, and eventually Jim returned to life as a sparring professor.[122]

Corbett may have helped prepare fellow Olympian Bill Kenealy for his November 29 fight with Joe Choynski. There is some evidence that Corbett worked with Kenealy, for in early August 1887, the *San Francisco Chronicle* called Kenealy Corbett's pupil. However, there are other reports that said Professor Watson trained Kenealy, and, it was Watson who worked his corner against Choynski, not Corbett.[123] Corbett might have stopped training Bill after the Burke contest, or he may have just been a sparring partner or assistant to Watson. The Choynski-Kenealy fight was a back and forth battle in which both men were decked multiple times until Choynski knocked out Kenealy in the 4th round.[124]

Although John L. Sullivan had badly broken his arm in January, as of May 1887 he still was not accepting challenges. When he did not accept Jake Kilrain's challenge, some newspapers, such as the *New York Clipper* and *National Police Gazette*, began calling Kilrain the champion. The general public still looked upon Sullivan as the champ.

Mike Donovan had sparred Sullivan in early August 1887. Donovan later told a reporter that Sullivan had "wonderfully improved in science of late."

> He told me to hit him as hard as I could, and I gave him two or three right-hand swipes on the jaw that ought to have felled a bull, but they never fazed him. He holds his hands higher and better than he did, and he is the cleverest big man the ring ever saw. He ducked away from several blows with a quickness that astonished me. He can stand off ten feet and fiddle in a way that disconcerts you and breaks your

---

[122] *Daily Alta California*, September 5, 1887; *San Francisco Chronicle*, September 5, 1887.
[123] *San Francisco Chronicle*, August 8, 1887.
[124] *San Francisco Chronicle*, November 30, 1887; *Daily Alta California*, November 30, 1887; Fields at 25.

guard. Then he comes at you like a battering-ram, you get it on the jaw and down you go. You can't help it.[125]

In late 1887, Sullivan went on a European sparring tour.

On January 27, 1888, the Olympic Club held an amateur boxing tournament. "W.J. Kennealy" was the only entry in the heavyweight class, so he was awarded the gold medal. "Kenneally" (alternate spelling) instead sparred Corbett in a "very neat and gentlemanly exhibition." Clearly, at this point, Corbett was not a competing amateur. He held a different and higher status as a teacher, who then sparred with an Olympic pupil.[126]

In early February 1888, Walter Watson resigned from the Olympic Club. Corbett had been impressive enough such that the club hired him to be its boxing instructor. According to a secondary source, he was hired at a salary of $150 per month and left his position at the bank.[127] On the 15th, Jim was the timekeeper at an Olympic wrestling tournament.[128]

On March 9, 1888, the Olympic Club was crowded to capacity for its Ladies' Night entertainments, which included 3 rounds of sparring between "Professor" Corbett and William Kenealy. Bill's excellent work gained him many admirers.[129]

Later that month, it was noted that "under the able instruction of Professor James Corbett, the popular boxing teacher of the Olympic Club, the boxing class has increased largely during the past few weeks." There was an average of twenty names on the boxing book during each class, and frequently thirty-five or forty.[130]

On March 10, 1888 in France, champion John L. Sullivan fought Charley Mitchell to a 39-round London Prize Ring rules bareknuckle draw that lasted over three hours in the cold rain. Despite the fact that he fought for over three hours, because it was a draw and John L. had not annihilated Mitchell, Sullivan's condition was criticized. It was believed that his excessive drinking and eating were finally catching up with him. After all, in 1883, a prime Sullivan had stopped Mitchell in only 3 gloved rounds.

> Sullivan has taught us afresh that physical vigor cannot be preserved by burning the candle at both ends. After years of dissipation, Sullivan pretended to reform, and then we were told that he was as good a man as he ever was. The student of physiology knew better. A man cannot trifle with his body…. He abused his system in every way…. The moral is that men who would retain their physical or mental

[125] San Francisco Chronicle, September 26, 1887.
[126] Daily Alta California, January 28, 1888.
[127] San Francisco Chronicle, February 13, 1888; Daily Alta California, February 13, 1888; New York Clipper, February 25, 1888; Fields at 25-26.
[128] Daily Alta California, February 16, 1888.
[129] Daily Alta California, March 10, 1888; San Francisco Evening Post, March 10, 1888; San Francisco Chronicle, March 10, 1888.
[130] San Francisco Chronicle, March 26, 1888.

powers must lead regular lives. If they indulge to excess the shadow of decay will early fall upon them.[131]

In April 1888, Australian heavyweight champion Peter Jackson, who was black, came to America and quickly became affiliated with San Francisco's California Athletic Club. After seeing him spar for the first time in early June against Con Riordan, impressed observers said, "Fear alone…will prevent Sullivan from meeting him…. The white fighters will draw the color line tighter than ever, now."[132]

The era's social standard was that blacks and whites did not mix on an equal level in any area of life. Racial separation was the theme of the day. Blacks and whites attended separate schools and churches, were not allowed to legally intermarry, and were separated in all ways socially.

In sport, whites simply did not compete with blacks. However, boxing was the one sport where that norm was not consistently observed. Some boxers felt that they would be degrading themselves by competing with a black fighter. Others simply used the color line as a way to avoid meeting good black fighters. Still others felt that boxing was not a forum for the color line to be drawn, citing earlier mixed race bouts as precedent. Over the next few years, Jackson would establish himself as a top contender for Sullivan's crown by fighting both black and white fighters.

During April 1888, Corbett was again being praised as a popular boxing teacher. His class was steadily increasing in size. One club member said, "Corbett takes more interest in the class and stands more punching good-naturedly from his pupils than any teacher which the Olympic Club has ever had. He's a good one." A week later it was said, "The names of pupils inscribed on the boxing-book last Saturday afternoon numbered forty – count 'em – forty." The class size had grown so much that by late April the Olympic hired the clever boxer William Dick as an assistant professor to help Jim out. At month's end, the Olympic raised its initiation fee from $10 to $25, but kept the monthly dues at $2.50.[133]

Being a professor brought Corbett a high social standing, as many, including America's top universities, were recognizing the sport's educational value. Even students at Boston's Harvard University, the oldest and most prestigious college in America, took boxing classes, which were growing in popularity. "Harvard students have taken to sparring more this year than ever before." Joe Lannon and even black George Godfrey had been teaching there.[134] As Corbett wrote years later,

If every young man in America would take up boxing as a pastime we would have better men and better citizens. In my many years'

[131] *San Francisco Chronicle*, March 26, 1888.
[132] *San Francisco Daily Examiner*, June 5, 1888; *Referee*, April 20, 1892.
[133] *San Francisco Chronicle*, April 9, 16, 23, 30, 1888.
[134] *San Francisco Chronicle*, April 16, 1888.

experience in athletics I have come to the conclusion that there is more actual benefit to be derived from it than from any other form of exercise.

It develops every muscle in the human body, it quickens the brain, it sharpens the wits, it imparts force, and above all it teaches self-control.[135]

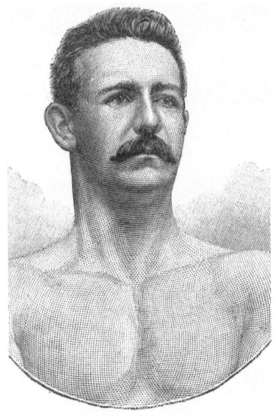

JOE McAULIFFE.

In early April, it was reported that the clever and popular Professor Corbett had been engaged by professional Joe McAuliffe to spar with him. McAuliffe was in training for his upcoming fight with Frank Glover, set to take place in May at the California Athletic Club for the title of Pacific Coast champion and a $1,750 purse. Corbett began working with McAuliffe on April 8. Joe was complimented for choosing Jim as a sparring partner. "A better selection could not have been made." Another newspaper later said that Corbett would "undoubtedly teach him many new and telling points."[136]

---

[135] James J. Corbett, *Scientific Boxing* (New York: Richard K. Fox Pub. Co., 1912), 11.
[136] *San Francisco Chronicle*, April 2, 9, 1888; *Daily Alta California*, April 23, 1888; *New York Sun*, February 4,

Such sparring was good for Joe, but it was also good for Corbett. McAuliffe was a highly regarded heavyweight contender who stood 6'3" and weighed almost 220 pounds. McAuliffe's record included an 1887 KO44 Mike Brennan (three hours) and a late 1887 KO3 Paddy Ryan (who Sullivan had twice knocked out in championship bouts). McAuliffe had power and endurance.[137]

There was even some discussion of how Corbett might do against either McAuliffe or Glover. Corbett was called "a likely lad, who has increased wonderfully in science and who is quite heavy and clever enough to make it decidedly interesting for either Glover or McAuliffe."[138] On May 22, 1888, Joe McAuliffe knocked out Frank Glover in the 49th round. A week later, there was further discussion of a potential bout between Corbett and McAuliffe. The *Chronicle* said that although Corbett was a clever boxer, the odds would be against him in such an undertaking.

Professor Con Riordan had issued a challenge to Corbett, and one writer sized up that potential match as well.

> Con Riordan has challenged Professor Corbett for a contest to a finish, and if Corbett can obtain the consent of his parents for a contest to a finish, Riordan will be accommodated, as Corbett is very anxious for a go at Riordan, who has tried to draw him into a contest for the last few years…. Corbett can get all the backing he needs, and it is dollars to doughnuts that if the match comes off he will fight Riordan to a stand-still in less than ten rounds.

Corbett was more than willing to fight Riordan, but the Olympic Club would not allow it, "owing to the manner in which the latter acted some months ago at the California Club." The article was alluding to an incident which took place at the California Club on November 25, 1887. Riordan was seconding Peter Hardy of the Golden Gate Club against J.V. Harrison of the Olympic in a 6-round bout. In the 3rd round, Harrison struck Hardy a chance foul blow and Hardy went down. There were loud cries of foul. Riordan jumped into the ring and floored Harrison with a blow to the jaw. A melee ensued and a there was a rush at Riordan, who ran out of the club, being followed by an enraged crowd which showered blows upon him. After the melee, order was restored and the bout was completed, with Hardy winning the decision, much to the chagrin of the Olympians, which felt that their man had won.

There was also discussion of a potential 8- or 10-round contest between Corbett and Peter Jackson at the Olympic, which at that point had grown to 1,250 members. "Directors of the Olympic are anxious to match Corbett

---

1890.

[137] *San Francisco Daily Examiner,* December 24, 1888, December 28, 1888; *San Francisco Chronicle,* December 29, 1888; Boxrec.com; Fields at 26. The McAuliffe-Ryan fight was to the finish at the California Club on December 23, 1887, for a $1,000 purse. *Daily Alta California,* December 24, 1887.
[138] *San Francisco Chronicle,* April 23, 1888.

for a ten-round go, but both men want such exorbitant figures that there is liable to be a hitch."[139]

Even as of 1888, Corbett was sufficiently well-thought of that there was discussion of his being matched with many top professionals. Obviously, he was perceived as a professional more so than an amateur. However, no professional match was made and Jim continued his duties as an Olympic professor.[140]

There was a large attendance at a June 29, 1888 benefit at the Olympic Club. It included boxing, fencing, and wrestling. Professor Peter Jackson sparred with assistant Olympic Club professor William Dick, "who evidently does not draw the color line." Professor Corbett engaged in a wrestling match. "Quite a feature of the wrestling was a collar and elbow match between J.J. Corbett and W.H. Quinn, in which each scored a fall." Quinn was an Olympic Club heavyweight amateur boxer, wrestler and weightlifter who was later listed as weighing 178 pounds.

Jackson and Corbett were originally scheduled to spar at the benefit, but Jackson had changed his mind. "There was considerable disappointment in not seeing Corbett spar with Jackson last Friday evening at the Olympic Club benefit, Jim being nearer his match than Mr. Deek." One report provided some insight into why Jackson had refused to box Corbett at the benefit:

> The relations between J.J. Corbett of the Olympic Club and Peter Jackson are somewhat strained. They were to have boxed at the benefit given for the widow of the deceased assistant professor of athletics of the Olympic Club, but Jackson, learning that Corbett had spoken disparagingly of him, refused to go on with him at the exhibition. Jackson is willing, however, to meet Corbett in a set-to of four rounds for points, or a go of ten rounds, in which he guarantees to stop Corbett in that time.[141]

It did not reveal what Corbett's insult was alleged to be. According to his autobiography, after observing Jackson box soon after he came to America in mid-1888, Jim had said that Peter was "a very clever man, but no cleverer than I am!" Apparently, Jackson had heard about what Jim had said, or a variation of the comment that made Peter think that he had been insulted. Certainly though, even at this early stage, Corbett was willing to enter the ring with Jackson, at least for a short exhibition bout. Nothing came of Jackson's challenge.[142]

The day after Corbett wrestled Quinn, on June 30, 1888, Corbett boxed an exhibition with the recently vanquished Frank Glover. The 23-year-old

[139] *San Francisco Chronicle*, May 28, 1888; *Daily Alta California*, May 21, 28, 1888, November 26, 1887.
[140] *New York Clipper*, July 7, 1888. On June 26, 1888, Corbett was a timekeeper for the Young Mitchell vs. Tom Cleary middleweight bout.
[141] *Daily Alta California*, June 30, 1888, July 2, 1888, August 6, 1888; *San Francisco Chronicle*, July 9, 1888.
[142] Corbett at 111-113.

5'9 ½" 180-pound Glover had been boxing for seven years. Prior to his 49-round loss to McAuliffe, he had lost an 1886 6-round decision to Jack Burke, but disputed it.[143]

FRANK GLOVER.

A local paper called the Corbett-Glover bout a benefit for Glover, so it was less than serious. Benefits were generally friendly sparring exhibitions put on to help make money for a boxer who had recently been defeated. Such boxers often lost big money in side bets, or won little or no money because their pay depended upon success. Therefore, often their conquerors and other fighters assisted them with follow up exhibition benefits.

"Professor" Corbett boxed Glover in a 4-round sparring match. Corbett was called a "sparrer of the gentleman order. Precise in his movements and quick, he managed to hit straight to the point frequently. In all the rounds he made a very good contest with Glover." After sparring Corbett, Glover went on to box 3 more rounds with his recent conqueror, Joe McAuliffe.[144] Later records list this as a win for Corbett, but it appears to have been just a friendly exhibition, not a serious contest.

On July 28, 1888 at a benefit held at San Francisco's Standard Theatre, Professor Corbett "donned the mittens for four rounds with Joe Bowers, and a lively and scientific display was the result, the professor, as might be expected, showing to the better advantage." This was the same welterweight/middleweight Joe Bowers who at the California Club four days earlier had lost a 10-round decision to Tom Meadows, and who earlier that year had scored a KO9 over Joseph Connelly.[145]

On August 13, Corbett refereed a bout between Dan Brady and Joe Soto. On August 20, he refereed a professional lightweight contest to a finish in which Tom Meadows (the man who had defeated Joe Bowers) stopped Billy Mahan.[146]

The night after the Meadows-Mahan contest, on August 21, 1888 at the Grand Opera House, Corbett engaged in a 3-round set-to with Frank Bush, who was called the latest importation from the East. "The set-tos were gone through with in a spirited manner and won the usual applause."[147]

---

[143] *San Francisco Chronicle*, May 22, 1888.

[144] *San Francisco Chronicle*, May 22, 1888; *San Francisco Daily Examiner*, July 1, 1888.

[145] *San Francisco Chronicle*, July 29, 1888; Boxrec.com. The benefit was for Tom Cleary, who had recently lost to Paddy Gorman.

[146] *San Francisco Chronicle*, August 14, 1888; *Daily Alta California*, August 21, 1888.

[147] *Daily Alta California*, August 22, 1888; *San Francisco Evening Post*, August 22, 1888. Later in the evening, Jim acted as timekeeper for W.H. Quinn's wrestling bout with Joe Acton.

On August 24, 1888 at the California Athletic Club in a fight fought for a $1,500 purse, Peter Jackson scored a KO19 over top American black, George Godfrey. Jim Corbett was Godfrey's chosen timekeeper, while sports writer W. Naughton acted in that capacity for Jackson, and Dave Eisman held the watch for the club.[148] Corbett's presence at Jackson's fights gave Jim an opportunity to analyze Peter's strengths and weaknesses.

From about August until mid-October, champion John L. Sullivan was suffering from typhoid fever, malaria, and various other ailments, being confined to his bed. At one point, it was feared that he might die. Medicine and life expectancy were on the short side of their development at that point. Even as of 1900, the average life expectancy for a male was not greater than 48 years.

On November 14, 1888, Corbett sparred the approximately 150-pound Robert McCord as part of an Olympic "ladies night" sporting exhibition. Ten days later, on November 24 at an athletic exhibition at Turner Hall, Corbett and McCord sparred 3 rounds.[149]

On November 29, Corbett was a marshal at an Oakland amateur athletic tournament, while Joe Choynski was an assistant marshal.[150] Jim was said to be hard at work training his pupils, preparing them for the Olympic's December 7th boxing night. "Professor Corbett is kept busy from morning till night putting on the finishing touches to several of the boys."[151]

Although in late September it had been reported that there was a probability that Professor Corbett and Joe McAuliffe would be matched to spar for points, eventually McAuliffe was matched to fight Peter Jackson.[152] Although McAuliffe had initially drawn the color line, he had been convinced to reverse himself and fight Jackson, in part as a result of pressure from the *San Francisco Examiner*. Some felt that drawing the line was an indication of fear, while others believed that Joe would "degrade himself by fighting the dusky Australian."[153]

In his autobiography, Corbett claimed to have sparred with McAuliffe once to help Joe prepare for his fight with Jackson, which occurred in late December 1888. Corbett said that he "knocked [McAuliffe] all over the place." Corbett's claimed superiority may have been correct. Peter Jackson said of McAuliffe that although he was a big fellow, standing 6'3" and worshipped in San Francisco, "I can't see anything clever in him. He has great staying power, and could hit you 'real hard' if you'd let him! But as far

[148] *Referee*, September 26, 1888.
[149] *Daily Alta California*, November 15, 1888, November 25, 1888; *San Francisco Chronicle*, November 8, 1890.
[150] *San Francisco Chronicle*, November 30, 1888.
[151] *Daily Alta California*, December 3, 8, 1888.
[152] *Daily Alta California*, September 24, 1888.
[153] *San Francisco Daily Examiner*, June 12, 1888.

as cleverness is concerned, I think Dooley could outfight him at every point."[154]

On December 28, 1888 at the California Club, for a $3,000 purse, Peter Jackson stopped Joe McAuliffe in the 24th round. Corbett witnessed the fight, watching Jackson and figuring out "a system of fighting him."[155] Corbett had a keen eye and was able to analyze fellow fighters. He knew that Jackson was the coming man and that he might have to fight him one day.

It is important to provide a context for and an insight into race relations, because such relations affected boxing. Just one week before Jackson's victory over McAuliffe, it was reported in a local paper that Kansas Senator Ingalls had said that the "negroes are growing blacker, and that the tendency is toward segregation." He and others feared that the black population might one day outnumber whites. "He fears negro supremacy." However, a San Francisco paper said,

> Neither the country nor the South is in any such danger. … Instead of a gloomy view, we think the future full of hope and promise. This fine country was not conquered from the red man for the black; it will never cease to be a white man's country, unless all history is false, and the superior race shall yield to the inferior.[156]

Another paper noted,

> Ingalls has sounded the keynote in declaring that there is an ethnological bar to the two races dwelling together upon terms of political equality. …
>
> They [blacks] must demonstrate their fitness for the duties of citizenship. Then that fitness is not yet demonstrated, and yet the denial of rights which it is confessed they are not yet proved fit to exercise is ascribed to "prejudice." … Lincoln believed that the only solution of the problem of the negroes' destiny would be found in their deportation and colonization in Hayti and Liberia, and it is opportunely recalled that General Grant thought of colonizing them in San Domingo. …
>
> But we begin to realize now that the colored people love the whites so much that they are determined to stay with them. The Governments of Liberia, Hayti and San Domingo are all monumental failures. The colored man cannot get along by himself.
>
> That is to say, the colored man, wherever he attempts to govern himself, is a failure. He can't get along by himself. …

---

[154] *Brooklyn Daily Eagle,* January 24, 1895; *San Francisco Examiner,* February 18, 1890; *Sydney Referee,* July 5, 1888.
[155] Corbett at 113; *New York Sun,* February 4, 1890.
[156] *San Francisco Chronicle,* December 24, 1888.

The white man can get along by himself. ... A white minority, anywhere on earth, finally conquers a colored majority...

But we need not discuss the matter. It is getting discussion enough by the men who rightly believed that the negro did not deserve slavery, and who now confess that they were so right in that proposition that they made the mistake of omitting to see that he also did not deserve citizenship.[157]

One black lawyer a few years later said that "the white people fear the negro. They are afraid to give him a fair chance in life. ... They show their cowardice by claiming his utter inferiority, and at the same time placing every conceivable barrier across his pathway." This was the era's racial climate.[158]

In boxing, John L. Sullivan had said that he would never meet Peter Jackson in the ring on account of his color. Although this was consistent with the general social norm, many felt that boxing tradition differed, dictating that

A champion of the prize ring must meet all comers. He wouldn't be any kind of a champion if he didn't, and the rules bearing upon fistic encounters, whether of the bare knuckles or of gloves, do not in the remotest way recognize color. The history of the ring shows this conclusively. England's phenomenal fighters and champions met all blacks that challenged them... Molineaux was never objected to because of his Ethiopian skin, and he was black as the ace of spades.[159]

The local San Francisco newspapers were very high on Peter Jackson and generally supported his right to challenge for the championship. However, some lamented Jackson's victory over McAuliffe on racial grounds. "Many regret that Jackson won, on the ground that no first-class Eastern pugilist will care to fight a colored man, and they think it will have a tendency to lessen the regard of outsiders for boxing if a black man demands the championship."[160]

When reporting Corbett's record as of May 30, 1889, the *San Francisco Evening Post* said, "One of the best fights that Corbett ever took part in was at the Orpheum Theater in 1889. On the occasion referred to he bested Professor William Miller, the heavy weight wrestler and all-round athlete of Australia in six rounds." Since the early 1880s, the 220-pound Miller had been an experienced wrestling champion and frequent gloved exhibitionist. In 1879 or 1880, he had boxed an exhibition with Paddy Ryan. In 1882, he

[157] *Daily Alta California*, January 4, 1889.
[158] *New York Sun*, February 14, 1892.
[159] *Daily Alta California*, January 14, 1889.
[160] *San Francisco Daily Examiner*, December 30, 1888.

toured Australia and New Zealand giving exhibitions with former world bareknuckle champion Jem Mace. Miller held a victory over Joe Goss and an 1883 KO40 over Larry Foley. In 1884, Miller boxed Peter Jackson in a 4-round exhibition. For Corbett, boxing a very large veteran fighter like Miller was good experience, and once again showed that he could compete with the big ones.[161]

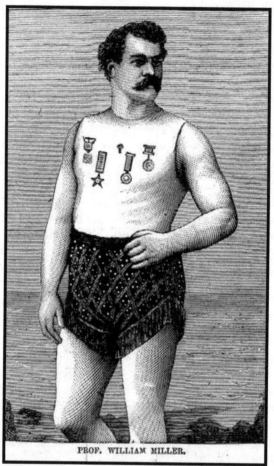

PROF. WILLIAM MILLER.

As of early 1889, Professor Corbett was training men such as Robert McCord, W.J. Zelner, William J. and E. Kenealy, and P.J. (or P.T.) Goodloe, in addition to a number of others, preparing them for an amateur tournament. Corbett was continuing his daily life as a boxing teacher, but his name was still being discussed in conjunction with potential matches against top pros.[162]

---

[161] *San Francisco Evening Post*, May 30, 1889; Cyberboxingzone.com; *Daily Alta California*, November 28, 1887. The exact date of the Corbett-Miller bout is unknown. Obviously it had to be prior to late May 1889. A secondary source claims the bout took place in 1887 and that Miller left America in October or November 1888. There is evidence that Miller arrived in American in late November 1887.
[162] *Daily Alta California*, January 12, 1889.

From January to March 1889, there was talk of a possible match between Corbett, "undoubtedly a really clever sparer," and Peter Jackson. "Corbett has betrayed an eagerness to measure his science with that of 'Peter the Great.'" Such a match was intriguing, because there was "a very strong desire to see what Corbett can do, as he has never been fully tried. Against such a general and ring tactician as Jackson he would have an opportunity of showing what there is in him."

The ongoing discussion of a Corbett-Jackson match focused on a potential 10-round points bout. However, because they were affiliated with rival clubs, neither club could agree upon terms regarding which club should host the match, the amount of the prize money, or who would be allowed to attend. There was also concern that there would be bias in any decision, based on which club hosted the match. Jackson said that he would only fight under the auspices of the California Athletic Club, and the Olympic refused to allow the bout at the Pavilion. The Olympic said that it would host the match and provide seats for California Club members. The California Club refused to allow the match to take place there, insisting on the Pavilion.

> So the proposal to have Professor Corbett measure his skill with that prince of scientific boxers, Peter Jackson, falls to the ground, as by a strange coincidence did similar proposals to match Corbett against Glover, McAuliffe and other fighters in times gone by. 'Tis strange, 'tis passing strange. The latest and most feasible plea of pitting Joe Choynski against Jim Corbett in a contest "for blood" has more of a true ring about it than all the previous twaddle.[163]

The writer was implying that there really wasn't a genuine intent to match Corbett with these men.

Still, the locals were very high on Joe Choynski, and interestingly enough, were actually more excited about a potential match between Choynski and Corbett than Jackson with the same. The 163-pound Choynski had in February 1889 scored a KO14 over 170-pound Frank Glover. This was important because the much larger and hard punching Joe McAuliffe had required 49 rounds to take out Glover. Of Choynski, in early March 1889 it was said,

> A brilliant future is predicted for the young Californian... Already they are talking of matching him against another native son, Jem Corbett of the Olympic Club, whose reputation as a sparrer is first-class. These two men have met before, and Corbett has managed to come out a little ahead, but the vast improvement shown by Choynski during the past year is expected to more than overcome the

163 *San Francisco Chronicle*, January 28, 1889, February 25 1889, March 11, 1889; *Daily Alta California*, February 25, 1889, March 11, 1889.

differences which formerly existed. Joe would not have any trouble in finding all the backing he desired for a match with the Olympian ...

Should the match be made it would undoubtedly attract more attention than a match between Corbett and Jackson, which was first talked of.[164]

During March 1889, the Olympic Club published a set of rules that would govern its amateur contests in the future. Middleweight was set at 158 pounds, while heavyweight was anything above that. Ring size was a minimum of 16-feet up to a maximum of 24-feet. The referee would decide bouts only when the two judges disagreed. Bouts would be 4 three-minute rounds, but an extra round could be fought if thought necessary to render a decision. The points for decisions would be based upon direct clean hits with the knuckles and for defensive moves such as guarding, slipping, ducking, counter-hitting or getting away, but points would also be subtracted for clinching to avoid punishment. When the points were otherwise equal, the man who did most of the leading was to be given the edge. Disqualification could result from clinching, hugging, butting, wrestling, striking foul blows, flicking or hitting with the open glove, or hitting with the inside or butt of the hand or wrist or elbow.[165]

Demonstrating its growing tension with professional clubs, in late March, the Olympic passed a resolution forbidding its members from taking part in exhibitions with professionals, under penalty of being expelled. "The Olympic Club by reason of its age, standing and membership considers itself in a position to dictate the course of amateur sports in this city."[166]

At some point, likely during March, Corbett became ill and took a hiatus from teaching, resuming his duties at the start of April 1889. One paper as of May said that Corbett had been somewhat ill for about three months.[167] The Olympic hired De Witt Van Court in late March to instruct the lightweight classes, allowing Professor Corbett to work with the middle and heavy weights.[168]

In late April 1889 at the California Club, Peter Jackson scored a KO10 over Patsy Cardiff, who had fought Sullivan to an 1887 6-round draw (Sully broke his left arm). Sullivan was already set to meet Jake Kilrain in a July 1889 bareknuckle bout. After Kilrain, Peter Jackson was at that time considered the next logical contender to Sullivan's throne.

---

[164] *Daily Alta California*, March 4, 1889.
[165] *Daily Alta California*, March 4, 1889.
[166] *Daily Alta California*, March 25, 1889, April 1, 1889.
[167] *Daily Alta California*, April 1, 1889; *San Francisco Evening Post*, May 29, 1889.
[168] *Daily Alta California*, March 29, 1889.

CHAPTER 5

A Tough Professional: The Local Rivalry of Future Greats

In April 1889, the California Club's Board of Directors offered a $3,000 purse for a June contest to the finish between Jim Corbett and their instructor, Joe Choynski. However, Corbett was under contract to the Olympic Club, which would not allow professional contests in its own rooms, nor allow its members or instructors to take part in bouts at professional clubs. In order to avoid this problem, in mid- to late-April, Jim and Joe signed for the match to take place in private, at neither club. Concern was expressed about this, because technically a private bout left both men liable to be arrested for a felony. However, Corbett believed what was really behind the "concern" was that the local professional athletic clubs wanted to make sure the fight took place in one of their rooms. One man opined that the professional clubs "fancy they have a monopoly of a certain class of contests." Legally, they did. Ironically, it later turned out that the boxers would have made more money if they had held their contest in a professional establishment.[169]

Joe Choynski, the son of Polish Jews, was one of the nemeses of Corbett's youth, although he was two years younger than Jim. Corbett had defeated Joe two or three times when they were both novices, as well as in March 1887. Although Choynski had a strong amateur career at the Golden Gate Club and elsewhere, he had recently been boxing as a professional for the California Athletic Club. By 1889, both men had come a long way in their boxing knowledge, and both had strong local reputations.

Choynski claimed that he began boxing at age 14 and that one of the first men he ever met was Con Riordan. Riordan was a 165-pound boxing professor at the Golden Gate Club, and likely helped teach Choynski to box. Riordan had sparred with the likes of Steve Taylor (November 1886) and Peter Jackson (June 1888), and was at one point a Jackson trainer/sparring partner.[170]

Choynski had a number of good wins to his credit: 5-1887 KO2 Jack McAuley; 7-87 KO Tom Moran, KO2 Joe Connelly for the Golden Gate

---

[169] *Daily Alta California,* April 22, 1889; April 29, 1889; *San Francisco Evening Post,* May 4, 1889.
[170] *National Police Gazette,* July 5, 1902.

Club's amateur championship; and 11-29-87 KO4 Bill Kenealy for the west coast amateur crown.[171]

In June 1888, Choynski boxed 4 rounds with Peter Jackson. A report said that no local pugilist was as clever as Choynski, and that his quick work forced Jackson to make some effort. It also indicated that Choynski had previously boxed with Joe McAuliffe and had made a "clever stand" against him.[172] In mid-November 1888, Choynski scored a KO2 over a fighter named George Bush.[173]

In February 1889, Choynski fought Frank Glover, who had previously been stopped in 49 rounds by Joe McAuliffe, and had subsequently sparred Corbett 4 rounds. During the last few days of his training for the Glover fight, Peter Jackson coached Choynski.[174] A 163-165-pound Choynski dropped the 170-173-pound Glover multiple times en route to a 14th round knockout victory.[175] The *San Francisco Evening Post* said that Choynski won easily, punishing Glover, who at the end of the fight was "one mass of blood and a couple of his teeth were knocked in. Choynski was in splendid condition and at the end of the fight he seemed to be as fresh as at the beginning."[176]

The Glover fight even gained Choynski national recognition. The *National Police Gazette* reported, "California has found a man in Joe Choynski who is worthy of the name of a first-class pugilist. As a fighter he is a cool and collected student of his opponent, a straight and effective hitter, a good judge of distance and a dead game man."[177]

Choynski was "anxious to obliterate the memory of one or two short frock encounters which Corbett loves to recall." Corbett was "confident of coming out ahead as he was in his previous encounters with his present opponent, when he had everything his own way. At the same time, he does not lose sight of the fact that Joe has improved at least 100 percent since the date of their last meeting."[178]

The local interest in the Corbett-Choynski fight was huge, because both men had "a large following of young and ardent admirers." Both were from San Francisco, from prominent clubs, and it was said that they were evenly matched. "The rivalry between them has been of long standing, and as each has a great number of friends the fistic contest is imbued with an interest that does not attach to ordinary professional battles for a purse." All of

---

[171] *San Francisco Evening Post*, May 30, 1889.
[172] *San Francisco Daily Examiner*, June 27, 1888.
[173] *Daily Alta California*, November 15, 1888.
[174] *Sydney Referee*, April 10, 1889.
[175] *National Police Gazette*, March 23, 1889; *Daily Alta California*, February 27, 1889.
[176] *San Francisco Evening Post*, May 30, 1889.
[177] *National Police Gazette*, March 30, 1889.
[178] *San Francisco Chronicle*, April 29, 1889; *Daily Alta California*, May 6, 1889.

these factors made the fight have more interest than any previous local encounter.[179]

According to Corbett's autobiography, the reason their fight engendered such strong local interest was because it was about more than just Choynski vs. Corbett, but about differing factions: California Athletic Club (where Joe trained) vs. Olympic, a pro vs. a previous amateur, Jew vs. Gentile, labor vs. capital (Corbett having worked for a bank), and Golden Gate Ave. vs. Hayes Street.[180]

Choynski trained in the same camp that the top middleweight, George "the Marine" LaBlanche, was training. Corbett initially trained with Young Dutchy, almost immediately "showing a big improvement." However, after Dutchy's wife took ill, Billy Delaney and Peter McIntyre took over the training duties. This began the long-standing professional relationship between Corbett and Delaney. Corbett went into intense training less than a month prior to the fight, although he had generally been an active well-conditioned athlete, so it would not have taken him very long to get into prime shape.

The gamblers were about equally divided upon who would win. As the fight approached, it was said that Choynski's "stock has gone up during the week, and

WM. DELANEY, CORBETT'S TRAINER.

he is now slightly in the lead in the betting, of which there has been a great deal in a quiet way." California Club members backed Joe quite heavily, while Olympic Club members bet on Jim. Another report said, "It is estimated that over $25,000 has been placed in the hands of local pool sellers on the result of the fight, but no odds have been offered in favor of either contestant." The night before the fight, "public opinion seemed to be equally divided as to who would be victorious."[181]

Peter Jackson predicted that fellow California Club member Choynski would defeat Corbett, saying of Joe,

[179] *San Francisco Chronicle*, April 29, 1889, May 6, 1889; *Daily Alta California*, May 13, 1889.
[180] Corbett at 62-70.
[181] *Daily Alta California*, May 13, 1889; May 27, 1889; *San Francisco Evening Post*, May 30, 1889.

True he is lighter, but then Joe is a cool, scientific fighter, an unusually hard hitter, and a dead-game man. Corbett, you know, made some talk about meeting me some time ago, but I hardly think he anticipated doing so, as he pretty well knew that the Olympic Club would not consent to it under the terms we would have to meet.[182]

Another opined, "Choynski is a harder hitter than Corbett, and if he gets in a few blows with his right, Corbett will stop."[183]

Joe Choynski

There were reports before the fight that it was a real grudge match, that the two competitors had a serious disdain for one another. However, some time after they had settled matters, one Olympic Club member provided his insight into how the Corbett-Choynski match was made:

[182] *Sydney Referee,* July 3, 1889.
[183] *San Francisco Evening Post,* May 30, 1889.

Jim and Joe, though old rivals, had squared matters, and as a matter of fact Jim was giving Joe instructions in boxing only a few months ago, shortly before Choynski's fight with Glover. I know of my own knowledge that those stories about being unable to meet on the street without insulting each other were false. What brought the fight about was this: Choynski had a setto in Alameda with Peter Jackson, and gave the brunette a very hard rub. Jackson complimented Joe on his prowess, and having heard some talk of rivalry between Choynski and Corbett, remarked that Joe could do up Jim in five rounds. Choynski's friends noised Jackson's words about until Corbett heard them. He promptly asserted that the best way to settle the question was for Choynski and himself to don the mittens. This was then talked about until finally a match was inevitable. Now, there's the whole story.[184]

On the morning of May 30, 1889, 22-year-old James J. Corbett fought a professional fight against 20-year-old Joe Choynski. According to the *San Francisco Evening Post*, which had a same day fight report, the bout took place in a 24-square-foot ring on the second story loft of a barn in San Anselmo, Marin County. Some later said it took place in the Fairfax area. They had to fight in such a location because the bout was scheduled to be to the finish and not promoted by any athletic club, and therefore technically illegal.

Although the fight was supposed to be held in secret, word of its location leaked out and a crowd of several hundred attempted to see it. However, athletic men guarded the barn and only newspaper reporters and invited guests were allowed inside. Regardless, before the bout began, it was announced that the county sheriff had sent word that although he would not make any arrests; he would not allow the fight to go on. They went ahead with the fight anyway.

According to the *Post*, Choynski said that he weighed 163 pounds. Corbett weighed 182 pounds. The *Chronicle* listed Corbett as a bit over 6' and weighing 185 pounds. Choynski was listed as nearly 5'11" and 165 pounds. Joe was clearly shorter and smaller, but his muscular build made him appear heavier than he was.

The *San Francisco Examiner* said that Corbett wore pink tights (not taboo at the time) and Choynski black ones. The *San Francisco Chronicle* said that the smiling Corbett wore pink trunks with a sash that had a band of green entwined with red, white and blue (Irish and American colors).

The gloves were "stuffed excuses," weighing a mere two ounces, providing almost no padding. The *Chronicle* called them hard gloves, meaning that they were just leather, with nothing inside. Patsy Hogan was the referee.

The bout began between 10:41 and 10:45 a.m. It was an extremely hot day. "In fact hot does not begin to express a fair idea of the temperature in

---

[184] *San Francisco Evening Post*, June 8, 1889.

the half sheltered shed."[185] When they shook hands, Corbett offered to bet Choynski $500, but Joe declined.

The following account is an amalgamation of multiple local sources, including the *San Francisco Evening Post* (EP), *San Francisco Examiner* (SFE), and *San Francisco Chronicle* (SFC).

Joe Choynski

1st round

Corbett was described as nimble on his feet, resembling Charley Mitchell in style. "He stood well up with his left lightly poised and his whole attitude that of the practiced and clever boxer." Choynski spread his legs wider and leaned back more, with his left extended and right ready to fire.

Corbett took the offensive at first, moving forward and feinting. Both landed some light blows and avoided others. Choynski was nervous and threw his right when too far out of range. Corbett stopped left leads, smiled, and led with one or two mere taps. The pace was slow.

Joe backed around the ring on the defensive, occasionally shooting out lefts to the body as the wary Professor Corbett dodged. The only effective

---

[185] *San Francisco Evening Post*, May 30, 1889.

blow of the round was a Corbett swift left to Choynski's jaw. Joe took it well though and smiled. "The remainder of the round was a harmless spar, with Corbett still working his man and Choynski on the watchful retreat."

2nd round

The round was fierce and entertaining, the only one of the four of its kind.

At the start, Corbett had a sneering smile on his face, while Choynski looked anxious. Corbett assumed the offensive to begin the round, while Joe kept away. Jim landed lightly to the neck with some harmless taps.

They soon drew to close range and began fighting in earnest. After Joe missed a right, Jim countered to the mouth and made Joe shake. Corbett again took the aggressive, but "lost his caution" and a Choynski right smash to the chin rubbed off skin and drew first blood. However, it was "scarcely an instant before Corbett's gloves were covered with blood from another smash that landed clean on Choynski's mouth." There were a series of fast and savage rallies, with "hate and dislike in every blow." Each man was slugging, trying to knock the other out. Corbett had the advantage in the rally, having superior speed and weight, landing some solid rights to the ear.

Choynski went down in this round, each local source giving its version:

EP: Joe rallied, but Jim stepped to the right and Choynski went by with a rush. "Corbett led for his neck. The blow went past without harm, but Choynski was rattled and stumbled to the floor." He rose before ten and they went at it again. Joe was slightly unsteady, while Jim was smiling and confident.

SFE: As Joe was ducking, Corbett caught him solidly on the chin and staggered him. Jim followed up but Joe clinched. On the break, Jim threw him off fiercely and Joe fell backwards to the floor. Choynski rose and then rushed him savagely.

SFC: They continued going at it, until Choynski "suddenly went down, being half pushed and half struck down." Joe immediately rose and rushed into a clinch.

After clinching, Corbett ignored the referee's repeated calls to break, instead continuing to hold and hit the kidneys and body, to cries of foul from the spectators and Joe's seconds, who thought that it was not fair. The referee had to engage in vigorous efforts to break them apart. Breaking away, Jim hit the body, taking off some skin. The referee cautioned Jim.

Corbett landed a left to the face, but received a hard counter over the heart. Still, Choynski had the worst of it. Joe's mouth appeared to be swelling fast, while Corbett's gloves were "one mass of blood." "There was one more clinch and rally, Corbett hitting when he had a chance, as he had a perfect right to do, but the spectators seemed to think he had no right to hit when they were clinched, but ought to break away."

Corbett clearly won the round. Joe seemed to have been shaken by two blows to the face, and he appeared more distressed than Jim did. It was an exciting round, the impression being that a chance blow on either side could have ended matters.

3rd round

The round was an "unemotional spar, Corbett backing his man round the ring slowly and Joe watching for an opening." Although Jim took the lead and drove Joe around the ring, he did not attempt to go inside, taking few chances, poking leads at a distance that fell short or missed because Joe was shifty. Choynski kept drawing him in, but Jim would not go for it. Corbett forced things, but both kept far enough away that neither was able to land for a while. Joe swung his right viciously, but Jim caught it with his shoulder. Joe did clever work in eluding Jim's leads, although generally Jim forced and feinted but did not throw.

The round was quite tame, no harm being done by either man. The only blows landed were a couple mere slaps to the face. The referee broke up one clinch. At this point, some felt that it would be a slow and dull fight. They seemed to have gained respect for one another's punching power, and it had developed into a tactical match. Between rounds, both corners told their man to take it easy, anticipating a long fight.

4th round

The round was not very brisk, essentially being a repetition of the 3rd, with neither doing damage. Joe missed his right, for Jim's keen eye enabled him to step back at the proper time, commanding the crowd's admiration. Corbett made an occasional lead, while Joe acted wary. Not much was done, but Choynski's face puffed up badly. The spectators became a bit disappointed, although the persistent way Corbett followed and Choynski retreated on the alert gave the impression that a hot rally could occur at any time.

After the one minute rest following the round's conclusion, just as time was called to begin the 5th round, the lookout spotted the sheriff coming down the lane, and the illegal fight was suspended. They removed the gloves and substituted them with large, soft pillows, to give the impression of a harmless spar. However, the sheriff was not fooled, telling them that a fight could not take place there, and that they had to leave. He informed them that if they intended to have a fight to the finish, it would need to take place in another county. Corbett told the sheriff, "I am glad to meet you...but I would have been a heap gladder if you had come here ten minutes later." Both sides consented to a postponement of the fight for a few days, particularly after the railroad refused to transport them out of the county.

The *Chronicle* said that Corbett's only damage suffered was a loss of skin to the chin and a sprained thumb. The *Examiner* said that Corbett was relatively unmarked, while Choynski's lip was swollen and he had sore ribs. It was agreed that "Choynski had received a little more punishment than

Corbett, but it was argued that this was the result of his method of fighting on the defensive.... The contest has so far decided nothing except that there will be a hard fight when the men finally finish." However, it also said that 4 careful rounds were fought, little damage was done, and the advantage was slightly in favor of Corbett. The *Evening Post* said that the opinion on the streets of San Francisco was that "the combatants had not been given an opportunity to display their respective merits."[186]

Afterwards, Choynski said, "I admit that I got the worst of it," but still felt that he could win, saying that a few rounds did not amount to much in a real fight. "You see I was feeling my man, and was trying to draw him into a rush. He didn't hurt me much. In fact he can't hurt me. I know I can last longer than he can, and besides that I have been in the ring before." Joe had a swollen nose, a cut lip, and a lump behind his right ear.

With his slightly swollen thumb and a little scratch on his chin, Corbett said,

> I didn't expect to see him run away from me the way he did. My opinion is that he was badly scared when he entered the ring. He appeared to be nervous and unconfident, as was shown by the number of times he led and fell short. He was depending altogether on a heavy right hand swing to settle the business, but I didn't give him a chance to put it in. He can't hit me at all; of that I feel pretty sure; and when he can't do that he can't whip me. His only hope is a chance blow during a rush when we are at close quarters.[187]

The day after the fight, the *Evening Post* reported that interest in the fight was increasing rather than diminishing. A couple days afterwards, the *Chronicle* reported that the leading topic of conversation on the streets was the unfinished contest and the prospect of its being resumed.[188] Despite Corbett's better performance, "The pugilists still think very favorably of Choynski, though admitting that Corbett is bigger and more clever." Both went back into training for a few days.[189]

The two fought again a mere six days following their suspended meeting, on the morning of June 5, 1889 on a barge anchored off Dillon's Point, opposite Benicia, in the Carquinez Straits. The ring was pitched on the barge's deck. 254 persons witnessed the bout.

Although the articles of agreement called for two-ounce gloves, either Joe or a friend failed to bring his pair. Corbett said in his autobiography that Choynski wanted the fight to be bareknuckle, perhaps having learned that Corbett had hurt his right thumb in the 4th round of their prior bout. Jim was not about to fight bareknuckle under such circumstances, and the bout

[186] *San Francisco Evening Post*, May 30, 1889; *San Francisco Daily Examiner, San Francisco Chronicle, San Francisco Evening Post*, May 31, 1889.
[187] *San Francisco Chronicle*, May 31, 1889; *San Francisco Evening Post*, May 31, 1889.
[188] *San Francisco Evening Post*, May 31, 1889; *San Francisco Chronicle*, May 31, 1889, June 1, 1889.
[189] *San Francisco Chronicle*, June 3, 1889.

had been arranged to be gloved. However, he did not object to Choynski's fighting without gloves. After some discussion, it was decided that Choynski would wear skin driving gloves, the closest thing he could get to being bareknuckle.[190]

The local primary sources agreed that Choynski's gloves could not be found. Corbett's manager said that the stakes and fight would therefore be claimed for Jim. However, Corbett said that he would waive all claim and wanted to get on with the fight. Denny Costigan suggested that they fight with bare knuckles. That suggestion was actually rejected by Jack Dempsey; one of Choynski's seconds, fearing that such a fight would leave them liable for a prison sentence. The courts were typically doubly harsh when it came to bareknuckle fights.

Choynski found a pair of soft driving gloves. Corbett graciously allowed Joe to have whatever gloves he wanted. "Let him take the driving gloves, and I will wear the two-ounce gloves I have got on." Corbett preferred and used the two-ounce gloves in order to protect his sore right thumb, and Joe indeed used thin dog-skin driving gloves. It was agreed that Corbett could elect during the bout to remove his gloves and put on a smaller pair of driving gloves. However, Jim kept the two-ounce gloves on for the bout's duration.

Before the fight began, Patsy Hogan, the same referee as from the week before, told the men that they were required to break and step back when there was a clinch. Reacting to claims that he had favored Corbett the first

[190] Corbett at 70-75.

time regarding hitting in the clinches, Hogan said, "I will now make the following rule, in addition to the Marquis of Queensberry, which I will strictly follow, and that is, in case of a clinch I will order the men to break away, which they must do and step back one pace and clear." Typically, under Queensberry rules, hitting in the clinches was allowed. Corbett asked what would happen if they hit in the clinch. Hogan said he would issue a caution, but if it happened a second time he would declare it a foul (which meant the fighter would be disqualified).

Corbett was listed as weighing 180 pounds to Choynski's 172 pounds. The fight began at 6:48 a.m.

The following round by round account is an amalgamation of the local sources, including the *San Francisco Evening Post* (EP) (which gave the most complete same day report), *San Francisco Examiner* (SFE), *San Francisco Chronicle* (SFC), and *Daily Alta California* (AC). Differences are noted where significant.

1st round

This time it was Choynski who did the leading and pressing, forcing the pace at the start, while the "cautious and agile" Corbett used his jab. Both sparred for an opening at ring center, but neither landed.

2nd round

It was cold and the men were blue. Choynski looked "sober," while Corbett was smiling. Joe was again aggressive, forcing the fight, landing hard rights to Corbett's ribs, which made a large red blotch. Jim took the offensive a bit, using hard left leads. Some hot exchanges followed, but neither did much harm.

3rd round

Choynski went down in this round, each source giving its own version:
EP: Choynski went down from a push blow in the mouth. It was not a clean knockdown. Later, Jim landed a light counter that made Joe's mouth bleed. Jim's corner was joyous.
SFE: This round was more exciting, as Corbett rushed and swung with his left. The force of the blow, along with Joe's legs getting tangled, caused Choynski to trip and fall down. There was a lively exchange at the end which brought first blood from Joe's chin.
SFC: This was another intense round. Joe moved back from a left, and Jim followed and floored Choynski with a smashing left on the stomach. Joe rose smiling. He was defensive, but Jim eventually caught him on the jaw with both hands. This was a strong Corbett round, and from that point on, Jim took the lead.
AC: "Corbett opened this round by swinging in his long left, catching Choynski on the jaw, the latter going down. Choynski, however, was up in a

second." After Jim landed a straight left on the nose, Joe said, "That was a good one."

4th round

EP: Choynski was wild and short with his punches. Corbett hit him with a straight smash in the face and ducked beautifully. Corbett countered a Choynski lead. "The round amounted to nothing, but showed Jim's superiority as a boxer. Joe could not reach him with any force."

SFE: Corbett began the round with jabs, and received a hard right to the ribs. Jim landed a hard left to the forehead, snapping Joe's head back, but apparently this blow broke Corbett's hand. (Handwraps did not exist at that time. They merely slipped their hands into the small, minimally padded gloves.) Just before the end of the round, Joe landed a hard left to the body.

SFC: Jim was aggressive and landed a counter to the mouth that brought blood from Choynski. Corbett also jabbed the nose and jaw.

AC: Choynski landed some blows to the body and head, a rib shot leaving its mark.

5th round

Corbett had the best of the round. Jim landed a hard blow on the nose, drawing first blood from that organ. Whenever Joe led, Jim countered him. Corbett's leads to the nose made the blood fly. Jim hit him three times in a row with the left and "Joe became groggy and could hardly stand. He got an awful stab in the nose, and another that made him reel, but he did not go down." Corbett kept hitting the nose with his left, which brought the blood streaming down in a deluge. Joe tried for a knockout with big rights, but generally could only land them to the ribs against the defensively intelligent Corbett. The *Chronicle* claimed that this was the round that Corbett broke his left hand.

6th round

As they did in the previous round, Choynski hit the body while Corbett struck the mouth. Jim smiled when Joe landed some good punches to the stomach and ribs. They spoke to one another. Jim responded to a blow, "That was pretty light." He also said after landing a left uppercut, "Joe, you have got your eye on that bottle." Choynski landed a rib shot and said, "Don't get rattled Jim."

7th round

Joe slipped and Jim landed a few smashes to the mouth, causing Choynski's lips to look very large. "Up to this time Jim never used his right." In the middle of the round, a left to Choynski's nose "brought another deluge of blood." Although Corbett's ribs and shoulders showed the marks of Choynski's blows, Joe found it increasingly difficult to land,

and took another jab to the nose before the end of the round. By this point, it looked like Corbett would win.

8th round

Overall, little significant work was done, as both were cautious. When Choynski pressed, he was wild with his right, throwing himself off balance. Jim hit the nose with his left and brought the gory blood stream flowing. Jim landed several times to Joe's sore mouth and nose, which looked horrible. Corbett successfully stabbed away in subsequent rounds.

None of the other sources mentioned this, but the *Chronicle* claimed that when Joe tried to jab, Jim hit him on the stomach and again floored Choynski, who rose quickly. Corbett crowded him until the end of the round.

9th round

There were again varying accounts as to whether and how Choynski went down in this round:

EP: Corbett continued hitting the nose, while Choynski missed his right. "Jim made a fine left lead in the ribs and the right in the jaw, and knocked Choynski clean down. Joe was much punished and did not look pretty. He also seemed rattled."

AC: Corbett landed lefts to the nose and evaded Choynski's left. "Corbett again touched up that nose and with a quick move with his left sent in a blow on Choynski's side that sent him to the floor."

SFC: Those wanting to bet on Corbett found no takers, even at odds of 50 to 20, for most thought Choynski would be defeated. Joe fought desperately, trying to get close and land his right, but the Corbett left "slaughtered him." Choynski bled so badly that it ran down his chest and stained Corbett's glove, such that it "looked as if it had been dipped in carmine." The blood started to make the floor slippery.

The *Examiner* mentioned no knockdown. Although the *Chronicle* did not mention a knockdown in this round, it did say that Choynski had gone down in the previous round from a body shot, so either it or the other sources might have been off by a round.

10th round

Corbett backers offered odds of 50 to 25 (2 to 1) on Corbett. Joe was wild and missed his right, but landed on the ribs with his left. Jim punched the nose several times. One left to Joe's nose sent blood spattering over both men. Choynski's lips began badly protruding. His cheeks were swollen and his right eye black and closing. Another flush hit made him look gorier than ever, although he continued fighting vigorously. "His face looked dreadful. The blood poured from his mouth, and it looked as if only the call of time saved him. He was badly beaten, and Jim was unhurt."

11th round

Choynski's face was red and bleeding. His nose suffered, and his legs appeared to be giving out. Corbett simply leaned back away from Joe's blows, which seemed to have lost their force. Joe choked on his own blood, causing him to spit out mouthfuls of blood all over the ring. Jim's trunks had turned red.

12th round

Choynski charged in, but Jim peppered him with multiple lefts. Joe tried to hit the ribs, but Corbett "proved a master of the art of getting away. A light tap drew the blood in streams, but Joe was game and stood up and took a horrible jabbing. His face was one bloody mask." Choynski was unable to defend the left jabs, and the blood spurted from his nose. The blood loss weakened him. "A game but overmatched man was the verdict." Corbett avoided Choynski's right, laughing. In a clinch, both slipped and went down, Jim falling on top of Joe.

13th round

After having been cut up "unmercifully" in preceding rounds, at this point Choynski became desperate and attacked furiously. Despite Choynski's attempted rushes and hard swings with both hands, he still received counter jabs. Corbett was "cool and crafty." Joe was badly punished and glassy-eyed, as Corbett tried to knock him out.

Still, Choynski made a bit of a comeback in the round. During one of his rushes, Joe got the best of a rally, landing a left and right to the mouth that sent Jim to the ropes. Choynski also landed a hard punch on the eye. Corbett clinched, and as a result of their wrestling, they went down, with Jim falling on top of Joe. Corbett helped Joe up. Choynski again rushed him to the ropes and landed several light blows. It seemed that Choynski had fatigued himself expending the energy required to do all that rushing. "This was the best round Joe fought, but it seemed rather late. Jim puffed heavily." The tide had shifted just a bit in this round.

14th round

Choynski rushed, but Jim was wary and made his work fruitless. Joe landed a good right but received a counter to the nose. Corbett's eye was black, while Joe's face and body were covered in blood. Choynski could hardly stand or see, seeming weak. "His lips stood out a full inch and his nose was a pulp." Corbett forced the fighting. Choynski was groggy and badly punished, but he fought on.

Although Joe was almost knocked out, Corbett began tiring. Choynski rushed and landed to the face and eyes, dazing Corbett. Jim's left to Joe's nose made it bleed freely. Both were covered in blood. "This was a bloody round and about forty sports turned away and walked to the stern of the barge, unable to stand the sight of blood."

15th round

Odds of 100 to 10 were offered on Corbett. Joe remained cheerful, but Jim resumed jabbing away, hitting Choynski four times with ease. Seeing his man fatigued, Corbett made a rush, hitting with both hands, forcing Joe onto the ropes and keeping him there with multiple blows to the face, sending Joe's body and head backwards over the top rope, leaning towards the crowd.

However, Corbett fatigued himself from his own efforts. "Suddenly Corbett began to weaken, and if Choynski had a blow in him he could have won. It was a most remarkable change." Both men seemed weak. Jim was exhausted and reeled around the ring. Joe staggered and swung wildly. The fight appeared up for grabs at this point. Choynski "now fought desperately and gamely. Corbett was very tired and winded as time was called."

16th round

By this point, Joe's face was misshapen, his cheeks puffed up, eyes closing, and lips protruding. Although initially both men seemed weak and winded, Choynski rallied and looked to be coming on. However, Joe slipped down on his own blood and took a count. "Choynski got up and fought gamely, Corbett keeping off, being tired." After some sparring in Jim's favor, Joe landed an awful smash to the nose. Jim was very weak. However, they went at it "hammer-and-tongs" at the end of the round.

17th round

The day grew hot. Joe improved in strength, but still missed, for Jim was careful. Joe's face was red and puffed, blood streaming from his nose and mouth, "bubbling at every breath drawn." Jim landed several times to the nose, but Joe landed a swinging left under Jim's left eye. This was an even round, but Corbett's condition improved a bit at the close.

18th round

EP: To this point, Choynski had taken enough punishment to knock out ten men, but still came up fighting, appearing at that time to be the stronger of the two. "The blood literally poured from his nose and mouth, but his courage was indomitable, and now the tide seemed to be turning against Corbett, whose legs were showing distress."

SFC: Corbett improved during this round, smashing Joe on the nose. Choynski weakened from the excessive blood loss. The blood was even spattering over the spectators.
AC: From the 18th to the 21st rounds Corbett continued punishing Joe terribly in the face. Jim's left glove was red.

19th round

EP: Jim landed a left smash to the stomach and another to the nose. This round was like the past five, Joe doing the most work but receiving the worst of the hits, which were all left leads to the nose and stomach. "Jim, in fact, had no right hand fit to use. It was badly hurt."

20th round

Corbett seemed to be getting stronger again, hitting Joe's nose. Choynski's nose and mouth continued streaming blood, which nearly choked him. Joe showed dogged courage, for he kept pressing, occasionally rushing, but he was being slowly jabbed to death. Choynski rushed Corbett, but when Jim ducked and Joe dashed against him, Choynski fell back onto the bloody, slippery floor. The round ended with Joe landing a hard right to the neck.

21st round

EP: Joe rushed but could do no harm, for Jim was strong again and landed a blow that dropped Choynski. In a rally, Jim fought him down with a half wrestle. They sparred for wind until the bell.
AC: Joe slipped down and took the ten seconds allowed.

22nd round

EP: Not much work was done, though Corbett landed a good blow to the stomach. Joe kept fighting desperately and gamely.
SFE: Not much happened in the 21st and 22nd rounds, but in the 22nd, Joe slipped in his corner and took the count to get some rest.
SFC: The 22nd through 24th rounds were in Corbett's favor. In spurts, Joe tried infighting, where he did his most effective work. Corbett however grew nimbler on his feet and avoided most of the rushes and blows.
AC: From the 22nd to the 24th rounds, Joe fought gamely and rushed Jim to the ropes.

23rd round

Joe's face was a purple mask. They sparred for wind. Choynski tried to keep out of reach, but Corbett landed four consecutive lefts on the mouth. "Stab, stab, stab in this sore nose was the treatment Joe received, and still he fought."

24th round

EP: Choynski made a rally, which Corbett stopped with a clinch. "Joe was again hit in the mouth, not hard smashes but good, square straight leads that made Joe wince."
SFE: The pace picked up, with Choynski making a determined attack. He knocked Jim slightly groggy with a rush of rights and lefts. Jim clinched, and on the break pushed Joe off with his left fist on the nose, to a disallowed cry

of foul. Jim countered a rush with his left between the eyes and again to the body. Joe landed a smash to the chin as the round ended.

AC: Jim staggered Joe with a left to the nose.

25th round

The game Choynski rallied and forced the fight, landing a good right and left to the head. Corbett was tired, and Joe landed on his wind, ribs and face.

However, eventually Corbett rallied and drove him back, uppercutting the forward ducking Choynski three times. Corbett attacked and chased him around the ring, butchering Joe in murderous fashion. Joe could barely stand, for a tap made him reel around the ring. Jim landed almost at will, but he could not knock him down. "Joe's face was like a chopped liver steeped in blood." Still, Choynski fought on.

26th round

EP: They got some wind and Joe made a rush and a clinch. Jim's left hit the nose, stomach, and again the nose. "It was cruel to keep him in the ring."

SFE: Joe's eyes were nearly closed, but he rushed gamely to no avail. Jim seemed stronger and began forcing Joe around the ring, jabbing often. Joe rushed again and landed a right and left. He rushed Jim to the ropes, but took a jab to the nose.

SFC: Some hard lefts again caught Joe.

AC: Jim's face showed signs of the punishment from Joe's rushes, for his cheek was puffed and his lips swollen. Jim stabbed the nose with the left. Joe rushed but did not land. Corbett landed a hard blow to the body.

27th round

EP: Joe made a couple rushes and Corbett clinched. Corbett knocked Choynski down. Joe rose, and twice more Jim smashed him and cleverly evaded a rush. Eventually, Choynski was knocked out and could not rise by the ten-count. He was up twelve seconds after being down.

SFE: The round did not last very long. Joe was too weak to hold his hands up and tried to keep away. He was pressed to the corner. Choynski tried to get away with a rush, but was hit with a counter left that weakened his legs. Joe saw another left coming and ducked, but it hit his forehead and he was dropped. When he rose, Corbett followed up. Joe tried a desperate rush, but as he ducked when delivering a left swing, Corbett uppercut him with the left to the jaw, dropping him for the ten-count.

SFC: Between rounds, Joe's seconds gave him some brandy, and he rushed in to begin the 27th. Jim was not very strong at this point, but was better off than Choynski. After rushing Jim onto the ropes, Joe landed a right to the head. However, when he attempted the blow again, Corbett dropped him with a right to the neck. Joe struggled to rise, and again rushed in. Jim crowded him back to the ropes and floored him with a left and right delivered in close to both sides of the head. "The right-hander sent the game lad down for the last time." Joe tried but failed to beat the ten-count. AC: Choynski rushed Corbett to the ropes, landing his right and left to the face. A clinch followed, and they broke.

> Corbett now sent in a straight left-hander that caught Choynski on the eye and he sank to the floor. Choynski got up, and, as game as any man that ever entered a ring, rushed at Corbett. A clinch and another fair break. Corbett was getting tired, and with a determined manner worked Choynski into a corner, and, sending in that never-failing long left, caught Choynski on the chin, and he fell in the corner.

Choynski tried to rise, but only managed to get to his knees at ten. He rose within the next two seconds. It was 8:40 a.m., almost two hours after the fight had begun (just under 1 hour and 47 minutes).

The *Examiner* said that Corbett had swollen lips, broken hands, a black eye, and a lump on his forehead. Choynski's lips were split and fat, his eyes nearly closed, and his hands swollen.[191]

The *Chronicle* said that Corbett's only damage suffered were sore ribs, swollen left side of his face, and broken left hand. It said that Corbett showed himself to be much the cleverer sparrer, and except in the 15th round, when Jim seemed fatigued, he was never in danger, escaping with barely any punishment.[192]

The *Alta* called it a brutal fight, worse than one with bare knuckles. A bone in the back of Corbett's left hand was broken, and his right was badly swollen at the wrist. His left eye was black, his right cheek swollen and his lips puffed. Jim said that he broke his left in the 5th, and it hurt every time it landed, but he could not use his right at all. Joe's face was swollen and his eyes black.[193]

The *Evening Post* said that Corbett had practically won the fight with one hand, "never striking a blow with his injured right, and using it only to guard his ribs. He was not punished at all, save that he was tired and short of wind." Jim did have some scratches on his body from the hard driving gloves, and a bruise over the left eye. Summarizing the fight, the *Post* said that Corbett was the cleverer and larger man:

> It was not a brilliant fight in the sense of hard, clean hitting and clever stopping or countering, but was simply a mill in which an inferior man made a reputation for gameness and fought a hard fight without showing ability to do his opponent very much damage. Corbett's remarkable weakness in the middle of the fight was due to weakness, and not at all to punishment, for the few blows he got in the ribs and stomach were not heavy ones, and ought not to have done him any

---

[191] *San Francisco Daily Examiner,* June 6, 1889.
[192] *San Francisco Chronicle,* June 6, 1889.
[193] *Daily Alta California,* June 6, 1889.

harm. All through the fight Corbett's defense was beautiful. He is one of the cleverest with both hands and legs that has ever been in the big class in this town. He has a wonderful way of getting back from a drive or counter, ducks like a bell diver and can evade almost as fast as Jem Mace. And he needed all his skill, for in the fifth round he hurt his left hand on Choynski's head, and it swelled so badly that the poky jabs he made at Choynski's nose and mouth were all the hitting it was safe for him to indulge in. He showed a great deal of respect for Joe's right all through the fight, and was never once in jeopardy of a knockout blow except when he showed the sudden weakness noted before, and which almost left him at Joe's mercy, but Joe was not able to hit. Corbett had the lead in the fight all the time except when Joe made his occasional rushes. He made Choynski fight on the retreat, and Joe is not so good in that line as many other men. He won the fight by repeatedly jabbing Joe in the nose with his left over the guard, and Joe did not seem to be able to protect the sore place with his hands.

No matter what tactics Choynski had pursued he would have been beaten. ... He would have whipped Corbett had he been able to hit him, but he could not hit him. ... [A]ll talk about Corbett's gameness must cease after this fight. When a man mills for more than an hour with two broken hands and faces the fighting there is no need to ask of what kind of stuff he is made.[194]

In a post-fight interview, Corbett said,

I knew I could whip him with one hand. ... I didn't have any soft snap after the fifth round, when I hurt the only weapon I had – my left hand. But I had my mind made up to fight, even if my arms fell off. My! but he's game, ain't he? I always knew he was a hard man, but I never gave him credit for so much gameness.

Jim also said that Choynski was a good one, and that anybody who didn't think so had better try him. "Joe had me dazed at one time, and at another I had cramps in my thighs, and if I had not been cool and used the good judgment of my seconds I would have been whipped."

When asked about the glove situation, Jim said,

Well, I knew I could lick him, no matter what was on my hands. I was afraid the fight was going to fall through when I learned that Choynski had no gloves, and would have agreed to his going on with bare knuckles, rather than not had the fight settled.

Explaining his loss, Choynski simply said, "Oh, I couldn't hit him." A collection was taken up to help Joe out financially.

---

[194] *San Francisco Evening Post,* June 5, 1889.

A crowd of 300 later followed Jim to the Olympic Club, where he was given congratulations and serenaded by a band.

The *Alta*, speaking of the fight and the men five days later said,

> The contest will go upon record as one of the best ever given on this coast. Both men displayed an amount of gameness and cleverness never looked for by their most ardent admirers. While Choynski suffered defeat, he has gained more reputation and friends than he could in winning a dozen battles from such men as Glover, Bush, Cuffe and others he has vanquished. If he still intends to follow the ring as a profession, he has a bright career before him, which is not the least dimmed by this his first defeat. As the matter now stands Corbett greatly out-classes him, and would have won the fight much sooner had he not met with the accident to his hands.[195]

The bout was significant enough such that it was reported as far as Australia.[196]

In his autobiography written decades later, Corbett said that he received more punishment in this fight than in any other battle; that it was his toughest fight. Choynski attacked from the beginning, but Corbett "had his face looking like a piece of liver." Jim broke his left hand early on. Ironically, although the left was in great pain, the previously injured right hurt worse and was used less often than the left. Choynski would occasionally land a good right to the eye, and had Corbett's face "busted up."[197]

Every now and then, Corbett would feint or show the right, but then throw a left hook as Joe moved away from the right, moving directly into the left. Corbett claimed the hook was a new punch, which he originated (although it was not - but the fact that he would say that tells you something about Jim's ego). The hook did not hurt his broken hand as much. Much of the fight was slugging, as Corbett said that he was still developing his skill. Joe freely bled from his cut up face, especially at the mouth and nose. Corbett's eye was nearly closed from swelling.[198]

Corbett said that he was hurt in the middle of the fight by a punch to the right eye, which left him somewhat groggy, but he was able to roll or "ride" with the subsequent blows to diminish their impact. Corbett clinched often in the following round, for his legs were still wobbly. He claimed to be masterful at the art of clinching, even knowing how to relax and rest in the clinch while Choynski used up his energy trying to push. He eventually recovered, and they continued fighting at a good pace.[199]

---

[195] *Daily Alta California*, June 10, 1889.
[196] *Sydney Referee*, August 7, 1889, quoting the *Alta*.
[197] Corbett at 75-76.
[198] Id. at 76-79.
[199] Id. at 79-84.

By the 27th round (Corbett incorrectly said 28th) both were fatigued. Corbett observed that Choynski's gait was different, that he was quite tired, and saw it as his time to land a big one. Corbett had reserved some energy specifically for a moment like this. Jim used right leads to make Joe move to Corbett's left, setting him up for a hook. Off of a lead right, he threw a hook as hard as he could and dropped Choynski for the ten-count. At least that is how an older Corbett remembered it.[200]

In 1902, Choynski said of the Corbett fight that it began with over two hundred spectators, but it took so long that by the end there were only ten. Under Queensberry rules (three-minute rounds with one-minute rests), the fight had lasted about 1 hour and 45 minutes. "That was one of the hardest fights I ever had in my life, and I guess I've been in as many as any man in the game."[201] He was correct. Over the years, Choynski fought the who's who of boxing, never ducking anyone.

Of Choynski, Corbett years later said that he was "one of the gamest and best fighters that ever lived, though a little bit too light for the heavyweight class. He was really as good as most champions I have seen, and this statement covers a period of nearly fifty years."[202]

Corbett had a valid point. Amongst his vast experiences and many good results during his career, Choynski would go on to score an 1892 KO15 over top American black George Godfrey, lose an 1894 5-round "draw" with Bob Fitzsimmons (Joe decked Bob in the 3rd, but was himself dropped and on the verge of being knocked out by Fitz in the 4th and 5th rounds when the police stopped it), draw in 20 rounds in 1897 with future champion James J. Jeffries, knock out future champion Jack Johnson in the 3rd round in 1901, and in 1903 box a 6-round no decision draw with future champion Marvin Hart. Despite being only a large middleweight, Choynski was known for both his skill and power, being able to hold his own with and hurt many of the era's best heavyweights, even when he lost. No one ever forgot Choynski's punching power.

For Corbett, the Choynski win was significant, as it proved for the first time that he could endure a long and tough fight. James J. Corbett was no longer just a fancy amateur who was thought of only as a limited rounds fighter. The pretty sparrer was a tough professional.

However, the fight was so brutal that afterwards, both men said that they were retiring. It was reported that Jim had accepted a position in a prominent insurance company's office. He was also reinstated as a boxing instructor at the Olympic Club. An Olympian believed that despite the announced retirement, Corbett would fight again.[203]

[200] Id. at 84-87.
[201] *National Police Gazette*, July 5, 1902.
[202] Corbett at 38. Corbett's book was published in 1925.
[203] *San Francisco Evening Post*, June 8, 1889; *San Francisco Chronicle*, June 10, 1889.

CHAPTER 6

Teacher Again

One month after the Choynski-Corbett fight, it was reported on July 1, 1889 that Joe McAuliffe had hired Jim Corbett "to teach him how to use his props to more advantage," to assist Joe in preparing for an upcoming September bout against 190-pound Pat Killen. The powerful knockout-artist Killen held an 1887 KO2 over Duncan McDonald and an 1888 KO4 victory against Patsy Cardiff.

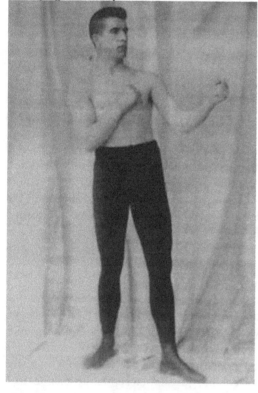

Corbett had previously sparred with McAuliffe in 1888 when Joe was preparing for bouts with both Frank Glover and Peter Jackson. After having suffered the December 1888 LKOby24 to Jackson, McAuliffe had come back with a May 1889 KO8 over former Australian heavyweight champion Tom Lees. In July and August, Corbett would once again train and spar with McAuliffe to help prepare him for the Killen bout.[204]

Prior to fighting Jake Kilrain, a lot of experts felt that John L. Sullivan was past his prime and would not be able to defeat him. John's left had not been the same since 1887, when he badly broke his arm. Not only had he been indulging to excess in life's enjoyments in recent years, particularly food and alcohol, but Sullivan had also been seriously ill and on his deathbed during mid- to late-1888 with malaria and typhoid fever. A man who had backed Sullivan in 1882 against Paddy Ryan said that he would not do so for the Kilrain fight.

---

[204] *Daily Alta California*, July 1, 1889.

You and I and hundreds of others are as satisfied as we possibly can be that Sullivan is not the man that he was, and that he never can be. No athlete, no matter what line he follows, can stand what he has been through and be the same physically. I have seen it a hundred times. Wine, women and tobacco will knock out any man, and it has done up Sullivan. Kilrain is as big, as tall, as heavy, and I believe as clever as Sullivan, and he is certainly in better condition bodily.[205]

John L. Sullivan

However, Sullivan proved the doubters wrong. On July 8, 1889 under the blazing hot Richburg, Mississippi sun, 30-year-old John L. Sullivan fought 30-year-old Jake Kilrain in a bareknuckle London Prize Ring rules bout, defeating him in 75 rounds lasting over 2 hours and 15 minutes. It was the last heavyweight championship fight fought under those rules.

---

[205] *Daily Alta California,* June 24, 1889.

Sullivan subsequently announced that he was retired, and was relatively inactive over the next three years, only engaging in some minor short and friendly sparring exhibitions, usually as part of plays. He became more of an actor and businessman than fighter, making more money in plays than he did as a boxer. His eating, drinking, and inactivity caused him to balloon in weight. This was time that Corbett utilized to gain boxing knowledge, experience, and sharpness.

Sullivan also had to deal with legal repercussions for his Kilrain bout. In August, a jury found him guilty of violating Mississippi's anti-prize fight law, and a judge sentenced him to one year in jail. He was free pending his appeal.

In the meantime, on July 15, 1889 at San Francisco's Mechanics' Pavilion, a little over a month after their 27-round war and a week after the Sullivan-Kilrain fight, Corbett and Joe Choynski sparred in a 4-rounder at a Choynski benefit. Patsy Hogan again served as referee. The local *Examiner* said that it appeared to be a friendly exhibition. They danced about the ring and did some "clever boxing" that pleased the crowd. The *Alta* said that it was 4 friendly rounds which were loudly applauded. The *Chronicle* said that the "bout was purely scientific, and served to settle all disputes as to the relative merits of the men, for from first to last Corbett showed his superiority as a boxer." 2,000-2,100 men and their lady escorts attended, and Choynski made $1,600.[206]

The *Chronicle* also reported that Jim insisted on receiving payment for sparring with Choynski. Corbett had apparently made "very little out of his battle with Choynski, and as boxing is his business, and his appearance helped equally to swell the gate receipts, he was entitled to some recompense." Corbett was becoming more of a businessman when it came to boxing, realizing his economic value.

Corbett had recently resumed his position as Olympic Club boxing teacher. "He has a large and promising class, and is a painstaking and successful teacher." It seemed that Jim was, at least for the time being, intent upon returning to that line of business, doing what he had been doing for the past couple of years.[207]

In late July, it was reported that Joe McAuliffe "is taking sparring exhibitions from Jim Corbett, which is a guarantee that his sparring will undergo a great improvement." A week later, in early August it was said, "Jim Corbett has McAuliffe in charge and will give him many useful hints in the art of knocking out." A week after that it was reported that McAuliffe "shows considerable improvement in his boxing since Corbett has taken him in hand."[208] Another August report said,

[206] *San Francisco Daily Examiner,* July 16, 1889; *San Francisco Chronicle,* July 16, 1889; *Daily Alta California,* July 16, 1889; *Morning Oregonian,* July 16, 1889.
[207] *San Francisco Chronicle,* July 22, 1889; *Daily Alta California,* July 22, 1889.
[208] *Daily Alta California,* July 29, 1889, August 5, 1889, August 12, 1889.

McAuliffe boxes daily with Jim Corbett, and is thereby adding considerably to his ability, as Corbett is not only the biggest, but by long odds the cleverest man he has ever sparred with in training.

A good idea of the size of McAuliffe can be obtained by seeing him exercise with Corbett, who though a strapping young fellow looks small in front of the Mission boy. While Corbett is much more clever than McAuliffe, he has all he can attend to in boxing with his big pupil, for when Joe unlimbers himself and lets fly either of his ponderous flippers something has to drop. The Professor generally drops his head and lets them go flying harmlessly over it, but once in a while he stops a rattler with his jaw that inspires him with great respect for McAuliffe's hitting power. In wrestling Corbett can make no impression on his pupil, who is about as easy to move as Bernal Heights when he plants his spacious brogans fairly on the floor and braces himself for a tussle.

It was good for Jim to be in there with a big, strong, powerful man, as much as it was good for McAuliffe to work with a fast and clever boxer.[209]

In late August, it was reported that Corbett had ceased working with McAuliffe, due to the fact that "he received notice from the Olympic Club to 'let go,' otherwise his place as boxing teacher might be declared vacant." The Olympic was not happy about Jim's divided attention.[210] Con Riordan took over as McAuliffe's trainer. During the second week of September 1889, Joe McAuliffe scored a KO7 over Pat Killen, winning his share of a $2,500 purse.

A February 1890 source indicated that Corbett had at one point bested Joe McAuliffe in a bout for scientific points, but no other information was given.[211] An 1895 source said that Corbett had once won a 4-round decision over McAuliffe.[212] In 1896, Corbett claimed to have boxed McAuliffe in a private bout. He said, "I know this much, I punched him full of holes out in the barn and I have a dozen witnesses who will bear me out."[213]

Apparently, McAuliffe saw the February 1890 newspaper report saying that Corbett had once bested him, and he was not pleased, denying that it had taken place.

Joe means that he will make Jim eat his words or deny that he ever sparred McAuliffe for scientific points. ... All his fights have been to a finish.... McAuliffe has only been defeated once, and that by Jackson.... Corbett has only fought one ring battle, and that with Joe Choynski, who would not be in it for a round with McAuliffe. On this

---

209 *San Francisco Chronicle*, August 12, 1889; *San Francisco Daily Examiner*, August 20, 1889.
210 *Daily Alta California*, August 26, 1889.
211 *San Francisco Examiner*, February 18, 1890.
212 *Brooklyn Daily Eagle*, January 24, 1895.
213 *San Francisco Bulletin*, June 30, 1896.

showing it is certainly unfair to boom the talented Professor away above McAuliffe, who has won his reputation by actual battles. ... The question now agitating ring-goers is whether Corbett, who is getting bigger and stronger all the time, cannot defeat McAuliffe in a finish as well as outspar him. This is something which can only be determined by an actual contest.... As to their sparring skill that is already decided to every one's satisfaction. Corbett is, if not the cleverest heavy-weight in the country, so close to Jackson in boxing ability that it would take a first-class umpire to decide a six-round match between them for points.[214]

Thus, it was clear that the press felt that Corbett was a better sparrer than McAuliffe when it came to points boxing, so good that he was on the same level with Peter Jackson, but the question was whether Corbett could defeat Joe in a *real* fight, in a fight to the finish.

Since late August 1889, Corbett had mostly focused on training his pupils, but he still engaged in the occasional sparring exhibition.[215] The Monday, September 23, 1889 issue of the *San Francisco Chronicle* said that the previous week, the Occidental Club had "tried out" its aspiring heavyweight named Atkinson. "Jim Corbett, who tested the aspirant, wound him up in one round, and the club has learned that skilled heavy-weights are not found in every lumber or coal yard." Later sources reported that this was 230-pound George Atkinson, sometimes incorrectly claiming that the bout lasted 2 rounds, all being unsure as to when it took place.[216]

On September 28, 1889, Professor Corbett sparred with Professor John Donaldson as part of a larger Olympic Club sponsored sparring exhibition show at the Grand Opera House. Nine years earlier, back in 1880, a then 160-pound 5'10 ½" Donaldson had twice boxed against John L. Sullivan; first retiring after 4 gloved Queensberry rules rounds, and subsequently retiring after 10 London-rules rounds wearing hard gloves. This respected boxing teacher had boxed various contenders throughout the decade, including Captain James Dalton, Steve Taylor, and Patsy Cardiff, all of whom had defeated him.

"The contest between Corbett and Donaldson was decidedly scientific, but Corbett only made sport of Donaldson in the manner in which he forced the fighting." A day later it was said, "Jim Corbett exceeded the expectations of all his friends, and showed that he is growing more clever every day. Donaldson, who is himself a clever big one, had more than his hands full with the young professor, who treated him in the most friendly manner."[217] Later sources report that they sparred 4 rounds. Some consider

---

[214] *San Francisco Chronicle*, February 24, 1890.

[215] *Daily Alta California*, September 22, 1889.

[216] *San Francisco Chronicle*, September 23, 1889; *National Police Gazette*, March 8, 1890, February 10, 1894; *San Francisco Examiner*, May 21, 1891; *New York Sun*, September 8, 1892.

[217] *San Francisco Chronicle*, September 29, 30, 1889. *Brooklyn Daily Eagle*, June 9, 1895, *New York Times*,

this a decision win for Corbett, as he was clearly better. Corbett and Donaldson became friends and in subsequent years would become regular sparring partners.

Professor John Donaldson, 1881

Two newspapers reporting his record as of late 1889 said that Corbett had defeated fifteen men as an amateur. He stopped Captain Daley in 1 round, Frank Smith in 3 (not quite accurate), drew with McDonald, bested Buffalo Costello in a 4-round private affair, drew with Burke, knocked out Mike Brennan in 4 rounds (not true), stopped Choynski (his fourth victory

---

January 26, 1894 and *National Police Gazette*, March 6, 1890 mention that Corbett defeated Donaldson, but do not provide any details.

over him) in 27 rounds, defeated Australia's 220-pound Professor Miller in 6 rounds, and Professor John Donaldson in 4 rounds.[218]

On October 12, 1889 as part of an exhibition given by the San Francisco Fencing Club at Union-square Hall, Corbett sparred 4 rounds with J.B. Smith, one of his pupils, "which proved a very pretty sparring bout, and gave the ladies an opportunity to see how things are done within the magic square, without any of the attendant brutality."[219]

That month, one of Corbett's clubmates told a reporter that Jim wanted to wager that he could stand up to John L. Sullivan for 6 rounds. Some Eastern journals copied that item.[220] Clearly, Jim was growing bolder and more confident.

Professor Corbett continued coaching and training at the Olympic, even going on a cross-country run with the boys in late October.[221] On November 28, Jim was again a marshal at the Olympic sponsored amateur athletic games.[222] However, his life as a teacher was about to take another hiatus.

[218] *Portland Evening Telegram,* December 27, 1889; *Morning Oregonian,* December 12, 1889.
[219] *Daily Alta California,* October 7, 13, 1889.
[220] *San Francisco Chronicle,* October 21, 1889.
[221] *Daily Alta California,* October 28, 1889.
[222] *San Francisco Chronicle,* November 29, 1889.

CHAPTER 7

Return of the Professional
Hippodromer

In early December 1889, the *San Francisco Examiner* called James Corbett "immeasurably clever, scientific; and a jabber and getter away without an equal." It said that Corbett had laid out a plan of action for the next two years wherein he would put on weight, improve his skills, and then make a bid for the world championship.[223] Corbett's ambition was growing.

On December 10, 1889, despite his popularity as an instructor, Corbett resigned his position at the Olympic Club in order to pursue his professional boxing career.

> Corbett has become dissatisfied with the monotonous duties of the post of boxing teacher at a salary of $150 a month, and has determined to become a fistic star of the first magnitude. The enlarged romances about the fabulous sums earned by Slogger Sullivan and the antipodean Hercules Peter Jackson have imbued Corbett with the idea that his lot was not a happy one, and on the spur of the moment he resigned. ... His sudden withdrawal from the Olympic Club was solely due to the furtherance of his plans as a professional boxer. He started last night for Portland, Or., where he is to meet Dave Campbell in a ten-round contest, the boxers to divide the gate receipts. ...

> The resignation...naturally occasioned quite a stir...as among the younger members the athletic professor was rated as quite a hero and the most likely successor of John L. Sullivan as the champion of the world. It appears that Corbett was much dissatisfied with the financial result of his hard-glove fight with Joe Choynski. The match with Choynski was for $1,000 a side, but there was no gate money, so that after all expenses were paid Corbett had just $100 to recompense him for the labor and pains of two hard battles. His discontent was increased by the fact that the California Athletic Club had offered him $3,500 to have the fight take place in its ring.... Recently there has been considerable talk about Corbett's capacity to hold his own with the best boxers in the world, and the result has been to start the

---

[223] *San Francisco Examiner*, December 5, 1889.

Olympic Club professor on the road once more as a full-fledged professional.[224]

Top professional boxers had been making good money, and Corbett wanted a taste. It was said that a popular San Francisco minister made $3,500 a year. Peter Jackson for three fights in less than a year had made $7,500, in addition to thousands more for teaching boxing, "which would seem to indicate that in this wicked city the man of God is not valued as highly as the man of muscle." $1,000 in 1889 was the equivalent of $20,525.09 in 2005.[225]

Corbett traveled to Portland, Oregon. While there, one writer spoke with Jim regarding his reasons for resigning from the Olympic. "He says he was handicapped while in the Olympic Club, but now, as he has left the club, he is at liberty to do as he pleases."[226] In a later interview, Corbett said that he had resigned because the California Club would not only have paid him for the Choynski fight, but would have engaged him as an instructor at $250 a month. The Olympic Club directors knew of the proposition and persuaded him not to accept, to remain with them, that it would be money in his pocket. However, the end result was that his expenses were not paid and the club still owed him money for some salary. Corbett's friend President Harrison had recently resigned from the Olympic, and so, "still feeling galled over the unfair treatment I had received, I stepped out too."[227]

Over the course of two nights, on December 11 and 12, 1889 in Portland, Oregon, Corbett engaged in two 6-round bouts for points against William Smith, also known as "Australian" Billy Smith. The 21-year-old Smith had begun his career in 1885 in Australia, and had generally fought as a 5'9" 154-pound middleweight; although the local press said that he was currently weighing 175 pounds. While in Australia, in 1886 Smith had possibly boxed Bob Fitzsimmons 4 rounds (4-round sparring exhibitions were frequent there). In 1887 and/or 1888, Smith scored a KO7 and KO6 over Starlight, a black middleweight, and in 1887 scored a KO6 over Bill Slavin, Frank Slavin's brother. Smith had a great deal of other experience, including an 18-round draw with Billy McCarthy.

Smith arrived in America in late September 1889, and in November scored a KO9 over Frank Glover. Smith said that he was willing to forfeit $100 to anyone in Oregon who could defeat him in a 6-round contest for points.[228] Corbett accepted his offer.

[224] San Francisco Chronicle, December 11, 1889.

[225] New York Sun, February 4, 1890; The Inflation Calculator, http://www.westegg.com/inflation.

[226] Portland Evening Telegram, December 12, 15, 1889.

[227] San Francisco Chronicle, December 13, 1889. President Harrison had submitted his letter of resignation on November 18, 1889, which was accepted by the board on November 25. Daily Alta California, November 26, 1889.

[228] Portland Evening Telegram, December 9, 1889; Boxrec.com; San Francisco Chronicle, September 29, 1889; Sydney Referee, August 4, 1887; Daily Alta California, October 28, 1889.

Liisted as weighing about 180 pounds in fighting condition, the 23-year-old Corbett was "known as perhaps the most scientific sparrer in the country today, being recognized as such by Jack Dempsey and other equally as noted pugilists." The local *Morning Oregonian* said of their boxing on the 11th that Corbett and Smith fought a 6-round scientific sparring exhibition for points only, "no slugging being allowed." It was called a wonderful exhibition, as Smith showed "agility and pluck," while Corbett handled himself with the ability of a lightweight, sparring cautiously, allowing his opponent to rush in, and then countering. The referee awarded the 6-round points decision to Corbett.[229]

The *Portland Evening Telegram* said that their bout was "the finest display of scientific boxing ever witnessed in Portland," and that there were frequent outbursts of applause. Both men were in good condition. "Corbett had the advantage of Smith in weight, height and reach, but the plucky Australian demonstrated that he is a fighter of no mean ability." Despite Smith's pluck, Corbett won the contest.[230]

The following evening, on December 12, 1889, Corbett and Smith boxed another 6-round contest, and Corbett again won the decision. The local *Portland Evening Telegram* said, "Corbett had the advantage of Smith in every way, yet the Australian, who is full of grit, and very scientific, made the heavy-weight do some hard fighting."[231] *The San Francisco Chronicle* confirmed that the two bouts were 6 rounds for scientific points only, as no knockouts were allowed there.[232]

Later that month, the San Francisco press assessed Corbett's professional prospects. "There is no doubt that Corbett has extraordinary qualities as a boxer, but whether he can become the successor of Sullivan is a question that can only be settled by a series of hard nights and an experience of life not usually beneficial, either socially or personally." Ed Smith of Colorado (a.k.a. "Denver" Ed Smith) had posted a forfeit for a match with Corbett or Choynski, but it seemed that Jim had already made other plans.[233]

The Portland press reported after the Billy Smith bouts that their local man, Dave Campbell, had been training for the past four months, and wanted to box Corbett in a 10-round contest. Campbell was a veteran middleweight who back in 1885 had been knocked out by Jack Dempsey in the 3rd round. Dave later assisted Dempsey as a sparring partner in

---

[229] *Morning Oregonian*, December 10, 1889, December 12, 1889.

[230] *Portland Evening Telegram*, December 12, 1889.

[231] *Portland Evening Telegram*, December 13, 1889.

[232] *Portland Evening Telegram*, December 13, 1889; *San Francisco Chronicle*, December 13, 1889. *The Morning Oregonian* listed Corbett's record to that point, although it may have had some inaccuracies regarding the results and bout order: W3 Frank Smith, W8 Duncan McDonald, KO2 Captain Daley, KO4 Mike Brennan, KO Choyinski with bare knuckles, W6 Professor Miller, W4 Professor Donaldson, W4 Choyinski, W4 Tom Johnson, and KO27 Choyinski. *Morning Oregonian*, December 12, 1889.

[233] *San Francisco Chronicle*, December 23, 1889.

preparation for his fights, gaining valuable experience. Campbell had defeated a number of lesser-knowns and had even boxed John Chow to an 8-round draw, although it was believed that Dave had scored more points.

DAVE CAMPBELL

Corbett confirmed his willingness to box Campbell 10 rounds, "the winner of the greatest number of clean hits or points to win." The match was made and it became the "principal topic of conversation," although really it was already known in San Francisco even before Jim left that Corbett was traveling to Oregon for the purpose of boxing Campbell.

Some said that Corbett was too heavy for Campbell. However, Dave was well enough respected such that no one was willing to give odds against him. "Everyone knows Corbett's reputation. He is a good man, probably one of the most scientific in the country…. Yet it is admitted by his best friends that he will have no 'picnic' with Campbell. Dave is an expert boxer." Corbett was cognizant of the fact that "Campbell is one of the best, if not a better man than he has ever met." Campbell said that "he is satisfied that he is a better man than the San Francisco heavyweight."[234]

Campbell was at that time being trained by Duncan McDonald, who had previously boxed Corbett in 1886 in what some considered a hippodrome. Given what was later revealed about this fight, McDonald's involvement might have been more than coincidental.

A week before the fight it was said, "Campbell is looking better than he ever did, and will no doubt give Corbett an interesting fight." Another said, "Campbell is known to be a very hard hitter and a good sparrer."[235] Campbell was the local man, and would no doubt "have the sympathy of

[234] *Portland Evening Telegram*, December 12, 13, 15, 1889; *Morning Oregonian*, July 29, 1889, August 26, 1889; *National Police Gazette*, November 7, 14, 1885; Boxrec.com.
[235] *San Francisco Examiner*, December 21, 1889; *Daily Alta California*, December 16, 1889.

somewhat 'clannish Portland.'" The local paper predicted that the cheers of his admirers would inspire him to do his utmost, which would make him "a harder nut to crack than some people imagine." "Campbell is, moreover, quick to a degree, and for a heavy man delivers and gets out of danger like a feather-weight.... His pluck and stamina has never been questioned."

> Corbett, while not so abstemious in his style of living as his opponent, has not neglected himself... his condition being always fairly good from his practice with his pupils..... A more calm and deliberate fighter than Corbett never stepped into the magic square, and the opinion of Jack Dempsey that for science Corbett leads the division, lends additional force to the belief that Corbett will make a fight of no mean order.[236]

The day before the fight it was reported that the bout was for points only, that those "who expect a bloodthirsty contest or a knock-out will be disappointed, as the Pavilion managers will not permit such."[237] Such a stipulation had been reported regarding the Billy Smith bouts as well. This requirement may very well have affected Corbett's performances. He had to hold back and not slug or attempt a knockout. Oddly enough though, as will be seen, apparently not many realized that such a requirement existed. However, as will also be discussed, there may have been an additional agreement at play that was not revealed until later on.

A secondary source said that Corbett and Campbell fought for a $500 purse. However, the *New York Clipper* said that Corbett was to receive a fixed 60% of the gate receipts. Earlier that month, even before Corbett traveled to Oregon, the *Chronicle* reported that they were to divide the receipts.[238] Such a stipulation was atypical for a competitive contest where there was to be a winner and loser, and was one indication of things to come. Typically, the winner's share was greater than the loser's share, providing an incentive to both boxers to do their utmost to win. In the event of a draw, the split was usually 50/50. At that time, fixed percentage splits were typical for less than serious exhibitions where the boxers agreed to work with each other to put on a good show and make a few bucks, but neither had to fear a loss or coming away with the loser's share. This also helps explain the manner in which Corbett fought.

A couple weeks after his bouts with Billy Smith, on December 28, 1889, still in Portland, Oregon, Corbett fought Portland's Dave Campbell in a scheduled 10-round bout wearing five-ounce gloves. Corbett weighed about 180-183 pounds to Campbell's 168 pounds.

The local *Morning Oregonian* reported that the 1st and 2nd rounds were even. The 3rd round was much in Corbett's favor. However, Campbell

---

[236] *Portland Evening Telegram*, December 23, 1889.
[237] *Portland Evening Telegram*, December 27, 28, 1889.
[238] Fields at 34; *New York Clipper*, December 21, 1889; *San Francisco Chronicle*, December 11, 1889.

clearly won the 4th round, landing well to the body. Corbett won the 5th round, focusing on the head, while Campbell mainly hit the body, once making Jim grunt from a right to the stomach. Corbett won the 6th, drawing blood from Campbell's nose. The 7th round had some "hot fighting" and was even. Through the first seven rounds, Corbett was leading, according to this account, winning three rounds to Campbell's one, with three even.

However, the tide started to shift. The 8th round was again active, but Campbell won it. In the 9th, Campbell went at Corbett "hammer and tongs and seemed to be able to hit his man whenever and wherever he pleased," clearly winning the round. Corbett showed more fight in the 10th, but Campbell still landed more than Jim and was said to have won the round.

The referee declared it a 10-round draw. However, this local report felt that the local fighter Campbell had won, scoring it three rounds Corbett, four rounds Campbell, and three rounds even. It did note that Corbett forced the fighting the whole way, and had Campbell moving all the time. The smaller Campbell gave way and was generally on the defensive. It said that it was Corbett's fight up to the 7th round, but felt that the clear way Campbell had won the last three rounds overbalanced the advantage Corbett had gained.

Disagreeing with the local paper, in calling it a draw, the referee said that both men were as fresh at the end as in the beginning and had an equal number of points. At the decision, the crowd hissed (in support of Campbell). Corbett began arguing, feeling that he had won. Campbell offered to box another round to settle it, but the Chief of Police would not allow it. Corbett called the decision "shameful" and said, "Campbell was not in the fight. He did not hit me three blows during the set to. Didn't I do all the forcing and all the leading? ... He did not even give me a good sweat." Naturally, Campbell thought the fight was his, feeling that his body punches were more effective than Corbett's work.

A subsequent report questioned why Corbett had allowed Campbell to come at him late in the fight, failed to follow up when he did land, and allowed Dave to slip away out of corners without an effort to prevent him from doing so.[239] Had Corbett carried Campbell?

Portland's *Evening Telegram* discussed Corbett's reaction to the decision and the *Morning Oregonian's* account of the fight.

> After the fight, his wrath was directed principally against the referee and the crowd who yelled for Campbell, but when *The Oregonian* made its appearance the following morning with a report of the fight, in which Campbell was shown to have gotten the best of the match, Corbett's rage knew no bounds. He was brim full and running over with fight and would not be pacified. He declared that Campbell did not hit him over three times during the ten rounds, and claimed that

---

[239] *Morning Oregonian*, December 29, 30, 1889; *San Francisco Examiner*, December 29, 1889.

he simply played with Dave and refrained from smashing him many times when he had an opportunity to do so.

There is probably considerable truth in what Corbett claims. It is very probable that he did start in to play with Campbell, but he played too long. There is not a person who witnessed the match Saturday night but who will admit that Corbett is a much more clever man than Campbell. In fact, Corbett showed himself to be a fighter who need fear no one. But he didn't whip Dave Campbell Saturday night, and if it was his own fault, as it apparently was, he has no one but himself to blame for it.

If it is true, as Corbett says, that he only played with Campbell and did not take advantage of many opportunities to score points on his antagonist; then there are good grounds for the belief of many, that the fight was a "fake." But if it was, it was all a fake on Corbett's part, for there is no one who believes that Campbell's splendid showing was other than "on the square."

Had Jim engaged in another hippodrome? At the very least, Corbett was required to hold back from attempting to stop Campbell. The pavilion owner confirmed that he had told them that it was a purely scientific contest and that no knockout would be allowed. Certainly though, this was a close enough fight for both sides to have arguments in their favor. Ultimately, the *Evening Telegram* did not feel that either man had faked the fight. However, it said that Corbett had made a mistake and was punished for it.

Regardless of the decision, the local paper still called Jim "without doubt one of the most scientific boxers who ever stepped into the ring…. It is not impossible that two or three years hence Corbett will be occupying the place in which John L. Sullivan stands today."[240] Thus, he was still seen as a likely contender for the crown. Those words turned out to be prophetic.

The *San Francisco Chronicle* reported that the 10-round draw was "considered no test of the merits of either man, as it was well known that the affair was purely an exhibition to draw gate money."[241] Still, a subsequent report said that Jim had added nothing to his reputation, and in fact had "lost many friends by his conduct in the glove contest."[242]

Two weeks after the bout, the *Chronicle* provided further insight into matters:

It is whispered around among Corbett's friends that the Professor…was compelled to sign an agreement that the fight was for scientific points and not a slogging match. Corbett proceeded in good

[240] *Portland Evening Telegram*, December 30, 1889.
[241] *San Francisco Chronicle*, December 30, 1889.
[242] *San Francisco Chronicle*, January 6, 1890.

faith to carry out his contract…with Campbell, who refused to go on unless it was agreed to make the contest a purely scientific one. In the concluding three rounds, however, Campbell rushed the fight and made such a good impression with his townsmen that Corbett has been, so to speak, in the bouillon ever since. Now Corbett threatens if he is not vindicated in some way he will haul out his private contract with the club managers and Campbell and show up the whole business.[243]

One week later, a further report followed.

They have not yet ceased to discuss the Campbell-Corbett match… The latest publication relative to the fiasco is in the *Sunday Welcome* of Portland. The article is headed:

"The Fake Exposed – The Corbett-Campbell Contest a Job From the Turn-Loose – Dave Not in It – Corbett Forced to Sign a Paper at 7 Saturday Night Not to Knock Out Campbell – Dave Admits to Asa Hamilton That Corbett Is Too Clever – A Bright Light on a Dark Subject." The article goes on to say that "Campbell knew himself that he was overmatched and made the best of it by binding Corbett not to put him to sleep, and has been heard privately to express the opinion that Corbett was one too many for him. And why should he not be?

"Campbell was among his own friends and in his own home and owed to the people here not to suggest a fake, and Corbett by agreeing to it has hurt himself irreparably with those who go in for honest sports.

"The cold truth of the matter," according to the Oregon critic, "is that Corbett is so greatly superior to Campbell that he had to hold himself in continually, for to have given full force to his powers would have been to knock out Dave and thus lose all share in the gate receipts, which, under the circumstances of his coming here and training expenses, he couldn't afford to do. Corbett's great mistake was to sign the paper not to knock Dave out, for that made him particeps in the fraud on the public, although he would accept of no counterpart document signed by Campbell that David should lose all the money pending the result should he put the Californian to sleep."

The effect of the Campbell-Corbett fiasco has been to scare a lot of San Francisco sloggers from rushing to Portland in quest of an engagement. They are all afraid that a metropolitan slogger would be

[243] *San Francisco Chronicle*, January 13, 1890.

put down at once as a faker and his exhibition queered from the very start.[244]

The odd part about all this was that the local Portland papers had stated *before* the fight that it was a contest for points and that no knockout would be allowed. Certainly though, it seemed that Corbett had not put in his best performance, owing to an agreement that he made before the fight. Corbett was good at working with many of his opponents. It was not unusual for a top fighter to be bound not to score a knockout. Sullivan himself had made some such agreements, although he generally battered those opponents and almost knocked them out. Still, some used the Campbell bout to attack Corbett's integrity. Perhaps they felt that Corbett had held back way too much.

Back east, the *New York Clipper* reported that the fight "was a farce from beginning to end…. Corbett showed the most science, but the display was so tame as to disgust the spectators, who numbered about twenty five hundred, so that the principals, and others who had a finger in the pie, fared very well financially."[245]

Almost a year later, in September 1890, there was further discussion about this fight, which was used to further damage Corbett's reputation. Jack Dempsey claimed that his buddy Campbell had held his own with Corbett the year before, and denied that there was an agreement that there should be no knocking out.

However, a letter was produced indicating that Corbett had suggested to Campbell well before their match that they work together in order to make some money. Corbett didn't simply offer to not knock him out, but actually offered to keep it even. The letter was dated November 29, 1889, one month before they fought, before Corbett had even left San Francisco, and it said:

> Friend Dave: I suppose you will be surprised to receive a letter from me, but I have met a lot of people from Portland….and they all tell me that you and I can make big money if we box ten rounds. Now, Dave, if you are anxious to make money, I know you and I can pull a big crowd. I will box you ten rounds; or more, or less, and fix it a draw, or if you don't want it that way, why, let it go on its merits; but if we box a draw we can go to Seattle and Tacoma and make some good stuff…. I want to make some money, and I know you and I can do it. All I want you to do is stick to your word. Whatever you want to do, say it in your letter, then we will understand each other.

Thus, Corbett had indeed proposed a hippodrome to Campbell, agreeing to box to a draw result and split the gate receipts, which could then lead to

[244] *San Francisco Chronicle*, January 20, 1890.
[245] *New York Clipper,* January 11, 1890.

their touring around giving additional money-making exhibitions. This is likely what Jim had done with Duncan McDonald, who interestingly enough, was in Campbell's corner. For his proposal, Corbett had to endure some criticism.

> A more compromising letter I never knew a fighter to write. Fancy John L. Sullivan writing anything of the kind. The big fellow has been guilty of a good many faults, but he never for a moment contemplated hippodroming the public or of putting up a job on it. Mr. Corbett will have a hard time explaining this letter. In fact it admits of no explaining.[246]

However, Corbett again insisted that he was forced to sign an agreement not to knock out Campbell. But did he do more than that? Had he intentionally carried him to a draw? Fortunately for Corbett, these revelations came about after he had already convinced many national experts that he was a fantastic boxer, so his career was not fatally damaged.

---

[246] *Daily Alta California,* September 29, 1890.

CHAPTER 8

The Calculated Rise

By early 1890, Jim Corbett wanted to face someone with a big reputation.[247] At that time, Jake Kilrain had been touring the country, challenging any heavyweight who would face him in a 6-round bout. Depending on the version, either Kilrain challenged Corbett or Jim challenged Jake, but either way, the match was made, set to take place in New Orleans, Louisiana.

According to Corbett, Jack Dempsey told him, "Kilrain will never lay a glove on you. You'll make a sucker out of him." Perhaps this encouragement, combined with the fact that Corbett wanted to step it up and improve his reputation on a national level, particularly after the Campbell draw, motivated his taking the fight. Besides, it was for only 6 rounds, and Corbett was considered an expert short rounds sparrer.

Jim took a train to New Orleans, arriving there on Tuesday, February 12, 1890. The local *Times-Democrat* described Corbett as having "a pleasant and rather refined-looking face, and a gentle, well-bred manner."[248]

Although Louisiana law technically made boxing illegal, because the sport was so popular, the law was not often enforced. On March 14, 1890, one month *after* Corbett boxed Kilrain there, New Orleans passed an ordinance officially legalizing boxing. Gloved bouts would be allowed in athletic clubs as long as no liquor was served, no boxing took place on Sunday, the club donated $50 to charity, and $500 was posted before each contest.[249]

According to Mike Donovan's 1909 book, when Corbett arrived in New Orleans, Donovan had the opportunity to speak with him. Donovan had sparred with John L. Sullivan many times in the 1880s, and was amongst the first to predict that Sullivan would be champion. Corbett shadow-boxed for Donovan and displayed "the wonderful footwork and skill which afterward caused him to be spoken of as the cleverest heavyweight in the world." Mike told Corbett that he had come along just in time to beat Sullivan. According to Donovan, Corbett seemed a bit surprised and felt that he would not be able to defeat him, having seen Sullivan against Paddy Ryan and George Robinson in San Francisco.

---

[247] One secondary source said that sometime after boxing Dave Campbell, Jim had been sparring at the Golden Gate Athletic Club, sometimes with Joe Choynski Fields at 35, 37.

[248] Fields at 35, 37; Myler at 32-33; Corbett at 94; *New York Clipper*, February 22, 1890; *Times-Democrat*, February 14, 1890.

[249] William H. Adams, "New Orleans as the National Center of Boxing," *Louisiana Historical Quarterly* 39 (1956).

Donovan responded, "I told him that Sullivan now and Sullivan at the time he beat Paddy Ryan were altogether different propositions...that every year he remained idle would make John L. easier to beat, while he would be gaining knowledge and experience."[250] Corbett was in New Orleans to take on Sullivan's last opponent, which could help Jim gauge where he stood relative to Sullivan.

During his career, the 5'10 ½" Jake Kilrain had weighed anywhere from 195 to 220 pounds. Kilrain had in 1883 stopped top black fighter George Godfrey in 3 rounds, fought 1884 draws with Charley Mitchell and Jack Burke, scored an 1886 KO1 over Frank Herald, and 1887 KO11 against Joe Lannon. Some newspapers recognized him as the world champion when he issued an unaccepted 1887 challenge to Sullivan. Jake subsequently fought Jem Smith to an 1887 106-round bareknuckle draw (lasting 2 ½ hours) in which he had the best of it, causing his stock to rise even further. Many had even predicted that he would defeat Sullivan. However, he eventually lost a July 1889 75-round bareknuckle fight to Sullivan (lasting about 2 hours and 15 minutes). On February 2, 1890, two weeks before taking on Corbett, Kilrain stopped Felix Vaquelin in the 3rd round.[251] Jake Kilrain was a very experienced and highly respected fighter, considered amongst the heavyweight division's elite.

On February 17, 1890 in New Orleans, Louisiana, Jim Corbett took on Jake Kilrain in a scheduled 6-round points bout. All local primary sources reported that Corbett weighed 183 pounds to Kilrain's 201-205 pounds. Upon looking at Kilrain and hearing his announced weight, Corbett responded by saying, "Then you can put me down for 170 pounds," reflecting his belief that Jake was 10 pounds larger than his reported weight. The local *Daily Picayune* said that Corbett looked even less than his listed 183.[252] The *Times-Democrat* a few days before the fight listed Corbett as standing 6'1 ½" and 180 pounds in condition. It agreed that Kilrain was large and brawny and the disparity in their sizes was evident. Jake said he weighed 205 pounds.[253] Kilrain was 31 years old to Corbett's 23 years of age.

The local *Times-Democrat* said that about 500 people paid $5 and $10 for seats to witness the fight at the Southern Athletic Club. Before the fight, Kilrain said that he had never seen Corbett box, but knew of his prowess. At 9:25 p.m., wearing white tights, black stockings and high laced fighting shoes, Jake entered the 24-square-foot ring that was set on a stage. Jim arrived five minutes later to the cheers of the crowd, wearing blue tights and

[250] Donovan at 137-138, 140.
[251] *Times-Democrat*, February 3, 1890.
[252] *National Police Gazette*, March 8, 1890; *New Orleans Daily Picayune*, February 18, 1890; *San Francisco Chronicle*, February 18, 1890.
[253] *Times-Democrat*, February 14, 18, 1890.

a blue knit jersey. The winner was to receive $3,500 and the loser $1,000. They fought with five-ounce gloves.[254]

Jake Kilrain

The two local papers' descriptions of the bout gave the impression that it was competitive, although they both concluded that Corbett was the superior boxer.

1st round

Corbett began smiling. "Scarcely had the men taken their stands when Corbett drove his left into Kilrain's face, which startled the Baltimore man

---

254 *Times-Democrat*, February 18, 1890; *New York Herald*, February 18, 1890.

in no small degree." Corbett hit him twice more with the left to the same spot before Jake could recover, and the "ex-champion of the world awoke to the fact that he had his hands full."

Kilrain landed some rights to Corbett's left side, but Jim landed his left jabs to the face. Kilrain attacked and tried to work on the inside, but Jim held and neutralized him. Corbett landed a left to the stomach. They clinched again.

On the outside, Corbett moved away from Kilrain's blows "like a flash." "The exchanges were brisk and the clinches numerous, and in all of them Corbett showed himself a quick, sure hitter, while Kilrain appeared stiff, having no control of his hands." Jake tried working on the body, while Jim "contented himself with pummeling Kilrain's face into a lithograph sheet for a minstrel show. He showed himself extremely light on his feet, and whenever Kilrain led heavily he would dodge and smash the Baltimore boy in the face."

When they came together, Jim would push Jake away, but Kilrain tried to land on the inside until ordered to break. Kilrain attacked the body and clinched, wanting to work and keep the fight in close, grabbing roughly to the crowd's displeasure, which cried foul to Jake's infighting. By the end of the round, "Corbett, though not having landed often, had slightly the better of the proceedings." Many were surprised at how well Jim was doing, apparently including Jake.

2nd round

Corbett opened with a "rattling" left to the eye but received a swinging right to the side and a stinging right to the neck, which Jim took with a smile. Corbett was never fazed. He would shoot out his left and jump away.

Corbett cut Kilrain in this round, each local source giving its own version. The *Daily Picayune* said that Kilrain threw the right to the neck, but as he was doing so, Corbett shot out a left and caught him with a stunning punch over the left eye, causing an ugly cut. *The Times-Democrat* said that Corbett landed a right to the left eye, splitting it open about a half-inch in length, bloodying his glove.

Jake was dazed and moved about for a bit. Jim landed a right to the ear and a left lunge in the stomach, but received a counter right to the side. Jake followed and landed a blow to the chest. Kilrain forced the fight and rushed in, but received a left under the right eye, causing it to swell and blacken.

Kilrain seemed to lose heart a bit and tried clinching, but Jim held well and prevented infighting. Corbett landed a heavy left to the ribs, and was able to use counter lefts to the face and nose. Jake hit the body and clinched. Jim landed a right to the nose. Corbett showed superior agility, landing twice on the body and twice on the head "before Jake could tell what had happened. This ended the round with Corbett decidedly the best off and Kilrain badly winded, from his severe and fast fighting." The audience cheered Corbett.

Kilrain without moustache

3ʳᵈ round

Corbett came up smiling, wearing that smile throughout the contest. Kilrain landed to the stomach to begin the round. Jim hit Jake's left eye, which was closing fast. A blow to Kilrain's mouth made his lips swell. Jake smashed Jim's side. Corbett landed a right to the ribs and a left to the face, and another left to the body. After landing hard on the back of Jim's neck, Kilrain attacked with a rush and landed to the body. Corbett was not concerned, and they countered each other. Jim attacked but was met with body blows and a left to the face. Corbett answered with a double left, first to the body and then up to the nose.

Corbett played for Jake's left eye. Kilrain landed to the stomach and face, but received a counter to the nose "which caused him to see a multitude of stars judging from his appearance." The two exchanged and landed a few blows. They continued countering each other, and Jim landed two right slaps to the face to end the round.

4th round

Corbett danced forward and back. Kilrain forced matters, and in this round, landed more to the neck, breast, sides and ribs. The crowd cried foul to Kilrain's infighting. The referee ordered them to break. Jim found it more difficult to find an opening, and Jake kept attacking.

The *Times-Democrat* said that despite his aggression, Kilrain received a right uppercut to the left eye, which drew more blood. The *Daily Picayune* said that on the inside, Kilrain grabbed with his left and used his right, but Corbett uppercut with his right, striking Kilrain's eye and raising a lump.

Corbett landed a right to the face and blows to the stomach and neck. "The Californian did some very clever work with his left and landed in one-two order on Kilrain's ribs before he could get away." Jake landed some good blows, but the "round ended with Kilrain badly distressed. His lips were puffed up and his eyes closing." Still, overall, this was Kilrain's best round.

5th round

Corbett landed to the stomach and left side of Jake's head, and again to the neck. Kilrain clinched to avoid punishment. Jim pushed him off and ducked a vicious blow. Kilrain "caught him about the neck and deliberately struck him with an uppercut blow in the face. The crowd yelled 'foul' and the men broke." Kilrain was upset when the referee broke them from the clinches, because he wanted to fight on the inside more. Corbett evaded him and slipped away from the inside. Jake landed the right to the neck, but received a lightning left to the body from Corbett, as well as a right to the body as Jim was getting away.

It seemed to be a competitive fight, with Kilrain mostly landing body punches, while his head shots only landed on the neck. Corbett eventually landed a right and left on the chest and face, as well as four "rattling blows" before Kilrain clinched. Jake held and hit on the inside, and Jim asked if that was legal. Corbett landed an uppercut to his swollen face. Jake landed to the neck, but Jim countered him in the face. Corbett dodged and they clinched at the bell.

6th round

The crowd cheered Jim as he rose to begin the round. They exchanged body punches. A Corbett straight left to Kilrain's nose made Jake wince. Corbett landed his right to the side of the body and head. Jake landed to the stomach and side of the head. Jim struck the head and "got in another heavy blow on the discolored right eye of the ex-champion, receiving a terrific drive in the side, which could be heard all over the room." Jake picked it up, twice hit the face with his left, and also landed a right to the neck. Corbett continued countering as Jake pressed. The round ended with the men in a clinch.

The crowd clearly was on Corbett's side, cheering his name when it was over. The referee awarded the fight to Corbett, saying that the fight was to be decided on scientific points, not strength of blows. His decision brought cheers from the audience. Jim never lost his smile and was unmarked. Kilrain had a black eye. One observed that Corbett was very fast, but not a hard hitter.

Kilrain agreed that Jim was clever, but not powerful. He felt that superior reach allowed Corbett to touch him and score. Jake tried to get in a good blow, but "owing to the fact that Corbett held his hand in such a peculiar fashion he could not land with his accustomed force." Kilrain complained that the referee did not allow infighting, which helped Corbett. He believed that only five rounds had been fought, claiming that he had been holding back for the final round, "but the reporters told him he was wrong." Kilrain wanted a rematch in a longer fight.

Corbett was jubilant, for Kilrain was the most celebrated pugilist that he had ever met. Although it had only been a limited rounds bout, this win made the experts take notice of Jim.

> Several prominent sporting men expressed themselves as surprised at Corbett's agility, and class him above Kilrain. They compared him to Dempsey and Burke as a boxer and to Sullivan in hitting abilities. Cleary acknowledged that he was a very clever fighter, but said: "I knew that he was a good one five years ago."[255]

Back home, the *San Francisco Examiner* reported that although it was an exciting fight with five-ounce gloves, "a savage set to from beginning to end," it was all one-sided on behalf of Corbett. Corbett "proved himself a cool, magnificent, wonderfully scientific fighter, and blackened both of Kilrain's eyes." It noted that Jim was too skillful, blocking, countering, feinting, moving, ducking and eluding, and attacking to the head and body.[256]

On the east coast, the *New York Herald* said that Corbett was an "exceedingly clever fighter, in fact much the better sparrer of the two. From start to finish Corbett scarcely received a damaging blow, while Kilrain's face bore abundant marks of the Californian's handiwork." Kilrain was described as having a cut, blackened and partially closed right eye, a cut and bruised left eye, and swollen nose and lips. Corbett showed few marks. "The general opinion is that Kilrain was outfought and outgeneraled from

[255] *Times-Democrat*, February 18, 1890; *New Orleans Daily Picayune*, February 18, 1890.
[256] *San Francisco Examiner*, February 18, 1890.

the start."[257] Owing to Kilrain's lofty status, this upset victory gained Corbett national prominence.

Corbett was interviewed a day after the fight.

> When asked why he continued to lead for Kilrain's head with his weak hands, Corbett said that the contest was one for points, and he knew that every blow on Kilrain's face could be easily seen.

> Of Kilrain's ability he said but little. While acknowledging the Baltimore man to be both strong and skillful, he thought that too much credit had been given him.

> Corbett's left hand is slightly hurt from coming in contact with Kilrain's face and head and two knuckles are knocked out of place. He said that since his fight in June last with Joe Choynski...his hands have been somewhat sore... He will rest for a number of months before he engages in any fight to a finish, to allow his hands an opportunity to grow stronger.[258]

In an interview about a month later, Corbett said of Kilrain,

> He did not appear to be in it in the go between us.... In the first three rounds I fought shy of him, thinking that he was holding off, but when he came up for the fourth round I saw that I had him and did my best. There appeared to be no force to his blows, and I had no trouble in getting in on him. ... He was bleeding freely at the nose and mouth and from several cuts on his face.[259]

Two and a half years later, Kilrain called Corbett "one of the shiftiest men I ever saw," and said that he was "surprised at his cleverness," admitting that he was outpointed. However, he felt that if it was a finish fight the result would have been different, commenting that Jim did not like infighting, which the referee did not allow, that body punches made him wince, and that Corbett was not a hard puncher. He predicted that Sullivan would defeat him.[260]

Even John L. Sullivan took note of the post-fight reports, but belittled Corbett's victory.

> I know this man Corbett, and I don't think for a minute that he can whip Kilrain, Queensberry rules, with small gloves. Kilrain has been having a good time lately and was out of condition. There was no in-fighting allowed, and Corbett, having a longer reach, got in some hits and got away. He is a clever fellow, no doubt, but if there is anybody in any part of the country who thinks that Corbett can stay ten rounds

[257] *New York Herald,* February 18, 1890.
[258] *Times-Democrat,* February 19, 1890.
[259] *New York Sun,* March 19, 1890.
[260] *National Police Gazette,* September 3, 1892.

with Kilrain with two-ounce gloves, why, I've got $5,000 which I will bet against $4,000 that he can't.[261]

William Muldoon, who had trained and cornered Kilrain for the Corbett bout, and who had previously trained Sullivan to his victory over Kilrain, gave his thoughts on Corbett.

> Corbett was away the superior of Kilrain the night they fought, he says, and he calls the Californian a second Jack Dempsey. Corbett has as much generalship and cleverness as a heavy-weight as Dempsey has as a middle-weight. When time was called he jumped for Kilrain, and was on top of him almost before he could get out of his corner. Kilrain only hit Corbett one square blow in the six rounds. When asked what he thought of Corbett's chances against Sullivan Mr. Muldoon said that Corbett was not such a hard hitter as he ought to be to fight Sullivan. The trouble with Sullivan would be that he could not hit Corbett. The Californian was twice as clever as Kilrain, he thought, and is just the man to whip Jackson.[262]

Thus, even then, Muldoon saw Corbett as a man who would be competitive with both Sullivan and Peter Jackson, which was a very high compliment.

The *San Francisco Chronicle* noted the significant impact of Corbett's victory and opined,

> Corbett's signal defeat of Kilrain has placed him at once in the front rank of heavy-weight boxers, and the Easterners are curious to know just how good he is. The young professor is likely to be overrated instead of underrated...

> They are already talking of the young professor as being the man to defeat Sullivan. The reporters have been interviewing Muldoon and other athletic celebrities who are quoted as saying that Corbett is the coming champion of the world and that Sullivan and Kilrain are stale and past their prime. ... Corbett's showing with Kilrain puts him in competition, with a jump, with the best big men in the country.[263]

Speaking of Sullivan, in March 1890, the Mississippi Supreme Court overturned his criminal prize-fight conviction. A fresh indictment was found in June, and Sully plead guilty and paid a $500 fine. Sullivan had been semi-retired since his July 1889 Kilrain fight, and his status would continue that way. One reporter who spoke with John in March 1890 said, "Reading between the lines of his conversation I am satisfied that he is thoroughly tired of the ring."[264]

---

[261] *San Francisco Chronicle*, March 3, 1890.
[262] *San Francisco Chronicle*, March 17, 1890.
[263] *San Francisco Chronicle*, March 10, 1890.
[264] *New York Sun*, March 9, 1890.

After his Kilrain victory, Corbett returned to San Francisco. On February 27, he was in attendance at a California Club fight card. Upon entering the hall, Jim was "cheered to the echo" and introduced as "the California wonder."[265]

Corbett settled matters with the Olympic, agreeing to resume his professorship there. However, at Mike Donovan's request, Jim was given a leave of absence to travel to the east coast to make money for a while. He left San Francisco again on March 8.[266]

Joe McAuliffe was "nettled" by the sudden boon to Corbett's career and in March issued a challenge to fight him to a finish for $10,000 a side. However, he felt that "Mr. Corbett being reinstated as an instructor of the Olympic Club, will probably hide from a finish fight behind a contract. In that case I will spar Mr. Corbett ten rounds…and will agree to stop him inside of that time or lay no claim to any part of the purse."

The match-up was assessed. "While the professional pugilists here, almost to a man, think McAuliffe can defeat Corbett in a finish fight, very few believe that Joe can distress the young professor greatly in ten rounds if Corbett chooses to make a waiting battle and avoids slogging."[267]

As predicted, Corbett said that it would be impossible for him to accept McAuliffe's challenge, for he was under contract to the Olympic for one year, at a salary of $3,000 per year ($250 a month), which prevented him from accepting serious challenges until its expiration. Of course, Corbett had already traveled to the east coast anyway, where he remained for a month, further establishing his reputation there. He was required to return to the Olympic by May 1.[268]

Oddly enough, Corbett was also quoted as saying on his way east,

> I do not care to become a professional fighter. They all get whipped in time, and then what are they? At present I am the professor of boxing in the San Francisco Olympic Club, which is the gentlemen's club of the city. I get a handsome salary and am satisfied. Just at present I have a lay-off, and as Donovan offers me an easy opportunity to make a few thousand, I've concluded to do it.[269]

Corbett arrived in New York on March 17, 1890 as the guest of Professor Mike Donovan, who had been in his corner for the Kilrain bout. The 42-year-old Donovan was the New York Athletic Club's boxing instructor, and was a well-respected, skilled fighter and teacher.[270]

Corbett likely sparred Professor Donovan a number of times in money-making exhibitions. The *New York Sun* said that Corbett and Donovan were

---

[265] *San Francisco Chronicle*, February 28, 1890.
[266] *New York Clipper*, March 15, 1890; *San Francisco Chronicle*, March 6, 8, 1890.
[267] *San Francisco Chronicle*, March 10, 1890.
[268] *New York Sun*, March 19, 1890.
[269] *San Francisco Chronicle*, March 24, 1890.
[270] *New York Sun*, March 18, 1890.

set to spar in Boston, Brooklyn, Philadelphia, Baltimore, and Washington.[271] A secondary source says they sparred 3 rounds in New York on March 20, 1890, but they apparently boxed on other occasions as well.[272] Donovan later claimed to have sparred with Corbett every day for a month. Such experience was valuable, because the middleweight-sized veteran Donovan had sparred John L. Sullivan many times, in 1880, 1881, 1884, 1885, 1887, and 1888.

Mike Donovan

In his book, Donovan claimed to have given Corbett some instruction. "His improvement was remarkable, owing to his unusual intelligence and quickness to grasp new ideas." Mike was impressed with Jim's defense.

---

[271] *New York Sun,* March 20, 1890.
[272] Cyberboxingzone.com; *Referee,* June 18, 1890.

"Corbett's head was always hard to reach. In fact, he might well boast that no one was ever able to mark him."[273]

At the time, after sparring with Jim, Donovan told the newspapers,

> I regard Corbett as the cleverest big man I ever sparred with, and I have no hesitation in saying that he is the coming champion. When I boxed Sullivan at the Howard Athenaeum in Boston in February, 1880, he was practically unknown to the pugilistic world. I said then that Sullivan was the coming champion...Corbett today is the man that Sullivan was ten years ago, and now it is his turn, and I regard him, as I said before, as the future champion.[274]

That was a high compliment indeed. Donovan also said that Jim had fought fifteen battles and lost none of them. "Corbett is a curiosity as a prize-fighter, as is any man who stops scratching books in a banker's office in order to deal knockout blows in the prize ring. He is as little like a pugilist in manner and appearance as a man can well be." The subtitle of the article was entitled, "Corbett as the Coming Champion."[275]

Back in San Francisco, the *Chronicle* said that Corbett had "caught on" and was an "athletic lion" in New York. It reprinted a March 22, 1890 letter from Mike Donovan which said,

> I have Corbett here, not only as my guest, but the special guest of the club. ... We had three rounds the other afternoon in the presence of several of my pupils, and they as well as myself were surprised at the science he displayed. He is the cleverest big man I ever sparred with, and I am sure he is the coming champion. ... George, do you remember me telling you after the first time I boxed Sullivan that he was the coming man, and didn't my words come true? Which will be the same in this case.

It also quoted the sporting editor of the *New York World*, who observed Corbett and Donovan spar.

> I had the pleasure of seeing a rattling "go" between Jim Corbett and Mike Donovan at the New York Athletic Club the other day. Corbett is all that his friends claim for him so far as clever sparring is concerned. As to his hitting propensities little can be said except that in his fight with big Choynski in California he made a good showing in this respect. Wonderfully quick he certainly is, and I don't believe he could be awkward if he tried. His every movement is graceful, and after seeing him spar no one will dispute that he is an uncommonly shifty fellow. Mike Donovan...says that Corbett is the quickest big man he has ever seen. "Why, Kilrain isn't to be mentioned in the

---

[273] Donovan at 144-145.
[274] *Referee*, March 6, 1890, March 19, 1890.
[275] *Referee*, June 11, 1890, quoting April 11, 1890 edition of *The Evening Sun*.

same breath with this man for cleverness," says Donovan, "and I'll wager he can't hit a bit harder. Corbett is a package of grit and cleverness, and I tell you he can give any of 'em an argument. He's the man now that Sullivan was ten years ago, and it will be well for these prophets who predict holders of championship honors to look out for Mr. Corbett."

As nearly as I could learn, Corbett will not look for a match this year principally because the Olympic Athletic Club of San Francisco pays him $2500 per annum to act according to its instructions. Donovan thinks Corbett is Jackson's master... I doubt if Corbett can outpoint the Australian.[276]

Even Corbett's performance against Joe Choynski was gaining greater recognition, given how Joe was recently performing. In late March 1890, Choynski scored a KO2 over Billy Wilson, a respected black fighter. "The local estimate of Jim's fighting qualities has also been raised since Joe Choynski so quickly defeated big Billy Wilson."[277] Speaking of Choynski's victory, Corbett said, "I was glad to hear of it. A number of other heavyweights will go down under his sledgehammer blows before Joe gets through with them. He is a great fighter."[278]

Corbett's confidence was growing, and in April 1890, he expressed a desire to take on Sullivan in a 4 rounder for a $1,000 purse. Sullivan said that he was willing, but on the condition that he would impose upon himself the duty to knock Corbett out within the 4 rounds or forfeit the entire purse. John L. had in part made his reputation by knocking out men within 4 rounds, offering them $1,000 if they could last that long, which almost no one did. "That such a meeting would draw a big crowd and excite a great amount of interest goes without saying." One writer assessed such a match.

> In Corbett, however, Sullivan will find a man fully as agile and clever as Charley Mitchell. Corbett will not stand till he is knocked down by one of the big fellow's rushes, but will be all over the ring in a round and boxing on the retreat... Of course there is the possibility that Sullivan may put him out with one of his famous punches, but it is only a possibility and too remote to be likely to happen in four rounds with Sullivan in very poor fix for any kind of a fight.

However, it was also believed that the bout was not likely to happen, because Corbett was leaving for home within two weeks, "which would be too short a period for Sullivan to prepare himself to face so good a man as Choynski's conqueror certainly is." Quite frankly, it sounded as if the

---

[276] *San Francisco Chronicle*, March 31, 1890.
[277] *San Francisco Chronicle*, March 31, 1890.
[278] *Referee*, June 18, 1890.

inactive and overweight Sullivan was simply bluffing. Still, the seeds of a potential match between the two were being planted.[279]

Jake Kilrain, like McAuliffe, was upset at all the attention that Corbett was receiving and offered to fight him in a rematch of a greater number of rounds, but Jim declined. Kilrain said, "I see he is doing considerable talk through the papers, but when cornered he always crawls out on the plea of having to go home. For my part I think he is the biggest bluffer I have ever seen." Of course, Corbett had already won his reputation off of Kilrain, and likely saw no reason to box him again.[280]

On April 9, Denver Ed Smith, who was coming off a 1st round knockout victory over Mike Cleary, issued a challenge for a match of 6 or 10 rounds against a host of contenders, but Jim Corbett or Dominick McCaffrey preferred. Less than a week later, it was Corbett and McCaffrey who entered the ring together. In May, Smith took on Peter Jackson and was dropped multiple times en route to a 5-round decision loss.[281]

Just before leaving New York, two months after the Kilrain bout, on April 14, 1890 in Brooklyn, Corbett took on another former Sullivan title challenger in Dominick McCaffrey, who according to Corbett "at that time was considered one of the cleverest boxers in America."[282] In 1884, McCaffrey had won a close 4-round decision over Charley Mitchell. In 1885, although he was dropped a number of times, McCaffrey survived 7 rounds against Sullivan, losing a decision. However, in 1887, Patsy Farrell knocked out McCaffrey in the 2nd round, and in 1888, Dominick lost a 10-round decision to middleweight champion Jack Dempsey.[283] Still, McCaffrey had some notoriety based on his fights with Sullivan and Mitchell, and his boxing skill was respected.

Corbett had actually expressed his desire to box McCaffrey back in December 1889, when he sent a telegram to San Francisco's Golden Gate Athletic Club indicating that he would fight McCaffrey in April 1890 for $4,000 if given the chance.[284]

The *San Francisco Examiner* reported that McCaffrey was 27 years old, weighing in the neighborhood of 165 pounds in perfect condition, and, "though it is next to impossible to get at these things accurately, he probably weighed 175 pounds in costume when he faced Corbett." Mac was listed as standing 5'8 ½", and generally fought in the 160–175-pound range. Reports of Corbett's weight varied, generally from 185-190, with one claiming that he weighed as much as 203 pounds.

Little known is the fact that because of legal constraints, the bout was really an exhibition, rather than an official Queensberry rules fight. There

[279] *New York Clipper*, April 12, 1890; *San Francisco Chronicle*, April 7, 1890.
[280] *San Francisco Chronicle*, April 12, 1890.
[281] *New York Clipper*, April 19, 1890, May 24, 1890.
[282] Corbett at 92.
[283] *National Police Gazette*, March 19, 1887, February 18, 1888.
[284] *San Francisco Chronicle*, December 16, 1889.

was no official referee or timekeeper, but Steve O'Donnell assisted as "master of ceremonies," keeping time and acting informally as an official. There were not even formally designated cornermen. They wore large 8-ounce gloves rather than the usual 2-5-ounce gloves worn in serious bouts. The rounds were clearly shortened and the rests lengthened so as to prevent Corbett from knocking him out.

Dominick McCaffrey

All of these differences reflected an effort to avoid potential adverse legal repercussions. New York law strictly required only exhibition bouts, with no slugging or knockouts allowed. Corbett and O'Donnell obviously did not want to break the law. The bout's eventual tameness might also indicate that there was a private agreement between Corbett and McCaffrey.

The *New York Clipper* said that it was announced beforehand that it would be "simply a contest for points, purely scientific in character." It was actually even less than that, although the paying spectators had expected or wanted more.

The following account is an amalgamation of the New York-based *National Police Gazette, Brooklyn Daily Eagle, New York Sun,* and *New York Herald.*

1st round

The first impression the 1,800 spectators had of Corbett was that he was too handsome and delicate looking to be a fighter. However, they soon changed their minds. It was obvious that McCaffrey was either afraid or something was wrong with him. He kept away most of the time, and only landed some light taps. Corbett landed his cracking left under the right eye and to the body. A Corbett straight left "twisted him like a rainbow." Mac countered and began leading more, but the damage had been done to him. They made a few exchanges and McCaffrey clinched, hanging onto Jim "like a barnacle to a ship's bottom, and time was called amid yells and hisses and shouts of 'That is not three minutes!'" The round only lasted 2 minutes and 7 seconds, which caused some to yell, "Fake."

2nd round

Corbett did the smashing and McCaffrey the hugging. "It was plain to be seen that the California Wonder was the master of the situation." Mac missed a right by a mile, and after that, he became extremely nervous and wobbled about the ring. Jim remained calm and confident, following up easily, but persistently. A smash to the face and stomach made Dom seem sick, acting so groggily that the expression, "He's been drinking," was heard. Corbett continued pasting him. Dominick was clearly rattled. Despite having McCaffrey at his mercy and on the ropes often, Corbett did not attempt to finish him, but let McCaffrey off the hook and allowed him to last.

Mac occasionally countered but Jim landed better blows to the face, usually under the right eye, as well as some to the breast. Jim only really banged Dominick when Mac tried to stand up to him. Mac seemed afraid and fell back or ducked his head very low. His blows missed badly and he only seemed to wind himself by them, while Corbett stepped back or to the side with a smile. McCaffrey dodged and held on for dear life. The crowd hissed and expressed its displeasure when time was again called early, after only 1 minute and 20 seconds.

3rd round

Corbett began the round landing a staggering punch to the nose. Mac could not land and ate two more lefts. Dom's nose was bleeding and he seemed weakened by the hammering. Even when Dominick landed one to the nose, he was heavily countered. Generally, Mac mostly missed, and was very weak.

The confident Corbett held his hands by his sides. Jim fought Dom to the ropes and pummeled him. After a clinch and break, Corbett slapped his right glove onto Dom's mouth and held it there, his long right arm extended. McCaffrey was unable to move until Jim stepped back. By the end of the round, Dominick was groggy from body blows, but it seemed as if Jim was holding back from finishing him. This round lasted 2 minutes and 30 seconds.

4th round

Corbett rallied and beat a tattoo on McCaffrey, who was "severely countered." Jim rushed Dom to the ropes and tried uppercuts, but Mac clinched. Jim broke away and landed rights and lefts, banging away, again fighting McCaffrey to the ropes. Mac fell on the ropes with his head and one arm over. The *National Police Gazette* said,

> Either from weakness or in attempting to avoid punishment, McCaffrey bent over the ropes. With an effort he turned his face toward his opponent as though to look if anything more was coming, but Corbett had stepped back and thrown up his hands in appeal to Steve O'Donnell to excuse him from doing any more damage. Steve said he guessed that would do, and seriously declared that "Mr. Corbett had the best of the bout."[285]

The *New York Herald* said,

> The fourth round closed with McCaffrey leaning over the ropes in despair, as a seasick transatlantic traveler hangs over the bulwarks. There were loud cries of "hippodrome" and groans and hisses at the conclusion. The crowd blamed Corbett for not punishing his man more and there was disgust at the tameness of the show.[286]

The round only lasted 1 minute and 13 seconds. Mac said that he was not in condition.

The *Brooklyn Daily Eagle* said that despite Corbett's holding back, during the round McCaffrey was groggy and made it known that he had enough. Corbett then stepped away and waited for time to be called, after just over a minute had elapsed.[287]

The *New York Sun* said the actual fighting time was only seven minutes and ten seconds (rather than the proper twelve minutes), and the three rest periods had totaled five minutes and ten seconds (rather than the proper three minutes), and yet Corbett had McCaffrey powerless.[288]

---

285 *National Police Gazette*, May 3, 1890.
286 *New York Herald*, April 15, 1890.
287 *Brooklyn Daily Eagle*, April 15, 1890.
288 *New York Sun*, April 15, 1890.

The *San Francisco Examiner* noted that the rest between the 3rd and 4th rounds was quite longer than the usual minute. This, combined with the short rounds, gave the impression that "there was to be no real effort at a knockout." Despite every effort to help Mac out with short rounds and long rests, Corbett's work still caused him to quit. "[W]hile Corbett is trying to punish him McCaffrey shouts to the officials to "Take him away." … Corbett sprang back and the men faced again in the center, when McCaffrey, dazed and uncertain, gives it up. He protests against the announcement in favor of Corbett a moment later amid derisive yells."[289]

This has typically been considered a 4-round decision, but really, this was more of a stoppage/retirement. No wonder the crowd called it a hippodrome. It seemed that Corbett just played with him, yet still beat him up, but eventually let him off the hook, with assistance from the timekeeper/master of ceremonies. It was clear that Corbett held back from finishing him because it was only supposed to be a scientific exhibition. Even still, McCaffrey had essentially retired before the well-shortened bout was over.

McCaffrey's protest over a decision being rendered was owing to the fact that the bout was only supposed to be an exhibition, and there was no official referee to render a decision. Thus, he felt that O'Donnell did not have the right to award the bout to Corbett.

The *New York Herald* said that it was a "tame and disappointing" exhibition and that Corbett could have easily knocked him out. Corbett smiled throughout, seeming to pity McCaffrey, and held back from throwing very often. Jim was listed as weighing 203 pounds, and McCaffrey looked small in comparison. It said that Dominick's tactics were essentially designed for survival only, hopping about, leaning his head back, ducking and running in to make a blind attempt at a punch, and then grabbing. To break free, Corbett would place one hand on Mac's throat and the other on his face, pushing his head back. Maybe there was something to John L. Sullivan's claim that McCaffrey only fought to survive.

The local *Brooklyn Daily Eagle* said that Corbett had it all his own way and that Dominick was no match. Every time Corbett struck him, McCaffrey would grab or run. It too noted that the rounds were improperly short.

The *New York Clipper* said that even though it was only a scientific bout, the crowd did not receive its money's worth. It called the bout unsatisfactory, blaming McCaffrey. Other than the 1st round, Mac was purely defensive throughout, hugging to avoid punishment, making it tame and uninteresting. Corbett did all the real work during the brief rounds, and Jim "satisfied everybody present that he is a remarkably clever boxer."[290]

One observer of the bout later said of Corbett,

[289] *San Francisco Examiner*, April 15, 1890.
[290] *New York Clipper*, April 19, 1890.

His left flies out like a piston rod. His deliveries are fine, quick and straight…his stoppings are excellent, and his flank movements, with his long strides and perfect poise and balance, are marvelously agile for a man weighing 185 to 190 pounds. McCaffrey was fought out practically in four minutes from the first call of time … McCaffrey seemed blown and amazed at a very early stage of affairs. When he failed to land, as he usually did, he lurched in for a clinch. Corbett threw him from him quite handily, I thought, but in the operation he had a way of roughing him over the face with the glove that was quite of the English fighters' variety. … Corbett was smiling, fresh as a daisy, strong and springy. … I should not want the contract of finding a Queensberry rule glove fighter to whip him. His demonstration of outclassing McCaffrey was far more complete than Sullivan's…. Make no mistake of counting upon Corbett as easy game for any holder of the much coveted fistic championship of the world. He is in the programme with any fighter living to give him an argument.[291]

McCaffrey was later interviewed:

I acknowledge that I was overmatched from start to finish by Corbett. He is by far a cleverer boxer than I am, and has a longer reach. Why, he did what I never saw or heard of before – placing his right hand against my nose and smashing me with his left. I was powerless to help myself in the mean time. I was licked from the first round.[292]

After the McCaffrey exhibition, Corbett returned to San Francisco to fulfill his new contract as the Olympic Club's boxing instructor. An Australian primary source said that Corbett was to receive $3,000 per year for two hours daily sparring work at the club. "Until his engagement expires Corbett cannot engage in any glove fight or fistic encounter unless the club gives him permission. Corbett says after this engagement with the club is over he will issue a challenge to meet any man in the world."[293] Corbett's professional career went on hiatus yet again.

At that time, there had been some discussion of a potential match between John L. Sullivan and Peter Jackson. San Francisco's California Athletic Club said that it was willing to meet Sullivan's demand for a whopping $20,000 purse for such a fight. Corbett predicted that John would not take the fight, and revealed his feeling about Sullivan's condition and ability to be properly prepared for a fight ever again. Corbett engaged a writer in some discussion, saying,

"Sullivan will not fight." "Nonsense," Said I, "Sullivan has declared that he will fight for $20,000." That sum having been subscribed by the athletic club, he will fight Jackson for it. "May be," said Mr.

[291] *Referee*, August 5, 1891; *San Francisco Chronicle*, April 28, 1890.
[292] *San Francisco Chronicle*, May 5, 1890.
[293] *Referee*, May 7, 1890.

Corbett, "but I don't believe it. Sullivan dare not train down to fighting condition now. If he were to train down as a man ought to for a fight it would kill him. He has indulged in all sorts of excesses and has tried his constitution to its uttermost. He has broken his health by these practices, and now he cannot quit drinking, try as he may. The result is that his whole physical being is laid under tribute, and he will find himself woefully lacking in physical responsiveness when he tries to train down to fighting trim.

Why, when he fought Kilrain he was far from being in prime condition. He wore a plaster on his chest and stomach, and was generally in bad shape. Had he been in condition he should have won that fight in twenty rounds. I think there are several men who can whip Sullivan now, but I don't think Sullivan will fight unless he becomes very hard up. However, if he fights Jackson I will stand to go broke on Jackson's winning. I have seen Jackson in all his fights and boxing bouts in San Francisco, and if he fights Sullivan I think he'll whip him. But I stick to my belief that Sullivan will not fight."[294]

Corbett had some keen insights, and this was his opinion *less than one year* after the Sullivan-Kilrain fight. One writer echoed Corbett's sentiments, saying,

This man Sullivan is beyond redemption. He has been drunk night and day for months, and he is now only a shadow of his former self. I cannot see how he ever can be got to fight again, besides he has a particular dislike to fighting colored men, which he expresses when drunk as well as sober.[295]

Sullivan did not fight Jackson.

Regardless of his condition, a potential match-up between Sullivan and Corbett was being debated as well. "The Eastern sporting writers continue to discuss Jim Corbett's qualifications for the job of defeating John L. Sullivan, and no two of the critics agree." Corbett would have to defeat Sullivan with intelligence, because he certainly did not have his power. "Corbett will not, I think, knock men silly by the crushing force of single hits as Sullivan has." One noted, "Joe Goss to his dying day declared: 'Sullivan is the best man that ever stepped in the ring. I bar none – Sayers, Heenan, Hyer, Morrissey, King or Mace, no man who ever lived. He is better than any man of them was the best day he ever saw.'" Certainly though, Sullivan was no longer the man that he was when Goss saw him (Goss died in 1885). Still, many experts had felt that John could never get into proper condition before the Kilrain fight, but Sullivan stood before him for over two hours in the broiling hot sun in a winning effort. As a

[294] *San Francisco Chronicle*, April 24, 1890.
[295] *San Francisco Morning Call*, May 11, 1890.

result, despite his food and alcohol excesses and his inactivity, many did not believe that the undefeated Sullivan could be defeated. They thought that Sullivan defied the laws of nature.

However, Corbett stated his belief that "as far as finish fights are concerned Sullivan's career is at an end." Phil Dwyer, who had financially backed Sullivan against Kilrain, said that he would back Corbett against Sullivan for any amount up to $50,000, and felt that it would be a safe investment. "You may not know it…but that man Corbett, in my opinion, outranks them all, and I took the pains to tell him so when he was here [in New York]. … I think Sullivan is retrograding sadly, and do not believe he will ever meet Jackson or any other first-rater."[296]

Jim arrived back home in San Francisco on April 26, having finished his "triumphal tour of the East." Four days later, and two weeks after the McCaffrey bout, on April 30, 1890 in Sacramento, California, Corbett again sparred "Professor" John Donaldson (They had previously boxed in September 1889). The local *Sacramento Bee* said that Corbett and Donaldson's sparring was very tame and disappointing, Donaldson having drunk too much wine. Corbett was clever, but he did not show his best points, possibly because he felt the need to hold back owing to Donaldson's condition. The local paper felt that the audience was entitled to something better than the hippodrome which they witnessed.[297]

Corbett resumed his life as a boxing professor. A May 1890 report noted that Corbett was quite popular and happy as a boxing coach.

> Jim Corbett's resumption of his old post as boxing instructor at the Olympic Club has created a fresh interest in sparring among the members. Great crowds assemble on class nights to see Corbett put his colts through their facings and the genial professor seems thoroughly at home teaching the young idea how to smite.[298]

Reflecting the constantly shifting political attitudes regarding the sport, in June 1890, California Governor Robert Waterman sent a letter to the state Attorney General taking a position against boxing in general and the California Club in particular. The governor wrote,

> [T]he State has been thoroughly and completely disgraced by the maintenance of an organization given up to degrading and disgusting exhibitions of brute force in so called scientific contests between so called scientific athletes, which are nothing more nor less than prize fights, in opposition to decency and the good order of society…. They should no longer be permitted to defame and degrade the soil of our State, and the mere fact that is advanced, that their patrons consist of those in the higher walks of life, should be a still further

[296] *San Francisco Chronicle*, April 27, 28, 1890; May 5, 12, 1890.
[297] *Sacramento Bee*, May 1, 1890; *San Francisco Chronicle*, April 17, 1890.
[298] *San Francisco Chronicle*, May 12, 1890.

incentive to put an end to the exhibitions alluded to, in order that their pernicious example may not affect those in the lower walks of life.[299]

The police began clamping down on boxing matches. However, boxing instruction was allowed to continue in athletic clubs. Naturally, sparring was a necessary part of that instruction, so the ongoing legal and political wrangling did not affect Corbett.

The California Club continued hosting tame exhibitions, but the status of serious fights was in limbo for a while. In July, the California Club decided to challenge the law by hosting a professional fight to make a test case of the issue. The club believed that it could draw the line between a test of skill and strength and a brutal prize fight, which it had been doing successfully for the past two years in the presence of the police. President Lem Fulda said that the club would continue hosting professional fights and would use its lawyers to fight to the bitter end.[300]

Members of the California Club witnessed a mid-1890 John L. Sullivan exhibition in the east and did "not express themselves as highly pleased with the champion's appearance. They found Sullivan giving boxing exhibitions in a swallow-tail coat with Joe Lannon, and they appear to think that this style of contest is about all that the eminent Boston slogger will be ever again good for."[301] The overweight Sullivan was mostly just performing in his play, which contained a tame and short sparring exhibition with Lannon.

In late July, there was further talk of a potential Sullivan-Corbett match-up. Phil Dwyer was willing to back Corbett for $20,000 against Sullivan, while Charles Johnston was willing to back Sullivan for the same amount against Corbett. However, Sullivan was tired of the game.

> The big fellow does not mind fighting, for he feels that he is the superior without doubt of any man in a twenty-four foot ring. It is the severe sacrifice that he has to make while training that sickens him. "Just think of throwing two good months of your life away to train for one fight," said the champion recently.[302]

During subsequent months, Corbett continued his teaching duties at the Olympic, as he had been doing since May. On September 3, 1890, a large audience witnessed an Olympic Club exhibition held at the Grand Opera House. Professor Corbett sparred with Robert McCord, the champion amateur middleweight of the Pacific coast, and they did "good and earnest work." McCord only weighed around 150 pounds, but at that time, middleweight was anything from 140 to 158 pounds.

---

[299] *San Francisco Chronicle*, June 17, 1890; *New York Clipper*, June 28, 1890.
[300] *New York Clipper*, July 5, 12, 19, 1890; *San Francisco Chronicle*, July 10, 1890.
[301] *San Francisco Chronicle*, July 8, 1890.
[302] *San Francisco Chronicle*, July 21, 1890.

Later that evening, Corbett wrestled with little Jack Woolrich, a member of the juvenile class, and it was the "most comical event of the evening," for the "professor looked like Gulliver beside his Lilliputian opponent." A number of other juvenile class members then joined in and jumped on Corbett, who was "finally overpowered by a host of pigmies, who forced him to the carpet by sheer force of numbers."[303]

It was in September 1890 that further revelations regarding the Campbell fight were published, including Corbett's letter to Campbell suggesting that they agree to fight to a draw. This naturally hurt Corbett's reputation.

In early October, it was reported that Professor Corbett was developing a number of boxers for the upcoming November boxing tournament.[304]

According to a non-local source, on October 8, 1890 at the Olympic, Corbett privately sparred the sugar tycoon John Spreckles, of the "immense firm of J.D. Spreckles & Bros." It was supposed to be a friendly bout, but amidst a vigorous interchange of rapid blows, Corbett accidentally broke Spreckles' nose.[305]

On October 9, 1890 at the packed Oakland Theater, the Acme Club held a ladies' night exhibition show in which a number of its members boxed against the Olympians. Corbett boxed 3 lively rounds with fellow Olympian, middleweight Robert McCord.[306]

Later that month, an upset Corbett made it known that he wanted to box Dave Campbell again, and he issued him a challenge. His letter to Campbell stated,

> I have read in the Eastern papers of your attempts to belittle my reputation through the forced draw battle in which you and I participated at Portland. It seems strange that you would dare to refer to that meeting, and if you did it would be honorable to have told the press and the public the means to which you resorted in a desire to save yourself.... I hasten to open overtures that will decide beyond a doubt the question of superiority between you and me. ... I will meet you in any kind of a contest...for any amount...and under conditions of your own choosing. In other words, this is but the second meeting you promised to accord me on the night I was forced to sign "that agreement."
>
> To be frank, I have always belittled you, as either a boxer or fighter, and even now I doubt your agreeing to a meeting under any conditions.

---

[303] *Daily Alta California*, September 1, 4, 1890.
[304] *San Francisco Chronicle*, October 6, 1890.
[305] *Milwaukee Evening Wisconsin*, October 10, 1890; Cyberboxingzone.com; Myler at 35. Special thanks to Pat Myler for his assistance in tracking down this date.
[306] *San Francisco Chronicle*, October 10, 1890.

The *San Francisco Chronicle* agreed with Corbett that Campbell was not likely to accept the challenge. "It is dollars to cents that the Oregonian will not accept, and it would be no credit to Corbett if he should beat the Webfoot champion...for he is not only a lot cleverer, but once and a half as big."[307]

Despite the fact that Corbett was under contract not to engage in professional matches, Jim was getting fidgety; wanting to further capitalize on his new prestigious status obtained from his Choynski, Kilrain and McCaffrey victories, and also to overcome some of the bad press surrounding his bout with Dave Campbell.

In addition to his Campbell challenge, at the beginning of November 1890, Corbett also issued a challenge to Frank Slavin, a highly regarded contender who earlier in the year had challenged Corbett. Although nothing came of the proposed Campbell and Slavin matches, clearly Corbett was interested in being something other than a professor.

---

[307] *San Francisco Chronicle,* October 20, 1890.

CHAPTER 9

Crossing the <u>Line</u>
to Face the Best

During Jim Corbett's professional ascendancy, the man who was most discussed as a potential challenger for Sullivan's title was Peter Jackson. Jackson was mostly residing in the San Francisco area, and despite the fact that he was black, was highly supported and touted by the local newspapers in his quest for the title.

Peter Jackson stood 6'1 ¼" and generally weighed in the 190–210-pound range. He was born in 1861 in St. Croix, British West Indies, but began his boxing career in Australia in 1881 at age 19 or 20, having his first fight in 1882. His only loss came in 1884, when the aggressive Australian champion Bill Farnan, who was 5'9", 32 years old and 165 pounds, knocked out a 23-year-old Jackson with body shots in the 3rd round.[308] A rematch between the two later that year resulted in a 6-round draw when the police stopped the bout. Jackson was at that time seen as scientific, but his ability to take a punch was questioned.[309] However, he continued improving, and in time became Australia's best fighter.

In March 1886, Jackson knocked out Mick Dooley in the 3rd round, two months before Dooley stopped future middleweight champion Bob Fitzsimmons in the 3rd round.[310]

In September 1886, a 25-year-old Jackson won the Australian heavyweight championship with a Queensberry rules KO30 over Tom Lees. This was significant because Lees had twice knocked out Jackson conqueror Bill Farnan, in 12 rounds in 1885, and in April 1886, after their 18 or 19 round bout lasting one hour and eighteen minutes was stopped by the police, the two finished the fight the next day and Lees stopped Farnan in the 4th round.[311]

Jackson's first official American fight was in the San Francisco area, in August 1888, defeating George Godfrey via KO19. The *San Francisco Examiner* said that Jackson's "fighting qualities astonished many of those present, while a few were disappointed with his hitting powers."[312] Generally, Jackson was praised as a highly skilled fighter, known for his

---

[308] *National Police Gazette,* August 30, 1884.
[309] *New York Clipper,* November 15, 1884, quoting *Sydney Bulletin,* October 4, 1884.
[310] *Sydney Daily Telegraph,* May 17, 1886.
[311] *San Francisco Daily Examiner,* December 29, 1888; *Australian Sporting Celebrities* (Melbourne: A.H. Massina & Co., 1887), 64; Boxrec.com; *Daily Alta California,* June 7, 1886.
[312] *San Francisco Daily Examiner,* August 27, 1888.

quick left-right combinations to the body and head, good uppercut, defensive skills, and endurance. He usually cautiously, consistently, and methodically broke his opponents down.

Peter Jackson

In December 1888, the 27-year-old 204-pound Jackson fought 24-year-old 219-pound Joe McAuliffe. In stopping the powerful McAuliffe in the 24th round, Jackson was called "too skillful, too quick, too scienced, too much of a general, and 'our big Joe' bit the dust." Peter "chopped him to pieces in as masterly a manner as was ever witnessed in the history of the squared circle... Jackson is a short-odds horse in the race for the world's laurels of modern fistiana. He has earned the chance, and earned it well."[313]

Those that lamented Jackson's victory did so upon racial grounds, feeling that if Jackson ever won the title it would hurt the sport. In fact, one newspaper later said that the pugilistic fever which had raged for the past ten years was abating, in part because of "the prominence darky fighters have assumed in the ring."[314]

---

[313] *San Francisco Daily Examiner*, December 29, 1888; *San Francisco Chronicle*, December 29, 1888.
[314] *San Francisco Daily Examiner*, December 30, 1888; *New York Sun*, February 16, 1890.

In April 1889, a 200-pound Jackson scored a KO10 over 185-pound Patsy Cardiff, who in 1887 had fought Sullivan to a 6-round draw. The local *San Francisco Chronicle* said that Jackson was superior to Cardiff in every respect from the very beginning, hitting the body and head with both hands. The *San Francisco Examiner* said that although Jackson was a clever boxer, he lacked finishing power, depending on defeating his opponent "by jabbing him into insensibility and not by a clean knock-out."[315]

In England in November 1889, Peter Jackson defeated English champion Jem Smith on a 2nd round disqualification, pounding on him before a frustrated Smith picked Peter up and threw him down. On December 24, 1889 in Ireland, Jackson scored a retirement KO2 over Peter Maher. Maher would be a top contender in years to come.

In May 1890, Jackson won a 5-round decision over 175-pound Ed Smith of Denver, knocking him down multiple times in the process. In the early 1880s, Smith had fought Charley Mitchell to a 1-hour and 40-minute draw battle.[316] Smith would later become a top contender.

On October 21, 1890 in Australia, 29-year-old Peter Jackson, "colored champion pugilist of the world," took on fellow Australian, 28-year-old Joe Goddard. The undefeated Goddard's victories included: KO11 Owen Sullivan, KO4 Jim Fogarty, and KO21 Mick Dooley, all top Australian fighters. Joe usually weighed around 186 pounds.

Jackson fought Goddard in a very tough, vicious, and grueling battle that saw him drop Joe twice in the 3rd round and once in the 4th, but Goddard came at him ferociously throughout the entire fight and often had Peter hurt, particularly at the end of the fight. At the conclusion of the 8-round bout, the fight was declared a draw. Most thought that if it had been a fight to the finish, Joe would have won.

The local Australian paper, The *Referee*, said that Goddard was a vicious, aggressive, strong rusher who kept the pace fast. He was said to have little skill, but more than compensated for it with "boundless energy, pluck, dash, and devil." He was also called "a modern Hercules, and planks his faith upon his grit and staying powers...he is the most perfectly trained man in the world." Here are the highlights of the fight story that it told:

In the 1st round, the demon Goddard was on top of Jackson, beating down his guard with a whirlwind of blows, smashing in lefts and rights to the body and head, causing Jackson to reel away, staggered and shaken. Jackson hit Joe often, but could not beat him back. It "was quite evident that the white man held his own, and many people were inclined to think he had a bit the best of the three minutes."

In the 2nd round, Goddard "bounded across the stage like a lion." They exchanged blow for blow and it looked as if one or the other would be knocked out. Goddard "bore down on him...and another frantic, desperate,

---

[315] *San Francisco Chronicle*, April 27, 1889; *San Francisco Daily Examiner*, April 27, 1889.
[316] *National Police Gazette*, March 18, 1892.

savage rally followed, in which Joe more than held his own until the cry of corners sent them apart."

Goddard again dashed at Jackson in the 3rd round. After a rally, "Jackson came away like an electric eel, and drove a superb left on the front of the chin, bringing Joe to the boards as if he had been kicked by an elephant." Despite this knockdown, Goddard sprang at Jackson and beat him back. "Joe held his own, fighting grimly, desperately, fiercely, as if the very pride of race and color had entered into his heart." However, "Suddenly Peter saw an opening, and shooting his right clean across he dropped his determined foe once more to the boards." Still, Goddard "rose and sprang at his man and drove him over the ring by sheer vim and pluck. Peter smashed him over the eye with the left and made it get on the bulge, but Joe smiled sardonically and went for more."

The 4th was also fierce. A flush left on the chin again dropped Goddard, but Joe rose and continued setting the pace. Peter dodged cleverly and landed his jab as Joe pressed. "Over and over again he flung himself full upon Pete and took his gruel like a white man, never flinching, never quailing, game, grim and almost reckless he fought as no man had ever been seen to fight in the Southern Hemisphere before." Despite the knockdown, the local newspaper said, "Goddard went to his corner with a decided lead."

Goddard gave him no rest again in the 5th, despite being driven back with long heavy lefts to the face. "All through the three minutes he was rushing and pounding, and it took Pete all he knew to keep his end up under the cyclonic pressure."

Goddard kept plugging away in the 6th, and had Jackson mostly defensive. "Jackson did mighty little besides dodge out of danger, for now it was a case of the huntsman hunted, for the knocker-out was in danger of being sent down."

In the 7th, Joe "punched him from one end of the ring to the other, Pete seeming fairly paralyzed by the tornado." It appeared that Jackson was weakening. "For a spell it looked as if Joe was going to win. Pete fell, but got up again quickly, and then the tongues of the throng were let loose." They fought "like dervishes, until the struggling, seething mass of humanity formed a sight such as one might hope to see in hell when it's nigh boiling point, but Peter was equal to the occasion."

In the 8th and final round, they went at each other, each trying to score a knockout. However, "Peter weakened, and Joe drove him all over the place. Hurling himself bodily on the great African boxer he sent him reeling from him like a child, and at the call of time it looked as if Pete had met his Waterloo."

One judge had it for Goddard, one for Jackson, and the referee decided to call it a draw. The local report said, "The fight was a grim one, but nearly all present agreed that Goddard had the best of it." It was said of Goddard, "He has now established a claim to be considered a phenomenon in his own style, and it looks as if that wicked natural style of his will carry him right into the front ranks of the very best fighters the world possesses." Goddard became a top contender known for his punch, toughness, and durability.[317]

Back in San Francisco, it was reported that Jackson had narrowly escaped from defeat and that Goddard had pluckily outfought him. Although Joe only weighed 182 pounds to Jackson's 197, he was the stronger man of the two. Jackson said, "I was far from well and hardly able to fight a round. It was fortunate for me the matter resulted as it did, considering the condition I was in." One paper opined,

> When he boxed Ed Smith in Chicago he floored the Denver man early in the battle, but Smith stuck to his work and improved toward the finish. On these public performances Jackson would have no show whatever with men of Sullivan's or Slavin's class as glove boxers, for both are knockers out who would make short work of him on the first symptom of fatigue.... Jackson claims...that he was not in proper condition... He made a similar claim when he met Smith. This, however, is no excuse for an aspiring champion.... If he neglects his preparation...that is his fault...
>
> The fact of the matter is that Jackson is not the most rugged type of boxers by any means..... [E]asy living tells quickly upon him. His successes in Europe and America changed him from a simple slogger into an athletic dude with a taste for good dinners, good clothes, fast horses and other rapid amusements... [A]thletic abilities once impaired are not easily regained.[318]

Goddard later challenged Sullivan to a fight when John was visiting Australia, but Sullivan declined. At that time, John L. was only engaging in 3-round friendly exhibitions with either Joe Lannon or Jack Ashton.[319]

The Goddard fight hurt Jackson's image a bit. What made things worse was that there was discussion of a rematch between the two in a fight to the finish, but Jackson left Australia and returned to America, which some took as a sign of fear or weakness.[320]

Fellow Australian Frank Slavin was also making a strong argument that he should be considered for Sullivan's crown. The 6' 188-pound Slavin's impressive resume included: 1887 KO10 Mick Dooley, D34 and KO9 Martin "Buffalo" Costello, and KO2 Bill Farnan (the only man to hold a win over Jackson); 1888 D8 Jack Burke (Slavin better) and KO1 Dooley; 1889 KO3 Jack Burke (who in 1885 went the 5-round distance with Sullivan

---

[317] *Referee*, October 22, 1890; See also *National Police Gazette*, December 6, 1890, December 13, 1890.

[318] *San Francisco Chronicle*, November 23, 24, 1890.

[319] Isenberg at 294; *Referee*, October 22, 1890; *National Police Gazette*, December 6, 1890, December 13, 1890.

[320] *San Francisco Chronicle*, December 29, 1890.

and in 1887 boxed an 8-round no decision with Corbett); 1889 D14 Jem Smith (London rules, Slavin better but fight stopped by police); and a recent September 27, 1890 KO2 Joe McAuliffe.

Slavin's quick KO2 knockout of the highly regarded McAuliffe was significant. Following Joe's 1888 LKOby24 to Jackson, McAuliffe had subsequently come back with a May 1889 KO8 Tom Lees (against whom Jackson scored an 1886 KO30) and September 1889 KO7 over Pat Killen (who had an 1887 KO2 Duncan McDonald and June 1888 KO5 Patsy Cardiff).

Slavin had demonstrated more punching power than Jackson. However, Slavin had ducked Jackson back when they were both living in Australia in the mid-1880s. The feeling at the time was that the next world champion was likely going to be either Jackson or Slavin. Slavin had been issuing unaccepted challenges to the semi-retired Sullivan.

Like McAuliffe, Slavin had challenged Corbett back in May 1890 (following Jim's victories over Kilrain and McCaffrey), but Jim did not accept at that time, owing to his teaching contract with the Olympic.[321] However, on November 3, 1890, Corbett wrote Frank Slavin a letter challenging him:

> A few weeks ago I read in the daily papers a telegram…in which you speak very disparagingly of John L. Sullivan. … Mr. Sullivan has proved himself the greatest fighter that ever stepped within a ring, and you certainly presume considerable when you attempt to criticize his achievements. … And, after expressing yourself quite freely regarding him, your insinuations are directed toward American fighters in general. Now, my dear sir, there's one American who has not accomplished one-half as much as Mr. Sullivan, but who deems it a pleasure to accord you a meeting.

Corbett admitted that Slavin was a hard hitter, but did not believe that Frank's victory over McAuliffe meant that he was invincible. Apparently, Jim wanted to take one big leap into the top contender status by knocking off a top guy. The *Chronicle* wrote,

> Corbett has always maintained that he could defeat McAuliffe. If Slavin goes on with his match with Jackson Corbett will meet the winner. The young Californian has evidently made up his mind to fly at the biggest pugilistic game in the world…. He is certainly as clever as the best of them, and the only question is whether he is strong enough to cope with a man like Slavin. He should be, however, for he is a bigger man every way than the determined Australian.[322]

---

[321] *New York Clipper*, May 24, 1890.
[322] *San Francisco Chronicle*, November 3, 1890.

On November 7, 1890 at an amateur tournament held at the Olympic, Corbett sparred 3 or 4 friendly rounds (depending on the source) with the Acme Club's unopposed tournament heavyweight champion, Jack Kitchen, "the professor extending himself just enough to show the difference between a first-class professional and a first-class amateur." Corbett had previously exhibited with Kitchen in late 1886. In mid-November 1889, a then 165-pound Kitchen had scored a KO4 over 170-pound William Kenealy.[323]

This Corbett-Kitchen exhibition and Jim's challenge to Frank Slavin was discussed in the following days:

> Jim Corbett's challenge to Slavin has provoked some hostile criticism of the Olympic Club professor. It is evident that a good many people will refuse to believe sincerely in Jim's fighting capacity till he has put one or two more finish contests in the ring to his record. As to the young professor's cleverness with the gloves there can be no doubt, for the Olympian has no superior in sparring ability. He demonstrated his cleverness to the club very satisfactorily the other evening at the tournament, when he appeared in a friendly four-round set-to with Jack Kitchen of Oakland. Kitchen, of course, is no John L. Sullivan or Peter Jackson, but he is a good, big, strong and willing young fellow who knows how to box, and would make a very creditable showing with any man not an expert with the gloves. In Corbett's hands he was just a punching-bag to exhibit upon. Corbett has grown very big of late, and is now strong and heavy enough to face the best man in the world. …
>
> Corbett is entitled to favorable notice for his challenge of Slavin as long as it does not appear that he is merely using other men's names and reputations to merely advertise himself without entertaining a serious desire to fight. There is nothing to justify such a suspicion. Corbett has so far met all his engagements like a man.[324]

Corbett negotiated and signed a contract to go on the road with a variety company, starting May 1, 1891 (when his Olympic Club contract expired). He would be paid $150 per week for the first ten weeks, and one half the profits thereafter as a partner. Another report said that he would travel with the vaudevilles for one year, giving representations of Greek and Roman statues, and sparring with an associate, likely John Donaldson. Jim said, "I think I can make some money, and after my year's contract is over I will be at liberty to fight."

---

[323] *San Francisco Chronicle*, November 8, 1890; *Daily Alta California*, November 8, 1890, November 15, 1889. The *Alta* called him John Kitchen. In April 1890, Corbett described Kitchen as weighing about 180 pounds, calling him "a wonderful amateur, and I consider him a good deal cleverer than many men who are traveling around the country." *San Francisco Morning Call*, April 6, 1890.
[324] *San Francisco Chronicle*, November 10, 1890.

Frank Slavin

Jim was still more than willing to fight Frank Slavin as soon as his Olympic Club contract expired. "A well-known New York horseman is ready to back Corbett for $10,000 against Slavin, Sullivan or any one else." However, "Corbett's friends think that the longer he delays fighting the better, as he is steadily gaining in weight and strength." Corbett said that the man he most wanted to fight was John L. Sullivan. However, Sullivan was out of the ring, for the time being.[325]

During November 1890, in its test case, California Club boxers Rochette and Huntington were tried for violating the law against engaging in a ring or prize fight, punishable by imprisonment for up to two years. A club representative blamed the press for all the trouble. "If the club loses the city press may claim the credit of abolishing a brutal sport in this city, according to Mr. Vice, and if that is so, certainly the press may congratulate themselves." After Rochette was acquitted, it was seen as a victory for the club and professional boxing. One local paper lamented, "To put the matter concisely, the opening skirmish of a battle between vice and virtue has taken

---

[325] *San Francisco Chronicle*, November 17, 1890; *New York Clipper*, November 1, 1890; *Referee*, December 31, 1890.

place, and, as not unfrequently happens, vice, clothed...in the garb of respectability, has won."[326] The doors were once again opened for the hosting of professional bouts in California.

On November 27, Corbett was a marshal at the annual local Olympic Games.[327] On December 11, 1890, during the Olympic's Ladies Night, Corbett boxed with A.G.D. Kerrill, and their sparring "seemed especially attractive to many ladies."[328]

During December, it was reported that the Slavin-Corbett match would likely be held in March 1891 for a $10,000 purse and $5,000 total side bet. Still, there remained some uncertainty as to when the bout might take place.

> The young professor...really believes that a match with Slavin is about the best contract he can get.... The only trouble appears to be that Corbett wants the match set for some far distant date. The young Californian has a shrewd regard for the American dollar and thinks he can make money next year by traveling with a theatrical company for several months and fighting Slavin at the end of the season.

As was or would become his pattern, Jim was never shy about putting off a fight to a more distant date in order to exhibit and make money in the interim.

Corbett regarded Slavin as far less scientific than Jackson, and felt that if he could survive for 6 rounds, he would defeat him. Mike Donovan picked Corbett to defeat Slavin. One local paper said, "With Corbett and Jackson here and Slavin willing to come some great fistic match is sure to take place."[329]

By the last week of December, it was reported that Slavin was less than interested in coming to America for a fight with Corbett.

> Jim Corbett has heard nothing new from Slavin, and it looks to sporting circles very much as if a meeting between this distinguished pair of boxers is a remote possibility. Corbett has no intention of fighting at an earlier date than May or June next. The most reliable news received so far is that Slavin has settled down in England and is desirous of staying there. Now that boxing is considered legal in the London sporting clubs...he would be less anxious than ever to make a long journey to fill an engagement, as his victory over McAuliffe has made him a lion in English sporting circles.[330]

Another paper said that Slavin had "a mind as variable as the winds," being unable to decide whether he wanted to remain in London or cross the

---

[326] *Daily Alta California*, November 17, 24, 1890.
[327] *Daily Alta California*, November 28, 1890.
[328] *Daily Alta California*, December 12, 1890.
[329] *San Francisco Chronicle*, December 15, 1890; *Daily Alta California*, December 15, 29, 1890.
[330] *San Francisco Chronicle*, December 22, 1890.

Atlantic to meet Corbett. It appeared that Slavin was content to remain in London, and Corbett wanted to make money for a while anyway before taking on a legitimate challenge. Still, Corbett wanted to arrange a big match.[331]

Since Peter Jackson and James J. Corbett were for years considered the San Francisco area's cleverest boxers, a match between them was a natural, and doing well would put Corbett at the front of the line for a title challenge with Sullivan.

In his autobiography, Corbett said of Jackson that he "was at that time considered without an equal as a boxer anywhere in the world." Corbett said that he first met Jackson in person in 1888, but felt that he would need to put on some weight before fighting him. Jim claimed that he eventually bulked up to 172 pounds two years later and felt ready to take Jackson on.

In truth, Jim had gained some weight in the intervening years, but not that much, and he did not begin as low as he alleged. The reality was that Corbett was about 180 pounds even in 1888, so it is more likely that Jim felt that he needed more experience before taking on the world's top contender. There had been some earlier discussion even in 1888 and 1889 for a 10-round bout between the two, but the match had not materialized, allegedly because of local politics between their competing clubs.

Jackson was world renowned, having defeated the top fighters from America, Australia, Ireland and England. Corbett was well aware that Jackson wanted to fight Sullivan but that the champion drew the color line. Corbett saw fighting him, when Sullivan would not, as his chance to gain a reputation and make himself the top contender.[332] Corbett's confidence had been growing, and the fact that respected men like William Muldoon and Mike Donovan told Jim that he was the man to defeat Jackson probably helped spur him on.

In mid-1890, when there were some negotiations for a Sullivan-Jackson fight, Corbett rendered his opinion of the match-up, which revealed his high opinion of Jackson and awareness that Sullivan was on the decline.

"You are credited with favoring Jackson against Sullivan?"

"I am, in a way. Sullivan I don't think will ever fight Jackson to a finish, for I don't believe that he can stand the training for such a fight. He realizes this fact himself, and is taking no care of himself. In my opinion he will never be the Sullivan of the past.... The man is but human, and can't stand all excesses."

"Peter on the other hand, takes all possible care of himself.... In science the Australian, in my opinion, is superior to Sullivan, but then

---

[331] *Daily Alta California*, December 29, 1890.
[332] Corbett at 109-113.

I am only one man, and don't wish at this early date to set myself up as a critic."[333]

Corbett had also been quoted as saying that if Sullivan and Jackson were to fight, he would bet on Jackson.[334] Jim had seen all of Jackson's fights in San Francisco, and had seen Sullivan fight in the mid-1880s.

Seeing that a Slavin match was not likely to materialize, on December 29, 1890, James J. Corbett signed a contract to fight Peter Jackson at the California Athletic Club on May 21, 1891 for a $10,000 purse, to be divided $8,500 to the winner and $1,500 to the loser. The excitement and anticipation was immediate. "This is unquestionably the greatest match ever made in the heavy-weight class, as the two men are known the world over as the most skillful boxers that the ring has ever produced."

The date of their match was set far in advance so that Corbett could fulfill his now scheduled theatrical engagement in the East, and so that Jackson could get into condition. Jim said he wanted full credit for defeating Peter, and did not want anything to diminish his victory, such as an argument that Peter was not in proper condition. After all, the local press was saying that Jackson had been leading the easy life for a year, and was still being careless in the manner in which he was taking care of himself.

Corbett again resigned his post as Olympic Club boxing instructor. The same night that he signed to fight Jackson, "Corbett was donning the mitts for the last time with many of the pupils he has rendered clever. Not a man among them but felt the greatest confidence in their old tutor's ability to whip the antipodean." Corbett would leave for the East in the next week, but return in time for two months of intense training under the care of Bill Delaney, who had handled him for the Choynski fight.[335]

It was said in early January 1891 that Corbett would be working with Professor John Donaldson on his statuary posing and sparring tour.[336]

On January 14, 1891 in New Orleans, Jim Corbett observed Bob Fitzsimmons knock out Jack Dempsey in the 13th round to win the world middleweight championship.[337] Fitzsimmons only weighed 150 ½ pounds, and Corbett probably did not realize that one day they would fight for the heavyweight championship.

The next day, on January 15, 1891 at a benfit in New Orleans, Corbett sparred Professor Donaldson. Both were described as wonderfully agile and clever. One local paper said, "Corbett ducked and dodged with all the ease and facility of a featherweight and let out several right and left hand swings and uppercuts which had they been intended to do execution would have proved a serious matter for his adversary." Another local paper wrote,

---

[333] *Referee*, June 25, 1890.
[334] *San Francisco Chronicle*, April 24, 1890.
[335] *San Francisco Chronicle*, December 29, 30, 1890.
[336] *Brooklyn Daily Eagle*, January 6, 1891; *Referee*, December 31, 1890.
[337] Corbett at 114.

135

Corbett showed great science, skill and activity, and the opinion of the audience was that he was the quickest big man on his feet they had ever seen. Prof. Donaldson, although overmatched, showed himself to be well up in the art of boxing.[338]

Pursuant to his theatrical contract, Corbett and Donaldson toured around giving almost daily sparring exhibitions. They worked in New York City and Brooklyn during early February. They were in Chicago during the third week of February. They were scheduled to head west, returning to San Francisco in late March for two months of preparation for the late May fight with Jackson.[339]

[338] *Daily Picayune*, January 16, 1891; *Times-Democrat*, January 16, 1891.
[339] *New York Clipper*, January 31, 1891; *Brooklyn Daily Eagle*, February 3, 1891. They sparred in Brooklyn on February 2, 1891; *Chicago Herald*, February 17, 1891.

CHAPTER 10

The Well-Contested No Contest

1891 was the year that Jim Corbett did what John L. Sullivan refused to do: fight the best black fighter and world's best contender, Peter Jackson. Sullivan criticized Corbett for fighting Jackson, believing that whites should not fight blacks. In February, when Jim met John in Chicago, Corbett quoted Sullivan as having said to him, "You're matched to fight that nigger? Well, you shouldn't fight a nigger!" Upset that he would fight in a racially mixed bout, Corbett claimed that his own father would not speak to him for months. It was generally believed that a white man lowered himself by competing with a black man.

Corbett felt that Sullivan sensed that he might one day have to fight Corbett, and tried to get a psychological edge by intimidating him. When they first met backstage of Sullivan's play, *Honest Hearts and Willing Hands*, John engaged in the stunt of trying to break Jim's hand by squeezing it hard when they shook. That evening, Sullivan took Corbett to a number of saloons and in each stated, "I can lick any --- in the world!" At one point John looked right at Jim when he said it. Corbett took that as a jab at himself and eventually had the guts to tell Sullivan to stop saying that in his presence, given that they were in the same profession. A stunned Sullivan was initially speechless, then laughed it off, but did not utter that statement again. John visited ten saloons and got drunk. Jim realized Sullivan's popularity. At each bar, everyone would crowd around Sullivan. "I think he was the most popular pugilist that ever lived." Corbett might not have been as popular, but he was much better at taking care of himself, rarely drinking and almost never smoking.[340]

On April 3, 1891, Peter Jackson's training had a set back. His horse became unmanageable and ran his buggy against the rail of a street-car track, throwing Peter out. Another version said the cart overturned when rounding a sharp corner. Jackson's ankle was badly sprained and his leg swelled. It required him to take almost an entire month off from training in order to heal.[341]

There was no forfeit money up for the match, which meant that if Peter had required a postponement, he would not have to lose any money for delaying the match. He could have asked for a postponement if he so

[340] Corbett at 117-122.
[341] *Daily Alta California*, April 6, 1891; *San Francisco Chronicle*, April 6, 13, 1891.

desired, but he did not ask for one. It was said that he did not need more than a month to get into the best of shape, that he had only required three weeks of work to defeat Joe McAuliffe (in 24 rounds).

On April 19, 1891 in Sausalito, California, Corbett boxed 4 rounds with Julian R. Brandon, the amateur heavyweight.

> Brandon says Corbett is looking better than he has ever seen him before, and thinks that he could not have a better man back of him than Donaldson. They boxed four spirited rounds, and Jim succeeded in giving Brandon a discolored left eye. Brandon says that any one who thinks Jim Corbett can't hit wants to stand up before him for a minute or so. Jim's legs have improved wonderfully.
>
> Donaldson says that Brandon has made the best showing with Corbett of any of the professionals who have sparred with him since his training.[342]

Jackson began serious training again at the end of April, less than a month before the fight. However, it was generally believed that this left him with sufficient time to be properly prepared. "Peter is both looking and feeling fine, and it now looks as if neither of the principles in the important contest will have the slightest cause for complaint on the score of condition." Even at that time, Jackson was a 2 to 1 betting favorite.

Still, Corbett would be the sentimental favorite. "As to prejudice, if there be any, it is all naturally on the side of the native son, as nine people out of ten in this city who take an interest in boxing would, of course, rather see the white native boy win than the colored pugilist from Australia. This is neither strange nor improper." Another said, "It seems as if national pride and a prejudice also in favor of the white as against the black, have had, so far, a good deal to do with the belief in Corbett's being able to get the best of Jackson." That said, few were willing to back their opinions with cash bets on Jim.[343]

The *San Francisco Chronicle's* Sportsman's Niche assessed the match up. It noted that most betting men and ring-goers believed Jackson would win. However, it was concerned about Jackson's leg, feeling that it would "prove a detriment in the violent work of a prolonged ring fight." It was also concerned about Jackson's condition. That said, it also had a fair amount of criticism to offer regarding Corbett.

> If the form shown by Corbett in his fight with Choynski is the best he can do he is not to be classed with Jackson as a ring fighter, whatever his sparring abilities may be. He never exhibited the workmanlike tactics and the free use of the right hand on the body that Jackson displays in all his fights. His friends attribute his one-arm fight to his

[342] *San Francisco Chronicle*, April 20, 1891.
[343] *San Francisco Chronicle*, April 27, 1891; *Daily Alta California*, May 11, 1891.

injured hands, and quite likely that is the proper explanation. In all probability, too, he has improved a good deal since that fight, and he needs it unless Jackson has deteriorated.

The Niche also felt that a defect in Corbett's tactics was "his rather loose guard of his body." Choynski had landed well to his ribs, and Jackson was known as having "no superior in any class at body fighting, and unless the young professor guards his ribs very carefully he will get a dose of the same medicine administered to Godfrey and Joe McAuliffe." Peter was also bigger and had the superior experience. It agreed that both men were clever, but dissimilar in styles.

> Jackson is a steady, cool, methodical fighter, who pushes his man, all the time looking for a chance to use both hands, and fond of crowding him into the corners and delivering body punishment. Corbett, on the other hand, is of the hit and duck away style, very showy in science and nimble on his feet, and oftener out of range than in it.

It predicted that Jackson would force the fight, while Jim would exhibit skill in defensive and retreating tactics as Peter attempted to corner him. However, it also acknowledged that Corbett "will fight and fight wickedly when it comes to 'mixing it up.'" Ultimately, its assessment of the fight was,

> [I]it cannot fail to be a great and clever battle, no matter who wins. Jackson's record is established, and any man who could defeat so good a boxer as Choynski and do it as cleverly as Corbett with injured hands is in the front rank of pugilists. The winner will indeed be entitled to pose as a champion, and if it be Corbett the victory will be doubly creditable.[344]

A week before the fight, Corbett was reported to be weighing 182 pounds stripped. Jackson was 209 pounds with clothes on, and expected to weigh around 200 pounds on fight night. A few days before the fight, it was reported that Jim was weighing 187 or 188 pounds to Peter's 197. Jim planned to have Delaney, Donaldson, and his brother Harry Corbett in his corner. Peter had Billy Smith and Sam Fitzpatrick.[345]

Frank Slavin said that he wanted to fight the winner. Jackson said that he was willing, but Corbett said that if he won, he would not fight again for a year and a half. It was typical for Corbett to take substantial periods of time off between fights.[346]

Shortly before the bout, the *Chronicle* provided its final thoughts regarding the match. It believed that Corbett was likely to be over trained

---

[344] *San Francisco Chronicle*, May 11, 1891.
[345] *San Francisco Chronicle*, May 14, 1891; *Daily Alta California*, May 18, 1891; *San Francisco Evening Post*, May 18, 1891.
[346] *New York Clipper*, May 16, 1891.

and Jackson under trained. Jackson's leg was not 100 percent, but it "gives no pain whatever, and Jackson can punch the bag for an hour at a time and do a twenty-mile spin on the roads without feeling any bad effects." Still, although it did not believe that condition would determine the match, it did feel that "if it comes down to a ding-dong battle of thirty or forty rounds condition will tell." Ultimately though, it noted that Jackson set a rapid pace in all of his fights, and believed that he would likely win within 15 rounds. Although Jackson was a light hitter when compared with Slavin, he could hit hard enough such that "when the dose is repeated often enough it will tell on the stoutest of them."

Peter Jackson

The *Chronicle* conceded that it was possible that Corbett might "spin out the fight by clever tactics, and make it a question of youth, endurance and training, tire out his heavier opponent and capture the purse." Although Jackson was a famed body puncher, it said that Corbett intended to punish Peter's body. From what it had seen of both men, "no man can punish either on any part of the anatomy without getting plenty of change in return." It observed that Corbett had generally exceeded expectations and felt that his townsmen had underrated him. "With his youth and great quickness Corbett may offset the advantages of his bulky opponent, but certainly it looks 100 to 80 that he will not."

One expert more supportive of Corbett said, "I saw him do better with Dominick McCaffrey than Sullivan did, and I saw him best Kilrain with such ease that I am satisfied he is a great fighter.... The fight is, therefore, in my opinion, likely to be hard and close."

Although the local sympathy generally would be with Corbett, it was noted that the affinity of the fight's host, the California Club and its members, would be with Jackson. After all, Corbett had been a star developed at its competitor, the Olympic Club, and Jackson had fought for the California Club while in America. There were personal reasons as well.

> The majority of them, beginning with President Fulda of the California Club, have very little local pride. Fulda took to Jackson very closely...and I know that he considers him almost invincible. He has no faith in Corbett's gameness.... Some say that his dislike of Corbett arises from the fact that Jim bested him with gloves.... He would like dearly to see Corbett punched out in short order.[347]

Also, given their belief in him, California Club members bet on Jackson, so they had an additional economic desire to see Corbett bested. These issues and sympathies may have had a hand in the fight's ultimate determination.

Two days before the fight, Jackson was seen hitting the punching ball for 20 minutes straight, his condition looking to be excellent, "while his smiting power was all that could be desired by those who have their money on him." Corbett walked 12 miles, punched the ball, and sparred with Donaldson.[348]

The *San Francisco Evening Post* gave its analysis of the two pugilists:

> As regards fistic talent, which, paradoxical as it may seem, includes in this connection clever footwork, Jackson has few equals. He is a boxer of the Jem Mace school, using both hands and arms in a perfectly easy and natural, as well as most effective manner. He is an excellent judge of distance, can time his blows to a nicety, has a rapid delivery, and moreover a wonderful faculty for avoiding returns. He

[347] *San Francisco Chronicle, May* 18, 21, 1891.
[348] *San Francisco Evening Post,* May 20, 1891.

"ducks" with precision, and when hard pressed can skip like a chamois. Jackson's left-hand deliveries at head and body are free and telling, while his right-hand heart punches have often turned the tide of battle in his favor.

Jim Corbett has very little in common with Jackson so far as his methods of attack are concerned. He is a stiff-arm puncher and a punishing hitter. By stiff-arm is meant that Jim does not shoot his left out straight from the shoulder, but holds his arm in a partly rigid state and delivers his most telling punches with a sidelong movement. He "gets there" as quick as a flash, however, and by leaning to the right keeps his own head out of danger. His incessant feinting with head, hands and feet is sufficient to keep a not over confident opponent in a state of nervous trepidation, and in addition wear him out by continued stepping back and dodging from imaginary blows. ...

Corbett is a marvel of quickness on his feet. He is as elastic as a rubber ball and apparently as tireless as a wooden rocking horse. He can duck with equal rapidity to Jackson and knows how to block a man from punishing him when closed. In the past he has not used his right hand with remarkable frequency, but all the same he knows how to place it with disastrous results on an opponent's jaw or ribs. ...

In the matter of temperament Jackson has an advantage over most knights of the knuckles. He is as cool as the proverbial iceberg when in action, and there is no instance on record where he has lost his head, no matter how fast or furious a contest may wage. ... Jim is of an excitable nature.[349]

On May 21, 1891 at San Francisco's California Athletic Club, 24-year-old James J. Corbett took on 29-year-old Peter Jackson. The bout was scheduled to be a Marquis of Queensberry rules fight to the finish with 5-ounce tan gloves. Both boxers were listed as standing 6'1 ½". A local morning of the fight news report listed Jim as 182 pounds to Peter's 197 pounds, and a next day report said that Corbett was 182 ½ pounds to Jackson's 199. Another local report said that Corbett was 186 to Jackson's 198. A next day out of state report said that the weights, "as near as could be obtained, were, Jackson 197, Corbett 185, though it was claimed by some that the difference was even greater than that." A report two days after the fight said that Jackson was 202 pounds to Corbett's 179.[350]

The day of the fight, the odds were 100 to 60 in Jackson's favor, and eventually he was a 2 to 1 favorite. Still, there were many who believed in Corbett's chances. "Corbett's youth, phenomenal quickness, perfect

[349] *San Francisco Evening Post*, May 20, 1891.
[350] Corbett at 126 and 132-133; *San Francisco Examiner*, May 21, 1891; *San Francisco Chronicle*, May 22, 1891, May 23, 1891; *Daily Alta California*, May 22, 1891; *Minneapolis Tribune*, May 22, 1891.

condition and marvelous skill are the grounds for his backers' confidence." Corbett was said to be "brighter, cleverer and quicker" than any other man that Jackson had met. Both were described as jabbers rather than sluggers.[351]

Corbett, 1891

Demand for seats was so high that the tickets were selling anywhere from $20 up to $50, the highest ticket prices ever paid for a boxing match. The ring floor was covered with padding, over which dark felt was stretched.[352] According to a secondary source, this was the first fight in which an electronic timer and bell was used.[353]

---

[351] *San Francisco Examiner*, May 21, 1891; *San Francisco Chronicle*, May 22, 1891.
[352] *Minneapolis Tribune*, May 22, 1891.
[353] Joseph R. Svinth, *Kronos: A Chronological History of the Martial Arts and Combative Sports* (Canada: National Library of Canada, 2004); Myler at 42.

Jackson wore a plaster of Paris protection under his trunks, the top of which showed just above the belt. This appears to have been the time's version of the large protector cups we have today. Sullivan wore the same in a number of his bouts. Jackson wore white drawers and blue stockings. Corbett wore nothing but "a breech clout. His colors were a red, white and blue ribbon around his waist." Basically, Corbett was almost naked, the breech clout being less than shorts.

The bout did not begin until 9:28 p.m.

The following account is taken from the local newspapers, the *San Francisco Examiner* (SFE), *San Francisco Chronicle* (SFC), and *Daily Alta California* (AC).

1st round

The men were "graceful" and the round was "as clever an exhibition of boxing by two big men as ever took place in the ring." They began cautiously, sparring at long range.

Both had low guards, Jim with almost none, his left hand held loose and swaying by his side, and his right resting on the stomach. Peter kept his hands much closer, his right resting on and across his body, with his left arm extended. Jim stood more erect than Peter.

Each fired only one or two shots, both seeming afraid to let out too much, fearing a blow at close quarters. Jackson assumed the aggressive and began to rush, but Jim was "as nimble on his feet as a fawn," and ducked away.

Jackson continued forcing the fight. Eventually, Corbett jumped into a clinch and threw his left to the stomach. Upon separating, Jim threw the left with a swing to the ribs and clinched again. He was good at punching and then clinching immediately. Corbett clinched well and often. He once even held with a firm grip around Peter's neck for almost half a minute, forcing referee Hiram Cook to step into the ring to separate them. Corbett was nervous during the first 2 rounds and "showed a decided disposition to clinch and hug."

Corbett hit Jackson three times in succession, avoiding counters with dodges each time. When Jackson landed even lightly, Jim would clinch. Three more times, Corbett was able to go up and down fluidly to the body and head with his left, dancing in and out like a featherweight, avoiding the returns. Jim ended the round by landing a flush left on the mouth.

2nd round

Each would shoot out a punch and then move away or clinch. When Jackson pressed, Corbett was able to duck, dodge, and avoid being cornered. Peter was wary as well, avoiding a couple rights. They grinned at each other.

Jackson made the pace, but Corbett hit him with a right to the ribs, followed by a lengthy clinch as Jim forced Peter to the ropes. On the outside, Peter landed a straight left to the stomach and avoided the counter. Corbett drove the left to the ribs and clinched. Jim again landed to the stomach as he charged into a clinch. After the break, Jackson landed a solid left under the ear. Jim feinted and moved about, keeping Peter guessing, occasionally stopping and going to the body with his left, and even once followed with an uppercut which brought cheers. Mostly though, Jim was on the retreat. Towards the end of the round, Corbett was crowded to the corner and hit by a right uppercut as he was ducking away. However, Jim gained some confidence when he landed two good blows to the ribs.

Although the round was another "remarkable exhibition of science," it "was not effective as a fighting display, there being little if any heavy work, the only telling blows being two scored by Jackson." Peter showed "a more systematic method of fighting and scored each point as coolly and cautiously as if he had a month to finish the battle in." That said, Jim demonstrated "extraordinary quickness with his hands and feet" and although appearing "a trifle less clever and effective as a ring tactician, he exhibited the most consummate science in boxing."

3rd round

When Jackson led, Corbett's graceful footwork enabled him to move away on his toes. Upon jumping back, Jim was also able to throw and land his left to the body. Peter threw for the head, but three times Jim ducked and landed his right to the ribs and left to the stomach, following with a clinch each time.

Peter rushed in and hit the ribs, though lightly because Jim was retreating. Jim landed to the ribs but received a blow to the ear. Peter crowded him, but Jim swung a left on the neck that shook Peter up. Jackson kept up a slow and methodical pursuit, leading with the left to the body or head, until Jim threw his left to the body and received a counter right to the ear. Jim rushed in and tried with both hands to the body, landing a light left and escaping a counter.

The crowd generally cheered Jim's effective work. Both were smiling and fresh at the end. The round was like the previous two, clever but cautious on both sides, although Jackson was the aggressor. There had been no heavy punishment, as neither scored with telling effect. By this point, most expected a long battle.

4th round

SFC: Jackson moved into close quarters and Jim clinched. A rally followed and Jim landed an ugly counter on the mouth and mixed it up grimly, landing several rights to the ribs that made Peter wince. There were hot exchanges of slugging, Corbett landing body punches that "plainly disconcerted the colored man." Jackson used clever counters and rarely missed a left to the head. He landed effectively, though Jim was even with him all through. The crowd cheered as they went to their corners.

SFE: Corbett scored three clean hits without a return, one a straight smash to the mouth and two swings to the body, clinching each time after landing. When Peter struck high, Jim ducked under him. When he went low, Corbett moved off to the side and Jackson was only able to hit him in the back. Jim's stock doubled. "Corbett was so awfully clever" that Jackson "could not do anything with him."

5th round

SFC: There was mostly long-range sparring and no punishment administered. There were two good rallies in the corner when Peter crowded close, but Jim fought him off. It was Jackson's round, "what there was of it," but Corbett was "as fresh as a daisy" and only showed some red marks where his neck had touched the ropes.
SFE: Peter landed two light blows to the face as Jim was on the retreat. The first close work followed. Corbett stopped Jackson's advance with a left to the body, and traded half-arm hits. He was "quite as good as Jackson, and the crowd cheered while Jackson clinched." Jim hit the mouth and then dropped back down to the body.
AC: In the 5th and 6th rounds, "there was some very hot work, the fighting being fast and exceedingly clever. Each man imbibed a wholesome respect for the other and was more wary. Both men played for the stomach."

6th round

Jackson "slowly and stubbornly" followed and crowded forward, looking for a chance to get to close quarters to hit the body, while Corbett coolly retreated. After several misses with the left, Peter worked Jim into corner and landed a right to the ribs, but received a blow to the mouth in return. Corbett landed a left to the ribs and escaped a return. The boxing was light, both falling a bit short with their blows, until Jim landed a left swing to the body at the bell.

7th round

The round was mostly long range sparring with nothing to choose between them. Jackson still forced the pace. Jim attempted to get Peter to lead, while Jackson merely threatened to do so as he slid forward. The only significant blow was a heavy punch to the breast landed by Jackson.

8th round

This was a lively round. Peter landed a right to the heart. Clinches, long range sparring, more clinches and left exchanges followed, Jackson scoring best, including an uppercut to the body.
After another clinch and break, Corbett fiercely rushed Jackson to the ropes and slugged him. Jim tried to hold him there and hit him, but Jackson drove him away with a punch to the nose. Another clinch and long range fighting followed.

There was a rally in the center of the ring, Peter landing the left on the jaw and Corbett responding with a left to the ribs and a left and/or right swing to the neck that shook Jackson up considerably. "Peter did most of the leading and scored repeatedly, but Jim was so clever in getting away that the punishment was ineffectual. Jim's swing on the neck was the beauty of the fight so far."

9th round

Some blood trickled from Jackson's lips at the beginning of the round. Corbett called attention to it and Peter laughed and punched at him, but nimble Jim eluded the blow.

This time Corbett did the work and took a strong lead. He rushed in and landed a left to the head, but caught an ugly left counter on his nose, which reddened it. In the next rush Jim landed a right drive to the stomach that made Peter pant, but Jim was again countered. Corbett held the lead throughout the round, and at the bell, as they returned to their corners; Jackson looked back over his shoulder at him.

10th round

Jim landed a left to the ribs, but Peter attacked more, landing his right to the ribs three times, a corker to the ear as Jim moved back, and also a left to the jaw. Jim missed to the body and Peter hit the ribs before a clinch. Pete pressed his man, with Jim backing quickly and evading head punches. Jackson seemed to have caught on to Corbett's left to the body, parrying it with his right. "This was a hard round for Jim, as Peter bored in on him all the time, and the local man's left swings missed fire." Jim was more defensive as he began to get hit more, but he still landed some good counters, including a couple lefts to the body.

11th round

SFC: This was another difficult round for Corbett. He mixed it up, but Peter's superior weight told in the counters. Jim landed a left swing to the neck and they tussled, with Corbett trying to clinch as if rattled. Jackson was cool and systematic, keeping things going until Jim was forced to rally in a corner. Both fell against the ropes. Regardless, neither showed signs of the punishment.
SFE: Corbett landed the left to the ribs and mouth. Jackson tried for the stomach, "but the young fellow seemed as able to take care of that as his head." Peter landed a couple blows to the side of the head at long range, and they engaged in some wrestling. Peter led for the head but Jim countered with the left and a right into the ribs that made Jackson grunt.

12th round

Jackson began on the attack, but after Corbett stopped him with a left to the body, they both only engaged in long range sparring, using light taps, taking a rest in this round.

13th round

They again rested, both content to skip about and laugh. Jackson landed his left to the chin, but after a clinch, Corbett knocked the smile off his mouth by a hard blow to the nose.

14th round

The SFC and AC agreed that Corbett landed several good blows to the wind and nose.

The SFE's version said that Jim landed solidly to the stomach but received one to the ribs. They exchanged slaps to the mouth. A pool of blood accumulated in Jackson's corner as a result of the leads to the mouth. Corbett had a swelled right eye and a very red back.

15th round

After a couple minutes of sparring, Corbett landed a left to the stomach and drew Jackson into missing three times. There were several clever exchanges, and a left sent Peter's head back. Corbett closed the round with a double left lead that landed and made Peter angry.

16th round

SFC: Corbett landed many body shots, including "three lightning–like blows that caused Peter's bellows to blow." Jackson forced Jim to a corner and landed a good face blow, but Jim returned to the wind and a vicious left swing on the ear. "It was about an even thing."
SFE: Jim landed a swinging right to the jaw that rattled Peter's teeth audibly. Jackson rushed and drove Jim to a corner with right and left rib-roasters. Peter could not hit the head though. Jim finally drove him back with a punch to the jaw, followed by another as Peter moved away.
AC: There was a lively interchange of blows, Corbett fighting Jackson into a corner. Just before the bell, Jackson landed a straight punch to the mouth that caused Jim to spit blood.

17th round

When Jackson rushed, Corbett either got under him or clinched. Jim landed a straight left to the chin, but Jackson countered him with a heavy left to the body which staggered Jim. Corbett responded with a vicious left swing on the ear. Peter landed several blows to the face and body and fought hard. After a break, Jackson landed a solid left to the jaw. Peter rushed and landed to the ribs. Corbett hit him with the left and right to the face. Short-arm work followed and Peter landed two to one on the body. Jim landed a good blow to Peter's chin.

It was a vicious round during which both were fighting with all their might, doing some heavy hitting, but Jackson had the best it and his stock rose. Corbett was tired but took it bravely. Both went to their corners breathing hard.

18th round

Corbett landed a heavy left to the ribs, and Peter responded with blows to the body and chin. Jim landed a left to the chin that staggered Peter. "It was one of the best blows of the fight." Jackson missed and Corbett hit his kidneys in the clinches. Jim landed three swings on Peter's head.

According to the AC, from the 18th to the 28th rounds the fighting was rather tame. Corbett rarely used his right.

19th round

The men did very little, only engaging in some smart boxing, "bearing no resemblance to fighting."

20th round

Corbett landed his right and left to the chin and wind, and Jackson responded with a straight left to the body. Corbett rushed Jackson to a corner and severely pounded on his jaw with both hands, giving him the most punishment up to that point. Pete clinched. However, in a subsequent exchange, Jackson split Corbett's lip.

21st round

Corbett kept attacking the body, landing twice with telling effect. Jackson returned with a hard one in the ribs. They fuddled around and Jim landed a couple of punches. The round ended with Corbett again reaching Jackson's wind.

22nd round

Corbett jabbed the breadbasket and landed a heavy blow to the forehead, where a lump was slowly rising. Jackson came back and landed a nasty counter left to the mouth/chin/cheek region. Jim's upper lip began to swell and show red.

23rd round

Nothing of consequence was done, as Jim was able to duck and avoid Peter's blows.

24th round

Corbett landed three quick successive body blows but received one to the ribs. Jim landed one to the nose, but no damage was done.

25th round

The pace was slow, both did little, and neither landed any blows.

26th round

Corbett landed three good lefts to the wind, his clever work drawing applause. Although Jim had not thrown his right for six rounds, he landed a hard one to the body.

27th round

Corbett landed twice to the body with the left and again on the chin, but received a right to the chest. Jackson countered well and staggered his man a bit, following up with a right, but Corbett got in a stinging left. It was Jackson's round, "but he was not wholly on top."

28th round

SFC: Jackson forced things and gave Corbett heavy punishment, landing to the chin and wind. Jim only used his left to counter. They exchanged blows and it became the most exciting round up to that point. Both were severely punished. Jim landed a right to the chin, but received a rib smasher in return. It was Jackson's round.

SFE: This was a lively round, as the two punched and clinched, but the blows were mostly muffled. Jackson had the best of it at first, landing a straight left and a fierce uppercut. Jim did some ducking and escaped.

AC: Corbett sailed in and forced the fighting, hitting Jackson in the stomach with both hands, and smashed him in the jaw and nose. He received return punishment, but not as much as he gave.

29th round

SFC: Corbett showed that he was a good fighter as well as clever boxer. He forced hard and landed repeatedly to the head and body with his right and left. Jackson was tired and distressed. Jim landed heavily in the wind and made Peter's "head swim with a swinging smash on the ear. It was Corbett's round all through."

SFE: This was another fierce round. They exchanged blows, and a right to the stomach made Jackson look weak. Peter was beaten back to the ropes and got the decided worst of a hot rally. By the end, Jim was tired and leaned on Peter, who was powerless to prevent it.

AC: Jackson was fought to a standstill, but Corbett suddenly lost his strength and staggered from exhaustion. Jackson was unable to take advantage, because he was winded and sore.

30th round

SFC: Corbett was recovered and forced Jackson heavily, jabbing him in the body repeatedly. Peter landed a swing to Jim's left ear, but Corbett went at him very hard and made Jackson look badly distressed. He rushed Peter to the ropes and hit him on the face and body with both hands. Corbett had by far the better of it.

SFE: The round began more slowly. Jackson landed twice to the face but Jim got him against a post and landed a right and left in quick succession. Both were too tired to do decisive work, but Jim's blows were harder, "and he punched Jackson's stomach until it seemed a miracle that he could stand up."

AC: There was some good fighting, but it ended tamely, with no decided advantage.

31st round

SFC: Jim went at him wickedly again with both hands. Peter tried to fight away, but Jim landed a solid right to the jaw that "nearly brought him down." Jackson recovered and rallied, fighting Corbett to the ropes, but then Jim turned it around until they were both tired. Corbett hit harder and faster in the round and looked stronger at the end, and "unless the fortunes of war turned he looked a winner."

SFE: They went slow at first, but then there were some pretty rallies in which Corbett's superior skill counted. The crowd cheered when Jim dodged Peter's hard drives. Before the round was over, Corbett reached the stomach again, "apparently as hard as ever."

All local sources agreed that the fighting became very tame from the 32nd round on. According to the AC, "The next thirty rounds were tame beyond description. There was little attempt at real fighting." The SFC and SFE agreed that there was mostly long-range sparring, both resting, throwing very few blows, landing even fewer, doing little of consequence until the 41st round. The boxers were clearly quite fatigued.

41st round

SFC: Jackson began fighting hard again, landing on the chin and body, forcing Corbett to the ropes. However, Jim made a rally and got back hard. Jackson landed a left swing to the chest, but Corbett landed a jab to the face and body. Jackson returned with a heavy chest blow.

SFE: They began fighting again. Jackson got the best of it at the start. He landed to the jaw with the left, right, and left again. Jim came back strong though, and knocked Jackson unsteady with a clean right. Jim had a little the best of it at the gong.

The *Examiner* said that the subsequent rounds were "extremely tiresome," with barely a blow struck. Corbett's hands were sore and Jackson's stomach tender, and neither took risks. They walked around and sparred at the air. Every time Peter led, Jim would counter to the body and Peter again became respectful. This continued through the rest of the fight.

The *Alta* said that there was some weak hitting in the 44th round, but not much else. "As round after round was walked and sparred out, the crowd began to yawn and thin out. They grumbled and swore at the fizzle."

The *Chronicle* basically agreed that nothing was done in the 42nd through 46th rounds, but noted that in the 46th, Peter landed a sudden left to the jaw that staggered Jim for a moment, but nothing else happened. The 47th round was a walk around. In the 48th, Peter drove Jim to the ropes, then Jim drove him back to the other side, and then Peter did the same. From the 49th to the 58th rounds, they sparred at long range, almost never throwing, and neither landing.

The *Examiner* said that in the 57th round, the crowd hissed and loudly demanded that the men wind it up or quit. Jackson tried to oblige them in the 58th, but he was hit in the stomach and it settled back down into "the same old dreary affair." Almost no punches were thrown for two rounds thereafter and members of the club started going to sleep, going home, or making sarcastic remarks. The *Chronicle* agreed that the crowd applauded sarcastically at Peter's feeble leads in the 58th round.

According to the *Chronicle*, in the 61st round, Jackson proposed a draw, and the referee, directors, and pugilists held a consultation at ringside. Corbett objected to a draw, and Jackson replied that he would continue to stay with him. The walk-around resumed. It said that by the 62nd round the referee saw that there was no further fighting likely to occur. He held up his hand and said it was evident that it could not go on as it was and come to a conclusion, "and as it has come to an unsatisfactory conclusion I declare it no contest." They had fought for 61 rounds over four hours and four minutes. A fight that had begun around 9:30 p.m. was ended at about 1:45 a.m.

Jackson seemed pleased that it was over, while Corbett objected to the conclusion. Jim said that he felt strong on his legs but that his hand was hurt in the 31st round. He was willing to go on and bring it to a finish. "To say that Corbett was indignant at the outcome of the contest would be putting it mildly."

The *Examiner* said that the referee called both over to him at the end of the 60th round and advised them to put some life into the fight. "This is not a walking match." Corbett replied sarcastically, "Ain't it, I thought it was." They walked around for another round. After the 61st round, some called for a draw, while others in the crowd objected. The directors and the referee then went into consultation. Each fighter was questioned as to his condition. Corbett's second said that Jim's hands were gone. Jackson conceded that he was sore in the abdomen and that his leg was swelling and giving him trouble. He said that he did not think Corbett could lick him, but that he was not going to whip himself by trying to whip him.

The referee then announced that the contest was becoming unsatisfactory and that both men admitted that they cannot go on to a satisfactory conclusion (which Corbett disputed). "You have had ample evidence that they cannot go on except as walkers, and I therefore declare the entertainment ended and that it is no contest." Some cheered and some groaned.

Corbett seemed inclined to protest, especially since the declaration of a no contest would mean that their financial reward solely "depended on the generosity of the club's directors." *The Alta* confirmed that the "decision deprives the contestants of any part of the purse, as the articles called for a fight to a finish or a conclusion satisfactory to the Directors."

Jackson was interviewed, and he said that they had fought hard for 30 rounds, but that there was not enough left in either of them to make a finish, meaning to knock each other out. Peter said that neither of them was taking any chances. "I tried to protect my friends who bet their money on me. I suppose my fighting days are over. Two draws in succession. It is too bad."

Corbett agreed that the first 30 rounds had tired them out. "I was the short-end man…and it was Jackson's place to whip me if he could…. I hit him every time he hit me. I was not going to take chances by forcing the fight in the condition we were in. I had my friends to look after."[354]

One *Examiner* report summarized that Jackson was not as skillful as Corbett, but his 15-20 pound weight advantage and experience kept things pretty even. Jim's "brilliant boxing" was evident from the 1st round. With $10,000 on the line, both were cautious at first, neither taking the offensive, each moving around and watching for an opening. Jackson found it difficult to land on Corbett the blows that he had easily landed against others. Both found it a challenge to land, but Corbett landed the greater number of blows.

It was mostly an outside fight. The one time that Jackson attempted infighting, Jim countered with a big body shot. Jackson retaliated, but Corbett's dodges were just as good as Jackson's. After that, Jackson mostly attempted to jab him. Jim moved his head and went at the body often. Peter usually landed on Corbett's shoulders. "It was a beautiful show of what men can do in the way of avoiding blows." Occasionally one or the other would land a good one, but they were usually not affected.

The boxers grinned at each other. Jim would move back and then counter with his left to the body. Jackson would try a counter uppercut, but Corbett clinched. Jim battered the body, but his blows did not seem to hurt Peter. Generally though, it looked like Jim's fight, getting in two blows to Peter's one, mostly with straight leads.

By the 20th round, it appeared that Corbett would be the winner, but then Jackson came back a bit and soon thereafter the fighting grew slow. One round would be lively with some good exchanges, but rounds that

---

[354] *San Francisco Examiner*, May 22, 1891; *San Francisco Chronicle*, May 22, 1891; *Daily Alta California*, May 22, 1891.

were more cautious would follow, when little took place other than walking around. Corbett's arm seemed hurt but Jackson was too fatigued to take advantage.

This report said that the fight ended in a draw, and that they had essentially quit because neither could do the other in. Corbett's hands were badly smashed, so he could not strike hard or often, and Jackson's stomach was so sore that he did not want to go near Jim.

The neighboring *San Francisco Chronicle* summarized by saying that Corbett's "ring ability, quickness and effectiveness" in the early rounds were a revelation. That said, it also felt that Jackson's superior strength, weight and experience made it appear through the first 12 rounds that he would be the winner. He hit Jim twice for every one blow that he was struck early on, but was unable to hurt Corbett. Jim stood him off, even in the hardest fought rounds. Peter "scored his points carefully" and Corbett made him earn everything such that by the end of 12 rounds things seemed to be switching around to Jim's favor.

Ironically, although it was believed that Corbett would be the cleverer one and Jackson the superior fighter, the reverse was true. Jackson exhibited "consummate skill," but his "fighting capacity was inferior to that of his lighter opponent, who showed superior hitting power and gamer qualities."

The first 30 rounds were "splendid" from a "scientific standpoint." In the 30th and 31st rounds, Corbett drove Jackson into the corner and almost "slugged him out by straight hard punching," but after that, over the next 30 rounds, the fight became "wearisome." Jackson had punched hard and fast early on, but became fatigued and saw that he could not do his man in. Corbett was fresher, but with his hurt hand and relative inexperience, backed off when he could have finished Jackson.

The *Daily Alta California* said that there were 30 rounds of hard fighting and then 31 rounds of lifeless attempts at sparring, the fight ending in a walking match. It said that Jackson had met his match.

Although it did not provide a round by round accounting, the *San Francisco Evening Post* gave its very nice overview of the fight:

> When the long drawn out contest…was terminated by Referee Hiram Cook this morning, those who had witnessed the affair were unanimous on two points, viz., that Corbett is a far better man than he has been given credit for, and that Jackson has passed the meridian of his fighting days. During the whole of the sixty rounds boxed there was not the semblance of a knock down, and the match in the main resembled more of a contest for points than a battle between two heavyweights who were considered eligible to compete for the championship of the world.
>
> Corbett developed a rare degree of cleverness, but his talent certainly favors the avoiding of blows more than the delivering of them. His ducking from Jackson's straight handers was simply phenomenal, and

the way he managed to throw his shoulders against the colored pugilist's stomach in ducking proves that Jim knows some of the most effective tricks of the trade. Jim, further, is about the shiftiest man on his feet that ever graced the California Club's ring, and in the one or two fierce rallies that marked the go he did the more effective work. After the twenty-ninth round the aspect of the match would have warranted odds of two to one being laid on Corbett's chances; but the lead he gained was only a flash in the pan, and thereafter the mill degenerated into a contest of condition.

Throughout the whole affair it was patent that Jim was the stronger of the pair. He was firmer on his legs and hit the harder blows. Jackson made frequent use of the heart blow, but this punch, which has stood him in such good need in the past, lacked steam, and he did not seem to send his brawny right in on Corbett's short ribs with sufficient force to redden the skin. The magnificent manner in which the Californian kept dipping to the right foiled Jackson in his attempts to use the right hand cross-counter at the head effectually, and the very few blows of this description that Peter got home did no harm.

Corbett's favorite blow throughout was a left-handed lunge at Peter's stomach, which he accompanied by a low duck to the right. He scored on Peter's "bread basket" repeatedly, but, despite all reports to the contrary, Jackson was not much distressed by the visitations. He drew too far back to be hurt much by Jim's well-meant assaults, and in many cases cleverly stopped Corbett by placing his left fair on the mouth and nose.

In the early rounds of the fight it looked as if Corbett had made up his mind to employ questionable tactics. He squeezed Jackson around the neck with his left arm, and seemed loath on several occasions to let go until the referee entered the ring and made him break away. Finding, however, as the contest wore on that he could hold his own, Jim discarded the practice, and the remainder of the match was marked by the fairest kind of fighting on the parts of both men.

Corbett certainly surprised those who thought he would become rattled. His demeanor throughout was that of a veteran ringster, and the cool methodical manner he acted in the couple of brisk spells of fighting wherein he had the advantage led his backers to think that he would keep his head and follow the lead he had gained, but at no stage after the thirtieth round did Jim prove dangerous enough to cause any commotion in the Jackson camp. The manner in which Corbett died away in his fighting after the middle of the contest led many to believe that he intended wearing Jackson out thoroughly and then going at him, and when the fiftieth round came along and Jim did not increase his pace it became whispered about that he had hurt his hands severely punching Peter's head.

Jackson certainly did the bulk of the forcing in the last half of the contest, but he failed to either corner Corbett or induce him to mix things for any length of time. That Peter was tired was extremely palpable. His legs dragged and he frequently dropped his hands to his side as if to rest his arms. Corbett did not seem nearly so weary. He hopped around in lively fashion and seemed but little distressed, and the only conclusion the onlookers could arrive at were that either his hands were disabled or he was fighting under instructions and biding the time when the dusky pugilist should give evidence of being thoroughly tired out before sailing in to finish him.

In comparing the methods of the two men the general opinion seemed to be that Corbett had the call in cleverness. He was certainly more rapid in his movements, whether delivering blows, hopping back or ducking, but if the question of superiority were to be decided by points it would require nice discrimination to determine which man scored the most. ...

The punishment received by both men on either head or body was extremely light. The lips of each were swollen from the smashes they received in the twenty-eighth and twenty-ninth rounds, which were the two best in the contest, but otherwise they showed no bruises or abrasions. When the number of blows scored by each is considered in this connection the only inference that can be drawn is that neither man is a punisher. Jackson since his arrival in this country has never been looked upon as a heavy hitter, and his display last night convinced those who have watched his career that he has deteriorated greatly as far as his smiting capabilities are concerned since he defeated Joe McAuliffe.

Peter's two favorite blows without a doubt are a left hand facer and a right hand heart punch. The former he found the greatest difficulty in placing on Corbett last night on account of Jim's well timed ducking. The heart blow he put in often enough, but Corbett was rarely coming towards him at the time, so that Peter's favorite hit was little more effective than a shove. Jackson stuck to his old plan of relying upon straight punches. He hooked Corbett once or twice with his left and went near catching Jim a couple of times with a right hand uppercut.

Corbett, as well as Jackson, developed the fact that he is not a heavy puncher. ... [T]he blows he got in on Jackson before he hurt his fists were not damaging ones. In outfighting his favorite head blow was a left-hand swing...

The opinion was freely expressed last night that even now John L. could make mincemeat of both Jackson and Corbett, while it was thought that in the Boston Boy's palmy days neither of last night's principals would have stood the ghost of a show with him. ...

At the commencement of the sixty-first round when it was patent that Jackson could not fight any longer and that the other man was in about the same fix, Hiram Cook called them to the center of the ring and lectured them on the lack of vim which characterized their work. Jackson replied that he was doing the best he could and did not propose to sacrifice himself to the younger man by fighting in a loose manner. Corbett also stated that he was "trying" and they were ordered to fight on. The round progressed and ended without a blow being struck.

The gong sounded for the sixty-second round and Cook stepped into the ring. He said that both the men had declared they could fight no more and that that their appearance and actions bore out their statements. The affair had proved unsatisfactory, and he therefore proclaimed it "no contest." ... Corbett did not claim at that time that his hands were hurt, but that his left forearm had been wrenched early in the contest and had been rendered almost useless to him. Jackson complained of a lame right shoulder, and also stated that his elbow was injured. ...

Corbett, while dressing, stated that his legs were good for 20 rounds more, and that if the "fight" had been allowed to proceed he felt confident he should have won eventually. Considering, however, that the match had degenerated into a walking contest, or a "will power versus sleep tournament," and that no blows were struck for round after round, the directors would hardly have been justified in standing aloof until one or other of the men fell down from sheer exhaustion.

Jackson, when seen in his room, looked thoroughly worn out. He said: "Perhaps I ought to fall back on the excuse that I am growing old.... I found after fighting thirty rounds that my [right] shoulder was almost disabled. ... Corbett is a very clever fellow," continued Jackson, "and I must give him every credit for it. He is a hard man to land on, and he knows how to give a fellow the shoulder when he ducks."

Corbett gained great praise for his coolness and ringmanship, while it was considered that he lacks punishing power. His supporters were dissatisfied that he did not force matters after the thirtieth round, as they consider he was stronger than Peter and must have won. As regards the cleverness of the men, the idea prevailed that Corbett had the call.[355]

According to Corbett's autobiography, Jackson began the fight on the attack, while the smaller Corbett used speed and footwork, ducking and clinching, dipping his left shoulder into the onrushing Jackson's chest to deter him. Jackson had a fearful left-right combination to both the body and head, which he fired quite often.

In about the 16th round (as Jim years later recalled), off a Jackson lead left to the head, a right to the body hurt Corbett. Jim used the next few rounds to figure out that Jackson landed that combination after landing a stiff left to the head, and that Jackson used the next lead left to draw Corbett's hands up to leave him vulnerable for the body shot. Corbett began to roll with Jackson's left and counter with a left to the stomach, which caused Jackson's right to the body to glance off his arm.

Jackson was a thinker too, and eventually he utilized a right uppercut to counter Corbett's left to the body. Corbett rolled from the uppercut and eventually countered it with left hooks to the head that discouraged Jackson from throwing it. It was a good pace and both used every trick they had.

Through the first 28 rounds, Corbett did not want to slug with Jackson, usually throwing no more than one punch at a time. In the 28th round, a Jackson right to the head hurt Corbett. Sensing danger, Jim let go with both hands in a lengthy flurry of punches that sent Jackson back across the ring, having hurt him. Both fought hard through the 35th round, but by that time, they were getting tired. As a result of their fatigue, they would fight in spurts, each occasionally testing the other. Both men tried to convince the other that they were fresher, exchanging glances at the conclusion of the rounds.

The referee left the ring for about 30 seconds in the 60th round, "a strange and illegal proceeding" which Corbett believed was an indication that he was consulting with acquaintances who had bet money on Jackson. In the 61st round, without any reason or warning, the referee stopped the fight and said, "No contest. All bets off!" Essentially, the referee had declared that they had not fought, which was preposterous. Corbett was willing to continue and had never agreed to stop the fight. They had been fighting for four hours.

Corbett claimed that after the bout, Jackson collapsed from exhaustion on the way to the dressing room, which led him to believe that he would have won had the fight continued. Corbett believed that the referee declared it a no contest in order to help save friends from financial losses. Jackson was at least a 5-1 favorite, and a lot of people had money riding on him, as not many thought Jim had a chance.[356]

---

[355] *San Francisco Evening Post*, May 22, 1891.
[356] Alexander Johnston, *Ten and Out!*, 87-90; James J. Corbett, *The Roar of the Crowd*, 132.

However, it is possible and quite reasonable that after four hours of fighting, the referee felt that they were both too exhausted and hurt to continue, and that no end was in sight. The day after the fight, Jackson said that they were both too tired to finish each other with punches.

Jackson was more concerned with his shoulder than his ankle. He did not blame the felt floor or the ankle injury for his performance or condition. "[A]s for the ankle I injured in the buggy accident I only felt one slight twinge of pain in it, and I am sure it did not affect my chances in the least." He said that he had done most of the leading and forcing, but that he did not always want to lead because of Corbett's cleverness, feeling the need to take care of himself.[357]

The local papers continued discussing the fight in the following days. Corbett disputed that he had said that he was unable to continue. He said that he told the referee and a director that he was willing to go on. When the referee asked if something was the matter, he said that he would only speak to him outside the presence of Jackson. To the side, he told him that his "left hand was a little off, and so it was, but I could have finished with it. I honestly think that the fight was mine throughout."[358] Corbett also later said that he told them that although his left was off, his right was good. Jim accurately claimed that Jackson said he was tired, but taking no chances against Corbett.[359]

The *Chronicle* reported that the referee's decision was that it was no contest, which technically is not a draw, but in reality, it was a draw. The real difference was economic. By declaring it a no contest, he was in effect saying "that the club has seen no battle and is in nowise, therefore, indebted to the pugilists for their hard night's work. All bets on the final result are, of course, off." The referee had essentially decided that there had been no fight. This lends credence to Corbett's later assertion that the referee's decision was designed to save friends from financial losses. It is safe to say that the California Club members supported and had bet on Peter, for the club was essentially Jackson's American home, and Corbett was from the competitor Olympic Club. The decision meant that not only would they not lose their bets on Jackson, but the club was no longer obligated to split the purse between the combatants, which was traditional in the event of a draw.

The truth probably lies somewhere in the middle. They clearly were not going anywhere with the fight for quite some time, and let's face it, no one wants to sit around for four-plus hours in the middle of the night (at least 1:30 a.m.) and watch completely exhausted men do nothing. That said, they had gone that far, and if Corbett was willing to continue, he should have been allowed to do so, especially given the money that was on the line and their physical investment to that point. The decision should have at least

[357] *San Francisco Evening Post*, May 23, 1891.
[358] *San Francisco Chronicle*, May 23, 1891.
[359] *San Francisco Examiner*, May 24, 1891.

been a draw, allowing them to split the proceeds. A 'no contest' was typically only declared when a fix was suspected or the fight interfered with in some way. There can be no doubt that they had fought honestly and hard.

The referee's explanation of his decision, "which he gave as the mouthpiece of the Directors, is that the men were physically unfit to go on. By their contract they were bound to give an exhibition satisfactory to the club Directors, and as they did not do so it was decided no contest. Calling it a draw would have entitled the men to a division of the purse." The Directors eventually agreed to pay each $2,500 of the $10,000 purse, but that was not satisfactory to Corbett, who rightfully believed that he deserved $5,000. He said that he would never again fight at the C.A.C. Corbett noted,

> Since the California Club's resuscitation after a battle with the courts the word fight has been tabooed with great emphasis. The Club's monthly entertainments have been put up as contests of science and endurance, and the directors most strenuously deprecated anything like a reference to them as fights. In this connection the humor of the thing occurs in the fact that the very first scientific encounter in the club's rooms is declared no contest because there was not a lot of blood spilled and a knockout to wind up with. That it was a scientific contest is beyond question, probably the most scientific ever seen in the squared circle.... The club's published policy of encouraging science and the decision do not hitch.[360]

Still, as a *Chronicle* writer correctly opined, "People may attempt to disguise the fact as much as they like, and athletic club directors may advertise that they want only contests of science, but the fact is undeniable all the same that nothing gives so much satisfaction as a hard, bruising battle evenly waged and finished by a determined knock-out."[361] A fight to the finish satisfactory to the club directors meant just that – a knockout. If the men were unwilling or unable to bring the contest to a decisive conclusion, then it was not a satisfactory bout.

In the days following the fight, the local papers criticized the 'no contest' designation. One said that the only circumstance that would have justified such a decision was if there was suspicion or evidence of a fake, but that was lacking.

> The referee could have declared the match a draw and thus ended it. He could have said to the men: "Finish this in five, ten or twenty rounds," whatever number he pleased. Then if they still were unable or unwilling to finish he could have decided the man most willing to

---

[360] *San Francisco Examiner*, May 23, 1891; *San Francisco Chronicle*, June 1, 1891.
[361] *San Francisco Chronicle*, May 25, 1891.

fight and most capable and who had scored the most points the winner.

Another option raised, not without precedence, would have been to stop it and order them to resume the fight at a future date. It was again noted that the failure to declare a draw affected the betting and the division of the proceeds.[362]

It should also be noted that referee Hiram Cook might not have been the most neutral arbiter. He had a definite association with the California Athletic Club, and had been one of its officers. In fact, he was its first president when it opened in 1886. If most of the club's members (Cook's friends) had bet on their man Jackson, that fact might have affected, or given the appearance of having affected the referee's decision.[363]

Still, it cannot be said that Cook was inconsistent. What historians have failed to discuss is the fact that Cook had made a similar decision before, in another fight at the California Club, and that Corbett was well aware of this.

On September 24, 1889 at the California Club, featherweights Tommy Warren and Frank Murphy boxed in a fight to the finish for a $1,800 purse. John Donaldson (Corbett's second in the Jackson fight), coached Warren. Jim Corbett and Joe Choynski acted as timekeepers. Hiram Cook was the referee.

The fight was a good one for 32 rounds, but thereafter became dull and boring. The men barely fought, and some felt that they were intentionally playing for a draw. Basically, both were exhausted and could not throw. At the end of the 64th round, referee Cook announced, "These two gentlemen have signed an agreement to give a satisfactory exhibition to a finish. Now, if they don't give a satisfactory exhibition to a finish they won't get a d—d cent." However, they continued doing nothing, and the crowd hissed. At 1:45 a.m., after the 68th or 69th round (depending on the source), the club directors assembled and Referee Cook met and spoke with them. Cook then went to the center of the ring and said,

> The directors of this club have just said that the fight has to be to a satisfactory termination. Now if these last ten rounds have been toward a satisfactory termination I would like to know it. If I were the Board of Directors of the club I would throw these men out and not give them a – cent. I don't think this fight is to a satisfactory conclusion, and I am done with it.

Both men said that they were fighting as best as they could, but Cook nevertheless left the ring. John Donaldson said, "These fellows wanted a knockout every fight, but there are some men who can't be knocked out." The bored and tired crowd, as well as the press, supported the referee,

---

[362] *San Francisco Chronicle*, May 25, 1891.
[363] *San Francisco Chronicle*, December 12, 1886.

feeling that the men were not giving their best efforts. Some felt that they were attempting to engage in a fraud for gambling purposes. The Board of Directors decided not to pay the boxers anything.[364]

Because he was present at that fight, Corbett was well aware that if a fight became too dull and it appeared that it was not going to be brought to a finish, that what eventually happened to him could happen. The circumstances of the Murphy-Warren fight were eerily similar to the Corbett-Jackson fight. Jim could have objected to Cook as the referee, which he did not, or asked for a stipulation that if such a circumstance were to occur that the purse would be divided. He did not. However, in Corbett's defense, in the Murphy-Warren fight there were beliefs that the fighters were faking, whereas everyone believed that the Corbett-Jackson fight was on the level.

Following the Corbett-Jackson bout, none of the newspapers mentioned the Warren-Murphy fight. The closest thing to a reference to this fight was in a later statement issued by President Fulda, wherein he said,

> On two occasions we were compelled to order competitors out of the ring for conspiring to hoodwink the club. ... Instead of appreciating the efforts of the club to build up square sport, the men who wished to appear before it tried all kinds of tricks to get our money without giving us what they were paid for. All our contracts with people whom we engage specify that they shall endeavor to win and shall satisfy the directors that they have used their utmost powers to do so. It is true that some of our directors have bet on contests. In the last one, between Jackson and Corbett, vice-president Leek bet a hat. Directors Vice and Fish had each small amounts on the result; but that their judgments were influenced by that fact cannot be believed when it is known that both went to sleep and slumbered through many rounds. Indeed, Director Vice told me that he left the rooms before the decision was reached. Money is no object to the club.[365]

Ultimately, the Corbett-Jackson fight should not have been called a 'no contest.' At worst, it should have been declared a draw, or the men should have been allowed to finish it. The no contest designation was generally believed to be meant to save the club's backers from losing their money on Jackson, and/or from having to pay out the full purse. This hurt the club's reputation. According to a secondary source, soon thereafter, it was revealed that certain members of the club had been siphoning funds, and a few months later, it declared bankruptcy.[366]

Both Corbett and Jackson showed immense respect for one another. In his autobiography, Corbett stated his belief that Jackson was one of the

---

[364] *San Francisco Chronicle*, September 25, 26, 1889; *Daily Alta California*, September 25, 30, 1889.
[365] *Referee*, September 2, 1891.
[366] Fields at 47.

most intelligent pugilists that ever stepped in a ring, black or white. "In all my career I never had a man make me travel so fast or make me think so quickly!"[367] Jackson told Corbett that he was the quickest man that he had ever seen, that it was like boxing a ghost.[368] Years later, Corbett called Jackson "the greatest fighter I have ever seen."

The bout was subsequently described as the greatest ever for lovers of boxing skill, but tame to those who enjoy slugging. Most felt that it was a good fight for 30 rounds, but that it became dull after that. Some said that Jim was too clever to be appreciated by the mob.

> A cleverer boxing match between heavyweights probably never took place, but as an exhibition of fighting the contest was not exciting. The display of skill was admirable, but, except in the thirtieth round, when Corbett suddenly turned the tables on Jackson and slogged him into the corner, the spectators never once howled with the delight that overspreads the ringside when a knock-out seems likely.... It was a splendid exhibition of skill, but it is very doubtful if many of the patrons of fistiana who saw it would pay $50 again for another such treat.

Still, Corbett's reputation rose immensely. "Corbett is today credited with being the cleverest man in the world as a boxer." Another said, "Corbett is now the leading American heavyweight, Sullivan being out of the arena." Jackson admitted that he had underrated Jim by considering him merely a scientific lad. "I found him a man, and a mighty clever one. As for lacking experience, I fail to see where it comes in. He has more tricks of evasion than most men that have spent a lifetime in the ring." Corbett claimed to have been in better condition and stronger than Jackson at the end. He felt that it was his right to tire out Jackson more and to take his time about it.

The general gist of the reaction from observers of the fight was that Corbett's stock had gone up and Jackson's gone down. Most of the compliments were for Corbett and the consensus was that he had the best of it.[369] The Olympic Club president said,

> Where Jackson stood yesterday Corbett stands today, the premier boxer of the world.... I have no hesitation in saying that it was Corbett's fight throughout. He outfought Jackson, outgeneraled him, outpointed him, and would have whipped him in the end, barring a fluke. I regard him as the greatest exponent of the manly art that the world has ever produced.[370]

---

[367] Corbett at 131-132, 135.
[368] Id. at 144-145.
[369] *San Francisco Chronicle*, May 25, June 1, 1891; *San Francisco Examiner*, May 23, 1891.
[370] *San Francisco Chronicle*, May 23, 1891.

A *Chronicle* expert stated, "The opinion is unanimous that Corbett was the virtual winner... Corbett came out of the battle with whatever laurels were to be gained by such an unsatisfactory termination."[371] The *Alta* said,

> Corbett showed himself Jackson's equal in strength and ring tactics and his superior in agility and endurance.... Corbett and his friends...regard the affair as a practical victory. Jackson's backers are very glad to get their money back, and do not conceal their relief that a draw was made under the circumstances.[372]

Those interviewed by the *Evening Post* generally felt that Jackson had deteriorated and was not the same man that he had been.[373]

An *Examiner* expert said,

> Now I feel sure that, while fair play was given Corbett, the sympathies of President Fulda and many of the most influential directors of the club were with Jackson. The great mass of betting members of the club had their money upon him, and, knowing this, I make this assertion without the fear of successful contradiction. If there had been a chance on earth for Jackson to win, the fight would not have been stopped. This draw, then, was a virtual victory for Corbett.[374]

Three days after the fight, Corbett issued a statement regarding his views of the bout. He noted that Jackson was a careful man who did not force things, relying on his staying powers. Jim said that he followed Jackson's example. That said, Peter was offensive more often than Jim was. Corbett allowed him to lead, but would counter with a punch of his own. After about 6 rounds, Jackson focused on the heart region, but was unable to land but once. Jim noted that Jackson was most interested in defending his stomach, so that is where he went, with some success. Corbett would go up to the head once in a while to get Peter to raise his guard and leave an opening for the body. Corbett said that the only blow that bothered him at all was a right to the stomach in the 20th round. Jim's hurt left hand gave him some trouble in about the 35th round, but the right was fine.

Responding to those who said that the last 20 rounds were a walking match, Corbett believed that was the view of only those who did not know anything about fighting. His seconds told him that Jackson was tired and his legs giving way, that he could not last another hour, so he did not think it would be wise to force the fight when he knew that his strongest point was in reserving himself. He heard that Jackson's legs failed him on the way up the stairs to the dressing room after the fight, proving that his strategy was the proper one.[375]

---

[371] *San Francisco Chronicle*, May 25, 1891.
[372] *Daily Alta California*, May 23, 1891.
[373] *San Francisco Evening Post*, May 23, 1891.
[374] *San Francisco Examiner*, May 24, 1891.
[375] *San Francisco Examiner*, May 24, 1891.

However, in fairness to Jackson, another reporter felt that although Corbett may have outlasted him,

[A]t the rate he was fighting he could not have won until the colored man fell down from sheer exhaustion. It would have taken hours. That eventually Jackson would have to fall down and that Corbett would finally win had the men been left together there is no doubt, barring some unforeseen chance. It looked, however...as if both men were decidedly glad to get out of the ring.... They had fought over four hours and it still looked dubious to each of them what the end would be, and naturally they were glad the physical ordeal and the mental suspense were over. Jackson and his backers were only too well pleased, for both feared defeat, and Corbett, having practically scored a victory by fighting the Australian champion to a standstill, was decidedly loath to take desperate chances of losing the great advantage he had gained.

If Jim had been at the business longer he would never have given the referee such a chance to stop the battle.... he would never have let the colored Hercules get a breathing spell after his display of weakness in the thirty-first round. He would have continued to force the pace...for Peter was getting feebler every round, and if ever a man wanted to quit in hasty order he did.[376]

An Australian paper, the *Referee*, reported,

It was a most painfully slow affair.... Of course now and again the men livened up and fought a good round or two, but for the most part they contented themselves with clever graft, feinting, ducking, stopping and getting away, until the large crowd...got most heartily sick of the whole show, and called upon the referee to stop the show. Both men made a heap of use of their feet, and displayed remarkable agility for such big fellows, but the crowd wanted to see some real punching for the big purse, and this the two gladiators did not seem either able or willing to show. From the outset it was very apparent that they had a great respect for each other. Many rounds were allowed to drag away wearily before a good solid punch was ladled out on either side....

The general opinion was expressed that Sullivan in his best day could have made mighty small work of the pair of them in the one night....

Should they again meet, Corbett will be the favorite in the betting, as it is generally considered that he is on the up grade, while Peter is supposed to be past his meridian.[377]

---

[376] *San Francisco Chronicle*, May 25, 1891.
[377] *Referee*, May 27, 1891.

Another Australian reporter said, "A draw with Peter Jackson is, so far as Corbett is concerned, a virtual victory for him. It makes him the peer of Jackson in prestige, and it at once establishes him, at the same time, as the leading representative glove fighter of America."[378]

California Club President Fulda was naturally not quite as high on Corbett, but even he begrudgingly had to admit Jim's ability. He gave a statement a few weeks after the fight.

> At the commencement of the match, almost immediately were the rules violated by clinching on the part of Mr. Corbett, who so continued throughout the first and second rounds, compelling the referee to enter the ring and forcibly part them, no attention being paid to his orders to separate....

> As the match progressed I soon discovered that it was not mere nervousness, but studied design, as the clinches were accompanied by wearing twists and bearing of weight upon his adversary, which were the teachings of such an experienced ringster as Professor Donaldson, Corbett's second, particularly the close embrace and pressure of his body sideways against that of Jackson.... It is an old ring trick, intended to prevent the return infliction of any effective body blow. Again, the throwing of one's shoulder under the guard of another is a very excellent way of putting in a sly blow with the shoulder. It is a slight, but effective, breach of the rules, and can only be effectively performed by one on the defensive....

> Aside from these faults Corbett did very clever work, which entitles him to great praise and established the fact that he was able to dispute the title of premier boxer of the world with all. His skill is phenomenal and unquestionable. In point of the number of blows landed I think he scored the most, generally counters, but there are other conditions necessary to make a champion pugilist besides mere landing of blows – namely, effectiveness.... [T]he aggressive or attack was confined almost entirely to Mr. Jackson...and in a competition for points would have entitled Jackson to considerable allowance, but if for points both men might have boxed differently.... Granting that during a match honors are even, the one on the aggressive would be declared the victor. Be this as it many, there is nothing compulsory upon the part of either competitor as to the method to be pursued, either aggressive or defensive, in a professional match, unless for points, and cuts no figure in this particular case.[379]

Still another old follower of fighters gave his perspective, also not quite as high on Corbett, but indicating both his strong and weak points:

[378] *Referee,* August 5, 1891.
[379] *San Francisco Chronicle,* June 15, 1891.

I saw the Jackson-Corbett contest…. But the fight I saw is not the one I see reported in San Francisco daily newspapers or in the Associated Press…. The contest was a very clever one for about thirty rounds, or, in other words, while Jackson continued to fight Corbett. When Jackson ceased chasing the Californian the fighting ceased. I can explain Corbett's handling of himself upon no theory except that he went into the ring not to whip Jackson but to keep from getting whipped, and he was both clever and strong enough to accomplish his purpose. Jackson saw that after 30 rounds of trying it was useless to chase Corbett further. … Corbett is strong and wonderfully shifty. He is a very hard man to land on, and a most puzzling man to get to when he takes the notion not to fight. He cannot punch as hard, however, as many of the middle-weights do….. My estimate of Corbett is that it will take a thoroughly good one in good shape to lick him, and that at the same time a thoroughly good one in good shape will not be licked by him.[380]

William Burns many years later said of the match, "I might add that this was the poorest fight I ever saw between two first class men."[381] However, Corbett felt that the onus was on Jackson to come after him.

Why didn't they let us go on? I was making the right kind of a fight. He was the favorite at 100 to 80, wasn't he, and I was supposed to be a "mug"? Well, why didn't he go in and whip me? I was waiting for him. It was his play to beat me, wasn't it? I was taking no chances. He couldn't beat me, and he knew it. … Anyhow, I shall have something to say about the championship of the world hereafter, now that Sullivan is out of it.[382]

When later that year speaking of the match, Corbett said,

When Jackson rushed at me I smashed him in the stomach and in the jaw, and clinched him as he was never before clinched. The clinching rattled him nigh unto death. He couldn't get loose, and he didn't know how he was held…. Let me tell you that Peter Jackson had no such man as Jem Smith, Patsy Cardiff, Joe McAuliffe, or George Godfrey before him…. When Jackson boxed these previously-mentioned men, all he had to do was to fool them and knock them down and out. When Jackson met me he had to look out so as not to get fooled and knocked out himself, quite the reverse from what he had been used to…. Between hitting and jostling him around and

[380] *Referee*, August 5, 1891.
[381] William Burns, *Incidents In The Life Of John L. Sullivan And Other Famous People of Fifty Years Ago*, 1928), 50.
[382] *New York Clipper*, May 30, 1891.

making him hit out at me without landing, I had Mr. Jackson way up on Queer-street.[383]

Regardless of perspective, his performance against Peter Jackson gained Corbett immense respect, credibility, and fame. He had fought the most feared, experienced, and well respected contender in the world on at least even terms, and many felt that he had proven himself superior to Jackson.

[383] *Referee*, December 23, 1891, quoting the Boston *Police News*.

CHAPTER 11

Staying Sharp

For more than one year following the Jackson fight, Jim Corbett did not engage in any serious fights, but rather toured the country performing in a play and giving sparring exhibitions. Corbett had become famous and was a fan draw, so it was easy for him to capitalize upon the demand for his appearances and remain active. He gave audiences the opportunity to see and assess him, further growing his popularity, and by having so many exhibitions, Corbett remained in good fighting form.

Four days after the Corbett-Jackson fight, John L. Sullivan arrived in San Francisco to perform in his play. He was said to be weighing 235 pounds, although some thought that he weighed even more. During the play, Sullivan sparred 3 rounds of "exceedingly short duration" with Joe Lannon. "At the present time John L. decidedly prefers talking about his new profession to discoursing on fighting subjects." He was set to tour with his play in Australia for a number of months, beginning in July 1891. At the moment, fighting a contender was not in Sullivan's plans.[384]

On June 16, 1891, Frank Slavin knocked out Jake Kilrain in the 9th round. This was somewhat significant because in March 1891, Kilrain had stopped top American black George Godfrey in the 44th round. Corbett had merely decisioned Kilrain and was not close to stopping him.

Just one month after the Corbett-Jackson fight, on June 24, 1891 in San Francisco, Corbett and John L. Sullivan sparred in an exhibition. A couple days beforehand, it was said, "Among boxers Sullivan's fighting days are considered over. It is not believed he will ever again enter the ring for championship honors…. Jim is expected to outspar him very handily."[385] Another said, "There is no doubt but what Corbett is cleverer than Sullivan, and in a setto with the big fellow he can make a pretty showing, but it is a question whether there would be much gayety left in him after Sullivan had landed a time or two." Still, it noted that Sullivan was big, fat, and short of work, so it was not likely that he was going to do very much. "If Sullivan is feeling at all mellow it is expected that he will freely express himself regarding 'niggers,' newspapers and heavy weight bruisers and wind up the recitation by proclaiming, 'I can lick 'em all.'"[386]

The pre-exhibition analysis turned out to be irrelevant, at least for the immediate future. For their exhibition, Sullivan insisted that they wear formal dress suits, an indication that he did not want it to be serious, and also an admission that John L. was far from being in fight condition even for a short bout. Sully probably wanted to size Jim up a little bit, but it was a bad move, because it wound up boosting Corbett's confidence.

According to Corbett's autobiography, it really was not much of a match, but he used it to learn a bit about Sullivan, choosing to stand in range and swap punches and not give away his own skilled footwork. The rounds were only about a minute long. Sullivan dropped his hands in the 2nd round and stuck his chin out, but Corbett then did the same to show him up. It was overall a tame, bloodless exhibition, but it gave Corbett confidence.[387]

The local *San Francisco Chronicle* reported that the fans were disappointed by the exhibition, having expected it to be more. It was called a "love fest" in which the boxers were "cheerfully hissed." Some called it a swindle and a fake, because people had paid $2 and $3 to see the real thing. Instead, the boxers wore large gloves and their dinner outfits, including their vests, pants, shirtsleeves, collars and neckties, to the surprise of the spectators. They barely ruffled each other's hair over the 3 rounds, as they mostly slapped and landed light blows.[388]

Sometime afterwards, Sullivan said that he could "do Corbett in a punch." Corbett later replied to the assertion,

> While I have great respect for Sullivan on account of his record, I have no hesitancy in saying that he is considered a good old has-been. The night we boxed he weighed 265 lb. He was remarkably active, however, and surprised everybody in the house.[389]

Following their exhibition, Sullivan went on another one of his patented drinking sprees.

---

[385] *San Francisco Chronicle*, June 22, 1891.
[386] *San Francisco Evening Post*, June 24, 1891.
[387] Corbett at 148-150.
[388] *San Francisco Chronicle*, June 25, 1891.
[389] *Referee*, December 23, 1891, quoting the Boston *Police News*.

John Lawrence Sullivan...seems to be working on the idea that he has a contract to drink all the whisky, beer, wine, gin and rum in the country. During the past few days he has been endeavoring to get away with this end of his job, but he has been knocked out, and if he ever again gets sober, he will realize that, although he has the drinking capacity of an army, there is more fire water in this little town than he can swallow.

It was said that Sullivan had been "beastly drunk" and stayed out all night until the following day, not passing out until noon. This was typical for him. "On his theatrical tours Sullivan is generally kept in such a condition as to admit of his performing by allowing him to soak himself with whisky at night after the performance is over. He sleeps next day until it is almost time to appear again before the curtain."[390]

Some questioned whether Sullivan ever wanted to enter the ring again. It appeared that he was more interested in easy money in the theater and drinking to excess. He was always an alcoholic, but he seemed to be degenerating. John said that he would be willing to meet Frank Slavin in September of the following year (1892), but some questioned his sincerity.

It now transpires that he wishes to put the battle off until about 1909, and it is extremely doubtful whether he is not simply working for an advertisement without having the least idea of ever again entering the ring. ...

During the course of his sojourn here of over a month he hardly drew a sober breath. The time was spent in a long, uninterrupted debauch.[391]

Two days after the Corbett-Sullivan exhibition, Sullivan was asked about Peter Jackson. He said of Peter, "He is a nigger, and that settles it with me. God did not intend him to be as good as a white man or he would have changed his color, see?"[392]

A newspaper one month later noted that although the negro population as a whole had been growing, as a percentage of the total population it had been diminishing. In 1810, the negro population was 700,000 or 19 % of the total U.S. population. As of the 1890 census, they were 11.9% percent of the population. "Facts such as these indicate that the negro problem will become less and less rather than more and more a political problem."[393]

In late July 1891, it was reported that since his late May fight with Jackson, Corbett had joined Thatcher's minstrels, "in which company he

---

[390] *San Francisco Evening Post,* June 26, 1891.
[391] *San Francisco Evening Post,* June 27, 1891.
[392] *San Francisco Chronicle,* June 27, 1891.
[393] *Minneapolis Tribune,* July 5, 1891.

sparred with Joe Lannon. The season has but recently closed in Omaha." Jim was said to be weighing 195 pounds.

Corbett was scheduled to eventually head to New York, where he would join Bill Brady's *After Dark* company in the middle of August, giving sparring exhibitions with Professor Donaldson for six to eight months. Jim said that after that tour, he would be ready to meet any man in the world.[394]

During the last week of July 1891, Corbett was in Minnesota to witness the Bob Fitzsimmons vs. Jim Hall fight. Unfortunately, the authorities refused to allow the technically illegal fight to take place.

While he was in St. Paul, Minnesota in late July, Corbett sparred with Joe Lannon. The 200-plus-pound Lannon was a frequent Sullivan sparring partner. He held an 1886 KO6 over former Sullivan challenger Frank Herald, but in 1887, Jake Kilrain stopped Lannon in the 11th round. Lannon fought George Godfrey to an 1889 15-round draw, but subsequently, Jack Ashton knocked out Lannon in the 19th round.

Lannon told one paper that he had sparred Corbett in St. Paul. Of Corbett, he said, "I believe he is the cleverest man I ever met, but, of course, he hasn't the hitting powers of Sullivan. Corbett is a fine fellow, and the man who thinks he is not a fighter is foolish."[395]

On August 5, 1891 in Chicago, Corbett boxed an exhibition with the experienced veteran Australian Jim Hall, who was known for his skill and power. In middleweight bouts, Bob Fitzsimmons had scored a January 1889 KO5 over Hall, but on February 11, 1890, Hall knocked out Fitzsimmons in the 4th round.[396] Fitzsimmons later claimed to have thrown the fight. Some agreed that there was something suspicious about the bout, while others felt that Bob was just trying to save face.[397] Hall had mostly scored knockout victories in Australia, fighting often there as a middleweight. His wins included: 1889 KO22 Starlight, W10 Jim Burge, D15 Australian middleweight champion Jim Fogarty (Hall better), KO4 Pablo Fanque, and 1890 KO16 Peter Boland. However, in August 1890, Hall was stopped in 11 rounds by Owen Sullivan, and in 1891 lost an 8-round decision to Billy McCarthy. When he came to America in 1891, Hall scored a KO1 over respected middleweight Alec Greggains.

According to the *Chicago Tribune*, Corbett weighed 200 pounds to Hall's 160 pounds. Wearing four-ounce gloves, they sparred 4 rounds of uneven lengths for a total of about nine minutes. The first 3 rounds lasted a minute and a half each, and the 4th over three minutes on account of the hisses of dissatisfaction over the fact that the other rounds had been short. Although Hall showed "quickness and good straight hitting ability" he at all times

[394] *St. Paul Daily Pioneer Press*, July 22, 1891.
[395] *New York Clipper*, August 1, 1891.
[396] *National Police Gazette*, August 23, 1890, January 24, 1891, February 22, 1896; *Daily Picayune*, January 12, 1891; *Sydney Referee*, January 23, 1889, February 12, 1890.
[397] *Daily Picayune*, September 4, 1892; *National Police Gazette*, February 18, 1899; Nat Fleisher, *The Heavyweight Championship* (N.Y.: G.P. Putnam's Sons, 1949, 1961), 119.

seemed "at a disadvantage – natural on account of the weight against him." Corbett was called the leading candidate for the heavyweight championship, "fast slipping out of Sullivan's reach."

Jim Hall

Corbett's style was described as

> [S]howy, clean cut, and his own. He is a stiff-armed puncher and a punishing hitter, as his ring career proves. He hits with a half rigid arm quickly and with a sidelong movement and head leaning out of danger. His foot work seems first-class, and his incessant feinting with feet, hands, and head at the same time should keep an opponent on his toes at all times. His judgment on distance seems first-class, and several times Hall appeared to lose his patience at the clever side slipping of the big Californian. The peculiar clinching game that stood Corbett in such good stead during the long fight with Jackson was shown a dozen times last night. It works perfectly, and an opponent is powerless to hit Corbett when the locking hug is applied.[398]

---

[398] *Chicago Tribune*, August 6, 1891. In 1893, Fitzsimmons would knock out Hall in the 4th round, but Hall would later come back with a KO7 over Frank Slavin.

Another local paper, the *Chicago Herald*, said that a crowd of 3,000 spectators witnessed the exhibition. Corbett forced the fighting in the 1st round. When the timekeeper sent them to their corners early, the audience howled in disgust. In the 2nd, Corbett feinted and landed a poke on the nose and a crack on the jaw. They engaged in some in-fighting, and Hall performed cleverly, landing many blows on the ribs. Both dodged well in the 3rd, and just as things warmed up, time was called, again to the fans' displeasure, because it only lasted a minute and a half. The 4th round lasted over three minutes, and both of these scientific men landed clever blows. After an exciting rush, they clinched, and upon breaking, their necks were red. Corbett left the ring surrounded by a crowd of admirers.[399]

The Chicago *Daily Inter Ocean* said of the exhibition,

> It was a friendly bout, and though some apparently hot interchanges were made, none of the blows landed by either man did any harm. Corbett showed up superbly, a thorough master of his art, and many were disappointed at the utterly helpless manner in which the big middleweight endeavored to "stand off" the tall Californian.[400]

Corbett later said, "Jim Hall is a wonder, I tell you. I boxed with him in Chicago the other night, and I have sparred with some clever men in my career, but by long odds Jim Hall is the cleverest boxer I ever tackled. I think he would have whipped Bob Fitzsimmons if they had fought."[401]

Corbett began exhibiting in Trenton, New Jersey on August 13, 1891 as part of the play, *After Dark*. On that date, he sparred 3 rounds with Jim Daly and 1 round with a lightweight named Murphy.[402] In March 1891, Daly "won" a 6-rounder with Joe McAuliffe because Joe had contracted to stop him in that time and failed to do so. Daly became Corbett's regular sparring partner during the *After Dark* shows. At each show, Corbett and Daly sparred 3 rounds in the concert hall scene. Bill Brady had assumed managerial duties for Corbett and made all the arrangements.

Corbett and *After Dark* began a week's engagement in Philadelphia on August 17.[403] Over the next several months, the play showed in Boston, Brooklyn, Harrisburg, Pittsburgh, Toledo, Chicago, Cincinnati, Columbus, and St. Louis, amongst other places.[404] While they were there, an October 13 *Brooklyn Daily Eagle* report said that the play contained an "exhibition of lively boxing" by Mr. Corbett.[405] One late October 1891 report said that

[399] *Chicago Herald*, August 6, 1891.
[400] *Daily Inter Ocean* (Chicago), August 6, 1891.
[401] *Referee*, December 23, 1891.
[402] *Daily True American* (New Jersey), August 13, 14, 1891; *New York Clipper*, August 22, 1891.
[403] *Referee*, December 23, 1891, quoting the Boston *Police News*; *Philadelphia Inquirer*, August 19, 20, 1891.
[404] Fields at 50-51.
[405] *Brooklyn Daily Eagle*, October 13, 1891.

Corbett had a 40-week theatrical engagement.[406] For the time being, Corbett was making money as an actor/exhibitionist.

Jim Daly

During that time, Peter Jackson was clamoring for a rematch with Corbett. In August, he said,

> I am ready to fight Corbett at any time, and in any place except New Orleans, and, further, will bet him $500 that he is not game enough to fight me again – or, in other words, finish the contest which he says he has already won. If he had me so badly beaten why doesn't he fight me again and settle beyond a question who is the best man?[407]

Jackson was well aware of the fact that the Corbett bout had tarnished his reputation. However, Corbett had already made his reputation off of their match, and therefore likely saw no need to fight Jackson again.

---

[406] *Referee*, October 28, 1891.
[407] *Philadelphia Press*, August 17, 1891; *New York Clipper*, August 22, 1891.

Still, Corbett had deposited $1,000 with the offices of the *New York Herald* for a future fight with anyone in the world, Frank Slavin or Charles Mitchell preferred. Corbett said, "I regard Mitchell as a scientific boxer and a good ring general, but there his accomplishments end.... I'd sooner meet him than any man I know, but it's dollars to cents that he dare not make a match with me."

Corbett was called a "phenomenal pugilist" who wanted soon to occupy the position of heavyweight champion. Jim envisioned two semifinal bouts and a final for the championship. He said that he would like to see Slavin meet Sullivan, and Mitchell could meet Jim. "Then let the winners of the two battles come together and settle once for all who is the real champion."[408]

An Australian newspaper felt that Australian Joe Goddard was a better contender than either Corbett or Jackson. Goddard had the October 1890 8-round draw with Jackson, in which he "would have knocked out the colored man if the contest had lasted a few more rounds." Goddard had also knocked out Joe Choynski in 4 rounds, twice, in February and July 1891. Both fights were total wars worth description.

In their first fight, Choynski dropped Goddard in the 1st round, but Goddard quickly rose and went right back at it. Each man was decked twice in the 2nd round. Choynski again dropped Goddard in the 3rd round, but after exchanging blows, both fell down in a heap. They blasted away and Goddard was hurt by rib smashes and slipped down. He rose and continued fighting. In the 4th round, Goddard attacked and sent Choynski down multiple times, finally breaking him. The round concluded, but Choynski was unable to respond for the 5th round.[409]

After this fight, Choynski scored a May 1891 KO2 over Mick Dooley and June KO2 over Owen Sullivan. Dooley held a May 1886 KO3 over Bob Fitzsimmons, and Owen Sullivan held an August 1890 KO11 over Jim Hall.

[408] *Philadelphia Inquirer*, August 20, 1891.
[409] *Referee*, February 11, 1891.

The second Goddard-Choynski fight in July 1891 was even more brutal than their first fight. It was a nonstop volley of bombs, each attempting to knock the other out in a back and forth battle. In the 1st round, the 173-pound Choynski landed a left that gashed the eye of the 184 ½-pound Goddard, "bursting it badly." Goddard in turn hurt Choynski with lefts on the chin and throat, almost flooring him. Blood flew from Goddard in every direction, and he was covered with gore as Choynski dealt him terrible punishment. It was "one of the most fiendish slaughters I have ever seen." Just before the end of the 1st round, Goddard dropped Choynski with a right.

Goddard began the 2nd round with a left that sent Choynski reeling. Choynski then went at him like a fiend, banging Goddard all over the ring. They were bathed in blood, and the spectators were spattered by it. Choynski went at him for fully a minute and eventually knocked Goddard down in a heap. He rose and they went at it toe to toe until a right to the ribs made Goddard double up. However, Goddard landed a left to the throat that snapped Joe's head back, and a right to the jaw sent Choynski down. Goddard went at him, but Choynski came back, giving him some "fearful gruel," and by the end of the round, "Goddard took enough punishment to whip any ordinary man ten times over."

In the 3rd, Joe's left opened another gash under Goddard's eye, and the blood poured all over him. However, Goddard's right to the ribs made Joe gasp. Choynski in turn landed a right to the ear that staggered Goddard. Choynski sprang at him like a demon and landed an uppercut that "sent the giant's teeth together like broken bottles." A right and left hook sent Goddard reeling back. He followed up, trying to finish Goddard, but a return right and left on the ribs sent Choynski down. After Joe rose, Goddard followed up, but was met with a blow that "would have killed an ordinary man." They fought as if they were fighting for their lives. Toward the end of the round, Choynski pulverized Goddard.

Goddard went right at Choynski to being the 4th round, rushing forward in a demoniacal manner. They fought with everything they had, and for a couple of minutes it was give and take. Eventually, Choynski reeled and went down. He was floored a second time, and finally, three rights to the jaw sent him down for the third time in the round, and Choynski was counted out.[410]

Many were impressed with Goddard's power, indomitable will, toughness, courage and conditioning. Of course, Goddard had been decked in his fights with both Jackson and Choynski, while Corbett, with his more careful style, was not. Still, Goddard was considered perfect for a fight to the finish.

---

[410] *Referee*, July 22, 1891.

The Melbourne Athletic Club offered a $5,000 purse for a Corbett-Goddard fight. However, Jim said that the amount was not sufficient, that he could make more on the minstrel stage. He also said that Goddard was not in his class. To this statement, one Australian reporter said that Corbett "has proved himself to be anything but a game man, and his constant bragging is disgusting everybody with him." Corbett was called "a skillful and pretty boxer, but cannot hit hard, and is not a fighter of the highest class by any means." Some believed that Goddard was better than Corbett. *"Judging from the battles of Goddard with Jackson*, Choynski and Corbett with the same two men, *the Barrier's champion* [Goddard] *is not in the Californian's class. He is two or three grades above him."*[411]

Still, even in Australia, Frank Slavin was considered superior to Goddard. In the late 1880s, possibly 1888, Slavin had once sparred with Goddard. Some secondary sources report that Slavin might have stopped him. One American source reporting in 1892 provided Goddard's version of events.

> Goddard is not very complimentary to Slavin. When the victor of Kilrain was in Victoria, New South Wales, Goddard was in business there, and upon invitation went to Slavin's show to spar three light rounds with him. Goddard says he had no idea that Slavin wanted to go in for a knockout, and was not thinking of it when Slavin sailed in hammer and tongs and came near putting him out before he knew what was up.[412]

Certainly though, at that time, three Australians were amongst the most respected contenders for the crown: Jackson, Slavin, and Goddard. In late September 1891, Goddard fought Tom Lees to an 8-round draw, being floored three times in the 1st round, which was said to have lowered Goddard's stock.[413] However, in May of that year, Goddard had scored a KO9 over Lees.

From July to October 1891, John L. Sullivan had been in Australia, giving 3-round sparring exhibitions with Jack Ashton there. Sullivan was looking quick and strong despite being fat and out of shape. As had been the case over the last couple years, he wasn't taking any serious bouts. In early October, Joe Goddard won an 8-round decision over Ashton.

On October 23, 1891 in Philadelphia, before 500 members of a local athletic club, Jim Corbett sparred both Billy Rocap, "whose standing as a boxer is one of the club's principal sources of pride," as well as Clarence Cramer, who was called an "Adonis." William Rocap of Philadelphia won

---

[411] *Referee*, September 2, 1891. Italics in original.
[412] *Times-Democrat*, September 5, 1892.
[413] *Referee*, September 23, 1891.

the first amateur U.S. National Championships in the 115-pound weight class in 1888, a feat which he duplicated in 1889.[414]

The following night, Corbett coached his chief sparring partner, Jim Daly, in a bout against Peter Maher. In the 1st round, Maher knocked Daly out of the ring. Despite the fact that he that he returned again within ten seconds and was ready and willing to continue, the referee stopped it.[415] Daly later said that he had secured the verdict in many bouts in which he had been knocked down, including fights with Joe McAuliffe, Pat Farrell, and Billy Gabig.

Around this time, there was discussion of a potential match between Maher and Corbett, but the negotiations eventually fizzled out.[416] Maher would later be a part of Corbett's career in an odd way.

On October 25, 1891, still in Philadelphia, Corbett again sparred Clarence W. Cramer (whom he had boxed two days earlier), and then sparred with H.W. Schlichter. Following the sparring, Corbett had a wrestling bout with Lon Kitchen, a clever middleweight who Jim threw. After that, Jim played hand ball, "at which game he is an expert," and ended his work with a long swim. That night, he headed to New York in order to continue with his play and occasional exhibitions.[417]

In November 1891, Peter Jackson and Frank Slavin signed articles of agreement to fight in London, England before the National Sporting Club in June 1892. The *New York Clipper* wrote,

> As regards Sullivan's previously expressed determination never to fight a colored man, we are of the opinion that he has since become convinced that persistence in his unjustifiable attempt to create a color line in P.R. matters would only make him appear ridiculous, besides casting a reflection on his courage, and for that reason we are satisfied that he will readily consent to meet Jackson in case the latter bests Slavin.[418]

That same month, in San Francisco, Sullivan sparred 3 short rounds with Paddy Ryan. John was fat and out of shape, but still quick. In December, Sullivan sparred 3 rounds with Joe Choynski. Afterwards, one man opined,

> I like John very much, and I believe that he could whip any man living if he would take care of himself. From what I have heard about him for the past few months, however, I am convinced that he has set his mind on going to the dogs as fast as he can.... He appears to think

[414] *Philadelphia Inquirer,* October 24, 1891; USA Boxing rulebook, U.S. Men's Champions.
[415] *Philadelphia Inquirer,* October 25, 1891.
[416] *New York Clipper,* November 21, 1891, December 19, 1891.
[417] *Philadelphia Inquirer,* October 26, 1891.
[418] *New York Clipper,* November 28, 1891.

that he can thrash anybody, and he continues to try and drink all the liquor there is in every town he visits.[419]

Sullivan continued with his ongoing theatrical career, performing in the play *Honest Hearts and Willing Hands*. Corbett was exhibiting with *After Dark*.

In late December 1891, it was reported that although Corbett was willing to meet Charley Mitchell in a fight to the finish, Charley was only willing to engage in a 6-round scientific points sparring match. Corbett agreed and the bout was scheduled for February 11, 1892.[420]

On December 26, 1891 in New York, Corbett sparred in an exhibition show at the packed New York Athletic Club. He first sparred 1 round with the club's instructor, Mike Donovan, with whom he had previously sparred in March 1890. "Although Donovan is an exceptionally clever man, he was little more than a child in Corbett's hands. Jim showed off to great advantage, and was heartily applauded for his cleverness." Jim then sparred 1 round with Bob Center, who was "one of Donovan's crack pupils."

> [Center] got a trifle daring and tried to show off before some of his clubmates but it was all a mistake, as the big, good-natured Californian let him run against his right once or twice, and upper-cut him with the left until he saw more stars in ten seconds than he had ever seen before in ten years. The youth will bear evidence of the bout for some time to come, judging from his general appearance when he left the ring.[421]

During the first week of January 1892, Corbett and Daly were appearing in *After Dark* in New York City.[422]

The Corbett-Mitchell bout was soon put in jeopardy. While in New York, it was announced that the police would not allow slugging matches there. The police said that the moment Corbett and Mitchell attempted to fight or engage in anything more than a tame exhibition, they would be arrested. "We have stamped out professional fighting in this city, and are determined that it shan't be resurrected again."[423] At first, the boxers decided to go on with it as a scientific sparring exhibition, but Mitchell subsequently pulled out of the match. Jim later said that Mitchell "flunked" and was afraid to meet him.[424]

In mid-January, Corbett gave boxing exhibitions in Philadelphia for a week. On January 14, 1892, Corbett and Daly gave a "remarkably clever exhibition" before 800 members of a local athletic club. Corbett "made an

---

[419] *San Francisco Examiner,* December 21, 1891.
[420] *San Francisco Examiner,* December 23, 1891; *New York Clipper,* December 26, 1891, January 2, 1892.
[421] *New York Clipper,* January 2, 1892.
[422] *New York Clipper,* January 2, 1892.
[423] *New York Clipper,* January 2, 1892.
[424] *New York Clipper,* January 9, 1892; *Boston Daily Globe,* January 25, 1892.

unusually good impression by his skill and dexterity in avoiding his opponent, and by his lightning-like work."[425]

On January 15, Corbett sparred the much smaller Billy Rocap (with whom he had sparred in October 1891). When asked by a reporter whether his "people" knew that he was a fighter, Corbett responded, "Good gracious, no! My mother's heart would break if she knew I was a prizefighter, she thinks I am a bank robber."[426]

On January 18, Corbett sparred Joe Donohue. "It just took three punches by Corbett to convince Mr. Donohue that he was too tired to continue on his feet any longer. Time, 20 seconds." Jim Daly boxed 3 rounds with John Clark, and then boxed 3 "clever" rounds with Corbett.[427]

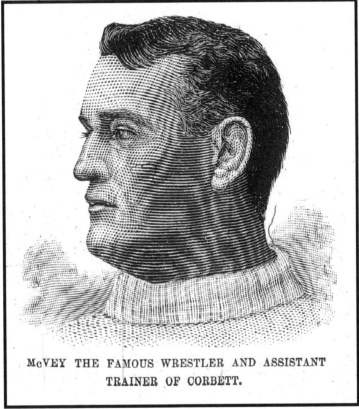

McVEY THE FAMOUS WRESTLER AND ASSISTANT TRAINER OF CORBETT.

On January 19, continuing his Philadelphia engagement, Corbett sparred John McVey of Trenton (a.k.a. Jim "Con" McVey). Of this exhibition, one local paper said, "It was very funny. McVey tried his best to knock Corbett out, but his heavy swings were cleverly stopped, and he was outpointed in every round." Another said the 3 rounds were more amusing than hard

[425] *Philadelphia Public Ledger*, January 15, 1892.
[426] *Philadelphia Press*, January 16, 1892.
[427] *Philadelphia Press*, January 19, 1892.

hitting, because the police required no knocking out. McVey was sadly out of condition, and Corbett "kept tapping him in a most aggravating manner, while with a twist of the head he would put it out of reach of McVey's wild swings."[428] The much larger McVey later became a regular Corbett sparring partner.

On the 20th, Corbett boxed "Bubbles" Davis. Davis made no effort to hit Corbett, while Jim by only using his left kept Davis on the run throughout the 3 rounds. Another account said that Corbett only engaged in tapping, but was still able to show what he could do with the gloves.[429]

On January 21, Corbett "hit Bob Caffey all over the face and body. The Californian's cleverness being well appreciated by the audience."[430]

On the 22nd, Corbett once again met experienced veteran Mike Donovan. Donovan was much shorter and lighter than Corbett, being more of a large middleweight, and was thought to be over 50 years old, but made up for it with his science.

One account said that Corbett and Donovan did not engage in slugging, but pleasing, expert scientific boxing. Donovan was able to hit Corbett in every round, and both showed themselves to be clever. Another account said, "It was a wonderful display of the manly art, and each good stop or blow was loudly applauded."[431]

Corbett ended this Philadelphia engagement on January 23, 1892. He sparred 3 rounds with Bob Caffey or Caffrey (local source spellings vary) and 3 more with John McVey, both of whom had sparred Corbett earlier that week. Caffey was said to be used up pretty well before the 3rd round. McVey weighed considerably more than Corbett, but was punished badly and was very tired in the 3rd round.[432]

As a result of these exhibitions, it was said that Corbett had proven that "he is beyond question the cleverest heavyweight this country has yet produced." He had given each man that he had faced that week a good thumping, defeating them all with ridiculous ease, with the exception of Donovan, who was able to make a good showing.[433]

Corbett and Daly subsequently headed to Boston to exhibit there for a week with their vaudeville company. A reporter there said of Jim, "There is no doubt but what Corbett is one of the cleverest men in the pugilistic world."

Jim wanted to reach the top, but was happy to be making easy money against lesser fare. Corbett said, "While big purses are offered me to spar

---

[428] *Philadelphia Inquirer*, January 20, 1892; *Philadelphia Press*, January 20, 1892.
[429] *Philadelphia Inquirer*, January 21, 1892; *Philadelphia Press*, January 21, 1892. Davis had an 1890 LKOby9 to Joe Choynski.
[430] *Philadelphia Press*, January 22, 1892.
[431] *Philadelphia Inquirer*, January 23, 1892; *Philadelphia Press*, January 23, 1892.
[432] *Philadelphia Inquirer*, January 24, 1892; *Philadelphia Press*, January 24, 1892.
[433] *Philadelphia Inquirer*, January 19, 24, 1892.

some of the lesser lights, I think it better in the long run to wait and get a match with the men in the championship class."

Corbett picked Peter Jackson to win the upcoming June big match with Frank Slavin. Regardless of who won, Corbett said that he intended to challenge the winner to fight at whatever club in America or England would offer the biggest purse.[434]

On January 25, 1892 at Boston's Howard Athenaeum, Corbett exhibited 3 rounds with Jim Daly. Every seat was occupied. The 1st round contained some light sparring and a few vicious lefts by Daly that were cleverly ducked by Corbett, "who has, it must be said, a clever head." In the 2nd round, Corbett hit Daly with three beautiful lefts, but Daly fought creditably. "The third round was a rattler, but Daly was a mere toy in the hands of Corbett who, more by accident than anything else, caught him an upper cut that made teeth rattle." It was said that Corbett would box John McMahon on the 26th.[435]

After completing that week's engagement on the 30th, Corbett provided some insight into his attitude about and reason for fighting.

> I lay claim to no love of fighting for fighting's sake. The money to be earned in professional pugilism was, you may be sure, the only inducement that led me to renounce a very congenial and fairly lucrative position that I had in San Francisco. While I seem to be so much of an attraction in a play house that I can make $500 to $800 a week, my duty to myself seems to be, I think, to take in the money.[436]

This statement explains Corbett's decision-making process in years to come. He generally made the decisions that made the best business sense, which is why he later became more interested in exhibiting and acting than fighting.

On February 5, Corbett signed a contract agreeing to meet the winner of the Jackson-Slavin contest, the fight to be held in New Orleans for a $15,000 purse. Jackson responded by saying, "I have said before that I will not fight in New Orleans...not that I don't think I would get fair play, but because of the feeling there against my race." Jackson consistently refused to fight in the South.[437]

Corbett was upset that Charley Mitchell had pulled out of their match. Charley instead went on a sparring tour with Frank Slavin. Jim said that he would exhibit at Madison Square Garden anyway.

On February 16, 1892 at New York's Madison Square Garden, Corbett imposed upon himself the task of stopping three men within 3 rounds each: William Spillings, Bob Caffey/Caffrey/Coffey (spellings vary), and Joe Lannon, the former Sullivan sparring partner and fairly well respected

---

[434] *Boston Daily Globe*, January 25, 1892.
[435] *Boston Daily Globe*, January 26, 1892.
[436] *Referee*, March 30, 1892, from an interview with *The Police News*.
[437] *New York Clipper*, February 13, 1892.

fighter. Corbett had on previous occasions sparred with both Lannon and Caffrey.

JOE LANNON.

Madison Square Garden was packed, with 8,000 in the building just for the preliminaries, and even more were present when Corbett entered. The crowd paid from $.50 up to $1.50 to watch the exhibition, and the profits of the show were said to have reached $10,000.

200-pound William Spillings of Rochester had a bulky form that was "too bulky for a man to fight with." The *New York Daily Tribune* (NYDT) said he was knocked unconscious in just fifty seconds. The *New York Sun* (NYS) said, "In two minutes Corbett floored him twice by judiciously administered cracks on the jaw, and then Spillings concluded that he had enough."

225-pound Robert Coffey/Bob Caffrey of Philadelphia, with his "surplus of adipose tissue," "went to sleep in short order," lasting even less time than had Spillings. "Corbett hit him a couple of punches within forty-five seconds and that ended him."

The spectators were upset at the ease of it all and cried, "Fake! Anybody can lick a couple of stiffs like those." Spillings and Coffey were described as novices who laid down as soon as they received a couple comparatively light punches.

Next up was the experienced 227-230-pound Joe Lannon, each local source providing its own account of his bout with Corbett:

NYDT: Although Lannon managed to last the 3 rounds, he was "badly used up" and damaged.[438]

NYS: Lannon had the sympathy of the house, for he looked like a fighter. Corbett, on the other hand, did not. "Corbett is such a good-looking fellow- so tall, lithe, clean-skinned; and prettily outlined- that it is hard for an old-timer to associate him with their own good fighters, and most of them were with the man who looked the gladiator."

In the 1st round, Lannon landed some "smashes that were hummers." The crowd cheered far more when he landed than when Corbett did. Lannon was on the defensive for a while, and Jim landed some lefts. Corbett clinched several times and often would not give Joe a chance to get away, which caused the crowd to hiss him.

In the 2nd round, Lannon landed a strong left to the stomach which Corbett "plainly felt." Jim grew angry and attacked, landing stiff ones to the body and head. Lannon went to the ropes, but Jim did not follow up. After Joe landed a whack on the ear, Corbett became wild and missed five punches.

The 3rd round saw Corbett's strength begin to tell, and Lannon was growing fatigued. Jim hammered on him and there was some infighting, but Joe's punches were weak. Still, Jim was wild and missed a number of times in this round as well. At the bout's conclusion, William Muldoon, the master of ceremonies, "decided that Corbett has won the bout on scientific points, and the general opinion among experts was that he had, but there were many present who thought he had no right to a favorable decision because he did not knock Lannon out."[439]

New York Clipper (NYC): Lannon stood up well during the 3 rounds, "balking all of Corbett's attempts to knock him out by stopping or warding off the latter's right hand swings, and giving him a number of very solid punches in the body and on the head in return for the hits administered by the Californian." Lannon did so well that Corbett frequently misjudged the distance and missed Joe. Jim's blows did not seem to have much force and he was unable to stagger Lannon, even though Joe was clearly out of shape. Corbett's supporters were surprised at how well Lannon did.

Although Corbett did outpoint Lannon, the performance brought him criticism.

---

[438] *New York Daily Tribune*, February 17, 1892.
[439] *New York Sun*, February 17, 1892.

A boxer who cannot do better than he did with a man who was defeated by Jack Ashton, and who is known to be simply a plaything for John L. Sullivan, cannot with reason be regarded as in the highest class, clever though he undoubtedly is. Other qualities than science are necessarily included in the composition of a thorough fighter, and some of these are apparently lacking.[440]

Of course, Corbett was not a knockout artist like Sullivan, and was not likely going to stop a man who had been accustomed to the blows of John L. The critique also failed to acknowledge the fact that it took Kilrain 11 rounds and Ashton 19 rounds to take Lannon out.

Back in Philadelphia, at the Lyceum Theater on March 2, 1892, Corbett boxed Jim Brady of Buffalo, "driving him all around the stage." Brady was a veteran heavyweight whose career included: 1884 LKOby3 Charley Mitchell; 1885 W4 Patsy Cardiff; 1886 D4 Cardiff and LKOby1 Pat Killen; and 1887 L7 Joe Lannon. A couple weeks later, a non-local source said that against Corbett, Brady "quit on the second round."[441]

In a heavyweight bout on March 2 in New Orleans, Bob Fitzsimmons defeated Peter Maher in 12 rounds. When asked his opinion of Fitzsimmons, Corbett said that he was not surprised that Fitz had won. "What did Maher do that he should have been so heavily backed...?" He said that Fitz was a "corking good man" and "in my opinion he is now justified in fighting any of the heavy weights..... He is game, clever, and a hard hitter, and would probably make it warm for anyone."

Corbett said that if Fitzsimmons wanted to fight him, he was willing to do so. He said that given that Fitz was weighing about 170 pounds and he was 180 pounds, there would not be much of a size difference. One paper reported, "Fitz, however, is averse to again going out of his class for a fight, so that it is not probable that they will come together, at least not for a finish battle."[442]

The following night, on March 3, still in Philly, Corbett boxed 3 "very scientific rounds" with Billy McLean before a large audience.[443]

In his autobiography, Corbett claimed that there was a local Irish fighter whom he was concerned about, so he conspired with his manager and the timekeeper to make the rounds longer so that he would have time to break him down, because it was one of those deals where Corbett had to knock his man out. Corbett knew that the fighter could not hit him, but was concerned about whether he could take him out, so he wanted his opponent to work and throw punches to wear himself out, while he played defense. When the man started to slow down, Corbett teased him so as to anger him

[440] New York Clipper, February 6, 27, 1892.
[441] Philadelphia Press, March 3, 1892; Boxrec.com; Times-Democrat, March 15, 1892.
[442] Philadelphia Press, March 4, 1892; New York Clipper, March 12, 1892.
[443] Philadelphia Press, March 4, 1892.

and make him throw more punches. Jim said things to the Irishman like, "I never saw a Protestant I couldn't lick." Corbett liked playing head games.

Pursuant to his pre-fight plan, Corbett was informed when the five-minute 1st round was about to end, and stopped and landed a hard hook to hurt his man. A right to the jaw in the 2nd round almost had him out, and at that point, the fighter decided to retire. Corbett did not want to give the real name of the fighter whom he dubbed "Mike McGuinness" because he said that he had been threatened with litigation after telling this story in vaudeville engagements. However, based on a review of his record, it is likely that the fighter was Mike Monahan or Monaghan, whom Corbett stopped in the 2nd round.[444]

A local Philadelphia report said that Corbett fought Mike Monahan on March 4, 1892. Monahan was a hard hitter, but could not reach Corbett. "Corbett played with Monahan for nearly two rounds and then he knocked him out. Tonight Corbett meets another good man."

Another local account said that it was one of the hottest bouts seen in the city for some time. Mike Monaghan had said that he "was going to try to 'do' Corbett and the latter knew it. The first round was lively, but in the second Monaghan kissed the stage three times and then the management stopped the contest. Corbett then boxed two rounds with Daly." A non-local report of Monahan's history said that he had won a state heavyweight tournament, and had made a good showing when he had boxed Jake Kilrain.[445]

The following day, on March 5, 1892, heavyweight champion John L. Sullivan, generally believed to be retired and done with serious fighting, issued his famous challenge:

> To the public in general and Frank P. Slavin, Charles Mitchell and James Corbett in particular:-
>
> On the 25th day of August, 1890, I formed a partnership with Duncan B. Harrison and entered the theatrical profession. ...
>
> Ever since the existence of the contract...this country has been overrun with a lot of foreign fighters and also American aspirants for fistic fame and championship honors who have endeavored to seek notoriety and American dollars by challenging me to fight, knowing full well that my hands were tied by contract and honor.... But now my turn has come; our season ends about June 4 and we do not resume again until September 12. This gives me over three months' time to prepare.
>
> I hereby challenge any and all of the bluffers who have been trying to make capital at my expense to fight me either the last week in August,

---

[444] Corbett at 158-163.
[445] *Philadelphia Inquirer*, March 5, 1892; *Philadelphia Press*, March 5, 1892; *Times-Democrat*, March 15, 1892.

this year, or the first week in September, this year, at the Olympic Club, New Orleans, La., for a purse of $25,000 and an outside bet of $10,000, the winner of the fight to take the entire purse. I insist upon the bet of $10,000 to show that they mean business, $2,500 to be put up inside thirty days, another $2,500 by May 1, and the entire $10,000 and as much more as they will bet to be placed by June 15… First come first served.

I give precedence in this challenge to Frank P. Slavin, of Australia, as he and his backers have done the greatest amount of blowing. My second preference is the bombastic sprinter, Charles Mitchell, of England, whom I would rather whip than any man in the world. My third preference is James Corbett, of California, who has achieved his share of bombast. But in this challenge I include all fighters, first come first served - who are white. I will not fight a negro. I never have; I never shall.

I prefer this challenge should be accepted by some of the foreigners…as I would rather whip them than any of my own country men.

The Marquis of Queensberry rules must govern this contest, as I want fighting, and not foot racing, and I intend to keep the championship of the world where it belongs – in the land of the free and the home of the brave.[446]

The $25,000 purse which Sullivan demanded in order to fight was astronomical for the time. Previously he had endured criticism for demanding so much money, being perceived as his way of pricing himself out of the market so as to avoid having to fight. However, apparently the New Orleans' Olympic Club was willing to meet his demands. The $10,000 winner-take-all side bet was also huge. He likely set the bet high enough such that no one would be willing to match him, or be able to find financial backers confident enough to risk parting with that kind of money should their man lose. Or it could be said that John wanted the "bluffers" to put their money where their mouths were. A challenger and his backers had to be confident enough that they were willing to come away with nothing if they lost, and to lose a lot of money in the process.

Sullivan really was not interested in boxing at that point, being content to continue with his lucrative stage career, which was easy money for him. He had been enduring criticism for three years for not accepting challenges, so he knew that he had to show a willingness to fight in order to maintain his lofty status. In his mind, the financial incentive to fight had to be large enough to be worth taking the risk and enduring the necessary training,

[446] *Philadelphia Press*, March 6, 1892; *Philadelphia Inquirer*, March 6, 1892; *Brooklyn Daily Eagle*, March 6, 1892; *New York Clipper*, March 12, 1892; *Referee*, April 20, 1892; Corbett at 164-166.

particularly when he was making such good money on the stage and enjoying the easy life. He possibly felt that the terms were sufficiently large as to prove prohibitory. However, if someone met them, he would have to accept or lose face.

Corbett immediately stepped up and said that he was pleased that Sullivan had challenged him, and wanted to fight him for the championship. "He says, first come, first served. Now I'll jump right in and put up the money." Jim was upset that John had classed him with bluffers. He had not previously challenged Sullivan "because he said he was out of the ring," and because he did not want people to think he was a bluffer like Mitchell and Slavin, who had not accepted Corbett's challenges. Jim said that he would be ready to fight whenever Sullivan wanted. "I can meet him at 190 pounds, and can, I think, train down and get into condition much quicker than he can."[447]

Corbett quickly deposited forfeit money, which each fighter typically deposited with a newspaper, which was later given to the other man should one or the other fail to be ready to fight on the designated date, or if they were to fail to make subsequent deposits. After making his deposit, Jim wrote Sullivan, "You challenged me and classed me among the 'bombastic members of our profession.' I now respectfully ask you to stand by your defiance. You said first come, first served. My money is up; therefore I am entitled to first chance." Sullivan immediately wrote his backer to cover Corbett's forfeit, and said that the fight would take place in late August or early September.[448] The fight was on.

[447] *Philadelphia Inquirer*, March 6, 1892; *New York Clipper*, March 12, 1892.
[448] *Brooklyn Daily Eagle*, March 9, 1892.

CHAPTER 12

Downing a Legend

By being the first to jump in and accept John L. Sullivan's offer, James Corbett secured the championship match. His backers were confident enough in Jim such that they were willing to put up and risk big money on him. The fight was for a massive purse of $25,000 and a side bet of $10,000 each, the winner to take all of the money. It was "the largest sum ever fought for in the history of pugilism."[449]

Men like Mitchell and Slavin had "failed to show the color of their money." Slavin said that he was already matched to fight Jackson. However, there had been indications even back in January that he could not obtain sufficient backing for a Sullivan match. Despite all the previous talk, the reality was that Slavin's backers were only confident enough to put up their money on Frank against anyone *but* Sullivan. Slavin hadn't even fought Jackson when they were both living in Australia. Charlie Mitchell attempted to negotiate. Sullivan had insisted "that Mitchell prove the sincerity of his professed belief that he can master him by backing up his braggadocio with a stake the loss of which would break his heart." Mitchell was unwilling. He had twice failed to defeat Sullivan anyway. Only Corbett had "acted in a business like, straightforward manner," immediately posting a deposit.[450] Corbett and his backers were either crazy enough or confident enough to take the risk.

Although Peter Jackson had the more impressive resume overall, since Corbett had equaled and done well with Jackson, Jim was a worthy and deserving contender. More importantly, Corbett was white, and that rendered him eligible to be considered for championship honors. Jackson was black, which automatically disqualified him. In early January 1892, Jackson scored a KO3 over Captain James Dalton, a former Sullivan challenger.

Immediately after the Sullivan-Corbett match was made, analysis and perspectives proliferated, for it was the all-absorbing topic. The *New York Clipper* said, "Sullivan will, of course, be the general favorite, but the Californian has impressed many shrewd judges very favorably."[451] Mike Donovan thought it was a smart move on Corbett's part, given Sullivan's deterioration. He said that he told Corbett that Sullivan "is so slow he can't get out of his own way. His stomach muscles are all gone, and he is flabby.

---

[449] *New York Sun,* April 4, 1892.
[450] *New York Sun,* January 5, 1892; *New York Clipper,* March 19, 1892, January 9, 1892.
[451] *New York Clipper,* March 19, 1892.

You can lick him in a punch."[452] Regardless, Sullivan was very popular with the masses, and according to Corbett, many Irish American citizens hated Irish Jim merely because he had the "insolence" to fight their hero.[453]

John L. Sullivan

Bob Fitzsimmons thought that Sullivan, "fit and well," would whip Corbett, but said that John "will have to do some training, as Corbett is a clever all-round man."

---

452 Donovan at 164.
453 Corbett at 171.

It seems to me, from what I have heard of Sullivan, that he will not do his work like a man who is going to meet a good and clever boxer. It may be that Sullivan will underestimate Corbett. If he does that, and will not train, he will be beaten, for Corbett is a remarkably clever man, and can hit a hard blow. Sullivan has no "cinch" with him at any stage of the game.

Fitz's manager, Jim Carroll, agreed with Bob. "We all know that John L. is a wonder. He has done many men in four rounds; but you must remember that this man Corbett is fast, shifty, and a puncher, and I like such odds as three to one."[454]

Sullivan's financial backer, Charley Johnston said,

Sullivan is perfectly confident.... He is not drinking at all now, and weighs about 250 pounds.... I still believe John L. Sullivan to be the hardest puncher in the game. Corbett is young and ambitious, but it will take all of his vitality to withstand a few of the blows that I am sure Sullivan will land, and yet I regard Corbett as the best man of the lot, as Slavin would be an easier mark than the Californian.[455]

The general feeling was that Sullivan would win if he was in proper shape. Reflecting this, Mose Gunst said,

Everybody that I talked with is of the opinion that Sullivan will win. ... Jim cannot punch hard enough or long enough to put him out. Corbett has a chance, but a poor one, of making a draw as he did when he met Peter Jackson. As all know, he is very clever and shifty on his feet and may manage to keep away from John, but the big fellow is apt to land on him, and if he does the battle will end in short order.[456]

One noted that the bout was "not for the P.R. [prize ring] championship, but for the 'boxing' championship, under the Queensberry rules."[457] Sullivan wanted a fight to the finish, and that was perfectly agreeable to Corbett.[458]

Corbett told the press his feelings regarding the match.

I think that I can defeat him; I always thought that I could. Ever since we boxed a friendly bout together in San Francisco I have had my mind made up that I could whip him. I think he will prove an easier man for me than either Slavin or Jackson would. I don't wish to appear boastful. I want the title of champion, but don't think that I

[454] *New York Sun*, March 23, 1892; *San Francisco Chronicle*, April 4, 1892.
[455] *New York Sun,* April 4, 1892.
[456] *San Francisco Chronicle*, April 4, 1892.
[457] *New York Clipper*, March 26, 1892.
[458] *New York Clipper*, April 2, 1892.

will gain anything by whipping Sullivan. The majority will say it was not Sullivan but the wreck of the champion that I met.

Corbett said that he was weighing 193 pounds and would start westward on an exhibition tour, making one-night stops at major cities.[459] Everyone wanted to size up Sullivan's next challenger, which helped Jim earn good money.

A March 12 dispatch out of Philadelphia said that Corbett had been there for two weeks, giving exhibitions against all-comers, easily defeating them all, including Jack Langdon (who had fought Mike Cleary), Mike Monahan, Jim Brady, Jack McVey, Sailor Brown, and an unknown Port Richmond heavyweight.[460]

On March 21, 1892, Corbett and Charley Mitchell got into an altercation at New York's Miner's Bowery Theater, where Jim was filling a sparring engagement with Jim Daly. Corbett and Daly's afternoon sparring was "extremely lively. Cheers rang though the house again at the conclusion of the bout, which was full of ginger." In the evening, an intoxicated Mitchell arrived at the theater with his sparring buddy, Frank Slavin.

> Mitchell rushed up to the American, applying the vilest epithets, causing Corbett to finally say: "Go away; I don't want a row with a drunken man." To this Mitchell returned hearty curses and squared off. Corbett then went into the theatre. Mitchell paid for seats and also went in. He accused Corbett of taking away his match with Sullivan and other engagements. ...

> Finally they were pushed out into the lobby. At last Corbett said: "I can't stand this any longer," and started to get at the cursing Englishman. He made one powerful swing at Mitchell, which fell short. The shouts of the crowd and Corbett's anger seemed to sober Mitchell, and he made up his mind that it was about time to get away. He dashed out of the theater and ran up the Bowery. Corbett ran after him but soon returned to his work.[461]

Clearly, these two men did not like each other. Mitchell later claimed that Corbett's "personal feeling against me is vague. I alone have cause for a grievance. Corbett (or his manager) in an underhanded way secured an engagement at Harry Miner's Theatre to supplant Slavin and myself, who had a prior engagement to spar there."[462] The seeds had been sown for their later grudge match.

Until his late 1892 championship match, Corbett continued boxing in numerous short exhibitions across the country, generally with Jim Daly. It

---

[459] *New York Sun,* March 15, 1892.
[460] *Times-Democrat,* March 15, 1892.
[461] *New York Sun,* March 22, 1892.
[462] *New York Clipper,* November 19, 1892.

was said that Corbett "makes the bouts pretty hard work for Daly, who is quite well tired out at the end of the three rounds." Corbett and Daly concluded their week's engagement of sparring in New York on April 2, 1892.

Over the next week, they were set to spar in Hartford, Providence, New Haven, Syracuse and Buffalo, and would return to New York for a set-to at Mike Donovan's benefit on April 9. Following that, Corbett was said to be touring as far as San Francisco, and then would return and set up training quarters at Asbury Park, New Jersey.[463]

500 spectators who saw Corbett box Daly 3 rounds in Providence, Rhode Island on April 4, 1892 were impressed with Jim's pretty display of skillful scientific boxing. Jim demonstrated "remarkable speed in leading, countering, guarding, ducking and getting out of his adversary's reach on leads and rushes. Corbett's lightning like movements astonished the spectators." The observers felt that Jim was all that had been represented.[464]

At the close of his week-long New England sparring tour, on April 8, 1892, Corbett and Daly sparred 3 rounds in Buffalo, where even standing room was at a premium in the packed house. First, Jim refereed some amateur bouts. Later, the "California Wonder" gave his usual set-to with Daly that left a favorable impression.

> In action he is quick on his feet, very shifty, and one of the most scientific and cleverest boxers that ever stepped into the ring. The bout with Daly was an excellent exhibition set-to and a better one has seldom been seen in Buffalo. Corbett demonstrated his ability to guard admirably, duck cleverly, get away in good style, and do quick and active execution with his "dukes." He strides round the ring like a giant.

Another local paper noted Corbett's strengths, but still felt he could not defeat John L.:

> Nobody can question his cleverness. He displayed science last night seldom seen in a ring. He is shifty, quick as a cat, jumps like a lightweight, ducks cleverly, but would never impress an audience as a man likely to defeat Sullivan.... Three two-minute rounds were fought and the audience wildly applauded.

Afterwards, a humble Corbett gave a speech and said, "The man I am going up against is the best that has ever lived. I don't know as I will win, but I will be in the ring September 7, and if I am defeated will go the way of many other good men."[465]

---

[463] *San Francisco Chronicle,* April 4, 1892; *New York Clipper,* April 9, 1892.
[464] *Providence Journal,* April 5, 1892.
[465] *Buffalo Courier,* April 9, 1892; *Buffalo Evening News,* April 9, 1892.

On April 9 in New York, before a crowd of over 1,200, Corbett sparred 3 "lively" rounds with Professor Mike Donovan at his benefit. "Their cleverness called out round after round of applause, and was the windup of the finest boxing benefit entertainment ever given in this city." Another local paper said it was only a tame and friendly bout, but the most scientific of the evening.[466]

A lot of the pre-fight analysis of the upcoming title bout focused on Sullivan's weight and ability to get into proper condition. Since his July 1889 title defense against Jake Kilrain, the semi-retired John L. Sullivan had essentially been inactive for three years, not engaging in any serious bouts, boxing only occasionally in some short exhibitions with men like Mike Cleary, Joe Lannon, and Jack Ashton. These exhibitions were usually part of plays and were more along the lines of friendly sparring sessions, often with short rounds. John L. had boxed in 3-round exhibitions with Ashton in Australia in mid- to late-1891, and did box in single 3-round exhibitions with Paddy Ryan and Joe Choynski respectively in November and December 1891. However, John's profession had been acting. During much of that time, Sullivan's excessive drinking had caused his weight to balloon up to over 250 pounds. He acted as if he was retired, and often said so.

As of April 11, Sullivan was said to be weighing a quite large 242 pounds, while Corbett was weighing 180 pounds. In assessing the match-up, Joe Choynski said, "Corbett is a great fighter, and he has improved and grown larger since I fought him. If Sullivan is in shape he will win." However, Sullivan's former trainer, William Muldoon, "says that he doubts Sullivan's ability to get into the pink of condition, and he must do so to whip Corbett, as the latter is a far better man than Kilrain." Parson Davies said,

> I believe the Californian will worry the big fellow a good deal.... Corbett will set a merry pace for John and it will be a long fight. It may result in a draw. If Sullivan goes into the ring in any sort of condition he ought to win, but it's a dollar to a dime that he won't be in shape. Corbett is a strong, active fellow, as clever as any man who ever donned the gloves, and if his heart is right, there will be some fun in the arena.[467]

Corbett's manager said that Sullivan was overconfident as a result of his long string of victories. Corbett said of the fight and his chances,

> I have sparred with Sullivan. I know him and respect his ability as a fighter; but I think my chances are good. The Eastern papers say I am too small. I shall weigh 190 pounds, stripped, when I step into the ring. Mitchell, McCaffrey and Jack Burke were middle weights and

[466] *New York Herald*, April 10, 1892; *New York Clipper*, April 10, 16, 1892.
[467] *San Francisco Chronicle*, April 11, 1892.

they gave Sullivan the hardest fights he ever had. When Sullivan was 23 years old and weighed 188 pounds he knocked out Paddy Ryan in eight rounds. Was he too small? ... I am quicker, cleverer and have a larger reach than John L. He may be able to strike a harder blow but I have faith in my ability to avoid his knock-out punches.

Jim said that he would go into serious training in early June under the tutelage of Bill Delaney, who had trained him for the Jackson and Choynski fights. He said that he would train up in weight rather than down.[468]

A prime Corbett

[468] *Rochester Democrat and Chronicle,* April 13, 1892.

On April 13, 1892, a thousand or so spectators in Rochester, New York watched Corbett and Daly spar (reported a week before as being a scheduled 5 rounder). "Many passes, leads, counters, dodges, upper and under cuts and body blows were illustrated in a clever manner." That said, the general impression was that Corbett was "entirely outclassed by the great John" and that "he has undertaken a contract that he cannot carry out."[469] Corbett and Daly continued with their sparring tour.

During April, the confident Sullivan said that he had stopped drinking and would begin training about June 30th. That would leave him only two months to overcome three years of less than serious work. He seemed overconfident. "I will not work as hard or walk as much as I did for Kilrain. Rope-skipping, football playing, tossing a ten-pound ball, and fighting the bag will cover my work. Of course I'll win-easily."[470]

On April 23, 1892 in Chicago, a crowd of about 2,000 watched Corbett spar 3 relatively tame rounds with Daly (the police refused to allow any rough work). Corbett looked solid and "hard as nails," not carrying superfluous flesh. He demonstrated his shiftiness and cleverness with hands, head, and feet.

> It occurred to seasoned judges who had not previously been so impressed that he can keep Sullivan guessing and that it will bother the big fellow a whole lot to hit him. He had Daly blowing before the end of the first round and the big Philadelphian had to hustle to keep up the pace.

Corbett was scheduled to commence serious training on June 10. He was reported to be weighing 190 pounds and expected to enter the ring only a few pounds lighter.[471]

John L. Sullivan arrived in Chicago on April 24, 1892, still touring with his play. He said, "I am going up against a hot game...and so, for that matter, is Corbett. Of course, I expect to win." Sullivan said that he was weighing 248 pounds and had not touched a drop of liquor in three months.[472]

In his autobiography, published just before his match with Corbett, Sullivan said,

> Ever since I was matched against Jim Corbett various alleged authorities throughout the country have been predicting my fistic downfall on the ground that I could never get well enough to fight

[469] *Rochester Union and Advertiser*, April 9, 14, 1892.
[470] *Chicago Tribune*, April 19, 1892.
[471] *Chicago Times*, April 24, 1892; *Chicago Tribune*, April 24, 1892; *Chicago Herald*, April 20, 23, 1892. It was advertised that Corbett was to meet Peter McCann that evening in a 4-round contest, but they were not allowed to box.
[472] *Chicago Herald*, April 25, 1892.

again with the old-time vim which has marked all of my struggles in the ring.[473]

Sullivan disagreed with the skeptics, and was apparently working his way into some sort of shape. He was appearing in Philadelphia in early May 1892, performing in his play, *Honest Hearts and Willing Hands*. It was said that a month ago he was weighing 257 pounds, but had dropped down to 240. He was sparring with Jack Ashton.[474] However, his sparring was merely part of the third act of the play, and they only worked 3 rounds. That said, a report of the May 16th showing of the play in Brooklyn said,

> [John was] quick and active throughout, and, of course, hit Ashton almost when and where he pleased. And he landed some very hard blows, too. The general opinion of the audience seemed to be that Sullivan would defeat Corbett easily and showed the champion to be the same old favorite.[475]

Corbett and Daly's tour included sparring in Milwaukee, Minneapolis, Vancouver, Tacoma, and Portland, up until mid-May, when they arrived and remained in San Francisco for ten days. He was then to return to New York, arriving at the beginning of June, giving exhibitions on the way back.[476]

Corbett arrived in San Francisco on May 14. In an interview, Jim said that although he had bad hands, he had been hitting straighter, which not only better protected his hands, but added force to his blows. That evening, Corbett sparred Manfred Olsen of Galway, Ireland, who "dropped in the first round without being hit." Jim then boxed 3 rounds with Daly, who had earlier sparred a black fighter.

Corbett was said to be looking fat, and "still uses a round-arm swing, and does not seem to be able to get in the straight blows he claims to have recently adopted in place of his old swings." Many felt that Jim had no chance with Sullivan. "Though Corbett may use up every inch of the twenty-four foot ring in keeping away from Sullivan until the latter becomes tired, it is doubtful if there are enough inches for him to skip about in." It was also opined that Jim did not have enough force in his punches.

On May 19, Jim sparred Daly at the Olympic on "ladies night," when the women far outnumbered the men present.[477]

When his week's stay in San Francisco was up, the local paper said that over the next two weeks Corbett would give exhibitions in Los Angeles and San Diego, and throughout Arizona, New Mexico and Colorado, before

---

[473] John L. Sullivan, *I can lick any sonofabitch in the house!* (Carson City: Proteus Publishing Co., 1979) 201, a reprint of the 1892 autobiography by Sullivan called *Life and Reminiscences of a Nineteenth Century Gladiator*.
[474] *Philadelphia Inquirer*, May 8, 1892.
[475] *New York Herald*, May 17, 1892.
[476] Fields at 54-55.
[477] *San Francisco Chronicle*, May 20, 1892.

going to Asbury Park, New Jersey, where his training headquarters would be.[478] A secondary source said that they also exhibited in Canton, Ohio.[479]

On May 30, 1892 at London, England's National Sporting Club, Peter Jackson took on Frank Slavin for the heavyweight championship of England and Australia. Slavin was so well thought of such that he "was looked upon as a sure winner" against Jackson. Slavin's excellent performances against Bill Farnan, Jack Burke, Jem Smith, Joe McAuliffe and Jake Kilrain gave them good reasons to make him the 2 to 1 betting favorite. He had demonstrated solid conditioning and very good power. However, one San Francisco expert said,

> With the exception of Sullivan, I regard Jackson as the greatest fighter in the world. The big fellow [Sullivan], however, is the best man of them all….. Jackson…is too clever a man for Slavin, and will not let him reach him…. Jackson is not a rusher or quick fighter. He is like Jack Dempsey, and finishes his men slowly.[480]

A San Francisco report a year earlier had agreed, saying,

> The general opinion is that Slavin would find it exceedingly difficult to land on Jackson, and that the colored man would cut him to ribbons, as he is not, like Corbett, a fighter who avoids punishment.

> Slavin is a one-blow puncher…and mind what I tell you, as soon as he comes in front of a man who can guard his body the Australian will not be in it. Slavin's punch is a heavy right-hand drive on the ribs. He depends on landing that blow in order to win. Either Jackson or Corbett could avoid the delivery, and either of the two would give him a very lively mill.[481]

The Jackson-Slavin bout was scheduled for 20 rounds with 4-ounce gloves in a 20-square-foot ring, for a purse to be divided 1,750 pounds to the winner, and 250 pounds to the loser (approximately $8,750/$1,250). Jackson weighed 192-196 pounds to Slavin's 185-188 pounds. One of Jackson's seconds was Joe Choynski, his sparring partner.

The *New York Times* reported that Jackson kept his long left constantly in Slavin's face in the 1st round, although not with much force. Slavin attacked viciously in the 2nd round, but Jackson kept him off with his left and was able to neutralize him on the inside. Peter fired his left and right in succession to Slavin's body. Frank's eye began closing in the 3rd round. Slavin kept boring in, but could not land his right on Jackson. The pace was very fast, but Jackson usually had the best of the exchanges.

---

[478] *San Francisco Chronicle*, May 15, 16, 1892.
[479] Fields at 54-55.
[480] *Referee*, April 20, 1892.
[481] *San Francisco Evening Post*, June 27, 1891.

In the 6th round, Slavin cornered Peter and landed two strong punches to the ribs, but Jackson got out of the corner and landed a left. Slavin's eye was nearly closed during the 7th from the repeated lefts. Jackson continued pounding on him with both hands in subsequent rounds, even though Slavin kept firing away and trying hard, occasionally landing a good punch.

In the 10th round, a right to the throat sent Slavin to the ropes. Jackson attacked with both hands, dazing him. Peter fought Slavin "all around the ring and succeeded in knocking him out in the first two minutes of the round." Jackson had displayed "wonderful science," though Slavin's "sudden collapse in the tenth round was an utter surprise to the majority of the spectators, who had thought that Jackson could win only by points."

> [Slavin], as he lay helpless and disfigured on the floor of the stage, appeared to be almost dead…. He lay motionless on the hard boards, with his eyes tightly closed, his face badly swollen and discolored, and his body covered with the blood which flowed from the cuts caused by the sledge-hammer blows dealt by Jackson.[482]

Some, like the *Referee* in Australia, billed the Slavin v. Jackson bout as being for the world's championship.[483] The *National Police Gazette* had previously named Slavin as the world champion as far back as 1890, when Sullivan had failed to accept his challenges. Defeating a fighter with the very impressive credentials of Frank Slavin certainly highlighted and confirmed the worthiness of Peter Jackson as a top contender, if not champion.

Beginning on June 6, Corbett and Daly sparred in New York for a week, during the performance of the play *Sport McAllister*. A doctor who examined Corbett on that date said that he stood 6'1 ½" and weighed 195 pounds. Bill Delaney said that they would leave New York on the 13th to set up training quarters in Asbury Park, New Jersey.

For his training, Delaney said that Corbett would take an 8-mile morning walk. In the afternoon he would walk about 15 miles, and also do some running. He would then punch the bag, skip rope, and play handball. Later, he would engage in wrestling and neck pulling. He would then box a couple rounds with Jim Daly. "I predict that Jim will be as perfect a conditioned man as ever stepped into a ring. He must be, for he is going to meet the best man that the world so far has produced."[484]

Sullivan also went into serious training in early June, when his theatrical season ended. One late June report said that Sullivan had reduced his weight from 243 pounds to 230 pounds in one day.[485] By late July, Sullivan was said to be weighing 221 pounds.[486] Some reported that he was weighing

---

[482] *New York Times*, May 31, 1892; Harold Furniss, editor, *Famous Fights, Police Budget Edition*, Volume 7, No. 91 (London: Frank Shaw, publisher, 1901-1904), 194-200.
[483] *Referee*, July 13, 1892.
[484] *New York Clipper*, June 11, 1892; *New York Sun*, June 7, 9, 1892.
[485] *Brooklyn Daily Eagle*, June 29, 1892.
[486] *Brooklyn Daily Eagle*, July 20, 1892.

206 pounds in late August 1892. One critic later questioned the prudence of losing so much weight so quickly, and training for such a short period of time after such a lengthy period of inactivity. It likely had an adverse effect.

> No man's strength is so deceptive as that of the athlete who has been trained down to condition in too short a time. Sullivan had not trained for three years... During all that time he had been drinking like a fish, and his weight never fell below 259 pounds.[487]

Some said that although Sullivan was the greatest fighter of his day, his time had passed, that he would meet his master in science, and that even if he could be gotten into shape, he would not be able to hit Corbett.[488]

Corbett and Daly gave sparring exhibitions on July 20 and 21 in the New York area, making a few bucks. In early August, John McVey, the heavyweight wrestler who had sparred Corbett in January 1892, was added to the training camp. On August 13, 1892 in Trenton, New Jersey, Corbett and McVey sparred as part of the *After Dark* company performance.[489]

As the fight approached, in late August 1892, Corbett continued sparring and training with Daly and McVey, and the newspapers frequently reported on Jim's activities. On August 19 at Asbury Park, New Jersey, Jim "wrestled, pushed, pulled, clinched, and broke away from big McVey for a half hour, and then went in for the punching bag." Jim also did some running sprints. Daly said that Corbett was in perfect shape.[490]

On August 20 at Newark, New Jersey before a packed house, Corbett engaged in Greco-Roman wrestling with McVey (or McVeigh), who weighed 235 pounds to Corbett's 188 pounds. Despite their size disparity, Corbett displayed his strength, "literally dragging the burly McVeigh all over the stage. In spite of his great exertion, Corbett was not even winded" at the end of six minutes. After some intervening exhibitions between locals, Corbett boxed Jim Daly for 3 rounds, putting on a "rattling good bout." Corbett threw straight lefts and rights, as well as uppercuts with "dash and brilliancy," and did some "phenomenal ducking from Daly's right-hand swings." The bout was "as pretty a one as ever was seen, and fairly electrified the vast audience."[491] The next day, Corbett said that he was weighing 191 pounds and would not enter the ring against Sullivan weighing less than 188 pounds.[492]

In the subsequent days leading up to the fight, Corbett continued giving sparring exhibitions with Daly and McVey. On August 25 at Asbury Park, in the morning, Corbett worked the wrist machine, pulled the weights, punched the bag, and wrestled with McVey. The same activities were

[487] *Brooklyn Daily Eagle,* September 11, 1892.
[488] *New York Clipper,* July 23, 1892.
[489] *New York Clipper,* July 30, 1892, August 13, 20, 1892.
[490] *New York Sun,* August 20, 1892.
[491] *New York Sun,* August 21, 1892; *San Francisco Chronicle,* August 21, 1892.
[492] *San Francisco Chronicle,* August 22, 1892.

repeated again in the afternoon. On the 26th, still at Asbury Park, Daly and Corbett received "thunderous applause" before they gave a "very pretty exhibition" of 3 "lively rounds" which were "heartily enjoyed." Corbett's "wonderful agility and science were shown to great advantage."[493] On the 28th at Loch Arbor, New Jersey, about 1,000 people showed up to watch Corbett train. He played handball, took a six-mile walk and ran back, and hit the bag for 30 minutes.[494]

On August 29 at New York's Madison Square Garden, Corbett gave three separate training exhibitions throughout the day. He "exhibited remarkable skill and agility, and his feats of strength and endurance aroused the enthusiasm of the large crowd present." At around noon, Jim worked at pulleys, played hand ball and punched the bag, which was a leather fighting ball that hung from the ceiling. Spectators were impressed. "Why, they said this young fellow couldn't hit hard. If he ever hits Sullivan that hard he'll settle him." Punching power was something new to Corbett's arsenal.

After lunch, at around 2 p.m. before a crowd of 2,500, which eventually grew to double that size, including one hundred ladies, Corbett worked the pulleys for 20 minutes, threw the 8-pound medicine ball with Delaney and Daly, and then wrestled with 220-pound McVey, engaging in "pushing, hauling and neck-squeezing." "Corbett exhibited great strength and soon had McVey puffing and blowing hard, while this violent work did not even start the perspiration on Corbett – proof positive of his condition." Jim then played hand ball with John Lawler. Following that, he punched the bag for 20 minutes, "in a manner that drew out frequent bursts of applause. He astounded the spectators, not only by the rapidity of his blows, but also by their force. His right-handers were terrific." Another said, "His wonderful agility and his hard, clean hits elicited great applause." Corbett then ran around a track for 10 minutes.

That evening, another 4,500 spectators watched Corbett spar 3 rounds with McVey and 3 rounds with Daly. One report said they only lightly tapped each other. Another said that Jim was all over McVey, and the audience was excited by the clever manner in which Corbett ducked and got away. When Jim sparred Daly, he had the latter's nose bleeding, and Daly was very tired at the end of the 3rd round. "The audience shouted words of encouragement and hailed him as the coming champion of the world." Jim went through his long list of exercises that day "without being the slightest bit winded, and never did a man put in a harder day's work."[495]

Another report of the exhibition that evening said,

> Corbett so far outclassed the Philadelphian in speed and science that the bout was uninteresting. Daly then took McVey's place.... The

---

[493] *Asbury Park Daily Press*, August 26, 1892.

[494] *New York Sun*, August 29, 1892.

[495] *National Police Gazette*, September 17, 1891; *New York Clipper*, September 3, 1892; *Newark Evening News*, August 30, 1892; *New York Sun*, August 30, 1892.

dash and spirit that Daly infused into his work put Corbett on his metal and gave him a chance to show the spectators how clever he really is. The swings and straight leads that Daly makes showed the Sullivan men, who were there in great force, how quick Corbett could duck or jump out of harms' way if necessary. Several men were outspoken in their opinion as they left the garden that the champion would have to fight the battle of his life on September 7 to defeat Corbett.[496]

It was said that Corbett intended to enter the ring at his present weight, which was 187 pounds. This was the condition and sharpness that Corbett had going into his early September 1892 championship bout with John L. Sullivan.[497]

When Sullivan arrived in New York that same day, the crowd was huge. Sullivan's backer said, "The President of the United States would not attract that much attention from the general public." In Brooklyn, Sullivan and Jack Ashton sparred 3 short rounds, none of which lasted more than a minute. Although they were lively and Sullivan "hit left and right with great force," as well as demonstrated "a good deal of his oldtime speed," at the end of the 3rd, "the big fellow was breathing a little more rapidly than was desirable." And this was only after three minutes of total boxing.

Another report said that 4,000 paid to see Sullivan spar 3 friendly rounds with Ashton. One observed that the "big fellow was undeniably fat and his stomach protruded." Sullivan claimed to weigh 204 pounds. He didn't look it. A spectator commented, "I'll bet it's nearer 240 than 204." Another observer confirmed that John L. had rolls of superabundant flesh and noted that the crowd "had their doubts as to his ability to stand a long fight. He looked too fat to retain his wind during a siege of violent exercise." This was about a week before the fight.[498]

Corbett's manager William Brady said that after seeing Sullivan, he was more confident than ever, feeling that John looked fat and was breathing heavily and irregularly. He said that Jim was in excellent shape at 190 pounds, was hard as a rock, and could undergo vigorous exercise without being winded at all. Although he admitted that Jim was not the puncher that Sullivan was, he could hit hard enough to jar a man, quickly recover his defense, and could take advantage of an opponent in a dazed condition. "Corbett is one of the shrewdest generals who ever stepped into the ring, and has the rare knack of sizing up an opponent's tactics in a few seconds."[499]

---

496 *Birmingham Age-Herald*, September 1, 1892.
497 *Times-Democrat*, September 3, 1892, from an Asbury Park dispatch.
498 *Newark Evening News*, August 30, 1892. *New York Sun*, August 28, 30, 1892. *Birmingham Age-Herald*, September 1, 1892; *New York Clipper*, September 3, 1892. It was at that time that Sullivan's autobiography was published.
499 *Times-Democrat*, September 4, 1892.

Sullivan's former theatrical manager, Duncan Harrison, predicted that Corbett would win. He denounced Sullivan as a drunkard. He said that he had witnessed Corbett make a "monkey" out of Kilrain, and felt that Jim was shiftier and more scientific than Sullivan. He also noted that Jim "has not had to train down and tear his system to pieces by the severity of training to the extent that Sullivan has." Corbett, already in good shape, was easily able to improve his condition.

> Sullivan, on the other hand, has dissipated to a fearful extent. I do not know of anyone who has gone to the awful extremes that he has indulged in. Why, from my own experience, covering two years and three months, I tell the truth when I state that he scarcely ever drew a sober breath. I have frequently seen him drunk for five and six weeks at a time. ... On the conclusion of our season, on the 4th day o' last June, he weighted 261 pounds. It is stated that he now weighs 208 pounds, a difference of fifty three pounds. Of course that amount of reduction can't help but weaken any man. ... He has been on two big sprees since he commenced training, one of them lasting a week.

> It is claimed Corbett cannot stand Sullivan's rushes. Mark my word, if Sullivan rushes Corbett to any extent Mr. Corbett will have him at his mercy and jab him at will. It is also stated that Corbett cannot punish. I know to the contrary. No man has improved more in this respect than Corbett and, again mark my words, he will surprise you all by his execution in this respect.[500]

Another expert agreed that he liked Corbett's appearance better than Sullivan's. "It appears to me like pitting a good three–year old against a handicapper that has had his day. All good men, as well as good horses, meet their Waterloo, and I think Sullivan's time has come."[501] There were those who said that Sullivan was looking to be in fine form and his strength enormous. However, many felt that it was an illusion and that Sully was a mere shell of himself. One gambler said,

> His feet are still troubling him, and his fat condition…will make a long and winning fight impossible for him. I believe that, although he looks outwardly as strong as an ox, his powers of endurance have been undermined by his excesses of recent years.[502]

Sullivan's lengthy 15–20 mile daily walks to lose weight had left his feet badly blistered.[503]

115 pound bantamweight Dan Egan, known as the "Montana Kid," said that Corbett would win because he was "the cleverest big man with the

[500] *Times-Democrat*, September 1, 1892.
[501] *San Francisco Examiner*, September 3, 1892.
[502] *Times-Democrat*, September 2, 1892.
[503] *Times-Democrat*, September 4, 1892.

gloves in the world." He said that he had boxed Corbett in the California Athletic Clubrooms about six years ago. "Corbett broke that nose and I had to have the bone taken out. He can hit hard."[504]

Even Sullivan's own trainer, Phil Casey, admitted, "Sullivan had not done a hard day's work before in nearly three years." Still, he said that John had worked hard in training, with steadfast purpose.[505]

Regardless, those picking Corbett were in the minority. Despite his relative inactivity, weight gain and drinking, most experts and gamblers still actually backed Sullivan to defeat Corbett. It was a reflection of how phenomenal Sullivan's reputation had been over the past decade. After all, no one had been able to defeat him. He had overcome drinking and dissipation and even disease in 1889 when he defeated Kilrain, proving wrong those who then predicted that he could not win. They had learned their lesson, so to speak, and would not bet against him again. His legendary status made him a 3-1, then 4-1 favorite against Corbett.[506]

World middleweight champion Bob Fitzsimmons picked Sullivan. He also said that if Corbett won, he would challenge him.[507]

Joe Lannon, who had boxed in exhibitions with both, said that Sullivan hit him harder in practice than Corbett did when Jim tried to knock him out. He also said that Sullivan was as clever as Jim was. Furthermore, when Corbett was hit hard, "he forgets himself and goes all to pieces. I have been with him, and I know what I speak of."[508]

One writer said that Corbett was "one of the most scientific boxers in the business, and is as shifty as they are made and very quick on his feet." However, "it must be borne in mind that John L. knows something of the art himself, and is one of the quickest big men in the ring on his feet."[509]

Jake Kilrain, who had fought both, picked Sullivan. Kilrain conceded that Corbett was a clever boxer with a good reach, but felt that he lacked power.

> Corbett's hands are liable to go back on him. He hits with his hand open. In sparring with Corbett I found there was no steam to his blows. He would touch me and get away, but, while it looked pretty, there was no damage done.

Kilrain felt that Sullivan knew just as much about the game as Corbett.

> Now, as to Sullivan. In the first place he is a heavy, powerful man, very light on his feet. He is a good two handed fighter with an extra good right. Sullivan's weight and strength give him good advantage. If

[504] *Newark Evening News,* September 3, 1892.
[505] *New York Herald,* September 3, 1892.
[506] Corbett at 186.
[507] *San Francisco Chronicle,* August 22, 1892; *Newark Evening News,* August 13, 1892.
[508] *San Francisco Chronicle,* September 5, 1892; *Times-Democrat,* September 5, 1892.
[509] Sullivan at 208.

a man meets him he will drive him back, and by the time he is settled Sullivan is on top of him and pounds him down. That was the way he wore me down in our fight.... Do I think Sullivan is game and will stand punishment? I believe he is as game as a pebble. I know I hit him some punches that would have knocked out a dozen ordinary men, and he didn't mind them at all.... In any sort of fair condition I expect to see Sullivan win easy.[510]

Kilrain also said that Corbett did not like infighting and winced from his body blows.[511]

However, there were those who picked Corbett, especially the ones who saw him against Jackson, or who recalled how Sullivan had difficulties stopping scientific men smaller than Jim.[512] Peter Jackson believed that Corbett would keep Sullivan busy for a long time and that Jim had a "splendid chance" of winning.[513] One San Francisco report said,

Corbett's supporters, and he has a good number of them, rely upon their old belief that if Jim can't lick the man in front of him the man will never be able to lick Jim. This argument is based upon Corbett's cleverness on his feet.... Corbett's supporters build to a great extent on the supposition that Sullivan can never be got into condition.[514]

Corbett had proved his condition and ability to avoid being hurt in the Jackson bout. If he could last 4 hours with Peter Jackson, then he had a good chance to do so with a less than active and aging Sullivan. Some felt that he would fight for a draw. Corbett had the style to frustrate an aggressive fighter like Sullivan if John wasn't sharp. A Corbett supporter said,

A clever man like Corbett, with a good left hand will find Sullivan's frontispiece a very open mark if he rushes from the word go, as has been his habit in all his glove fighting..... Take a quick pair of legs playing shy of that right of John L., keeping him fighting wind and jabbing into his mug with a well-aimed left-hand as he charges forward, and it will be a new experience to him.[515]

In assessing the two, one writer who on September 1 had observed both in training said,

[Corbett] is easier, quicker, and more graceful, landing his volleys of blows with more accuracy of hand and eye. He shows less fatigue than Sullivan after a half hour's bout with the leather, his breathing being

[510] *Brooklyn Daily Eagle*, August 23, 1892.
[511] *San Francisco Examiner*, August 15, 1892.
[512] *New Orleans Daily Picayune*, August 31, 1892.
[513] *San Francisco Chronicle*, September 5, 1892.
[514] *Referee*, April 27, 1892, from a San Francisco report.
[515] *Referee*, July 13, 1892, quoting a *Boston Police News* report.

noticeably lighter. When Sullivan attacks the bag he uses great swinging blows, with an occasional quick, terrific upper cut that makes a spectator shiver. It takes a glace only to convince one that he is stronger than Corbett. The thunder of the leather as it batters the boards above is eloquent evidence that the champion's right arm has not its peer in the world. There is a marked difference between the force of Sullivan's right and that of his left, due probably to the fact that his left arm was once badly broken. Corbett's arms are equally powerful, and he depends on his left, with its superior reach, to stop Sullivan rushes. His success or failure in this will go far to determine his success or failure to win the battle.[516]

Another assessment said,

> There is naturally a great deal of discussion as to whether Corbett's youth will stand off Sullivan's great rushes and terrific blows. Sullivan's supporters think the fight will be a short one, and the followers of Corbett say that it will be a long one, as Corbett will not stay and mix it up with the champion during the early rounds, but will rather try to tire the big fellow and then defeat him at his leisure, all of which is beautiful in theory but extremely difficult in practice.

> Bat Masterson …is a Corbett man. … Bat said, among other things: "Sullivan is growing older, and Corbett is hardly in his prime, but you must admit that he is a great young one. I've bet $250 on Jim … If Sullivan thinks Corbett will stand and let him rush he will be greatly mistaken, because I happen to know that he won't."[517]

Five days before the fight, on September 2 in Asbury Park, Corbett's training was again vigorous. In the morning, Jim hit the punching bag. In the afternoon, he spent 25 minutes on the pulley weights. He then won three games of handball. Subsequently, he wrestled 40 minutes with Daly and McVey, and then sparred McVey for over 30 minutes. Another less local report said that he wrestled McVey for 38 minutes, until John finally gave in. McVey "was ringing wet with perspiration, while Corbett felt and looked as cool as an icicle." Despite his excellent condition and appearance, the bettors still backed Sullivan, placing wagers on him at 100 to 70 and 100 to 60.[518]

Jim subsequently headed south on a train towards New Orleans, the fight site. On the morning of September 4, just three days before the championship bout, over 1,000 persons met Corbett at the train station in Greensboro, North Carolina. After departing from there, in the baggage car, Jim threw the medicine ball with Daly and Dillon (likely Dennis Dillon).

---

[516] *Times-Democrat*, September 4, 1892.
[517] *New York Sun*, September 5, 1892.
[518] *Asbury Park Daily Press*, September 3, 1892; *New York Herald*, September 3, 1892.

Later that morning, Jim and Joe Choynski exercised together for more than twenty minutes, throwing the medicine ball, etc. "Choynski congratulated Corbett on his appearance, and gave the opinion that Sullivan would have a hard fight."

The train also stopped that day in Charlotte, North Carolina. Jim first jogged a mile and a half. He punched the bag for 30 to 40 minutes, and finished the day by sparring Daly for 40 minutes and then wrestling with him for another 20 minutes. Daly was unable to hit him, and Corbett's feints kept him guessing. Corbett "finished fresh, and every one pronounced his condition superb." "Corbett showed no symptoms of fatigue. He certainly possesses remarkable lungs." In the evening, he went for a 5 mile stroll and practiced some maneuvers with Mike Donovan.[519]

Sullivan was in New Orleans on September 4. According to a local paper, John was looking to be in grand form, and it felt that the stories of his being too fat were untrue. He hit a punching ball for 28 minutes, and then spoke to Bob Fitzsimmons for two minutes before skipping rope for six minutes. He seemed to be in good condition. After the workout, he was weighed at 214 pounds. Sullivan said that he did not enjoy training and that it would be his last fight, regardless of the outcome.[520]

Two days before the fight, on September 5 in New Orleans, Sullivan punched the bag for 36 minutes and skipped the rope over 700 times, but did not seem fatigued. Before exercising, he weighed 217 pounds. However, one newspaper said that rolls of fat were still there.[521] On that date, Corbett worked out in Spartanburg, South Carolina. He punched the bag, wrestled and sparred Daly, and tossed the medicine ball.[522]

In the days leading up to the fight, Corbett made it known that he would insist on Sullivan showing bare flesh from the navel up. Jim claimed that Sullivan bandaged up his stomach with heavy plasters for protection. Jim's trainer said, "This is to be a fight between men and not a trial of skill between upholsterers.... If it is allowed he might just as well come in the ring wearing a baseball mask." Quite a few boxers today who wear those huge protectors above their hipline should be reminded of this, as well as referees and commissioners.

There seems to be some evidence of Corbett's allegation. A report on Sullivan's fight with Kilrain stated that his "stomach and back were protected with a large strengthening plaster." Sullivan's people responded that he never intended to wear such protection for the fight and would not do so, wearing only his green trunks held up by a silk American flag.[523]

[519] *Birmingham Age-Herald*, September 5, 1892; *New York Herald*, September 5, 1892; *Times-Democrat*, September 5, 1892; *New York Sun*, September 5, 1892.
[520] *Times-Democrat*, September 5, 1892.
[521] *Birmingham Age-Herald*, September 6, 1892.
[522] *New York Herald*, September 6, 1892.
[523] *San Francisco Chronicle*, September 6, 1892; *New York Herald*, September 7, 1892; *Boston Daily Globe*, July 8, 1889.

The day before the fight, Corbett threw the six-pound medicine ball around for half an hour and skipped rope. He said that Sullivan was a 4-round knockout artist, that after the 6th round, he would have things his own way. Jim said he stood 6'1 ½" and would enter the ring weighing about 190 pounds.

Sullivan hit the punching ball for 25 minutes, firing left jabs and "chop-like blows. His right was used for short, quick swings, which seemed to tear into the leather-covered ball with force enough to break the rope." It was also observed, "In dodging and side stepping the champion was exceptionally clever." He then jumped rope over 700 times. Later in the day, he went through this exercise once again, and then took a swim with Bob Fitzsimmons.[524] No one mentioned it, but this amount of work seemed excessive the day before a fight to the finish.

THE OLYMPIC ATHLETIC CLUB BUILDING, NEW ORLEANS, LA.

On September 7, 1892, at the Olympic Club in New Orleans, Louisiana, a 26-year-old James J. Corbett took on the 33-year-old (one month shy of 34) heavyweight champion, John L. Sullivan. The bout was fought under the Marquis of Queensberry rules using 5-ounce gloves, and was scheduled as a fight to the finish.

---

[524] *Times-Democrat*, September 7, 1892.

The round by round account herein is an amalgamation of multiple sources, which mostly agreed upon what happened. These sources include the *New Orleans Daily Picayune* ("Picayune") and the *New Orleans Times-Democrat* ("Times-Democrat"), the local papers, the nearby *Birmingham Age-Herald* ("Age"), the *New York Times* ("Times"), *New York Herald* ("Herald"), and *New York Sun* ("Sun"), major publications from a major city, and Corbett's competing hometown newspapers, the *San Francisco Chronicle* ("Chronicle") and *San Francisco Examiner* ("Examiner"). From these sources, a general sense of what happened in each round can be obtained. As usual, there are some variations between sources, but those variations will be addressed only where significant.

The *Times* and *Sun* both said that Sullivan weighed 212 pounds to Corbett's 187 pounds, their weights as taken and announced before they stepped into the ring. The *Chronicle* said Corbett looked 195 and that Sullivan was 212. The local *Picayune* said that Sullivan was 212 to Corbett's 178 pounds, although this contradicted recent news reports that said Corbett intended to enter the ring in the high 180s. The local *Times-Democrat* said the weights as announced were Sullivan 212, Corbett 189. It said that Corbett weighed 178 *after* the fight. The *Age* said that Sullivan weighed 212 to Corbett's 189. The *Referee*, an Australian paper, reported that Corbett was 188 to Sullivan's 216.

Reports of crowd-size ranged anywhere from 7,000 to 9,000 to 11,500 persons, which contained everything from "the millionaire banker to the street fakir. Politicians, lawyers, merchants, gamblers, newspaper reporters and pugilists elbowed each other." Present to observe the bout was Bob Fitzsimmons, who would later fight Corbett.

Corbett was a 4 to 1 underdog, but the pools eventually closed at 3 to 1. Despite the lopsided odds in favor of Sullivan, "those who looked purely at form failed to see why the 'big man' should be selected as the infallible winner." According to his autobiography, Corbett was confident that he could go for a long time, and that "no man who has lived the life that Sullivan has lived can beat me in a finish fight."[525]

At Corbett's insistence, Sullivan entered the ring first, having told John L. the night of the fight that he was willing to wait all night unless Sullivan went in first. This enraged Sullivan, but he acquiesced and entered first to a huge ovation.[526]

According to his autobiography, Corbett tried to convince Sullivan that he was not concerned about him by bowing and waving to the crowd, smiling and laughing all the time. When the referee gave instructions, Corbett would not meet Sullivan's stare, but instead asked the referee about the rules and what would be allowed. After this discussion, he then turned

---

[525] Corbett at 187.
[526] Id. at 193-194.

to John L. and aggressively met his stare, which seemed to startle and surprise Sullivan. Corbett then turned his back and said, "Let her go!"[527]

According to the primary sources, Sullivan entered the ring first, quickly followed by Corbett. Sully wore short green trunks with a belt made of the Olympic Club's colors. His socks and fighting boots were black. One report said Jim wore light greenish brown trunks, green socks, and black boxing boots. Another said Jim wore nothing but a "rubber jack strap." The brown five-ounce gloves were put on in the ring.

Corbett's seconds were Billy Delaney, Jim Daly, John Donaldson, and even Mike Donovan appeared in his corner. Sullivan had Phil Casey, Joe Lannon, Jack McAuliffe and Charlie Johnson (or Johnston) as his seconds.

Jim looked pale, but wore a smile. Sullivan "looked as unconcerned as though about to eat his dinner." Although ultimately it had no impact, interestingly, Bat Masterson was asked to serve as the timekeeper, even though it had been reported that he had a conflict of interest: he had bet on Corbett. The fight began between 9:06 and 9:15 p.m. (depending on the source).

In the 1st round, Sullivan attempted to hit Jim, but Corbett stopped him and "danced all about," slipping away when John tried to corner him. Corbett's tactic was to remain purely defensive, keeping away, ducking, blocking and circling, to the jeers of the crowd. He had remarkable agility, and Sullivan could barely hit him. At every approach or feint, Jim would dart back or to the side, or simply run away. Jim ignored the hisses. Neither landed any blows, but Jim did not expend energy in attempts the way Sullivan did. Corbett simply smiled. John seemed angry. When he had issued his challenge to all comers, he said he wanted fighting, not foot racing. Yet, that was what Corbett was doing, to John's dismay and frustration.

Sullivan was the aggressor again in the 2nd round, as Corbett continued moving and successfully eluding, or ducking into a clinch. In one clinch, Corbett pressed his forearm under John's chin. After Sullivan rushed Corbett to the ropes, caught him a couple blows and followed with an uppercut, Jim flew "about the arena like a hunted deer." Both landed some blows in the round, mostly to the head. Jim also landed a right to the stomach while his left was around John's neck in the clinch. Jim continued smiling, moving about in a circle, while Sullivan looked serious, following him.

Sullivan continued his attack in the 3rd, smiling disdainfully at Jim's tactics. It was evident that Corbett was going to make a long fight of it. Jim landed two or three heavy stomach punches with the right, as well as some light head shots, all the while evading John's attack. This was the first round that Jim did any meaningful offensive work at all.

---

[527] Id. at 195-196.

Sullivan continued chasing and rushing Corbett around the ring in the 4th round, but was either hit by lefts or met with a left stiff arm in the face as Jim moved speedily about. Sullivan's blows were either glancing or missed. Once in a while Corbett would stop and land some punches with both hands, but not with much power. When John missed, Jim laughed and shook his hands mockingly at him. "Corbett's agility was remarkable. He seemed to escape Sullivan's leads with the greatest ease, but he did not work himself, and it was evident that he was playing a waiting game." The crowd hissed Corbett's defensive tactics again, which kept matters dull, but he was making John miss. "It was painful to Sullivan's admirers to admit that he was not the champion of old, being very slow."

The 5th round was the most exciting to that point. Sullivan began landing some hard blows until clinched, but still landed some short shots on the inside. As Sullivan rushed in again, Corbett abruptly switched tactics and brought out his vicious counter attack, stepping in and beating Sullivan to the punch, landing to the body and head, targeting both the nose and mouth with a rapid volley of punches, drawing first blood from Sullivan's nose with his left. Jim had been mostly defensive up to that point, so when Corbett suddenly savagely attacked, he likely surprised John, catching him unprepared. Sullivan clinched to save himself. The blood flowed from John's nose in streams. Sullivan continued pressing, but ate some good lefts and rights as Corbett fought him. The men were bathed in Sullivan's blood.

Jim hit and moved in the 6th, particularly targeting John's bloody nose, but he also landed some occasional body shots. Sullivan began slowing down and became more cautious, but still would occasionally rush in with some swings that missed. John's nose spilled blood. Jim remained elusive, but countered more often. "Sullivan was slow and appeared to have fully wakened to the realization that Corbett was not wholly adverse to mixing matters whenever the occasion required." Another said, "Corbett's quickness was marvelous, and he landed his left on the broken nose at the call of time." Still another said that Jim jumped around like a cat but not much was done in the round.

Sullivan tried hard to land in the 7th, but could not do so. Corbett was more aggressive in this round. He continued jabbing John's bloody nose and became more offensively ambitious, even landing a good right and rushing John to the ropes in a rapid rally. On the inside, Jim landed body shots and an uppercut. Sullivan "was tired when he went to his corner, though he had done nothing in the round but take punishment."

Corbett continued landing jabs to the body and head in the 8th, although John landed a bit more than usual in this round, including some rights and counters. However, the frisky Corbett countered and landed a left to the body and head, as well as a left and right to the nose or jaw, sending John back momentarily. Jim focused on the stomach and also jabbed the bloody nose, "while his excellent judgment of distance prevented Sullivan's well meant blows from doing any damage of consequence."

Jim kept landing his left to the nose in the 9th, but his tactics were not quite as successful early in the round. Sullivan mostly missed, but when he did land, "it was twice as heavy as his antagonist's." John landed some good lefts and a couple punches to the jaw or ear that made Jim more cautious. Overall though, Corbett's boxing skill prevented Sullivan from landing effectively or very often. There were some clinches. Corbett landed hard body shots during the infighting and continued landing his jab almost at will. Sullivan's lips were swelling. Despite outlanding Sullivan, one writer said that Corbett's blows "did not seem to weaken the big fellow, who appeared only tired."

By the 10th, Corbett was doing most of the hitting in the fight, keeping in range more this round, sending jabs into the nose. Sullivan did land occasionally, and a few of his blows landed well. However, the majority of John's blows fell short or their power was diminished on the quick moving Corbett, landing only lightly.

In the 11th, Corbett jabbed the body and head. Sullivan pressed hard for a moment and landed some blows, but was immediately countered well with a left uppercut to the chin, right to the ribs near the heart, and left to the side, all of which were effective and hurt. Corbett looked fresh, while Sullivan was bloody and clearly had the worst of the round. Jim was able to dance out of harm's way each time he landed.

Corbett began landing more lefts to the stomach in the 12th round. The body blows eventually lead John to lower his guard. Jim then went to the head, but followed to the body again. Sullivan landed some good blows, including a hard right to the ribs, but was always countered. The more effective work overall was being done by Corbett. Jim could quickly move in and out of range, attacking with quick blows when he desired, and smiling and laughing all the while as Sullivan pursued him. However, one counterpoint said, "Great cleverness was shown by Corbett in the way he jabbed and got away, but his blows did not seem to be effective." Tap and move was his strategy.

Corbett exhibited his ability to remain out of Sullivan's range in the 13th, ducking and moving away whenever John led, and the few times Jim was struck, he always countered. Corbett's style was like water gradually wearing down a stone. He cautiously moved, jumped and ran about, carefully picked his punches, and then sprung away out of danger after landing. Neither landed many blows.

Both landed well in the 14th as they exchanged a number of fierce blows, particularly early in the round. Although Sullivan landed a bit more often than usual in this round, his punches had lost some of their power and were ineffectual on the generally moving Corbett. Sullivan continued to be hit with the jab. Corbett remained comfortable, almost constantly smiling at

John during the bout. It was obvious that Sullivan would need to use his strength to overcome Corbett's great cleverness. Another version said of the round that no blow was struck "that would have broken a pane of glass."

In the 15th, Sullivan led hard but kept being countered and kept at bay by Jim's long reach. Sullivan rushed but was clinched, at which point John spoke to Jim. It was not uncommon for them to speak to one another. Corbett landed a right and left to the nose and jaw, bringing out the blood again. He also landed a hard left swing that hurt. They exchanged leads and counters, "mixing it up in lively style." Sully looked tired, and Jim landed a hard left to the stomach at the bell to the cheers of the crowd.

With his nose and mouth flowing blood, Sullivan kept trying to rush in the 16th round, but Corbett used his jab and kept away. Both landed some punches. Sullivan still seemed strong, trying hard to land a good one, but his breathing was labored. Jim jabbed the stomach and escaped returns with ease. Jim twice landed a left to the head and right to the body in combination and then clinched. During the clinch, John hit Corbett with a half-arm swing and the audience yelled "foul," but "Corbett refused to have the victory that way."

By the 17th round, John's face was very red. However, he continued pressing and landed some good punches, particularly to the body. Despite John's body punches, Jim remained as "spry as a kitten." Corbett stayed away more, but still landed his own occasional shots. Another account said that this was a very tame round, as neither landed any blow of significance.

Jim landed his left to the body, face, and head in the 18th round, as well as an occasional right to the body or head. John landed a punch to the ribs that "sounded all over the house" like a "bass drum," but Corbett countered with a left to his body. Overall, Corbett was landing more and was unmarked. It was still his round. Another account said that John twice landed smashes on the ear, but Jim responded by landing two scorchers to the jaw and following with three more.

The *Picayune* said that Sullivan began the 19th round looking dazed, while Jim was "fresh and smiling." They exchanged, but Corbett always landed. Corbett was encouraged by his ability to land as Sullivan's defense was weakening, and therefore he attacked more. Sullivan rallied, but Corbett again punished him to the body and head, sending John to the ropes. The *Age* said, "Sullivan is winded and has the worst of the fight up to this time."

The *Times-Democrat* said that Sullivan looked strong at the beginning of the 19th round, but his face and body wore evidence of the jabbing. Jim jabbed a tattoo on him. John tried to act as if the blows meant nothing to him, confidently awaiting a well timed rush. However, when he did so, Jim ran away as nimbly as a deer and landed a left to the stomach.

According to the *New York Times* and *New York Herald*, by the 19th round,

[Corbett] looked too clever for him and he laughed sarcastically at the champion as he leisurely boxed for an opening. Corbett landed two quick lefts in the stomach and Sullivan lost his temper from a staggering right, rushed at his opponent, but he looked like a beaten man.

The *Sun* said of the 19th round that Corbett's cleverness in tapping and getting away was greatly admired. Jim landed four jabs in succession. Sullivan landed a left to the breast, but Jim landed a couple rights, to the enjoyment and howls of the crowd.

In the 20th round, the *Picayune* said that Corbett went on the attack to the body and head. Jim's swinging lefts and rights sent Sullivan back to the ropes. John fought back, but Jim had a clear advantage. When John raised his guard, Jim went to the body. When the guard was lowered, Corbett went up to the head. Jim landed his double left - to the nose and then to the body. Sullivan fought back, but inevitably, Jim came on again with a rush of blows to the head, sending John to the ropes again. Sullivan landed a left, but was countered with a left to the mouth. The crowd went wild.

The *Times-Democrat* said of the 20th that a vicious left-swing terribly jarred Sullivan. Jim followed up with right and left three times, sending him back to the ropes. Jim landed heavily to the stomach and face. They fought fast and furiously, but it was all on Corbett's side, as Sullivan backed away, acting on the defensive. John was very groggy at the end. The crowd cheered and sensed that the end was near, for the punishment was telling on Sullivan.

The *New York Times* and the *Age* said that Sullivan appeared fatigued in the 20th round. He was beaten to the ropes by a right and left. "The champion was nearly knocked down with the left on the stomach and right on the head." Sullivan tried his right but received five punches to the head. Corbett continued hitting him. "The champion's knees were shaking, and he seemed unable to defend himself. Sullivan was fought to the ropes with heavy rights and lefts and the gong seemed his only safety."

The *Sun* said that Corbett fought Sullivan to the ropes, using a succession of lefts and rights to the stomach, jaw, and sides of John's head. Jim punished John repeatedly to the stomach, and landed to the ear and ribs with great force. Sullivan was groggy and weak, failing to protect himself.

The 21st round was the last. The *Picayune* felt that although Sullivan had been severely punished, he did not seem to be a beaten man at that point. Thus, it felt that the end was somewhat unexpected. However, John's head "seemed but a gory mass of flesh." He kept trying to land, but was unable to do so. Corbett must have sensed something, because he rushed him with a number of blows, driving John back. A left then right staggered him. Another left landed audibly and sent Sullivan down. John started to rise, but then fell back down again, out cold. James J. Corbett was the world heavyweight champion.

The *Times-Democrat* said that the final round was a succession of vicious rallies in which Corbett had the best of it. Sullivan was weak and groggy as a result of the consistent, "seemingly light, but really heavy and jarring jabs," which had been well directed and landed so often that they finally told. Those punches, combined with the uppercuts to the body, as well as the energy that Sullivan had expended in trying to land his vicious swings, had worn Sully out.

Sullivan was game, but had nothing left. John's legs seemed to quiver with weakness. His belly overlapped his trunks at the front, sides, and back. His face was red, nose, lips and left eye swollen, and the blood trickled down, leaving him a sad sight. Corbett on the other hand was unmarked.

> His cleverness in dodging, his quickness on his feet and his wonderful amount of wind had stood him in good stead, and though he had traveled four feet to Sullivan's one there was but the slightest possible approach to an impairment of his wind. He seemed as cool and as fresh as when he entered the ring.

Still, as usual, Sullivan led first, landing a left to the chest. Corbett defended some blows for a while. Sully feinted for the ribs with his right and landed a left swing, but received a similar hard left counter that hurt. Corbett then went on the attack as Sully moved back. Jim feinted his right for the head but shot the left into the stomach. Sullivan doubled up. Jim then drove the right to the jaw. John's hands dropped for a quick moment and Corbett was all over him with a rain of blows to the head, every punch seeming to land harder than the former. Sullivan tried to raise his guard but the blows beat it down. John's head bobbed back and forth from the lefts and rights. A final swing to the jaw dropped him. Jim stood a few feet away, ready to strike if John should rise again. Sullivan got to his knee and tried to push himself erect, but just as he rose and Jim was moving in, John went limp again and fell with a crash. He was counted out.

Another *Times-Democrat* description of the end said that Corbett landed the left and right to the jaw, jabbed to the stomach with the left, and finally landed a terrific right uppercut on the chin that dropped Sullivan.

According to the *New York Times*, in the 21st round, although Sullivan was bleeding from the nose and his lips were swollen, when the end came, "it was unexpected." Perhaps they just could not believe their eyes. Previously, Sullivan had been invincible. Yet,

> Corbett's finishing strokes were lightning in speed and force. Three times the left went into Sullivan's face. Four times the right smashed on the swollen nose and mouth. Then Sullivan collapsed. He went down hands first, then knees, then shoulders.

The article also said, "Sullivan was beaten down with heavy rights and lefts, falling to the ground. He attempted to rise and fight, but nature gave way and he fell and was counted out."

The *Age* said that Sullivan's blows were weak. Corbett landed his left on the stomach, and then rushed John to the ropes, knocking him around the ring. Sullivan was knocked down with rights. He tried to rise, but could not.

The *Sun* (providing two versions) said that at first, John edged in and Corbett edged away. However, Corbett landed a left to the nose that dazed John. Jim was out for blood and rushed in and planted a succession of blows to the head, face and neck. Jim momentarily jumped back with a smile, but soon attacked again. John backed away, trying to save himself, but he was exhausted and lowered his guard, receiving a fearful smash on the jaw, going to the ropes. The blood from his face "flowed in torrents and made a crimson river across the broad chest. His eyes were glassy, and it was a mournful act when the young Californian shot his right across the jaw and Sullivan fell like an ox."

Another version said that John staggered about until Jim attacked again, going in to finish him. "A right-hander on the ear and a left-hander on the jaw settled the business and the championship. The last blow sent the great John L. Sullivan to the floor with a thump." It was over after a minute and a half had elapsed in the round.

Sullivan was out for a couple of minutes. Water was poured over him and ammonia was placed under his nose. When he came to, he asked, "Say, am I licked? Did that young fellow do it?" After being informed that such was the case, Corbett came over and they shook hands.

Afterwards, addressing the crowd, Sullivan made a speech in the ring, saying that he had fought once too often, but that if he had to lose, he was glad that it was to an American. Sullivan's sportsmanship was admired. As Mike Donovan summarized, "Here was the man who had stood for twelve years the acknowledged physical king of the human race. In one brief battle his kingdom was swept away from him, but he took his defeat like a man."[528]

Bob Fitzsimmons provided his assessment of the fight. Early on he said, "Sullivan will never hit this fellow; he is too shifty for him." By the 5th round, Fitz felt that Sullivan would not last past the 7th round. In the 6th, Fitz observed, "That's the way Jim will win the fight; those continuous jabs will wear out any man." Of the finish, he said that Corbett hit the mouth and stomach with multiple blows. "Sullivan is gone – right and left on Sullivan's jaws; right and left again – Sullivan is down – just say that it was a rapid succession of right and left hand blows, and Sullivan unable to protect himself."

In summarizing the fight, the *Picayune* said that early on, Corbett danced, ducked and stepped away from blows, while the crowd hissed him. However, as the bout progressed, he took advantage of openings, punished John when the opportunity allowed, and stood his ground more than half

[528] Mike Donovan, *The Roosevelt That I Know* (New York: B.W. Dodge & Co., 1909), 186-187.

the time, mixing it up and constantly changing his plans in order to worry Sullivan. When he had finally weakened him, Jim "punched him out like a master," showing that he was a "king of speed and cleverness." Corbett was unmarked.

> [Corbett is] the evolution of the Sullivan era of glove contests… a keen analyst of men and methods. His art consisted not so much in the brutal battering down of an adversary, as the parrying of attacks, the accuracy of aim, the discovery of weaknesses, and the skillful acceptance of every opportunity for advantage. He represents the idea of the refinement of the science, of thinking and acting quickly in emergencies, of the perfection of self-defense.

The *Times-Democrat* said that the shifty Californian landed three blows to one and had sustained his reputation of being one of the quickest and most scientific boxers the world had ever seen. He started off warily, but became aggressive later. Sullivan made a heroic struggle, but finally went down under repeated blows. Jim's skill was too much for John's strength.

The *New York Times* called it a contest between science and strength, saying that Corbett's expert agility in dodging Sullivan's blows and eluding his rushes won it for him. Corbett was confident from the beginning, demonstrating his ability to stop Sullivan and avoid his punches, all the while looking happy and smiling. Corbett "ducked," "sprung," and even ran out of John's reach, but it was not a fight fought purely for survival. Corbett countered and moved away with "lightning quickness" before John could return his blows. He was more defensive early, his tactics designed to get Sullivan to wear himself out. John L. could not reach Jim. However, over the course of the fight, Corbett "battered his man badly." "The fight was fast and furious and Sullivan nearly fell on the ropes from left hand jabs on the head."

The *Sun* said, "From the start, youth, agility, and science were arrayed against advancing years, over-confidence, and strength, and Sullivan had no chance against such odds."

The *Chronicle* said that Sullivan was beaten "thoroughly and artistically," being "outsparred, outwinded, outpunched and outgeneraled." Jim won it from first to last.

> He started with a line of defense that he followed perfectly in spite of the jeers of the crowd, and when he had taken the measure of Sullivan's stamina he punched his antagonist to sleep in a hurry. Corbett more than upheld his reputation as a man of exceeding cleverness with the gloves.

The *Herald* said that Sullivan was brutally punished, his nose split, mouth swollen and cut, neck enlarged by the blows, and his body battered. He was outclassed in every area but brute strength. Corbett was able to dance away and dash in or out. Either way, there was nothing that Sullivan could do.

Sullivan said in an interview,

> I am gone now. I can't fight anymore, and that settles it. I had to go
> after him from the start to the end. He kept on running away. I swear
> that through the entire fight he did not hurt me until the last round.
> Then I felt a smash, and it seemed to me as if I was on a bridge and
> had fallen into the water. I tried to get out of it, but I couldn't. There
> wasn't a damn punch from him that hurt me until the last round, and
> that was where I received the knockout blow. That was all. He can't
> hit hard by any means, and I could not get at him. I had to go for him.
> …
>
> I went up once too often. Booze is a bad thing, I assure you. I could,
> seven years ago, at that fellow's age, have licked any one of them in
> the world, but that time has passed.[529]

He also said, "He hit me forty times and whenever he wanted to… I tried in
every way to hit him, but I couldn't."[530]

One observer said that Corbett coolly eluded Sullivan in the 1st round.
He danced about and when the audience hissed him, "he stopped suddenly,
held up his hands deprecatingly and gave the audience a look that seemed to
say, 'I came here to do a certain thing, and I mean to do it in my own way.'
He had his man gauged after that round." Once Corbett was sure that he
could avoid Sullivan when he wanted to, he focused on offense, alternating
between the face and stomach.

The observer also said that he had seen Sullivan against Kilrain, and
could tell the difference in Sullivan against Corbett. He felt that Sullivan had
deteriorated physically, and was badly trained. Ironically, in the loss, Sullivan
proved that he could absorb punishment.

Regarding the finish, this observer said that Corbett landed a powerful
right to the stomach that pained John L. and caused him to drop his hands.
Jim landed a left to the nose that snapped John's head back. He followed
with six drives with his left and right, Sullivan's head wobbling about. Then
Corbett drew back his right and landed a full-arm swing on the jaw.[531]

Corbett shortly after the fight discussed his strategy. He said that he did
not throw a punch in the 1st round, just using it to figure out Sullivan.

> He would lunge for me and I would gauge his force and speed and see
> just where his weak points were, then I would make a feint and try to
> bring out another weak point. In this way he showed me his entire
> hand. His best plan would have been to stand stock still and let me

---

[529] *New York Times, New York Herald, New York Sun, Daily Picayune, Times-Democrat, San Francisco Chronicle, San Francisco Examiner, Birmingham Age-Herald,* all September 8, 1892; *Referee,* September 14, 1892.
[530] *Daily Picayune,* September 8, 1892.
[531] *Times-Democrat,* September 11, 1892.

come to him…. I would have thought he had something up his sleeve, and I would have been very cautious how I went in.

His tactics were to use his footwork to size Sullivan up, throw John's rhythms and timing off, make him wear himself out in attempts, but also to use his footwork offensively, setting up his own attack. The crowd hissed at first, but he held up his glove to let them know that he was sizing him up, that they needed to wait.

Corbett wanted to keep Sullivan moving and not allow him to rest. "Whenever I would get away too far he would drop his hands in the expectation of getting a rest. Then…I would jump in again and up would go his hands." Sometimes when using this tactic, Corbett "went at him, knowing that he was not ready for me." Thus, Corbett used his in and out footwork to make John miss and keep him working, to disrupt his timing, and to surprise him with offense when it wasn't expected.

Jim further described his strategies. He was careful not to get hit by John's right. When he saw Sullivan setting for his right, he would either move away to throw him out of proper position for the punch, or Jim would step in with a quicker punch of his own. "I found that it took him some time to get in proper attitude for delivering a blow, and then I either gave it to him on the stomach with the left or on the face, always working around afterwards and keeping him moving his feet." He said that he generally would roll to the side from Sullivan's chopping left and counter with a left of his own. Corbett was not afraid to occasionally engage Sullivan, noting that whenever Sullivan's "eyes turned green and he looked especially ferocious I would make it a point to go in and mix up with him just to let him know that I was not afraid of him. This, I think, surprised him more than anything else." Jim felt that he could have knocked him out far sooner, but was advised by Delaney that Sullivan was still strong, to hit the body until he got weaker.[532] Corbett claimed,

> Sullivan is big and strong but I knew that he could not hit me. In the whole fight he never reached me with a blow…. I kept my right in reserve and cut him down with the left. When I saw I had him safe I ended it as soon as possible. I won by whipping him, not by keeping away.[533]

Of the finish, he said, "I really did not know how hard I hit him with my left until I saw the effect of the blow. Then I knew my time had come, and I went at him as hard as I could with both hands."[534]

Corbett later admitted that he had been hit with some good punches, but said that Sullivan was unable to cleanly land his hard right. He noted,

---

[532] *Daily Picayune*, September 13, 1892; *San Francisco Examiner*, September 9, 1892; *Times-Democrat*, September 13, 1892.
[533] *San Francisco Examiner*, September 8, 1892.
[534] *Daily Picayune*, September 9, 1892.

[Sullivan's blows felt like] kicks from a mule with boxing gloves on his heels. Sullivan does not deliver straight blows, or in fact any kind of blows, like another fighter. He down chops and uses his hand like a club somehow, and the blows make you think that the whole of his weight is in his arms.[535]

There is some existing footage of a much older Sullivan, as many as eighteen years later, hitting a speed bag with big swinging punches that had the weight of his body behind them. Corbett's description of how he threw seems apt in light of this short clip.

Jim considered quickness of eyesight and ability to judge distance the first requisite of a good boxer. He relied on ducking and using his legs for defense more so than parrying because he realized early on in his career that punches could sometimes get through his guard in spite of everything. This was especially true with very small gloves. As a result, he said that he had never been knocked down in his life.[536] Such tactics were perfect against Sullivan, because for years it was said that Sullivan was so strong that he could beat down any man's guard. Corbett did not rely on his guard.

Mike Donovan was in Corbett's corner that night, and years later recalled the fight. He said that Corbett was a dancing master, too elusive, skipping away, grinning at Sullivan, "making some contemptuous remark" and laughing at him. Corbett landed a left that sent the blood spurting from John's nose, and subsequently "jumped around like a grasshopper." Body shots in the 7th round made Sullivan double up in agony. Donovan told Corbett to finish him, but Jim listened to Bill Delaney, who told him to be cautious and take his time, fearing Sullivan's right. Donovan felt that Sullivan was weak and helpless, and growing weaker from his exertions and the extreme loss of blood from his nose. However, Corbett was content to stab away and move about, showing Sullivan respect, taking his time. "It was more like a game of tag than a fight." Finally, in the 21st round, Corbett rushed at Sullivan and knocked him out.[537]

Bill Delaney backed Donovan's version, saying that Corbett could have finished Sullivan sooner, but agreed that he persuaded Jim to take his time and not take any chances.

Corbett echoed his cornermen to a certain extent, saying,

I don't think Sullivan was himself after the second round. He was decidedly weak. He wanted to rest his arms all the time, but I wouldn't let him; I made him keep them up. He hit me most on the back of the shoulder. Some of his blows were so strange that I did not understand them. ... I came very near knocking Sullivan out in the eighth round. He was groggy, and I went in to finish him, and had

---

[535] *San Francisco Examiner*, September 9, 1892.
[536] *Referee*, November 1, 1892.
[537] Donovan at 177-184.

forced him to the ropes when the bell saved him. ... He had recovered by the next round and I determined to wait a little longer for a better opportunity. ... Jackson gave me a harder fight. He kept me busy all the time. There is no rest when he is in the ring.[538]

According to his autobiography, Corbett said that he decided to allow Sullivan to corner him early, while he was still fresh and had the energy to defend, so that he would know how to react when he was there later in the fight in a more fatigued state. This way, he would not be forced to learn about John L.'s tactics when he was tired. As he saw Sullivan setting up for a right, he sidestepped out of the corner, with the aggressive Sullivan after him. Corbett said that he allowed John to corner him in all four corners in the 1st round, using it as a time to learn, allowing Sullivan to think that it was his own pressure that was cornering Corbett.

Corbett did not throw much early, choosing instead to study Sullivan's moves and reactions. Because it was a fight to the finish, Jim did not have to worry about impressing anyone. Also, because the gloves were small, he had to be cautious against a dangerous puncher like Sullivan, carefully selecting his moments to attack. He allowed Sullivan to wear himself out trying to hit him.

The crowd thought that Corbett was just a runner at first, for by the 2nd round, he had not even thrown a punch, and they began hissing him. However, Jim called out, "Wait a while! You'll see a fight." This display of confidence angered Sullivan, who unsuccessfully chased after him like a bull, only landing glancing blows.

Eventually, Corbett again intentionally allowed John to corner him, this time intending to hit him with a good one. He looked around as if he was trying to get away, but just as he saw Sullivan setting up for a right, he beat him to it and hit him with a left thrown as hard as he could. It snapped Sullivan's head back, and Jim followed with a number of punches that sent John back across the ring into the other corner. He had broken Sullivan's nose. Despite the bloody nose, a determined Sullivan came out for the next round with continued aggressive ferocity.

Sullivan chased Corbett with big punches throughout the early rounds, but Corbett's footwork, head movement, and boxing skill proved too elusive. Sullivan always did well with other punchers and men who stood toe to toe with him. Against those who did not, a younger Sullivan had the speed and aggressive ferocity with his irresistible rushes eventually to get in on anyone. However, against a relaxed, defensively intelligent boxer, the aging and less fight sharp Sullivan had serious difficulties landing his bombs. Corbett utilized his whole repertoire, using combinations such as firing a jab to the nose, hook to the stomach, and then a hook to the head, in addition to using his side-stepping and footwork.

---

[538] *New York Sun*, September 9, 1892.

In the middle of the fight, a frustrated Sullivan attempted to hit him on the break, which was a foul that could have cost him the fight. When many in the crowd yelled "foul," Corbett responded, "I don't want it that way."

For the remainder of the fight, Sullivan continued making his bull-like rushes, but he rarely landed on the elusive Corbett. Jim noticed that Sullivan was starting to show fatigue and slow down by the 21st round. In that round, Corbett feinted a left, and then threw a hook that hurt Sullivan. He immediately followed with rights and lefts that dazed Sullivan further. Corbett then set himself and let go a hard right that landed and dropped Sullivan for the ten-count (and broke Corbett's hand, according to him). James J. Corbett had become the world's heavyweight champion.[539]

John L. Sullivan's loss represented the end of an era. He had been undefeated for about 13-14 years. His reputation had been built to such mythic legendary proportions that he was considered invincible. He was boxing. Therefore, the world was shocked at his loss.

Mike Donovan said, "[T]he American people have never lost and will never lose their admiration and affection for Sullivan. He was not only the most marvelous fighting machine the world had ever seen, but he was fearless and honest, always on the level. That will never be forgotten of him."[540]

Although Corbett's skill and accomplishment was admired, many felt that his victory was more the result of Sullivan's age, inactivity, drinking, and improper training. One critic commented,

> Taking into consideration the life he has been leading, Sullivan should have had twelve months steady work instead of twelve weeks. Previous experience had shown him that a 24 foot ring of all places was in no way suited to his style of boxing…. Men who had seen both Sullivan and Corbett fight were agreed that the Californian would have had no show with the Sullivan of ten years back, and on all hands they were loud in praise of the game stand made by John L.

Charley Mitchell, no friend of either, said, "It was not Corbett that beat Sullivan, it was nature and Sullivan himself. A few years back John would have knocked Corbett out inside four rounds." Frank Slavin said, "Corbett won as I thought he would. He was too young and quick."[541] Jack Ashton said, "Corbett is much cleverer than we gave him credit for. He hits a very much harder blow than we thought he could do. Sullivan is not the Sullivan of old." Joe Choynski felt that a good middleweight could have beaten the Sullivan that Corbett fought. Jake Kilrain said that Sullivan had lived high and carried too much flesh, and therefore had needed no less than five months of training to be properly prepared.

---

[539] Corbett at 196-203.
[540] Donovan at 198.
[541] *Referee*, November 16, 1892.

However, Charlie Johnson, Sullivan's backer, said that Sullivan was in excellent condition, but was simply outfought, and that Corbett had fairly earned his laurels. Still, Johnson also admitted that although John had retained his punching power, he had lost the speed in his legs. Pat Duffy said that although John was in good condition, he was not as good a man as he had been in 1889. "He was not prepared, however, to say that he could have beaten Corbett even if he had been at his best."[542]

A doctor said that Sullivan was actually overtrained. He opined that Sullivan had trained too hard over too short a period of time, rather than gradually working himself back into condition.[543]

One paper quoted Sullivan as saying, "He licked me square enough; but I'm old, I am. Let him go through what I have. Let him knock 'em all out for twelve years, and then see if he can do any better than I did."[544] However, Sullivan was also quoted as saying that Corbett was "cleverer than any fighter I ever met in my life. I let him hit me one or two body blows purposely, with the idea of catching him as he landed, but I couldn't touch him."[545]

The *New York Herald* said, "No man, certainly no athlete, can afford to indulge, even spasmodically, in those things which the laws of health and morality forbid, and continue in the full possession of the physical power with which Nature had endowed him." It said that Sullivan's overindulgence had "predisposed him to fleshiness, had caused him the loss of lung power and of the endurance that had once distinguished him."[546]

Jake Kilrain noted that although Sullivan was in condition, he was not the man that he was three years ago, because no man could do the things he had over the last few years and remain at his best. Even when Jake saw Sullivan at a George Dixon fight in late June 1892, John was under the influence of liquor, despite claims that he had stopped drinking. He criticized John's trainers, saying that he had not trained for enough months, and, "They seemed to think only of taking off his weight, without considering at the same time he was losing vitality."

Kilrain also criticized Sullivan's strategy, saying that it was not wise to rush, that doing so had been a fatal tactical error. Jake felt that Sullivan should have been calm, consistent, and methodical in his attack.

> Instead of following Corbett up in this deliberate and worrying manner, Sullivan made those savage rushes at him... I have always allowed that Corbett was a lot cleverer than Sullivan, who should have known it, too. But apparently he did not, for by his tactics he did not

[542] *Times-Democrat,* September 9, 1892.
[543] *Times-Democrat,* September 15, 1892.
[544] *Referee,* October 26, 1892.
[545] *New York Herald,* September 8, 1892.
[546] *New York Herald,* September 8, 1892.

appear to give Corbett credit for knowing anything about the business at all.[547]

The *Times-Democrat* oscillated in its analysis. At one point it said, "How much may have been due to Sullivan's age and, possibly, impaired vitality cannot readily be determined." However, it also remembered a young, prime Sullivan, which stood in sharp contrast to the Sullivan that fought Corbett.

> Sullivan was one of the quickest big men that ever lived; that with all his aggressive ability, which had in reality not been overrated, he was quick as lightning at parrying, ducking, dodging and getting out of the way generally. While his tactics were never to unnecessarily delay a contest, he well knew when it was desirable to rush and when it was prudent to bide his time. In brief, Sullivan, in addition to being probably the hardest hitter that ever stood in a prize ring, was also one of the quickest of big men, a thoroughly scientific boxer by instinct as well as training, and without a superior as a ring general. In this way many boxers of skill and comparatively good sense were ignominiously defeated.

It also said the following day, in more balanced fashion,

> Sullivan certainly did not show the form that was expected of him, and those who always jump at conclusions and then retail them as the most oracular of utterances, at once decided that Corbett is, after all, not entitled to any fame for having vanquished a man upon whom the hand of time and constitutional decadence had been so heavily laid already. On the other hand, there will be people of precisely the same class who will attribute everything to Corbett's marvelous powers. It is probable, though by no means certain, that the truth may be found somewhere between these two extremes.

Those who had seen Sullivan in 1889 and in 1892 felt that he had gone from a man of superior speed to one who was pronouncedly slow. However, the *Times-Democrat* felt that the analysis should take into account that "this was the first time Sullivan's speed had been compared to that of such a phenomenon as Corbett." It believed that it was difficult to tell whether Sullivan had slowed or just seemed slow in comparison to Corbett. "Altogether, it is very difficult to determine how far Corbett's victory was due to his own wonderful capacity as a pugilist and how far to Sullivan's supposed deterioration."[548] Such a debate would once again be repeated years later when Gene Tunney defeated heavyweight champion Jack Dempsey in the 1920s.

---

[547] *Times-Democrat*, September 14, 1892.
[548] *Times-Democrat*, September 8, 9, 1892.

Sullivan's age, lengthy inactivity, loss of interest, heavy drinking, weight gain, combined with overtraining in such a short period of time, and pro career that had lasted around 14 years, had left him at less than his best. He really had been at his peak in the early- to mid-1880s. Sullivan would have been faster, stronger, busier, and better conditioned a number of years earlier, and it is debatable as to how well Corbett would have dealt with that.

That said, Corbett had been schooled in a boxing club and had developed and honed his skills over many years to become the perfect foil to an aggressive fighter like Sullivan. It required the world's best defensive fighter to defeat a highly aggressive power puncher like Sullivan. Corbett was a skillful defensive master who utilized speedy, well placed punches, timing, beautiful footwork, elusive head movement, clinching, and relaxation. He was larger and stronger than some of the defensively skilled fighters who had lasted rounds with Sullivan, and it appeared that he had a better chin as well. James J. Corbett had the perfect style to give Sullivan trouble. Therefore, he might have given even a prime Sullivan the fight of his life. After all, Jim had more than held his own with Peter Jackson.

A few years later, Sullivan said, "[H]e licked a man that had tried to drink all the rum there was flowing in the United States, and even then nature went back on me."[549] Sullivan also generally said of the fight that he was never hurt until the end, that Corbett was not a hard hitter, but that he simply tired him out.[550]

However, over a decade later, in 1907, Sullivan in an oddly self-deprecating statement said,

> The fighting style of today is all shiftiness.... Corbett, it must be given to him was the first of the big exponents of the shifty game.... I didn't know anything about the Corbett stuff before I ran into it. I was warned about it by my friends, but I was bull-headed and incredulous, and I couldn't understand how mere quickness was going to win over me.... I honestly believed that Corbett would be a mark for me, and I trained for the fight on Bass's ale and big black cigars, so to speak.... I was...trimmed good, by the boy who was open-minded enough to study the fighting game from a new angle, and let nobody ever believe that his style of doing it didn't furnish me the surprise of my life. I believe that, even if I had trained faithfully and been in perfect shape for that fight, Corbett, with his panther agility and his new style of getting in and out again, would have handed it to me that time.[551]

---

[549] *Brooklyn Daily Eagle,* December 10, 1895.
[550] *Brooklyn Daily Eagle,* January 21, 1894.
[551] *Los Angeles Times,* May 12, 1907.

The truth was that a younger Sullivan had dealt with many movers and slick fighters. However, they were not as big and tall as Corbett was and were likely not quite as good at the outside game as Jim.

Still, even Corbett years later said of the fight,

> In justice to the man who had reigned so long as champion of the world...I got him when he was slipping; and that goes for all the champions down the line. It is very hard to tell, as you gaze down the list at all the defeated champions of the past, which was supreme.... Like the pitcher that goes too often to the well, the champ will go once too often to the ring, and be broken in the end. And all argument as to their respective merits is foolish and futile.[552]

---

[552] Corbett at 202.

CHAPTER 13

Resting on Laurels and the De Facto Color Line

Immediately after defeating Sullivan, the *New York Times* reported that the general expectation was that Peter Jackson was the next man that Corbett should face.[553] Jackson was obviously the number one contender. One expert for the *Daily Picayune* said that Corbett was a "wonderful fighter and it would take a Peter Jackson or Joe Goddard to defeat him."[554] Both Jackson and Goddard eventually challenged Corbett.

However, Corbett was not to be as much of a fighting champion as Sullivan had been in his prime. The day after the Sullivan fight, Jim said, "I will not fight again for a year at least. I can not; my time is taken up with theatrical engagements."[555] Regarding whom he would fight when he fought again, Corbett said, "Jackson I consider has the first and best claim to my attention.... I consider he is alone entitled to my attention." At that point, Corbett said that Charley Mitchell was a "stiff" who had been afraid of him. "He's unworthy of notice."[556]

However, within a week, Corbett changed his mind. "Corbett says the man above all others in the world that he wants to meet is Charley Mitchell. He has made up his mind to make Mitchell do more fighting and less talking."[557] A report almost a month after the Sullivan fight quoted Corbett as saying,

> There are really two men in the world today who have any claim to fight me, and they are Charley Mitchell and Peter Jackson, the colored man. Mitchell once insulted me, and I have always had it in for him.... I once fought Jackson and did not whip him, therefore he has a right to try conclusions with me again. I will not fight him, though, until I finish my theatrical season.[558]

Even Corbett admitted that Jackson would be a stiffer test than Sullivan. "Jackson gave me a harder fight than Sullivan. I had no rest when he was in the ring. Sullivan was decidedly weak." He also said, "I had no time to walk

---

[553] *New York Times*, September 9, 1892.
[554] *Daily Picayune*, September 8, 1892.
[555] *Daily Picayune*, September 9, 1892.
[556] *Times-Democrat*, September 9, 1892.
[557] *Daily Picayune*, September 13, 1892.
[558] *Daily Picayune*, October 1, 1892.

around with Jackson. He kept at me and I had to be on the alert all the time."[559]

Jake Kilrain thought that Corbett would be able to defeat both Joe Goddard and Bob Fitzsimmons (Fitz told Jake that he would fight Corbett), but felt that it was still an open question as to whether he would defeat Jackson. "I rather think Corbett would win in the end, but it is possible that the darkey would get the best of it."[560]

Sullivan gave his opinion as to what Corbett should do. "He can lick the negro and anybody, but he won't fight again. He don't have to fight again and if he fights the negro he is a sucker."[561] He also said, "If he ever is matched to fight Charley Mitchell or Peter Jackson he will defeat them to a certainty."[562] However, he was also quoted as contradicting himself, saying, "My advice to him is that if he wants to keep it [the title] he had better not meet the nigger Jackson. If he ever does he will get licked."[563]

Sullivan's opinions were a reflection of something deeper than a mere assessment of abilities, but rather a belief that the races should not compete. This was not an uncommon feeling about race relations. The day before Corbett defeated Sullivan, at the Olympic, a Canadian black fighter named George Dixon, who was the world's featherweight champion and the first and only black world champion at the time, defeated a white fighter named Jack Skelly in the 8th round. It was reported that blacks were so triumphant that,

> [T]hey are loudly proclaiming the superiority of their race, to the great scandal of the whites, who declare that they should not be encouraged to entertain even feelings of equality, much less of superiority. The Olympic Club management have about decided not to hold any more colored contests.

The *New York Herald* said that the making of a mixed race bout had caused "sharp criticism and much indignation" and it was felt that "if a white man puts himself on a level with a negro in a pugilistic contest he deserves to be thoroughly and completely thumped." It was believed that while such contests could occur in the North, "where there are very few negroes," such contests in the South could only "arouse a bitter feeling between the races which will lead to bloody affrays."[564]

The *Times-Democrat* wrote that it had been a serious mistake to match a white and black, one that it hoped would not be repeated. It noted that although there had been fair play, "it was a disagreeable duty to all Southern men present."

---

[559] *Referee*, October 26, 1892; *Times-Democrat*, September 9, 1892.
[560] *Times-Democrat*, September 14, 1892.
[561] *Daily Picayune*, September 8, 1892.
[562] *Times-Democrat*, September 14, 1892.
[563] *New York Herald*, September 8, 1892.
[564] *New York Herald*, September 8, 1892.

It was a mistake to match a negro and a white man, a mistake to bring the races together on any terms of equality, even in the prize ring...for, among the ignorant negroes the idea has naturally been created that it was a test of the strength and fighting powers of Caucasian and African. ... [T]he colored population of this city...because of [Dixon's] victory...are far more confident than they ever were before of the equality of the races, and disposed to claim more for themselves than we intend to concede. ... We of the South who know the fallacy and danger of this doctrine of race equality, who are opposed to placing the negro on any terms of equality, who have insisted on a separation of the races in church, hotel, car, saloon and theatre; who believe that the law ought to step in and forever forbid the idea of equality by making marriages between them illegal, are heartily opposed to any arrangement encouraging this equality, which give negroes false ideas and dangerous beliefs. ... Some may argue that there is no race question in the prize ring. We think differently. ...

Mr. John L. Sullivan has set a good example in this matter. ... [H]e has persistently refused to meet a negro in the ring. No one can believe that he has done this for any other reasons than his confidence that such contests place the races more or less on terms of equality.[565]

Clearly, many believed that boxing had symbolic social and racial value. William Muldoon, Sullivan's old trainer said, "There should be colored champions and white champions, and I would like to see the line drawn once and for all."[566] In places like Texas, mixed race bouts were legally banned until 1953.[567]

Immediately after defeating Sullivan, Corbett's trainer Bill Delaney said,

You can say that I am in a position to announce that Corbett will not meet Jackson again. He is averse to meeting a negro on principle; besides, all of his friends in the South do not want him to again face the black man. Jim is anxious to please them in everything, as they have proven true to him. Why should Jim fight Jackson, anyhow? He has virtually defeated him once, and that is proof positive of Jackson's inability to cope with him.[568]

Delaney also said that Corbett would pay no attention to any immediate challenges because he had engagements to fill.

---

[565] *Times-Democrat*, September 8, 1892.
[566] *National Police Gazette*, September 24, 1892.
[567] Svinth, *Kronos*.
[568] *New York Sun*, September 9, 1892.

Peter Jackson was the most deserving contender, but immediately there were excuses being put forth to avoid him. However, "Corbett himself said nothing about the Jackson matter."

Regardless of whom he would fight next, Corbett chose to take to the stage in plays and cash in on his new status as champion for a while. He did what Sullivan did late in John L.'s career, making as much money as possible with as little risk as possible. Corbett was already scheduled to begin performing in a play specifically written for him called *Gentleman Jack*, which would start in early October (His later popular nickname, "Gentleman Jim," developed as a result of this play).

Peter Jackson would first have to take a back seat for well over a year, and eventually would have to sit by as Corbett decided to take on Mitchell next. Corbett did not defend the title at all in 1892 or 1893, only occasionally boxing in limited, friendly sparring exhibitions.

Like Sullivan before him, Corbett had to absorb some criticism for not taking on Jackson. One paper wrote in late 1892,

> But does Corbett really expect the country to take stock in his sudden access of aristocratic exclusiveness, and to believe that his refusal to meet Peter Jackson springs from inherent distaste and conscious superiority? ... Such a refusal will be understood everywhere...as meaning that he is afraid of Jackson. There is no color line in professional pugilism. If Corbett avoids Jackson, after having met him once, the world will construe it as a back-out, and he will no longer be champion in any proper meaning of the term.[569]

Still, unlike Sullivan, Corbett did not say that he was drawing the color line.

> I see I have been quoted as saying I would not fight a colored man. That is not so. I have never said the first thing about the "color line." You know I fought Jackson, and I think the fight will prove that I whipped him.[570]

Either way, it was a rematch that never materialized, and Corbett did not appear anxious for it.

According to Mike Donovan, in the days immediately following his victory over Sullivan, Corbett gave exhibitions. It was easy money, for everyone wanted to see the new champion. Donovan claimed they gave performances in Birmingham, Alabama, Atlanta, Georgia, Charlotte, North Carolina, Washington D.C., and then New York.[571] A secondary source said they also stopped in South Carolina and Virginia.[572]

---

[569] *Referee*, November 9, 1892, quoting a Boston exchange.
[570] *Times-Democrat*, September 15, 1892.
[571] Donovan at 191-194.
[572] Fields at 65.

Corbett had hurt his right hand against Sullivan, but had not broken it as he claimed in his autobiography. The *Times-Democrat* noted that Corbett's right hand was swollen and hurt from the knockout blow in the final round. However, the fact that he gave exhibitions demonstrates that he merely hurt it. A doctor confirmed that his right hand, though sore, was not broken. At the time, Jim said of his swollen right hand, "I think it was from the last blow I struck. I was determined to knock Sullivan out then, and used all my force. My right landed too hard, and I have sprained it."[573]

The day after the fight, in New Orleans, Corbett played in *After Dark*. Just two days after the fight, on September 9, 1892 in Birmingham, Alabama, Corbett and Daly gave a sparring exhibition in an opera house that was "crowded to suffocation."[574] On September 10 in Atlanta, Georgia, Corbett and Daly sparred 3 rounds to a packed house.

They next headed to Spartanburg, South Carolina on the 11th. However, they did not exhibit there. Jim and his trainer took a run, but since it was Sunday, it was a violation of the Sabbath, and this caused a warrant for Corbett's arrest to be issued. They got back on the train and moved on. During the train ride, Alabama Governor Jones asked to meet Corbett and was surprised to see that Jim did not look like a prize fighter. Jim responded, "I am glad I don't look like a fighter.... I attribute my success more to science and skill than to any other cause."[575]

At that time, Joe Goddard challenged Corbett, saying that he did not think Corbett's victory over Sullivan meant much, and that he could defeat both Corbett and Jackson.

> Why, Sullivan fought like an old woman. He never was in it, and proved just what I have always said of him, that he was no good, and the most overrated man I ever saw. Why, young fellow, any good man could lick the Sullivan of today, and Peter Jackson would have made a show of him.

He also said, "It was plain to me, as soon as Sullivan stepped into the ring it was not the same John L. I saw in the antipodes; it was only a shadow of Sullivan."

Of Corbett, Goddard said, "Oh, he's a good one, but he is not too good. Peter can do him, and I can do 'em both." He also said that Jim was quick and clever and a good boxer, but "I believe that he is easy game for me, and that I could defeat him to a certainty."[576]

Goddard was consistent. Even before Corbett defeated Sullivan, Goddard predicted that Corbett would win the title and then avoid him and fail to accept his challenges. "I think if Corbett wins he will sleep on it, and

[573] *Times-Democrat*, September 9, 1892; *Boston Daily Globe, September 16, 1892; New York Sun*, September 9, 1892.
[574] *Times-Democrat*, September 10, 1892; *New York Sun*, September 9, 1892.
[575] *New York Sun*, September 9, 1892.
[576] *Times-Democrat*, September 11, 1892; *New York Sun*, September 12, 1892.

we will be old men before he will give me a chance. I think he was shrewd in meeting Sullivan, for the latter is the most over-rated pugilist alive." Joe had said that he was not all that impressed with Corbett. Goddard had twice stopped Joe Choynski in 4 rounds, while it took Jim 27 rounds to do the trick. Of course, Choynski managed to drop Goddard many times, something he never did to Corbett.[577]

The 6' 30-year-old Goddard had fought very well against Peter Jackson in their October 1890 8-round draw, and some claimed that he had the best of it and would have defeated Peter if it were a fight to the finish. He also had many good recent knockout victories, twice over Mick Dooley, in 21 rounds and 7 rounds (6-1890 and 11-1890), twice over Joe Choynski, stopping him in the 4th round both times (2-1891 and 7-1891), and a KO15 over Joe McAuliffe (6-1892)(after McAuliffe scored an 1891 KO15 over Patsy Cardiff). Goddard was definitely a legitimate contender.[578]

Corbett's response to Goddard's challenge was, "What license has Goddard got to challenge me, any way… He's not a champion. The men who have the first right to battle with me are Peter Jackson and Charley Mitchell. As I owe the latter a score, I will in all probability take him on first."[579]

The Coney Island Athletic Club said that it wanted to host a match between Corbett and Jackson. Analyzing the potential locations for such a match, one report said,

> There are only three clubs in the country which can afford to offer a suitable purse for such a battle – the Olympic of New Orleans, California of San Francisco and the Coney Island Association.
>
> Jackson will not fight at New Orleans on account of the prejudice which exists against his race; Corbett will not fight at the California Club because he claims he was unjustly deprived of a victory over Peter Jackson by the officers of that organization. By the logic of events, then, the rich plum would fall into the lap of the Coney Island Association.[580]

Of course, this analysis failed to recognize the fact that New York politicians were generally opposed to boxing there, and they were likely to take measures to prevent such a fight. The dearth of clubs legally and financially able to host the fight would impact whether it took place.

On September 12, 1892, just five days after winning the title, Corbett appeared in New York's Madison Square Garden before a crowd of 8,000, every seat being sold. With his right bandaged up, he sparred 3 short and light rounds with Jim Daly, "Corbett making scarcely any use of his good

[577] *Newark Evening News,* September 2, 1892.
[578] *National Police Gazette,* December 24, 1892.
[579] *New York Sun,* September 13, 1892.
[580] *Times-Democrat,* September 11, 1892.

right hand, but showing how rapidly and with what effect he could deliver the left…. He also convinced the spectators that he was extremely agile on his feet, as well as a remarkably good judge of distance."[581] One writer said, "Jim will scarcely ever take the place of John L. in the hearts of the people. It was evident that the tall Californian lacked the magnetism of the Boston boy." Still, he was capitalizing on his new status, as large crowds paid to see him.[582] Corbett continued making money traveling around giving daily short exhibitions with Daly. Jim was billed to exhibit in Baltimore on the 13th.[583]

On September 14, Corbett and Daly exhibited in Philadelphia. They were given a rousing reception by a crowd of 2,500, which included ladies. When he entered the stage, Corbett was wildly cheered for five minutes. The Jims sparred 3 spirited rounds. Corbett only used his left, sparing his bandaged right. "One hand was enough for the champion, however, and he gave Daly more than he could do to defend himself. Corbett's quickness on his feet was marveled at…. In the last round Corbett gave Daly an upper cut which made Daly snuff blood."[584] Daly and Corbett exhibited in Providence, Rhode Island on September 15.

Corbett's train arrived in Boston on the morning of September 16 to exhibit there that evening. A crowd of 10,000 was at the train station to greet them. Everyone wanted to shake the new champion's hand, and he obliged about 3,000. It was said that the reception equaled that which Sullivan had received in his prime, and Sullivan was from the Boston area.

Corbett told a reporter that he wanted to get at Charley Mitchell, that "after six months' rest I am going after him with a sharp stick." He also said that he was not afraid of Peter Jackson, "and when I think he is entitled to meet me I'll give him a chance for all the money he can raise. I worked hard for the honors I have, and it is only right that I should enjoy them for awhile." Corbett also said that the hardest fight that he had ever engaged in was the one with Choynski.[585]

That evening in Boston, sparring Daly, Corbett ducked, tapped and smiled, and was nimble and agile with both hands, not evidencing that he was lame in one. The packed house went wild every time he dodged a blow. One reporter said, "Corbett is, if anything, more agile than ever, which is saying a good deal." Daly was a good boxer, but the champion was far ahead of him. "His dodging tactics were marvels of quick, lightning-like movement, outrivaling Fitzsimmons, even, who is a past master in the use of the head. The rounds were brief, but lively, with, of course, no attempt at hard hitting."[586]

[581] *New York Clipper,* September 17, 1892; *New York Sun,* September 13, 1892.
[582] *Newark Evening News,* September 13, 1892.
[583] *New York Sun,* September 13, 1892.
[584] *Philadelphia Public Ledger,* September 15, 1892; *Philadelphia Inquirer,* September 15, 1892. Corbett was scheduled to return to Philly on November 14 to appear in his new play, *Gentleman Jack.*
[585] *Boston Daily Globe,* September 16, 1892.
[586] *Boston Daily Globe, September* 17, 1892; *Boston Herald,* September 17, 1892. It was said that Corbett

On September 17, 1892 in New York, just ten days after they had fought, champion Corbett boxed 3 friendly rounds with the ex-champion at a Sullivan benefit. Benefits were often held for the losers of fights so that they could make some money. It was Corbett who had won the massive stakes from the winner-take-all championship fight, so Sullivan had come up empty handed. As Mike Donovan said, "Corbett volunteered his services, not only with generosity but with excellent judgment. It is no exaggeration to say that millions of Americans were sore on him because he had beaten the old champion, and the surest way to gain popular favor was to show a kindly interest in the monarch he had toppled off the throne."[587]

When Sullivan entered, the crowd cheered for a number of minutes. When Corbett arrived, there was the same. The two shook hands in a friendly manner and the cheering continued. Sullivan gave a speech, which included the statement, "I have no excuses to make for my defeat. I was defeated; that is all there is to it, and the defeated man who makes excuses makes the mistake of his life." The crowd wildly cheered John's speech.

Writers called the boxing between Corbett and Sullivan "tame" rounds with "light taps." One description said that Corbett remained in range and exchanged light blows, although at one point in the 2nd round, Sullivan hit with a bit more power, Jim gave him a look, and then John ended the round by going to his corner. The final round featured Corbett ducking and countering with light blows, showing what he could do if he desired.

The New York Sun said, "Corbett looked young, fresh, buoyant, agile, and vigorous, while Sullivan's gray hair and serious expression of face made him appear very much older. The sparring was light, both men showing science without any attempt to hit hard." Some in the audience called to John, "Hit him, Sully," but he looked at them contemptuously. "The idea that Sullivan would endeavor to take advantage of a man sparring for his benefit showed that some persons did not understand the man from Boston." Obviously, it was just a friendly sparring exhibition, as it can be inferred that Sullivan would not want to seem a sore loser, and Corbett would want to appear a gracious winner and not take advantage.[588]

Corbett was scheduled to appear with Daly at Bridgeport on the 19th, Hartford on the 20th, New Haven on the 21st, Brooklyn on the 22nd, Danbury on the 23rd, and Troy on the 24th.[589]

Joe Goddard was pressing with his championship challenge, which was being ignored, saying,

> Corbett is champion and he may be a better man than I am, but that has got nothing to do with the case. He will have to meet at

would return to Boston on December 5 with his play.
[587] Donovan at 197.
[588] San Francisco Chronicle, September 18, 1892; San Francisco Examiner, September 18, 1892; New York Sun, September 18, 1892.
[589] New York Sun, September 19, 1892.

reasonable periods all comers who challenge him in good faith and put up a fair-sized forfeit. I have already posted a thousand-dollar forfeit. I will give Mr. Corbett due time for rest after his fight, time to fulfill his present show engagements and time to prepare to fight me. If then he refuses I will claim the championship, according to my right, and defend it against all comers.[590]

Goddard's manager, Billy Madden, said, "Corbett could be champion until he dies if he never fights. There are rules to make a champion fight, and I want to manage a champion of the world. Goddard says Corbett could not hit him hard enough to stop him in a week."[591]

Tradition dictated that champions were required to accept the first challenge backed by a $1,000 forfeit, and for the fight to take place within six months of the articles of agreement being signed. The *Clipper* opined in support of Goddard,

> A champion cannot ignore a proper challenge, nor do the rules governing such matters permit him to make a choice of an opponent, nor to defer the period of fighting till such time as may suit himself.... Otherwise a man who is the premier pugilist might declare that he would not fight for a period of five years to come, and yet expect to retain the title of champion.[592]

When asked what Goddard's chances were against Corbett, John L. Sullivan frowned and replied, "The blarsted foreigner has no show whatever. If they lick Corbett they must be good 'uns."[593] However, Bob Fitzsimmons felt that Goddard had a legitimate chance to win.

> Goddard can lick a whole lot of good men that know how to fight. The Barrier champion is not clever, and don't understand much about science, but he can fight and take more punishment than any man that ever stood in a twenty-four foot ring. And such a jaw! Why, he is the hardest man to knock out in the ring today. He would give Corbett a great fight, and while it is said that Corbett would tire him out making him hit the air, Corbett would break his hands trying to put Goddard out. He is bad medicine for the best of them.[594]

In late September, Corbett and Daly continued giving daily exhibitions. In one of those exhibitions in Brooklyn on September 22, 1892, the Jims sparred 3 short rounds. Corbett was said to be looking heavier than what had been represented, and was described as "agile, rapid and a neat hitter." Throwing clean and scientific blows, their exhibition was called superior to

---

[590] *Newark Evening News,* September 21, 1892.
[591] *New York Sun,* October 4, 1892.
[592] *New York Clipper,* September 24, 1892.
[593] *New York Sun,* October 4, 1892.
[594] *New York Clipper,* February 11, 1893.

what was generally seen. Corbett and Daly also sparred on the 23rd at Newburg, New York.[595]

They exhibited in Buffalo on September 29 before 1,800 – 2,000 enthusiastic spectators. When he appeared, Corbett was given an ovation for several minutes. He said, "I will now take a rest for a time, and when I fight again I will give Charles Mitchell the first chance." He was again cheered, and commenced his 3 rounds with Daly.

> [Corbett] displayed his great cleverness and gave a strong hint of what he can do when he enters the squared circle with strictly business intention. His quickness on his feet, artistic ducking, and general shiftiness came in for much admiration, and it was the unanimous opinion that he could "do" any of them – and especially Mitchell.

Another report said the 3 rounds only lasted one minute each. Corbett said that the exhibition "would have been more pleasing tonight but for the fact that Daly, my sparring partner, is in the sulks." Apparently, Corbett had been too rough with Daly, who was upset about it. Daly said,

> I had asked Corbett on several occasions to treat me with some degree of consideration while doing our turn; but he continued to punch away, and any objection offered by me was met with anything but a promise to do better. ... I am satisfied that Corbett can whip any man in the world, but he is a very unreasonable fellow, and is forgetting his friends.

Daly objected to Corbett's handling of him and the two parted ways. In December, a 163½-pound Daly scored a KO28 over Tom McCarthy.

Just before Corbett left Buffalo for Pittsburg, where he was set to exhibit on the 30th, Corbett said:

> I don't care for the championship belt, and if any one claims the title because I will not fight inside of six months he can have it. All I care for is, that the American people will still look upon me as the real champion. Sullivan only fought twice in seven years.... Next Monday night at Elizabeth, N.J.; I will open in my new play, "Gentleman Jack."[596]

Corbett's nearly one month sparring exhibition tour with Daly had ended, and the play written specifically for Corbett, *Gentleman Jack*, began showing on Monday, October 3 in Elizabeth, New Jersey.[597] During it, Corbett usually sparred Professor John Donaldson in a friendly but spirited manner. Corbett's more consuming and intensive theatrical career had

---

[595] *Brooklyn Daily Eagle*, September 23, 1892; *New York Clipper*, October 1, 1892.
[596] *Buffalo Courier*, September 30, 1892; *Buffalo Evening News*, September 30, 1892; *New York Clipper*, October 8, 1892, January 7, 1893; *New York Sun*, October 2, 1892. It is unclear whether the Pittsburg exhibition took place, given that Daly had left Corbett.
[597] *New York Clipper*, October 8, 1892.

begun, mirroring what Sullivan had done for the last few years. Over the next year, Corbett toured the entire country, giving performances of his play in almost every state in the nation, and even Canada.[598]

Corbett as he appeared in *Gentleman Jack*

Sullivan had become more of an actor at the *end* of his career, but Corbett, just when he was on top of his game, seemed more interested in acting than in fighting. Like Sullivan, Corbett realized that he could make a bundle of money just by acting. People wanted to see the heavyweight champion, the man who had defeated Sullivan, even if he wasn't fighting. Corbett later claimed that the play made $1,000 a week in profits.[599]

By late October 1892, the *New York Clipper* published its opinion that Corbett had forfeited the title by his failure to accept Joe Goddard's challenge. In early December, Goddard scored a KO3 over 24-year-old 170-pound Irishman, Peter Maher, who earlier that year had lasted 12 rounds with Bob Fitzsimmons.[600]

---

[598] Fields at 67-73, 236.
[599] Fox at 45.
[600] *New York Clipper*, October 22, 1892, December 17, 1892.

The fight that most knowledgeable boxing fans wanted to see was Corbett vs. Jackson. On October 31, while in Cleveland, Corbett said that he would not sign papers for a fight with Peter Jackson. He would not fight for a year, and when his theatrical season ended the following fall, he intended to sign to fight Mitchell.

On November 1, 1892 in Philadelphia before a crowd of 1,500, Peter Jackson sparred with John McVey in a tame fashion. It was "plainly manifest" that Jackson "could have made shreds of him had he so desired. The Australian parried, ducked and countered in a clever way." Jackson said that his greatest ambition was to fight Corbett.[601] After Peter learned that Corbett intended to box Mitchell next, it was reported that he was "much disappointed because of Jim Corbett's refusal to make the expected match with him."[602]

The Referee in Australia at year end said that the world's championship was in a state of chaos, and called Corbett the champion of America and Jackson the champion of England and Australia. "The heavyweight championship of the world thus lies between these two.... Will Champion James J. Corbett settle with Peter Jackson which of them is the world's master?" It noted that the National Club of Boston offered a hefty $20,000 for Jackson and Corbett to meet, but Corbett said that his theatrical contracts prevented him from fighting for a year. Still, he was taking on Mitchell next, not Jackson. A Boston writer said,

> I think that the new Champion of America justly regards Peter Jackson as the toughest antagonist in the world. Nobody can blame a boxer for wanting to get as much easy money as possible, and for postponing to as late a day as he can the running of hazards and of uncertain tests. Unfortunately, in our country, our champions are a law unto themselves. They refrain from matching themselves and avoid challengers so long as suits their convenience or whim.[603]

By December 1892, Richard K. Fox, publisher of the *National Police Gazette*, said that tradition dictated that a champion, in order to remain such, had to accept a bona fide challenge once every six months. *The Gazette* agreed with the *Clipper's* position that tradition dictated that the failure to accept Joe Goddard's challenge meant that Corbett forfeited the championship.[604] However, such tradition usually went ignored by the general public, only some newspapers recognizing it. Until defeated, Corbett was the champ in the public eye. Also, in Jim's defense, six months had not elapsed yet.

---

[601] *Philadelphia Press*, November 2, 1892; *Philadelphia Inquirer*, November 2, 1892.
[602] *New York Clipper*, November 19, 1892.
[603] *Referee*, December 28, 1892
[604] *New York Clipper*, December 17, 1892; Fox at 45.

Some newspapers were quite harsh in their criticism of Corbett, feeling that he still had a lot to prove.

> Mr. Corbett, because of his avariciousness or his cowardice has allowed his claim to the title to lapse. He beat a worn-out fighter and secured the proudest title a fighter can have, and he has been using that title to benefit him as a theatrical performer. He will not fight men who challenge him on the level and post money, but he will await the coming of dead cards. This is what Mr. Corbett will do: He will fight Charles Mitchell.... This is what Jim Corbett refuses to do: He will not again meet Peter Jackson within the six months called for by the rules... He will not make a match with Goddard...
>
> For about twelve years John L. Sullivan held the championship and in that time he fought about three hundred and fifty battles.... He never refused a match and when an aspirant for the title appeared and put up his coin John accommodated him. ... Mr. Corbett, because he had the luck to beat a worn-out champion and is possessed of a clever nut and a shrewd business manager, has taken a position on a pedestal and asks all to admire him. He will, of course, find some who will do so, but as a matter of fact he will find more if he will show some action. The American people want a champion who will fight, and it seems that Mr. Corbett will not do so. Jim had better come off his perch and fight or give way to Goddard or some other chap who likes scrapping.[605]

Reacting to the criticism, Corbett said that it made economic sense to act, that he would clear $150,000 in a year as an actor, that no other theatrical performer could equal that. Boxing purses did not come close either. Corbett said that Sullivan had done the same for the past number of years, and had only fought four actual championship battles in 12 years: Ryan, Mitchell, Kilrain, and himself, an average of once per three years.

> True, in exhibitions at the Madison Square Garden and other places [Sullivan] met all comers in four-round contests. So have I, and nobody took any particular notice of it, as the accomplishment of stopping unscientific, untrained humps in a short space of time has long since ceased to be a novelty. Now, when I stipulate that I shall have one year's rest between my battles I am sneered at and maligned by these pugilistic oracles.

Corbett said that Jack Dempsey (who had lost to Fitzsimmons) was the greatest fighter who had ever lived, that his record was even more impressive than Sullivan's. However, after fighting anyone and everyone for years and submitting to the desires of the experts, Dempsey was now

---

[605] *Chicago Daily News*, January 26, 1893.

"forgotten, unspoken of, and, from all accounts, in needy circumstances."
He had "fought every Tom, Dick, and Harry for any sort of a purse.
Observe the result: Dempsey today possesses more so-called friends than
any other pugilist living, but they do not open their pockets for him."
Corbett was determined to make the best financial moves that he could.[606]

One newspaper responded to Corbett's position, saying,

> His defense of his stand in declining to fight again inside of a year
> because Sullivan only fought four times within twelve is mere
> sophistry. Who can say that Sullivan refused to fight when challenged
> by men not merely "bluffing?" If John L. only fought four times
> within twelve years it was because there were only four men within
> that space of time who had the courage to face him and the money
> wherewith to back themselves when called.[607]

On January 19, 1893 in Los Angeles, Peter Jackson sparred 4 rounds
with Frank Childs, another black fighter, who was undefeated. Childs had a
February 1892 KO win over George La Blanche, a November 1892 KO3
over John Rivers, and a January 12, 1893, KO3 against Soldier Walker. In
years to come, Childs would become a prominent heavyweight.[608]

In February 1893, Jackson offered to fight Corbett to a finish for
$20,000. A $2,500 deposit was made and the terms were for a side wager of
$10,000 per side and the largest purse any club would offer. Jackson said,
"He claims that he is entitled to one year's rest from the date of his contest
with Sullivan. The terms of my challenge will allow him more than that
time." Corbett wired back that he would accept the challenge only if the
Mitchell match fell through.[609]

Jackson was clearly the best contender, and deserved a title shot. He had
proven to be Corbett's equal in their 61-round draw, had defeated Frank
Slavin, and, given Corbett's success against Sullivan, Peter would have had a
good chance to defeat a less than his best Sullivan as well. Jackson had
already unsuccessfully waited four years to obtain a match with Sullivan.
Once again, the reigning champion was putting off a match with him.

Unlike Sullivan, Corbett never specifically said that he would not defend
against a black fighter, but it appeared that he was at least avoiding a tough
challenge, regardless of color. Goddard's challenge went ignored as well,
and he was white. Certainly, both Jackson and Goddard would have been
tougher tests than Mitchell. Corbett's trainer, Bill Delaney, had said that Jim
would draw the color line.

---

[606] *Chicago Herald,* January 23, 1893.
[607] *Chicago Daily News,* January 27, 1893.
[608] *Los Angeles Express,* January 18, 20, 1893; *New York Clipper,* December 3, 1892, January 21, 1893.
[609] *Brooklyn Daily Eagle,* February 12, 1893; *National Police Gazette,* March 4, 1893; *New York Clipper,*
February 18, 1893.

The New Orleans *Times-Democrat* wrote that the admirers of pugilism wanted to know how much of Corbett's success was due to his own ability as opposed to Sullivan's physical deterioration.

> Corbett appears to be in no hurry to satisfy public curiosity on this point. ... In all of Corbett's actions and speeches he has demonstrated to the public most conclusively that he is a fighter for revenue only and only looks upon a match as a means to make more money.[610]

Any claim to the championship or top contender status that Joe Goddard might have had certainly disappeared when on March 3, 1893, Denver's Ed Smith knocked out Goddard in the 18th round. It was a vicious back and forth battle that saw both men hurt and decked multiple times throughout, but Smith eventually put Joe down for the count.[611]

Ed Smith had previously been defeated by Peter Jackson (L5 in May 1890), George Godfrey (LKOby23 in late November 1890), and had been bested by Joe Choynski in an April 30, 1892 exhibition. The Smith-Choynski exhibition was tame for the first 3 rounds, though Choynski had the better of it, and when a Choynski straight left in the 4th round dropped Smith, the police stopped it. "The blow was not really a knockout, but it badly dazed the Denver lad."[612] Choynski scored a KO15 over Godfrey on the last day of October 1892.

Peter Jackson clearly was the most deserving contender because he had previously defeated Godfrey (who had defeated Smith) and Smith (the man who had just defeated Goddard), had fought evenly with Corbett, and was coming off an 1892 victory over Frank Slavin (whose victories included: 1887 KO2 Bill Farnan - the only man to hold a win over Jackson; 1889 KO3 Jack Burke; 1890 KO2 Joe McAuliffe; and 1891 KO9 Jake Kilrain).

Corbett avoided Jackson and other top contenders and instead chose to take on Charley Mitchell. One paper in late 1892 criticized, "Undoubtedly he considers Mitchell an easier task than Jackson."[613] Furthermore, after Ed Smith defeated Goddard, Corbett was quoted as telling Smith that as soon as he defeated Mitchell, he would give Smith the next title shot, even though it was reported that Jackson had been promised the first fight after Mitchell.[614] "This verbal agreement between Smith and Corbett shuts out Peter Jackson, who was promised the first fight after Mitchell."[615] It seemed that Corbett wanted nothing to do with another Jackson match. Corbett would later reverse himself and say that Smith did not deserve a title fight, and they did not fight either.

---

[610] *Times-Democrat*, February 20, 1893.
[611] *New York Clipper*, March 18, 1893.
[612] *Philadelphia Inquirer*, May 1, 1892.
[613] *Referee*, December 28, 1892
[614] *Philadelphia Inquirer*, March 26, 1893; *Chicago Tribune*, March 26, 1893.
[615] *Chicago Herald*, March 26, 1893.

CHAPTER 14

The Foul

The scheduled James Corbett vs. Charles Mitchell fight date and location changed several times. Although Coney Island was initially supposed to be the fight site, in July 1893 it was reported to be set for December in Chicago for a $45,000 purse.[616] The date and location would eventually change yet again.

Throughout 1893, Corbett was touring with his play. During July, while in Chicago, Corbett said that he was ready to meet Peter Jackson any time. He also said that he would agree to meet Jackson in November, one month *before* fighting Mitchell. It was considered mere advertising for the bouts, not a serious proposition.[617]

The next day, on July 11 it was announced that Corbett and Jackson had signed articles to meet in late June 1894, one year later, in a fight to the finish for $10,000 a side and the largest purse offered by any club north of the Mason and Dixon line (Peter would not box in the South), the winner to take all of the money.[618]

Corbett gave boxing exhibitions at the Chicago World's Fair from July 3 to 18, 1893. They were supposed to continue, but the fair's president was opposed to boxing and ordered the exhibitions stopped. Corbett filed for an injunction to forestall the fair's directors from preventing his exhibitions, but the court refused to grant it, citing the contract term that gave the exposition the power to remove any show it deemed objectionable.[619]

As of August 1, Corbett headed east to Asbury Park, where he would train for the Mitchell fight. At that point, the match was once again set to be held at Coney Island, New York.[620]

On Labor Day in New York, September 4, 1893, Corbett sparred with John Donaldson at a Jack Dempsey benefit. World middleweight champion Bob Fitzsimmons was present, and Bob sparred with Dempsey.[621] Corbett continued working with Donaldson in various cities as part of the play *Gentleman Jack.*

Political and legal attacks on boxing were alive and well. In October, fearing that official interference would prevent it, the Mitchell fight, set for November in New York, was shifted to New Orleans, to take place in

---

[616] *Chicago Tribune,* July 2, 1893.
[617] *Chicago Herald,* July 11, 1893.
[618] *Chicago Tribune,* July 12, 1893.
[619] *New York Clipper,* July 29, 1893.
[620] *New York Clipper,* August 5, 1893.
[621] *New York Clipper,* September 9, 1893.

December for a $20,000 purse, winner-take-all.[622] However, in November, at the behest of the governor, Louisiana's attorney general decided to renew afresh the legal attack on boxing and brought a suit to enjoin the fight. The press backed this effort.[623]

A group of Jacksonville, Florida men said that they wanted the match, and the fight was moved there. Unfortunately, citizens groups in conjunction with the ministerial community in that city protested the fight, and the city attorney told the mayor that there were legal means to prevent it. The pugilists ignored them. In mid-November, the agreement was made to fight in Jacksonville in January 1894 for a $20,000 purse, winner-take-all. However, Florida's governor directed the local sheriff to take precautions to prevent the fight.[624]

On November 27, 1893 in Buffalo, New York, before a crowd of nearly 4,000, Corbett sparred John Donaldson 3 rounds. "The exhibition was a very pretty one and showed that the champion is one of the quickest men with the gloves alive today. A scratch on Donaldson's forehead was reopened by a punch and it bled profusely."

It was said that they would next perform in New York City before heading south on December 10 to train there for the Mitchell fight. Corbett said, "I think the fight will come off. Of course if the Governor of Florida sets out to stop it he will do so, but I think the people down there want it, for they see that it will help their town."[625] Big fights generally proved to be an economic boom for a city.

The New Orleans Olympic Club still hoped to host the fight there. They had scored the first point in their legal battle. It seemed that the attorney general was making contradictory arguments. He forgot that simultaneous to a suit to enjoin boxing at the Olympic as an illegal enterprise, there was a case pending before the court against the club for $16,000 in back taxes. "On this case for the payment of the taxes the State claims that the club is carrying on a legitimate business under the laws of the State." They would have to await the ultimate legal resolution, which eventually would be in the club's favor.[626]

Meanwhile, in December, Florida's attorney general said that prize fighting was illegal there, and that anyone who attended, aided, or abetted a fight would be indicted and punished. However, on December 19, 1893, the Jacksonville city council passed a law permitting boxing contests in that city

[622] *New York Clipper,* October 7, 28, 1893, November 11, 1893.
[623] *New York Clipper,* November 18, 1893.
[624] *New York Clipper,* November 11, 18, 25, 1893.
[625] *Buffalo Courier,* November 27, 1893; *Buffalo Evening News,* November 27, 28, 1893.
[626] It would not be until April 23, 1894 that the Louisiana Supreme Court upheld a jury decision that found that the law permitting boxing contests in athletic associations indeed permitted gloved boxing bouts, and that these bouts were not prize fights. However, it was said that attempts would be made to induce the legislature to repeal the law. *New York Clipper,* April 28, 1894.

as long as they were fought with gloves weighing not less than five ounces.[627]

Corbett trained at Mayport, a small town 22 miles east of Jacksonville, Florida. Manager Bill Brady, trainer Bill Delaney, and trainers/sparring partners John McVey, John Donaldson, Dan Creedon, Tom Tracey, and Joe and Tom Corbett (Jim's brothers) arrived in Mayport on December 14. The combination gave an exhibition that night, and would continue sparring and exhibiting up until the Mitchell fight. At some point, even Jack Dempsey joined the crew.

5'8" 158-pound Australian middleweight Dan Creedon was a worthy addition to the team, for his career included: 1890 D30 Jimmy Ryan and W8 Jim Hall (Hall contracted to stop him in 8 rounds but failed); 1891 KO7 Starlight, KO2 Jimmy Ryan, and W6 Martin "Buffalo" Costello; 1892 D23 Costello and KO6 Jim Ryan; and 1893 KO15 Alec Greggains.

Corbett said that he would begin his training days with 8, 10, or 15 mile walks or runs, and would hit the bags, box, wrestle, play handball, and use the wrist machine (turning a wooden shaft using the wrist only, hoisting a weight as the shaft turns). "I know that I can outbox Mitchell, and I'll be mighty sure when I go into the ring with him that he can't wind me. You will see, I think, a short, easy fight."[628]

In late December, Mitchell told a reporter that he was weighing 185 pounds, and intended to enter the ring at about 178 pounds. He sparred with Jack Fogarty in preparation.[629] A secondary source said that he also worked with Jim Hall, Harry Darrin, Pony Moore, Tom Allen, and Steve O'Donnell.[630]

In January 1894, Jacksonville's Duval Athletic Club, the fight's host, decided to have the bout's principals arrested in order to force a test case in the courts. Jacksonville's citizens wanted the fight, and sent the governor a petition opposing his anti-boxing stance.[631] Despite the fact that the local Jacksonville city council had passed a law allowing boxing matches if they were fought with five-ounce gloves, state governor Henry L. Mitchell still threatened to arrest the participants.[632] However, the day before the fight, a judge granted an injunction restraining the sheriff from interfering with the bout. The fight would happen.[633]

Charles Watson Mitchell had begun his fight career in around 1878, 16 years earlier. In 1883, John L. Sullivan stopped Mitchell in 3 gloved rounds. Over the course of his career, Mitchell had fought draws with Jack Burke, Jake Kilrain, and Patsy Cardiff, and had lost a controversial 4-round

---

[627] *New York Clipper*, December 2, 16, 30, 1893.
[628] *New York Clipper*, December 23, 1893; *St. Louis Daily Globe-Democrat*, March 11, 1894.
[629] *New York Clipper*, January 6, 13, 27, 1894.
[630] Fields at 77.
[631] *New York Clipper*, January 6, 13, 27, 1894.
[632] Fields at 76-77; Myler at 76.
[633] *Florida Times-Union*, January 25, 1894.

decision to Dominick McCaffrey. In 1888, under London Prize Ring rules, Mitchell managed to fight Sullivan to a 39-round bareknuckle draw lasting over 3 hours. Mitchell subsequently trained and sparred with Kilrain in 1889 when Jake was preparing to fight Sullivan.

In a February 1890 bout promoted as being for the heavyweight championship of England, Mitchell defeated the ancient and inactive but famous bareknuckle ex-champion Jem Mace in a 4 two-minute round gloved bout, dropping him a couple of times early until it was stopped by the police in the 4th round. The fight was meaningless, as Mace was over 60 years old.

The 32-year-old Mitchell had not fought in a legitimate fight since 1888, and thus had been inactive in serious bouts for six years.[634] He had only engaged in some light and short sparring exhibitions with Frank Slavin in 1891 and 1892, as well as some short exhibitions in 1893 with Jim Hall and some others. Therefore, like Sullivan, Mitchell was past his prime and not likely to be sharp owing to the effects of lengthy inactivity. Furthermore, he was smaller than Corbett in both height and weight, rarely weighing more than 175 pounds and only standing 5'9". Mitchell had the reputation, the lip, and 1888 result against Sullivan six years earlier, making the fight somewhat marketable, but he did not have the more recent results against top fighters that others had. At that point, he most certainly was not a legitimate title contender, and Corbett knew it.

Sizing up the men, the *New York Clipper* said that the betting odds would be 3 to 1 on Corbett. Still, it was said that Mitchell was "as clever and shifty as Corbett, more tricky than the latter," and despite the size disparity, he was also called a "better puncher and more determined fighter" than what Corbett had yet shown himself to be.[635]

Of the prospective Mitchell-Corbett fight, in April 1893 John L. Sullivan was quoted as saying,

> I think Corbett has undertaken a bigger contract than he realizes. Mitchell is fully as shifty a boxer as Corbett, and he can strike twice as hard a blow…. Corbett didn't land a blow at New Orleans that would have phased me had I been in anything like my old time form when I fought Charley Mitchell. I was simply all run down and Jim just hammered away until he wore me out…. Corbett will try to keep landing that left of his in the stomach, but I don't think it will work with Mitchell to the same damaging extent as it did to me.[636]

However, Sullivan later changed his mind. In November, he said, "To tell the honest truth, I think, barring accidents, that Corbett will just about

---

[634] *San Francisco Examiner*, February 8, 1890; *National Police Gazette*, February 10, 1894.
[635] *New York Clipper*, January 6, 13, 27, 1894.
[636] *Philadelphia Inquirer*, April 19, 1893.

hammer the life out of the Englishman." Speaking of Mitchell, at that point Sullivan said,

> When I say that he can hit hard and run fast the whole story is told. If he could land on Corbett enough he might hurt him, but I couldn't do it and I'm sure Mitchell can't. Corbett, on the other hand, has strong, long arms, strong fast legs. Mitchell can't run away from him.

Just before the fight, Sullivan said that although Mitchell was a harder hitter, he would not be able to get to Corbett, who was bigger, had a longer reach, and would likely win.[637]

Peter Jackson said of Mitchell, "I believe no gamer man ever stepped into a ring. He has grit and science also, and Corbett will find him a hard man to defeat."[638]

Before the fight, Corbett's former instructor, Walter Watson, described Jim's strengths. He said that he never saw anyone quicker than Corbett, and that Jim was a wonderful judge of distance. If he missed a punch and was unable to get away, he would clinch and get his forearm under his opponent's neck. One of Jim's best punches was his left uppercut, which mostly landed, especially when the opponent ducked to the right. He was also able to throw a stiff left to the body and then quickly come up to the face. Ultimately though, Watson said that Corbett's biggest strength was his ability to duck and slip out of reach. "He is the hardest man in the world to hit."[639]

Corbett and Mitchell had previously come close to fighting, but the match had fallen through either because of Mitchell or because of legal impediments. The two subsequently got into an impromptu outside the ring altercation. These men did not like each other, and certainly, based on his subsequent quotes, Corbett had long desired to administer a thrashing to Mitchell.

Over one year and four months after winning the title, on January 25, 1894 in Jacksonville, Florida, the 182-184-pound 27-year-old Corbett made his first defense of the title by taking on 32-year-old 5'9" 164-168-pound Charley Mitchell.

As is often the case, trying to decipher exactly what happened is like trying to solve a puzzle, but overall the accountings are fairly consistent. The two versions provided by the *Florida Times-Union*, a local Jacksonville paper, will be presented first, followed by different versions put forth throughout the country, as well as by Corbett's autobiography.

They fought for a $20,000 purse, but there was an additional side bet of $10,000 per side, meaning that the winner would earn $30,000. The crowd turned out to be much smaller than hoped for and expected; only

---

[637] *New York Clipper*, November 25, 1893; *Brooklyn Daily Eagle*, January 21, 1894.
[638] *New York Clipper*, July 1, 1893.
[639] *San Francisco Chronicle*, January 20, 1894.

containing about 2,500, with only one woman in attendance. This was probably because Corbett was at least a 2 to 1 favorite, the ticket prices were quite high, anywhere from $10, $25, and up to $35, and most importantly, because there was uncertainty as to whether the fight would be allowed to take place. As a result, not many traveled to Florida.

Charley Mitchell

Corbett in his autobiography claimed that he weighed 182 pounds to Mitchell's 168 pounds. Mitchell claimed that he weighed 164 pounds to Corbett's 190. *The San Francisco Chronicle* said the weights were not announced, but "it is believed that Mitchell weighed no more than 165, while Corbett's weight is given at 184 ½." *The San Francisco Examiner* said Corbett was 184 Mitchell's 165. *The New York Clipper* said Jim weighed 194 to Mitchell's 157 pounds. *The Daily Picayune* said Mitchell claimed to be 155 pounds. The Florida paper said that Mitchell "hardly weighed 165 pounds." It reported that Mitchell gave his weight as 174, but afterwards said he was actually only 165, saying that he had tried to mislead Corbett into believing that he was bigger than he was. "Corbett weighed 184, and he looked every ounce of it."

Before the fight, Mitchell angered Corbett with his taunts. He enjoyed needling his opponents to break them up psychologically, and had apparently angered Sullivan years earlier as well. According to Corbett's autobiography, Charley even arrived an hour late to the fight (an exaggeration), and then smiled and winked at Jim.[640]

Corbett entered the ring first, attended by Brady, Delaney, Donaldson, McVey, Jack Dempsey, and Dan Creedon. Mitchell arrived "some minutes later," wearing a "roguish grin on his face, and the first thing he did was to give Brady the laugh." Tom Allen, Jack Fogarty, Steve O'Donnell, Jim Hall, "Pony" Moore, and Harry Darren attended him. Corbett looked at Mitchell's nasty smile and "gritted his teeth."

Before the fight, Corbett refused to shake hands and "was laughing in an ugly way." Jim had been "abused roundly and called harsh names that only the original mind of the Englishman could invent." He wanted to avenge all the insults.

---

[640] Corbett at 209, 217-218.

Corbett wore "nothing but a jockey strap, a red, white and blue belt, white socks and low cut black shoes. Mitchell wore short blue trunks, white socks and black shoes." Their size difference was noticeable. They fought with 5-ounce gloves, and the bout began just after 2:00 p.m.

1st round

Florida Times-Union (FTU): Corbett laughed during the round, and Mitchell avoided him. Both were quick. Corbett was the aggressor, but the round closed with no damage done.

Another version said that no punching was done in the first minute. Corbett forced the wary Mitchell around and blocked his punches. In a clinch, he pushed Charley off and laughed. Both landed some blows, but Corbett had the decided advantage. A left made Charley's face red.

Daily Picayune (DP): Honors were easy, with both feeling each other out. In a clinch, it was apparent that Corbett was much stronger, as he shook Charley off like a child.

New York Times (NYT): Both were cautious, but Corbett was the aggressor as Mitchell backed off and worked around the ring and out of corners. They exchanged some blows, the most significant being a Corbett shot on the nose and another in the face that jolted Charley's head back. Although Mitchell was the one laughing before the fight, by the end of the round, it was Corbett who was laughing at him.

New York Herald (NYH): Mitchell was mostly defensive, moving away and clinching, but Corbett violently pushed him away by using his glove in his face.

New York Clipper (NYC): Corbett advanced gradually and forced Mitchell to break ground. Jim feinted, but Mitchell would not bite, looking to get away. Mitchell ducked a powerful right and laughed. Jim pressed and Charley landed a right to the stomach and left to the mouth that drew blood. He followed with two more body shots. Some felt that Jim allowed him to land in order to get a line on him. Jim eventually landed a hard right on the cheek that left a red spot. Mitchell was more defensive thereafter.

San Francisco Chronicle (SFC): Mitchell focused on the body and landed one solid shot to the face, but his punches had no effect.

San Francisco Examiner (SFE): Mitchell landed a left that brought some blood from Corbett's upper lip.

Corbett's autobiography (CA): Corbett said that Mitchell cut Jim's lip in the 1st round with a left, angering him further.

2nd round

FTU: One local version said that Corbett landed a right and left on Mitchell's face. He chased him to the ropes and Mitchell fell, possibly more as the result of lack of balance than force of blows. As Mitchell rose to his knees, it looked as though Corbett hit him. The Mitchell party cried foul, but the referee did not allow it. The referee warned Jim, and Corbett's seconds rushed in and dragged him to his corner as the gong sounded. As he was pulled away, Corbett tried to hit his own cornerman, Dan Creedon. This version said that no damage had been done in the round.

Another local version said that Mitchell began the 2nd round cautiously, but landed a right to the ribs. Corbett laughed. Eventually, Jim sprang in with a right swing that had all of his body weight behind it and knocked Mitchell down near the ropes. Charley kept one knee on the floor during the count. Corbett struck at him while he was down, but seemed to avert his blow at the last moment. Some said that he struck him, while others said that he just missed. Corbett's seconds entered the ring. Delaney grabbed Jim around the waist and Jack Dempsey "actually hit him to bring him to his senses. Big John McVey threw his whole weight against him." Mitchell got up and then Jim was released. The gong sounded while they were clinched. After the bell, Mitchell landed on Jim's ribs to even the score. Corbett walked to his corner, but Charley was carried.

A year later, Corbett said that a punch to the chin in the 2nd round essentially ended it, for Charley was groggy for the rest of the fight.[641]

DP: Corbett began forcing matters, and in a clinch, Jim put the heel of his right glove under Mitchell's chin and pushed him away. Jim landed a hard left to the stomach, which caused Charley to run away. This caused some spectators to shout, "Chantilly!" in reference to Mitchell's running around tactics against Sullivan in their match in Chantilly, France.

Corbett feinted with his left for the stomach, and then crossed Mitchell to the jaw, sending him down. One version said that the referee, by a great effort, prevented Corbett from committing a deliberate foul. Another description said that Jim struck him while he was still down, but that he only grazed the top of his head. The referee did not allow the foul because it had done no harm.

The seconds entered the ring during the confusion. When the bell rang, Mitchell was in the act of striking Corbett, who then attempted to retaliate despite the fact that the round was over. The referee and the cornermen had to pry them apart.

Another version said that after the round was over, Charley went at Corbett, hitting him with a glancing right just as he was getting into his chair. Corbett just shook his head as Mitchell was carried back to his corner.

NYT: Mitchell landed a left to either the mouth or body (depending on the version) to begin the round, and momentarily tried forcing the fight, but he fell short with his punches. Corbett then went back on the attack with a rapid pace and worked Mitchell into a corner, landing a left to the mouth. There was a rally and Corbett hit Mitchell with some punches on the neck.

At the end of the round, Charley was sent to the ropes, and after they mixed it up, Corbett dropped Mitchell with a straight left to the temple.

---

[641] *Minneapolis Tribune,* January 23, 1895.

While Mitchell was down, Corbett seemed to lose his head and almost lost the fight on a foul. He was frantic to get at Mitchell, trying to pounce on him every time Charley got to one knee in the process of rising. Corbett actually struggled with the referee, who tried to restrain Jim as he hovered over Charley.

NYH: A right dropped Mitchell. After sitting upright, Mitchell sneered at Jim, winked and grinned, and Corbett lost his temper and swung an uppercut that barely grazed. His seconds grabbed Corbett and he "struggled with them like a madman." Mitchell rose and clinched until the end of the round.

NYC: Corbett attacked ferociously and went for the head, while Mitchell focused on the body. They engaged in some infighting, Charley doing some nice ducking. Jim forced him to the ropes with a right and left, and Mitchell held. Jim threw ferocious uppercuts. After the break, Jim again attacked like "an infuriated panther" with punches to the head and ribs, driving him about the ring. A solid left to the jaw dropped Mitchell in a heap. Corbett went wild. As Mitchell started to rise, Corbett uppercut him, and Mitchell sank back down. Delaney sprang into the ring and he and the referee held Jim back. Mitchell rose at nine and held onto Jim's neck until the bell rang. Charley was dazed and bleeding.

SFC/SFE: The SFC presented multiple views of the fight, one saying that Mitchell went down in the 2nd round from a right to the jaw, the other saying it was from a left uppercut. One of its reports may shed some light upon the confusion (or add to it) regarding how the knockdown(s) occurred.

There may have been two knockdowns in this round. One report said that after he was dropped by the left uppercut, the round continued, and did not mention the melee at this point. The closest the *Examiner* came to mentioning a first knockdown was when it said that Mitchell was hit by a right to the body and then turned his back and slipped down along the ropes to the hisses of the crowd. The *Herald* did allude to an earlier slip where Mitchell almost fell. The *National Police Gazette* was not very detailed, but it said that there were two knockdowns in this, the 2nd round.

The *Chronicle* went on to say that after Mitchell arose from the first knockdown, Corbett landed very hard rights to the body in addition to many other punches. At one point, Mitchell ran away, and the crowd hissed. Corbett attacked ferociously and a right dropped Mitchell a second time. The *Picayune* said that Jim had worked him against the ropes, and then a right dropped him.

One SFC account said that Mitchell sat up at about eight seconds and Corbett landed a right that grazed the top of his head, but the referee disallowed the claim of foul because it had done no damage. Another said that while Mitchell was down, Corbett "punched at him several times with his left and hit him on the top of the head. His seconds rushed into the ring and tried to pull him away, but he fought them back." Both reports agreed that the bell ended the round at this point. It confirmed that Mitchell then landed a right as Corbett was returning to his chair. However, Corbett just shook his head. The groggy Mitchell was carried to his corner.

The SFE said that Mitchell was down for about twenty seconds due to the confusion. After the bell, when Mitchell hit Corbett in the back of the head, Jim did try to go back at him but was restrained. During the rounds interval, both the referee and Jim's seconds implored him not to foul.

CA: The aggressive Corbett first badly hurt Mitchell with a right to the body. He dropped Mitchell at the end of the round. While Mitchell was down, Corbett admitted that he slapped him in the head. However, Corbett claimed that Mitchell was rising at the time and setting himself to throw a punch, but upon seeing Corbett unleashing a blow, went back down just as the punch struck him. After the bell, when Corbett was headed back to his corner, Mitchell hit him in the back of the head. Corbett turned around and the two brawled until their seconds broke them apart. Neither received much rest between rounds.[642]

3rd round

FTU: Corbett rushed Mitchell to begin the 3rd. Mitchell tried but could not run away. As Charley tried to clinch, Jim landed a right that knocked him down. Charley rose in a very groggy state, and another right sent him down. He rose again, but a right smash to the jaw dropped him for the third time in the round. Charley went down on his face, out cold, with blood flowing from three cuts on his face. "His form twitched."

Another local version said of the round that Corbett "rushed at him like a mad bull, swinging a right and left, landing both with terrific force on Mitchell's neck and jaw and knocking him down clean." Mitchell rose, but was hit and sent down again. He rose again, but Corbett rushed in and hit him with a right to the jaw that dropped Mitchell for the third and final time in the round. "The blow was delivered running and had with it all of Corbett's strength and weight. It lifted Mitchell clean off his feet and up into the air. He came down in a heap bleeding at the nose and mouth. He fell on his side and lurched forward on his face."

The NYT said that after dropping Mitchell for the first time in the round, Corbett again lost his cool and the referee struggled to keep him away. Corbett's seconds jumped into the ring and pushed him back as Corbett seemed like a madman bent upon utter destruction.

The SFC said that Corbett danced over him "like an infuriated panther" but did not mention any odd occurrences in this round, saying that Corbett turned around and went to his corner. Another SFC account said the count was long and that Mitchell was down ten seconds even before the referee

---

[642] Corbett at 217-219.

began counting, owing to the confusion created by Corbett and his cornermen. The SFE said that the referee kept an eye on Jim and held him back.

The NYH mentioned nothing in particular happening after the first knockdown in the 3rd. One DP version said that Corbett nonchalantly walked back to his corner, not mentioning any attempt at fouling. Another DP report said that Corbett again lost his mind and swung out with his hands, until he was held back by his seconds. It too noted that Mitchell was down for quite some time, but he eventually did rise.

The NYC said that Corbett began the round attacking like an infuriated mad bull with a Gatling gun, constantly firing away. Mitchell held, but Corbett pushed him off and attacked in the same fashion, until a left to the jaw dropped him. The referee and Jim's seconds kept crazy Jim away. Dempsey slapped Corbett. Referee Kelly would stop counting to warn Jim.

As soon as Mitchell rose, Corbett attacked, hitting him on the mouth and dropping Charley again, most all of the sources agreeing that the knockdown punch was a right, which sounded like "the crack of a pistol." Blood ran from Mitchell's mouth and nose. He rose, but was very dazed.

Most sources agreed that Jim rushed in after the second knockdown and landed another right to the jaw that dropped Charley for the third time in the round. Mitchell then rolled over on his face, knocked out cold. The DP and NYC only mentioned two knockdowns. The DP said that Corbett leapt from his seat and dropped Mitchell face first by a right to the nose that had his full forward momentum. Mitchell was knocked out.

The NYT said Jim's cornermen again entered and held him back. Another account said that this time Jim turned away and did not look back, being congratulated and hugged by friends even before the count was complete. Still another said that he danced around like a crazy man. The DP did not mention anything in particular happening at the end.[643]

CA: They fought hard in the 3rd. Corbett dealt with hand troubles throughout his career (there were no hand-wraps then). Therefore, he usually waited until a well-timed moment, when his opponent was vulnerable or ready to go, to unleash big power. Corbett knew that he had his man and threw a very hard right that landed and sent Mitchell down, face forward, out for the count.[644]

The *New York Clipper* summarized,

> Seldom, if ever, have two pugilists entered the ring with a more bitter hatred toward each other…. Corbett forgot himself completely…and had it not been for the timely interference of his seconds he would unquestionably have lost the fight on a foul…. Corbett was in such a

---

[643] *New York Times*, January 26, 1894; *San Francisco Chronicle*, January 26, 1894; *San Francisco Examiner*, January 26, 1894; *New York Herald*, January 26, 1894; *National Police Gazette*, February 10, 1894; *Daily Picayune*, January 26, 1894; *Florida Times-Union*, January 26, 1894; *New York Clipper*, February 3, 1894.
[644] Corbett at 220.

terrible frenzy that he really did not know what he was doing. The first time he knocked Mitchell down he committed a deliberate foul, and his seconds, seeing the danger that threatened his brilliant victory, bounded into the ring and threw themselves between Corbett and Mitchell to prevent Jim, in his idiotic rage, from doing something he might regret during the remainder of his life. The seconds had no business in the ring, but that was due to the leniency of Referee John Kelly. … John Kelly is an honest man and a good fellow, but it is a question whether he ever refereed a fight before in his life…. Kelly meant well, but he had no business to allow Corbett's seconds to enter the ring, and had he kept them out it is more than likely that Mitchell would have won on a foul.

So far as pugilistic ability is concerned, however, there is no comparison whatever between the men. Corbett is the superior of Mitchell in every respect, and he smothered him so completely that, scientific as Mitchell is, Corbett made him look like a novice. The only chance Mitchell had of winning the battle was on a foul, and had there been an experienced and strict referee his chances of winning in that way were very rosy.

Corbett is a wonderful fighter, and doubtless the marvel of the nineteenth century. It is the opinion of many leading experts on pugilist matters that he is the most scientific fighter ever known, and that, if he defeats Peter Jackson with as much ease…it will be many years before he will meet another opponent worthy of his street. He is as quick as a flash and a good stiff puncher.

The *New York Times* called it a short but brutal contest wherein Corbett's superior science and hard hitting won out. It complimented Corbett's punching power, saying that "no one will ever say a word about Corbett's lack of hitting power. He punished Mitchell terribly, and with terrific force." Jim's punches had been so "lightning-like" such that his work had been "too rapid for most of the spectators to follow and understand." Apparently, it had been so rapid that even newsmen could not always agree on the specifics.

After the fight, speaking about his anger, Corbett said, "I never entered a ring in my life and I hope never again to do so, with more of murder in my heart than I had this afternoon when I got into the same ring with Mitchell." Corbett was upset at a name Mitchell had used to refer to him. Jim also admitted that he had refused to shake hands before the bout.

Regarding the fight, Jim said that he was able to neutralize Mitchell on the inside. "In the clinches at short range where he did his spiking, backheeling and roughing with Sullivan I found him the easiest to handle…. When he came in and closed on me I so pinioned and held him as to make it absolutely impossible for him to land." Most observers agreed that

Mitchell was past his prime and that the much larger Corbett had completely outclassed him.[645]

Regarding the claim of foul, at the time Corbett said,

> [T]here is nothing to it. He had his knee off the floor both times when I led at him, and a man in that position is up under the Queensberry rules. No, I did not hit Brady and Delaney in the ring. They were trying to push me back from Mitchell when he was up and I pushed them away rather forcibly; that was all. I was rather hot at Mitchell, as he called me the vilest kind of names when we stepped to the center of the ring.

However, Jim also said, "I forgot myself. My hatred of this man was so intense that when I started to fight him I forgot all about the rules."

Mitchell said that Corbett was the better man and that he had been fairly whipped. He called Corbett the cleverest big man that he ever saw. When questioned about a potential foul, he said, "[H]e may have fouled me. I don't know whether he did or not.... I have been in the ring seventeen years now, and I know a good man when I see one. Corbett is a dandy." Clearly, Mitchell did not remember anything about the knockout blow or potential foul because he had been concussed, causing him to forget what had happened. Still, he took the loss in sportsmanlike fashion.

The question that the fight raises is whether Corbett should have been disqualified. Under both the London and Queensberry rules, striking a downed fighter was grounds for disqualification. Corbett likely committed an intentional foul and let his rage get the better of him. His seconds, upon seeing this, entered the ring to prevent him from going further than he had. The referee apparently felt that his blow(s) did not do any harm and chose not to disqualify him. However, the fact that Corbett's seconds entered the ring could also have been grounds for disqualification because they entered during the round, something technically illegal under the Queensberry rules. Ultimately, because they did it to maintain order and prevent a disqualification, it was overlooked. Not much complaint was raised in the newspapers at the time, and historically this has not been a point of controversy or debate. However, there was a cognizance of the fact that Corbett had come close to becoming the first man to lose the Queensberry rules heavyweight championship by disqualification.

Like Sullivan before him, because he had defied those political forces that wanted to prevent boxing, Jim Corbett had to deal with the legal repercussions. Immediately after their fight, the police arrested both Mitchell and Corbett, along with their managers and representatives of the Duval Athletic Club. They provided appearance bonds, were released, and

---

[645] *Brooklyn Daily Eagle,* January 26, 1894.

trial was postponed for one month, until late February. Corbett took a train to New York.

Corbett, the Champion

CHAPTER 15

The Fight That Could Not
Or Would Not Happen

Following the Charley Mitchell fight, Peter Jackson was reported to be Corbett's next opponent. They were supposed to fight in June 1894, six months away. Corbett stated his alleged intentions. "I will jump right into the theatrical business again…but of course I am keeping in view my fight with Peter Jackson in June next."[646] There was some talk of the fight occurring in England so that legal difficulties could be avoided.

Jackson also spoke of the June match, saying that he would meet Corbett anywhere north of the Mason and Dixon line, but not in the South, fearing for his life due to the region's racial prejudice.[647] This condition had been known for quite some time.

Two days after the Corbett-Mitchell fight, on January 27, 1894 at New York's Madison Square Garden, Corbett was given a hearty reception by a crowded house of cheering admirers. Demonstrating his "agility and marvelous science," Jim sparred with Dan Creedon, who had assisted Corbett in his preparations for the Mitchell fight.[648]

Corbett subsequently returned to the theater, performing in the play *Gentleman Jack*, touring the country. During that play, he would usually spar John Donaldson 3 or 4 rounds. Places which were visited included Boston, Philadelphia, Pittsburgh, Harlem, and Washington D.C., amongst others.[649]

During the second week of February, when Corbett was in Philadelphia with *Gentleman Jack*, he was given an enthusiastic reception that was said to be even greater than that which used to be given to Sullivan. Corbett said that he had hurt his hand against Mitchell. For the first time since the fight, he punched the bag. In the last act of the play, he sparred 4 spirited and lively rounds with Professor Donaldson, which contained many blows that were more than of the "love tap" order.

There was further discussion regarding who would be Corbett's next challenger. He had been receiving a number of challenges from various contenders, including middleweight champion Bob Fitzsimmons and

---

[646] *New York Times, San Francisco Chronicle, Florida Times-Union,* all January 26, 1894.
[647] *San Francisco Chronicle,* January 27, 1894; *Newark Evening News,* January 27, 1894; *Daily Picayune,* January 27, 1894.
[648] *Florida Times-Union,* January 28, 1894; *New York Clipper,* February 3, 1894.
[649] Fields at 81-82.

Denver Ed Smith. Regardless of who would be his next opponent, Corbett had scheduled a tour in England.

> He recognizes the fact that if he meets and vanquishes Jackson he will be the champion of the world without doubt. ... When questioned regarding the challenge of Fitzsimmons, Corbett smiled and said: "When he whips Choynski I might consider his challenge, but until he does that I shall not pay any attention to him." Mr. Brady says that he is going to send a representative to London on Saturday next to arrange with the National Sporting Club for the [Jackson] fight. Corbett will sail for England about the 1st of April. In speaking of "Denver" Smith, Corbett said that he didn't consider him in his class. "I think he had better get on a fight with George Godfrey before he talks of challenging anyone else," the champion added.

Smith had previously lost to Godfrey, before defeating Joe Goddard. Of course, Corbett knew that when he had earlier told Smith that he would box him next after Mitchell. His tune had changed.

Corbett's manager Bill Brady discussed the Jackson match and the terms under which it had to take place.

> Jim is taking the most perfect care of himself, and you can rest assured that he will be in A No. 1 trim to meet Jackson next June. ... It must be to a finish. Corbett would take no chance of a decision against him in a limited round contest with Jackson or any other man. ... There is every reason to believe that a Corbett and Jackson contest would last longer than twenty rounds – perhaps.[650]

On February 24, 1894 in New York, Corbett and Charley Mitchell gave a 4-round scientific exhibition. As usual with these follow-up exhibitions, it was not a fight but a friendly sparring show for money.[651] The two had reconciled, perhaps in part motivated by the pending criminal charges against them. Corbett showed his generosity by helping Mitchell to make some money. After all, it was Jim who had won the entire purse from their fight. It was traditional for the victor to assist the loser in this way.

Corbett returned to Jacksonville, Florida, where on February 28, 1894, he was a defendant in a criminal trial, facing misdemeanor charges of engaging in a prize fight, and for assault and battery. A jury of six men heard the case, which was given to them to decide on March 1. The judge instructed them on the prize fight charge, "It is immaterial whether it was a glove contest, a sparring match or a boxing match, if it constitutes and amounts to a fight." The judge instructed the jury on the assault and battery count, "[I]f in the contest the blows were given with the intention to cause bodily harm, the consent of the party receiving the blows is no defense."

---

[650] *Philadelphia Press,* February 13, 1894; *Philadelphia Inquirer,* February 13, 1894.
[651] *National Police Gazette,* March 10, 1894.

After deliberating for sixteen minutes, the jury returned with a verdict of not guilty. It appeared to be a case of jury nullification.

The following morning, the Attorney General dismissed the cases against Mitchell and the Duval Athletic Club members. It was obvious that no local jury would convict them. "The Duval Club members are jubilant over the result, and intend making a strong effort to secure the fight between Corbett and Jackson. It is doubtful, however, if Jackson would care to do battle in that State."[652]

Corbett returned to exhibiting with *Gentleman Jack*, performing in places like Cincinnati, St. Louis, Newark, and Brooklyn. Jim was also set to tour the British Isles.[653]

In March, Corbett was expressing confidence that he would defeat Jackson, saying that he should be a 10 to 1 favorite. Jackson said that he was boxing Joe Choynski every night in preparation.[654] Corbett also said, "If an English club makes a good offer I will accept. The fight must be to a finish and I must have three months in which to train after the articles of agreement are signed."[655] However, the *New York Clipper* said that while he was in Louisville, Corbett also made a contradictory statement, changing his previous position, insisting that the battle take place in America. Jim was quoted as saying that he "desired it distinctly understood that the fight would not take place in England, or in any other country but the United States."[656]

On April 9, 1894 in Philadelphia, Corbett gave his last performance of *Gentleman Jack* in the United States (sparring with Donaldson in the last act) before setting sail for England to tour with the play there. Corbett said that the reported Louisville interview was false.

> I never said that I would never fight Jackson anywhere but in America. I want to place myself on record. I will fight Jackson anywhere when it comes to the finish. I want the fight to take place in America, but if Jackson cannot secure a battle ground here I will fight him anywhere in the world. ... I am not trying to crawl out of this fight and I want to fight Jackson just to prove to certain harping critics that I am the champion of the world.[657]

At that point, Corbett also said that the Jackson fight could not take place in June as previously planned. "It is useless for Jackson to talk about fighting in June. There is no club in view, and I cannot be expected to sit

[652] *New York Clipper*, March 10, 1894.
[653] Fields at 82.
[654] *National Police Gazette*, March 24, 1894.
[655] *Newark Evening News*, March 20, 1894.
[656] *New York Clipper*, March 31, 1894.
[657] *Philadelphia Inquirer*, April 10, 1894; *Philadelphia Press*, April 10, 1894.

down quietly and wait for one to come along."[658] Apparently, no northern club had made a serious offer to host the fight, or was legally able to host it.

On April 12, Corbett set sail for Europe. While there for three and a half months, he did not fight in an official championship defense, but just boxed in short exhibitions as part of his play. He made his debut in London, England on April 21. One report said that Jim Mace was secured as a sparring partner, in addition to John Donaldson, but generally, Corbett just sparred with John.[659]

In reviewing the play, an English newspaper said that "more utter rubbish than *Gentleman Jack* has not been seen on the London stage, but so much has been written about Mr. Corbett that vast numbers of people will feel a curiosity to see him." People paid to see the champ, regardless of the quality of his play. Regarding Corbett's ball punching scene, it was said,

> The rapidity of his hitting is altogether astounding. It would be interesting to know how many blows a minute he gets in – I do not think it is in the least exaggeration to say that he hits faster than one can clap one's hands, and yet I dare say many unpractised persons would very often miss the ball altogether, if they took a vast deal longer to aim at it. ...

> Corbett proclaims one of the great secrets of successful fighting to be the avoidance of an adversary's blows. Hit, but do not be hit, is his extremely sensible rule, and tame as the fight is in the last act of the Drury Lane piece, one can realize Corbett's marvelous quickness in getting away. I should be inclined to doubt whether there was ever a cleverer fighter. Donaldson hit fast, but though I suppose he really does aim at Corbett, and takes a little pride in landing a tap, Corbett always seemed to be gone before the blow got home. Sometimes he ducked, and sometimes he dodged, but the other man's blows almost always met nothing but the unresisting air.[660]

Another English report on the play a week later said,

> Mr. J.J. Corbett is an athlete in excellent condition, exceedingly smart upon his legs, and remarkably quick with his hands. He has mastered the ball which he punches...there is no doubt whatever of the performer's immense superiority over the flying windbag. He knocks it about unmercifully... it cannot escape those clean and rapid blows... For the few minutes during which it lasts this exhibition is interesting. ... In a play it is more like the circus than the prize-ring. It shows Mr. Corbett's condition, his smartness, his long reach, and his agility, however, and we get a further illustration of these qualities in

[658] *New York Clipper*, April 14, 1894.
[659] *New York Clipper*, April 28, 1894.
[660] *Illustrated Sporting and Dramatic News*, April 28, 1894.

the exhibition boxing with Mr. John Donaldson which follows. The match has been rehearsed, of course, to give the champion the advantage of the interchange, and it is as spirited as a contest of this sort can be; but it is not what I call boxing either. It takes place in a ring which is surrounded by three or four hundred spectators…. The scene has been described as a triumph of stage management. … With regard to the play and the performance of it…it is simply terrible.[661]

A romantic view of Corbett in Europe

Corbett certainly did not act as if he was preparing for a Jackson match, content to tour in Europe with his play from April all the way through late July. When he later spoke about his European tour, Corbett said that he had played in London and Paris, and toured provinces of England, Ireland, and Scotland. While there, he met a number of political dignitaries.[662] Corbett also said that there were no good heavyweights in England, and thought it odd that the referees wore full dress suits and sat in a box fifteen feet above the ring, speaking to the boxers from there.[663]

A mid-1890s Corbett biography said that he had visited London, Glasgow, Edinburgh, Liverpool, Manchester, Birmingham, Newcastle-on-Tyne, Brighton, Southampton, Sheffield, Belfast, and Dublin. While in Paris for ten days, Corbett offered to spar French savate champion Charloment

---

[661] *Illustrated Sporting and Dramatic News,* May 5, 1894.
[662] *Minneapolis Tribune,* February 3, 1895; Fields at 82.
[663] Corbett at 237-238; *National Police Gazette,* August 18, 1894.

(sometimes called Charlomat) 3 rounds. Jim even said that he would allow him to kick if he wanted, but the Frenchman declined.[664]

By late June, Peter Jackson was growing concerned that Corbett would be looking for an excuse to get out of their match. Jackson felt that Jim might use the challenge made by highly regarded middleweight champion Bob Fitzsimmons as an excuse for avoiding him.[665] In June, Fitzsimmons had done what Corbett had said that he needed to do in order to be recognized as a challenger, which was to whip Joe Choynski, doing so in 5 rounds. Jackson's concern was not unfounded. After all, Corbett had fought the middleweight-sized Mitchell instead of the larger true top contender Jackson, so Fitzsimmons could be used as well. The Florida Athletic Club's generous offer made this possibility more likely. It said that it would put up a purse of $35,000 for Corbett to fight there, and if Jackson would not consent to fight in Florida (a southern state); its same purse offer was good for a battle between Corbett and Fitzsimmons.[666] Thus, Corbett could make the same amount of money for what seemed, on paper, to be an easier test.

Bob Fitzsimmons was certainly a very well respected and highly regarded fighter. Fitzsimmons had won the middleweight championship in 1891 with a KO13 over "The Nonpareil" Jack Dempsey. In 1892, although dropped and hurt early, Bob boxed masterfully and scored a KO12 over hard punching Peter Maher. In 1893, Fitz scored a KO4 over Jim Hall, who later in the year scored a KO7 over Frank Slavin. In mid-June 1894, although dropped once in the 3rd round, Fitz repeatedly floored Joe Choynski in the 4th and 5th rounds, and was on the verge of knocking him out in the 5th when the police stopped the fight, and it was technically declared a draw. This was significant because Choynski had a late 1892 KO15 over George Godfrey, who held a win over Ed Smith, who had defeated Goddard. Although only a large middleweight, Fitzsimmons was known for his big punching power, stamina and recuperative powers, as well as his crafty skills and experience. He could box well on the retreat or attack.

Fitzsimmons believed that he could defeat Corbett in a finish fight, but said that he did not want to "give Corbett the chance of flunking out of a match with Peter Jackson. I would like to see the two come together, for, in my opinion, Jackson will win." Of course, he had also picked Sullivan over Corbett, but this at least demonstrates that a Jackson-Corbett fight was viewed as quite competitive and dangerous for Jim.[667] Fitzsimmons was well aware of Jackson's abilities because in the 1880s they had both trained in Australia at Larry Foley's gym. Jackson had actually given Fitz some boxing instruction.

---

[664] Fox at 57–59.
[665] National Police Gazette, July 7, 1894, reporting on a June 23, 1894 dispatch.
[666] New York Clipper, July 7, 1894.
[667] National Police Gazette, July 7, 1894, reporting on a June 22, 1894 dispatch.

Race certainly plays a factor in the analysis for the potential of a Corbett-Jackson match to take place, but it is difficult to quantify how much of a factor it really was. As it stood, boxing was not a generally legalized sport, so there were few places for them to meet anyway. Although boxing had often proved the exception, the general social rule was that whites and blacks did not mix. When a black defeated a white, in any area of life, even boxing, it was seen as a threat to the social order. Under these circumstances, not too many clubs or politicians would be anxious to support an interracial heavyweight championship, particularly given that most politicians were opposed to allowing boxing at all anyway, regardless of race.

There was an open cognizance of race in the sport, even in newspaper analysis. One writer in July 1894 opined,

> Up to date very few of the colored stars of the fistic world have gone wrong or finished second best in meetings with white men. Nearly all their matches have been with whites. The colored champions, Peter Jackson, Frank Craig, Joe Walcott, Bobby Dobbs, Jerry Marshall, and George Dixon, have seldom, if ever, given battle to men of their own race…. It is humiliating, perhaps, but the bald pate fact seems to be that in the roped arena Africa has walked away with the top knot in nearly every encounter with the boasted "superior race." Joe Choynski and Peter Maher, in the defeats they administered to George Godfrey, are pretty much the only exceptions to the rule of recent pugilism…. Is the cause that the white man in pugilism obstinately refuses to deny himself and to train scrupulously and be manageable like the colored one? Or is there really something in the difference of structure of the two races which makes a white man weaker in the parts above the belt that are, by the rules, made a fair target for fist smashes?
>
> Maher has toppled over Craig, Corbett should do Jackson, and Plimmer is very likely to lower Dixon's colors. A new supply of colored stock will then be needed.[668]

White boxer Peter Maher had just a couple days earlier in July scored a KO2 over Frank Craig, and he had avenged his loss to George Godfrey with a late May KO6. There were other white boxers that had defeated or fought well with black boxers. But this article demonstrated recognition of the existing significance of race when viewing boxing, and the potential problems posed to the social order of white superiority if blacks did too well with white fighters. Boxing already had serious legal difficulties, and those problems were certainly not going to subside if the sport allowed a mixed race heavyweight championship contest.

---

[668] *Buffalo Courier,* July 18, 1894, quoting *Boston Post.*

Still, there was a large contingent of fair-minded sportsmen and writers who genuinely wanted to see a contest between the best two fighters, regardless of color. Ironically, it would be Southern clubs which offered sufficiently large purses for a fight of the magnitude of the Jackson-Corbett championship bout. There were those willing to put race aside in order to make a match between the best.

After setting sail on or about July 20, Corbett arrived back in America from Europe on August 1, 1894. Shortly thereafter, Corbett met then Governor and Presidential candidate, William McKinley. Corbett noted that everyone knew who the heavyweight champion was, but few could recognize McKinley, who eventually became U.S. President.[669]

Upon his return, Jim said that John Donaldson was retiring owing to his old age and that Australian Steve O'Donnell (who had been a Mitchell sparring partner) would help him train for the Jackson fight.

Having won its court battle, the New Orleans Olympic Club offered a $25,000 purse for the Corbett-Jackson fight.[670] Its club president said that the club would see to it that Jackson received fair play. "It guaranteed fair play to George Dixon when he fought Jack Skelly, and Dixon won; and no one insulted him or interfered with him."[671]

However, concerned for his safety, Jackson refused to fight in the South. Thus, the opportunity for the fight to take place did exist, but Jackson's fear of what might happen to him as a result of racial prejudice was a barrier. Given the legal constraints on the sport, there simply were not many other options.

Corbett also presented a roadblock to the Jackson fight, changing his tune about when the fight could take place. Jim said that the London dinners had been too much for him, that he was not in good form, and although he was willing to meet Jackson anywhere in America or in another country, he would need yet another six months to get in condition to fight "the colored wonder."[672] Previously, Jim had said that he only required three months preparation time. Corbett wanted a lot more time, and Jackson did not want to fight in the South. Things were not looking good.

On August 13, Jackson, Corbett, and their representatives met in New York to negotiate a match. According to the *New York Clipper*,

> After each had accused the other of bluffing and not wanting to make a match at all…Peter reiterated the statement that he would not fight in the South under any circumstances…. There being no apparent possibility of any club in the Northern States offering a purse of the proper dimensions to satisfy these pugilistic high rollers, Jackson then proposed to have the fight take place before the National Club, in

[669] Corbett at 237-238.
[670] *New York Clipper*, August 11, 1894.
[671] *National Police Gazette*, August 18, 1894.
[672] *New York Clipper*, August 11, 1894; *National Police Gazette*, August 18, 1894.

London, Eng. To this Corbett dissented on the ground that that organization, nor any other in England, would arrange for a contest of more than twenty rounds, and he would fight only to a finish, as his former experience with the sable boxer had convinced him that he could not defeat him in twenty rounds, while he was satisfied that he could win in a finish battle. He desired to fight in the South only because the offer made by a New Orleans club was satisfactory, and there was no doubt that the contest could be brought off without any trouble. He offered to bind himself to give Peter the purse and stakes in case the latter was interfered with, but Jackson thought that even that would avail him little in case he should be killed before leaving the ring, which he believed was likely to happen in case he should defeat Corbett. ... Corbett, who professed to fear unfair treatment at the hands of English officials, then declared that he would not fight in England. This ended the matter.... Peter...was satisfied that Corbett did not want to make a match at all. So the conference terminated, and, from appearances, there is not the remotest probability that these men will ever again face each other in the prize ring. This is to be regretted, for they are justly regarded as the foremost boxers of the world, and their indecisive contest at San Francisco left the question of relative superiority undecided. The public can be left to judge as to which of the two is most at fault, but it must be said that neither one has acted as though he was anxious for an opportunity...and certain it is that their failure to make a match will have a tendency to injure the future prospects of both boxers.[673]

A *National Police Gazette* report said that during their negotiations, Corbett backed off of his position a bit, indicating that he would fight in England only if there were express conditions that the fight was to be to the finish, that if the fight was stopped prematurely or if he was interfered with in any way that the whole purse was to go to him. Probably to his surprise, Jackson agreed to those terms. However, Corbett once again said that he did not want to go to London, and they were at an impasse. Jim said, "I feel towards London as you feel towards the South."[674]

The *New York Sun* said that Jackson was upset that Corbett wanted yet another six months to fight, questioning the legitimacy of Corbett's desire to fight him. "Six months? Why not sooner? If he is so anxious to meet me he should not let the question of a few thousand dollars and theatrical engagements stand in the way." Jackson said to Corbett, "You're bluffing and afraid to meet me." Corbett then asked him if he would fight in the South, but Jackson said "No. ... I would not have a chance for my life. Somebody would shoot me before I got into the ring. I will fight North, or

[673] *New York Clipper,* August 18, 1894.
[674] *National Police Gazette,* September 1, 1894.

in England." Corbett did not want to fight in England because it limited bouts to 20 rounds.

Jackson said that he would wait until a club in the North bid for the fight, or they could fight in England and he would agree to insert a clause in the articles that the battle must be to a finish. Corbett still feared that an English referee would decide against him in some way, so Jackson gave in on that point and said that Corbett could select an American referee. Corbett consulted with Brady and Delaney and then said, "I refuse to fight in England under any circumstances. That is my ultimatum." Why didn't Corbett accept under those circumstances?[675]

Both fighters were open to criticism. Corbett had said that he would fight Jackson *anywhere*, even after he had returned from England. Yet, suddenly, Corbett refused to fight in England, and then insisted on the fight being held in New Orleans, in the South, exactly where he knew Jackson did not want to go, that having being a major Jackson condition for quite some time. Jackson stated that he did not think he would get out of the South alive if he won. Peter's position was not about boxing or trying to gain an edge, but a literal fear for his life. "The impression in sporting circles just now is that Jackson is perfectly right in refusing to fight South." The previous year, Corbett had signed articles of agreement for the bout to take place in the North. As Jackson said, "If he remembers, the articles called for a battle north of the Mason and Dixon line. Let him stick to the agreement."[676] Still, mixed race bouts had taken place in the South without problem, so Jackson's fear might have been unjustified. Perhaps neither really wanted to risk losing to the other.

However, even if Jackson had been willing to fight in the South, it seemed that Corbett was continually attempting to put the fight off to as far into the future as possible. It was not a mystery to him that he had an upcoming Jackson fight, so his failure to maintain his condition, if true, was his own fault. Obviously, Corbett was not anxious to have to meet such a tough challenger, wanting to capitalize upon his championship status for as long as possible with as little risk as possible, and waiting for Jackson to get older and staler, further past his prime. Perhaps to feign interest in the fight, he agreed to box in the very region where he knew Jackson would refuse to box.

In Corbett's defense, he realized that he needed to be in the best shape to defeat Jackson, and that it would require some time to get into that shape. He also knew fully well that he needed more than 20 rounds to defeat Jackson, and correctly believed that the title should not be at stake unless it was in a fight to the finish, which apparently was not allowed in England, despite any agreement that Jackson was willing to sign to the contrary. Corbett and his representatives had for some time said that he

---

[675] *New York Sun*, August 14, 1894.
[676] *New York Sun*, August 17, 1894.

would only fight Jackson in a finish fight. At that moment, Louisiana was the one place where a fight to the finish for a huge purse could legally be held (although boxing's legality there would continue to oscillate). Furthermore, regardless of Jackson's fears, George Dixon had fought at the New Orleans Olympic Club and was not molested in any way. If Jackson had really wanted the title badly enough, he too might have taken the risk and fought in the South.

A week later, there was a report that a Sioux City, Iowa syndicate was offering a $25,000 purse for the fight to take place there. However, "The mayor of the city emphatically declares that the fight shall not be brought off within his jurisdiction, in which he echoes the previously expressed sentiments of the Governor of the State."[677] Without any political support, it was not likely that they would be allowed to fight in Iowa. Jackson said that in order to fight there, "I must be guaranteed protection. That is, they must assure me that I will not be interfered with. I only suggest this, as it is most likely that something might happen whereby I might be arrested, or otherwise be prevented from winning."[678] Prospects of a fight taking place there did not look too good either. There simply were not many choices. Economics, political and legal opposition, rule limitations, and racial considerations were all obstacles to the fight's occurrence.

Contender Ed Smith was critical of both Jackson and Corbett, saying that he did not think either wanted to fight. Ed had challenged both Corbett and Jackson to a fight for a side bet of $10,000. "Corbett is the best man of the two, and of course I would rather fight him." Jackson held a 5-round decision victory over Smith, although Smith had improved and come on strong towards the end of their bout. Smith was more critical of Corbett, saying that Jim had refused matches with both he and Joe Goddard, whom Smith had defeated. Corbett had earlier promised Smith the next fight after Mitchell, but he did not box Smith either. Ed supported Jackson's refusal to fight in the South, saying that "would be foolish to do."[679]

Ironically, even John L. Sullivan was supportive of Jackson, feeling that Corbett only wanted easy money.

> [T]he ex-champion said that he believed Jackson to be sincere, but he hardly thought that Corbett cared to meet him, having plenty of money and an immense income, and for that reason a match might not benefit him. ... He thought that much of Corbett's talk was a bluff, and did not blame Jackson in the least for refusing to fight in the South.[680]

[677] *New York Clipper*, August 25, 1894.
[678] *New York Sun*, August 29, 1894.
[679] *National Police Gazette*, September 8, 1894; *New York Sun*, August 17, 1894.
[680] *New York Sun*, August 29, 1894.

Basically, Sullivan was using common sense for his insight into Corbett. If Corbett was making very good money with his theatrical engagements because of his undefeated championship status, it did not make good business sense to take on a man who had at least a chance to defeat him, whether it was Joe Goddard, Ed Smith, Bob Fitzsimmons, or Peter Jackson.

CHAPTER 16

History on Film

During the time that Corbett and Jackson were negotiating a potential match, Jim saw another opportunity to make easy money, against a man who was not going to be a tough test the way Jackson or other contenders would have been.

On September 7, 1894 in West Orange, New Jersey, exactly two years after he had won the title, and seven and a half months after his first defense, 28-year-old James J. Corbett made an unusual title defense in what could technically be termed an exhibition (they had to call it that for legal purposes), but it was a real fight...sort of. What made the bout significant was that it was filmed.

Thomas Alva Edison was fascinated with the idea of making pictures create the illusion of motion. Beginning in 1889 and culminating in 1891, Edison along with William K.L. Dickson invented the first movie camera and projector. Over the next number of years, they worked to improve their inventions, called the kinetograph (camera) and kinetoscope (viewer).

On or about June 14, 1894 in West Orange, New Jersey, W.K.L. Dickson and William Heise filmed Mike Leonard box Jack Cushing 6 rounds in Thomas Edison's Black Maria studio. The Black Maria was a small moveable theater which could swivel on its axis so that it could be adjusted to allow a sufficient amount of light to enter through the open ceiling. The walls were all painted black, so the entire theater resembled a large black coffin.

Some aspects of the fight were different as a result of the filming process. The theater only allowed for a ring which was a mere 14 square feet, and two sides of the ring went right up to the padded walls. The camera was stationary and did not have zoom capabilities. The rounds were only about 1 - 1 ½ minutes long, because the camera could not handle any more film than that before needing to be reloaded. Also, as a result of the camera's film reloading requirements, the rests were a bit longer than the usual one minute.

For film viewing, each round was contained and projected within one kinetoscope device. The kinetoscope was a peep show device that looked like a very large and long wooden box standing on the floor, with a small eyepiece through which a spectator could bend over and look down inside to see the short one-round film projected.

Edison sold copies of the films to New York's Holland Brother's Arcade, where observers paid 5 or 10 cents to see each round. But these fighters were nobodies. Edison needed a star to generate significant revenue.

Edison attempted to get former champion John L. Sullivan to stand before Corbett for 6 rounds, but John wanted too much money - $25,000.[681] Sadly, Sullivan would never be filmed in the ring, though he would many years later, in about 1910, be briefly shown in a formal suit swinging at a speed bag and engaging in a momentary friendly semi-shadow box with Corbett, mostly feinting , showing one punch but then switching to another, but not really throwing. The footage is of limited value because it was brief, Sullivan was 51 years old (John L. died at age 59), had been retired for many, many years, and he looked to be weighing well over 300 pounds. However, even under all those conditions, you can still get a sense for how quick and reactive he once was. For Sullivan to look that good even at that age and in that physical condition tells you just how fast and strong he was in his early 20s. Even an aged Corbett looks pretty quick and defensively reactive himself.

Edison instead agreed to pay a purse of $5,000 plus royalties to heavyweight champion James J. Corbett to fight local champion Peter Courtney 6 rounds before his movie camera. Actually, the agreement was for Edison to pay $4,750 to Corbett only if he could stop Courtney within the 6 rounds. Courtney was to receive $250 as his pay, although one source said that he was to receive $500 if he could last the 6 rounds. This made Corbett and Courtney, boxers, amongst the first persons to perform under a film contract.

A *New York Sun* reporter was on the scene for an exclusive, and had the most detailed report of matters. Boxing was illegal in New Jersey, so the participants had to act with some stealth.

> The handlers of the affair were most mysterious. They told Corbett on the quiet that the utmost secrecy must prevail or the whole crowd would be "pinched" for aiding and abetting a prize fight, a violation of the New Jersey State laws. Exposure, they explained, meant an almost certain sojourn behind the bars.

In the morning, a policeman asked Corbett where he was going that day. Jim said that he was just going for a run. The policeman was satisfied. Corbett said, "Whew! That was a narrow escape. If that fellow had known I was going out in Jersey to knock out a stiff, he'd have made trouble, perhaps."

Corbett had never before seen or heard of Peter Courtney, but apparently, Jim had been told that he was a "stiff." Courtney told this story of himself:

---

[681] *New York Sun*, September 8, 1894.

I don't think this here champeen will have such a picnic with me as he thinks. I was born in Pennsylvania and am 26 years old. A year and a half ago I went to Trenton to get a job, and that's how I got in the fighting business. There was a duck there named Ed Warner, and they said he was the champeen of Jersey. Well, Jack McNally, a boxing instructor in Trenton, give me a few lessons, and I just put this here Warner to sleep in just one round. Soon after that I did up Jim Glynn in two rounds, Jim Dwyer in three, Jack Welch in four, and recently I went agin Bob Fitzsimmons, who couldn't put me out in four rounds.[682]

Courtney had recently lasted 4 rounds with Bob Fitzsimmons in an exhibition, although Fitz clearly had the better of it. "Courtney admits that the fight was a trifle one-sided, but considers that he added a great deal to his reputation by staying four rounds with Fitz." That bout took place in mid-August 1894, when both Fitzsimmons and Corbett were in Trenton, New Jersey.[683]

However, Bob Fitzsimmons told a different story regarding Courtney. Fitz said that Courtney was going to attempt to stand before him for 4 rounds to win $100, but Courtney only wanted a friendly bout, and refused to face him unless he promised not to punch hard. The manager of the house said it would be better to have a bout than none at all, so Bob consented. "I could have put him out with a punch any time." Bob also related a different story regarding Courtney's experience.

> There was a big heavyweight up there. I cannot be sure about his name, but it sounded like Hulong, or Oolong, who put Courtney out in a round and a half. Courtney weighs about 190 pounds, and this other fellow is about fifty pounds heavier. Well, I met this Hulong, or whatever his name is, and it took me just two punches to put him out. There is a welterweight in Trenton who also knocked out Courtney, and afterward I met this same welterweight in Baltimore, and it took just one blow to settle him.[684]

Courtney had some good local knockout wins and was billed as the New Jersey state champion, but had not particularly done anything to legitimize himself as a Corbett challenger. Obviously, he was not someone for whom Corbett needed another six months to prepare. Jim had been back in America for only a month.

Corbett said that he intended to put Courtney out within the 6 rounds, as required in order to earn the big money. "It is stipulated that I must put the guy out in six rounds or I get nothing; … You can bet I'll do the trick, too, for it's too much money to let slip out of one's grasp." Still, those who

---

[682] *New York Sun*, September 8, 1894. Spelling and grammatical errors in the original.
[683] *Brooklyn Daily Eagle*, August 17, 1894, September 8, 1894; *National Police Gazette*, September 22, 1894.
[684] *Times-Democrat*, September 11, 1894.

based their opinion upon appearance felt that Courtney might be a tough nut to crack, for he seemed cool and confident. Even Corbett said upon seeing him, "He looks like a tough customer…and I think he'll take quite a punching."

Most primary source accounts of the bout said that Courtney weighed 180 pounds, with Corbett slightly heavier at about 184 pounds. *The Sun* reported, "Corbett weighed 195 pounds, he said, and Courtney 190." However, from the film it appears that Jim is heavier and taller than Peter, so it is likely that those reported weights were inaccurate and there was a greater disparity between them.

Corbett faces off with Courtney

There was some discussion regarding which gloves should be used. There were sets of two-ounce and five-ounce gloves. Corbett said, "I'm in a quandary. You see, each round only lasts a minute, and with these big bags on my hands I might not be able to put this fellow out." Courtney said he did not care which gloves were used. Jim was about to use the two-ounce gloves, but Jim McVey talked him out of it. "You will cut this man up awful, Jim, and then people would say it was brutal. Better wear the big mitts, and if you find you can't do him, you can shift with his consent to the small ones. But you can do him as it is, for you can make the pillows hurt." So, they wore the five-ounce gloves.

For the first time, the live action of a heavyweight champion was to be preserved. They walked over to the Black Maria at 11:40 a.m. It was a very hot day. As soon as Corbett entered the ring, he exclaimed, "My, but this is small. There's no chance to bring any foot movement into play here, that's sure. A fellow has got to stand right up and fight for his life." The 14-foot ring had a rope on two sides, with the other two sides going right up to the heavily padded walls. The floor was smooth and covered with rosin. The roof was raised to let in the sunlight, and the heat was overpowering. They began boxing at about 11:45 a.m., with the kinetograph buzzing.

Because of the filming and reloading process, the rounds were much shorter and the rests much longer than Queensberry rules normally required. "All battles decided in this arena must be fought under a special set of rules. A round lasts a little over one minute, with a rest of a minute and a half to two minutes between the rounds."

In the 1st round, Courtney savagely attacked, while Corbett cleverly ducked and dodged all the blows and laughed. Eventually Corbett came up with a counter attack, landing body shots and snapping Peter's head back with jabs until clinched. Courtney made another rush with swings, but could not land. Corbett drove him to the padding on the wall and landed a wicked uppercut on the chin just as the round closed. Time of the round: 1 minute and 16 seconds.

The 2nd round was a case of science versus slugging. Courtney rushed and swung hard blows, but missed them all. Courtney just missed a lunging right as Corbett stepped back. Corbett then advanced with punches, landing a right to the jaw, and then a vicious uppercut that hurt Peter. Courtney rushed madly and swung blindly as Jim kept out of harm's way. "Corbett was not hitting hard at all, evidently waiting for an opening to put in a sockdolager when Peter least expected it." Jim landed two lefts to the face and a ripping right to the wind. He laughed good naturedly at Courtney's attempts. Another source said that Corbett hit him with a right uppercut and forced matters with some well landed blows that sent Courtney to the padding on the wall. Time of the round: 1 minute and 24 seconds.

After the round, Corbett said to McVey, "This fellow is taking some awful punches without wincing, and I'm afraid the big gloves are going to make trouble for me. He is getting a good rest after each round and comes up like a new man."

In the 3rd round, Courtney kept rushing and swinging like a wild man, even landing a right to the stomach. Jim went on the attack, landing well and knocking Peter against the rope. On the rebound, Courtney was hit by a straight left on the eye and another left on the jaw that wobbled him. Corbett landed a flush left hook to the jaw that dropped Courtney. After seven seconds, Courtney rose and swung wildly, but could not land. Corbett showered blows on his neck and face, punching him severely, but Courtney was still game. Time of the round: 1 minute and 12 seconds.

Corbett's quickness in this round was wonderful. When he feinted Courtney always jumped five feet away, but when Jim really let fly a hard blow it came so quickly that Courtney couldn't avoid it. Peter's heavy swings were generally wasted, for Jim's judge of distance was simply perfect, and he escaped many a blow by pulling himself just far enough away to let Peter's fist fly past one or two inches from him.

When Courtney went to his corner, Corbett called across the ring: "Did I hurt you?" "Naw!" answered Peter. "There's a buzzing sound in me head, but I guess it's the heat." Everybody had to laugh, including Corbett.

One source indicated that there was a two-minute rest period to reload the film (which had to be done after each round). In the 4th round, Courtney was still strong and rushed. Jim clinched and laughingly threw him off. They mixed it up a bit and Peter landed more blows than he had in all the previous rounds combined. He landed a strong right behind Jim's left ear, but Corbett countered with a body blow that doubled him up. Time of the round: 1 minute and 29 seconds.

"It was now a certainty that Courtney would not last the six rounds, but his gameness was incomprehensible. He was taking some fierce punching on the neck and jaw, but he seemed to be made of iron."

In the 5th round, Courtney once again rushed but missed. Jim landed a right to the mouth that drew blood, and followed up with two body blows and a cross to the jaw that sent Peter against the wall. Courtney came back with a grazing right, but Jim "punched his man when and where he pleased until time was up, finally doubling him up again with a punch in the wind." Time of the round: 1 minute and 23 seconds.

After the round, Corbett whispered to McVey,

Now I'll put him out. I'm going to rush him and slug his jaws with both hands. His defense is weak and I can easily beat down his guard. I've got to do it quick, though, for there's only a little over a minute, and that's a precious short time in which to knock a man out. He is dead game and will take some frightful smashes before he goes to sleep.

A New Jersey source said of the 6th round that Jim made every blow tell, and the first that landed sent Peter to the floor. After that, a left to the body and right to the jaw knocked him down on his face again. "Courtney showed wonderful pluck, although he was knocked out; he made a great effort to get up. After a game effort he almost got on his pins, but it was of no use." He was counted out, and it took two minutes before Peter realized what had happened.

The *Sun* said that Corbett "cut loose at once in the 6th round. He rushed at his antagonist like an infuriated wild beast and began to beat down his guard." Jim "swung a pile-driving left that landed squarely on the jaw,

Courtney staggering from the force of the blow. Then Jim sent his right across on the chin and knocked Peter to the floor in the champion's corner." Still, the game Peter rose and attacked. Jim nailed him on the jaw with his left, and then "felled him like an ox with his right on the same place." Courtney rolled over, crawled to his knees, but then collapsed forward on his face in an insensible state. The referee counted him out.

Corbett picked Courtney up, carried him to his corner, and helped bring Peter to his senses by pinching his ears and slapping his hands. When Courtney woke up, he said, "This Corbett is much stronger and a harder hitter than Fitzsimmons, and can lick him, sure. I've tackled both and I know what it is." Jim complimented his pluck, but also said that they had only fought about two rounds, if adding up the total time that they had boxed.

Later in the day, a man asked Jim if he had knocked anyone out that day. Jim laughed and said, "No! No! I just had a friendly boxing match with my trainer, McVey." The men all breathed a sigh of relief when they left New Jersey's jurisdiction.[685]

One report said that 16,440 separate views (frames) of the fight were taken. Not much footage remains because the nitrate films disintegrated over the years. One problem with viewing old films is that they are often projected either more slowly or quickly than they actually occurred. This is the result of the transfer process, when the film is projected at a different rate than it was filmed, or copying it to a filming device that records it at a different rate than it was filmed. Thankfully, the Moving Image Division of the Library of Congress in conjunction with the Museum of Modern Art has reproduced and projected 37 seconds of the 150 feet of 35-millimeter film, mastered at the proper projection speed of 36 frames per second. The filmmakers are listed as W.K.L. Dickson and William Heise, Edison's assistants. At the proper projection rate, one can get a much better feel for Corbett's speed and skill than with the slow motion and shorter version typically seen in most documentaries and collections, such as in the Academy Award nominated *Legendary Champions*.

Regarding ring apparel, both men were bare-chested. Courtney wore tight pants that extended down just below his knees. All Corbett wore was a strange looking pair of shorts that were not really shorts at all. It was less than that, actually revealing the lower portion of his behind/rear end and having the appearance of a small girdle in front. *The Sun* said that this was a "red elastic breech clout." The ring they boxed in only had one rope.

The short film shows that Corbett continuously kept a smile on his face, looking completely relaxed. As he was attacked, Jim was able to lean and/or step back, turn or roll his head away from punches, and was also good at dipping. Although he kept his hands down, he was able to quickly lift his

[685] *New York Sun*, September 8, 1894; *Newark Evening News*, September 8, 1894; *New York Herald*, September 8, 1894; *National Police Gazette*, September 22, 1894.

arms up and out defensively in order to block, smother, or clinch. He could also fire off a left jab counter, which he then held out momentarily, in order to create a defensive cage and to maintain his height and reach advantage. He was also good at clinching or putting his left hand around Courtney's neck. From the clinch, he would push off and then punch. Corbett had a particularly good snappy right, slipping it up the middle off of being clinched. He was known for being good at firing his right coming out of a clinch. Offensively, Jim would counter as he saw Courtney throwing, coming over or underneath Peter. Corbett appears to have quick reactions to what Courtney does, countering or defending well. Jim was rapid with his punches and slippery with his head movement and step backs.

Because less than a minute of the footage exists, it is difficult to get a read on the bout as a whole, and based on what written accounts have said about the fight, these moments are clearly not the most significant. Thus, it is perhaps unfair to critique Corbett's skills with such a small window into the bout. A local source said that the first 3 rounds were tame and "both men appeared to be playing and making a great many fancy movements in order to make a better display in the record." The existing footage appears to be this portion of the fight - the men giving a show for the camera.

However, using what is available, if one wanted to lodge any criticism it would be that Jim's punch form, particularly the hooking punches, left something to be desired. This is much more evident when watching the slow motion version. His straight punches, particularly his right, were surprisingly quick and snappy, but overall, he did not seem to have big power, relying more on speed and timing than on strength, punch form and putting body weight behind the blows. His hook was fairly long and wide and not very smooth. Generally, the counter hooks with the right and left have more of an arm swing quality, and he doesn't really get his body behind them all that well. However, Jim could have been sizing Courtney up and possibly working with him early on for the benefit of the camera.

Naturally, because of the very small ring, he was not able to exhibit his dancing skills very much, which may have overall affected the performance and view of his ability. Of course, against the shorter and smaller Courtney, he may not have felt the need to move much. Courtney still could not hit him.

Even in this short segment, it is clear how Corbett's relaxed quick moves and fine understanding of ring generalship could give a slugger difficulties. Corbett demonstrates excellent skill and ring knowledge, understanding when to pull back or dip away from a punch, how to lift his hands up and outstretch them to block or keep his opponent at bay with a stiff arm, how to clinch and put his hand behind his opponent's head, how to punch out of the clinch, how to counter, when to throw, and how to position himself with a bit of footwork in order to land or make his opponent miss. He even dipped to the right, and then pivoted/swiveled to the right. Corbett is economical with his moves, very relaxed and supremely confident, wearing a smile through it all, seeming just to be playing with his man. Courtney seems very amateurish but game, swinging wildly.

Bob Fitzsimmons said that the bout was meaningless, that "Courtney is not a man of any class at all, and I can tell you he never will be. He does not even know how to put up his hands." He said that Peter was not even a man who could earn a living from pugilism, and never had. "I do not believe that Corbett was sparring with him in earnest during the first part of the bout, for I am sure from what I know of Courtney that Corbett could have punched him out any time."[686]

When later that year discussing the possibility of a match between him and Bob Fitzsimmons being filmed, Corbett said,

> It is impossible to fight before the kinetoscope. I fought before it once, and it is all bosh to say that a battle according to Marquis of Queensberry rules can be fought before it. Do you know that a round can only last one minute, and that there is a rest between the rounds of ten minutes before the instrument can be regulated to faithfully reproduce the actions of the contestants in a mill?[687]

However, Edison would continue improving his technology.

Although not technically completely following the Queensberry rules, clearly the Corbett-Courtney bout was a fight, and Courtney was knocked out in the 6th round. However, given the fears of legal repercussions, the bout was subsequently spun as a mere exhibition for the camera.

Afterwards, it was reported that a Newark circuit court judge was going to charge a grand jury to investigate the matter and would "instruct the finding of an indictment against principals and spectators if the published reports of the affair are found to be correct. Glove contests and stage exhibitions are prohibited in that county." The judge told the grand jury, "I will ask you gentlemen to investigate…and if, as appears very probable, there has been a violation of the law, the Court will certainly expect from this Grand Jury that it will be followed by an indictment, no matter who are the parties concerned."[688]

Although a grand jury investigated, no charges were brought, although they certainly could have been. Corbett and Edison were stars, and they were doing something that a strong portion of the public supported and wanted to see, even if it was illegal. Star power had previously helped Corbett escape a conviction for fighting in Florida.

The fight was the first heavyweight championship (sort of) recorded by a movie camera. Boxing was a natural for the stationary movie camera because its participants competed in a small space. It also made economic

---

[686] *Times-Democrat*, September 11, 1894.
[687] *Chicago Herald*, December 25, 1894.
[688] *New York Clipper*, September 15, 1894; *New York Sun*, September 12, 1894.

sense because boxers were very popular, and fans were willing to pay to see the champ in action. Therefore, boxing helped make films a money-making enterprise. This was the only way to see Corbett other than to show up at one of his fights, exhibitions or plays.

At first, fans could only view the films in parlors, one person watching one round at a time through a hole in a wooden box, paying 5 or 10 cents per round, each round being contained within a separate kinetoscope device. That is how they had to view Corbett vs. Courtney in 1894. However, in 1895, the Lumiere brothers' cinematographe in France, and in 1896, Edison's vitascope in the U.S. enabled multiple persons to view a film at the same time, in a theater on a movie screen. Still, even with the limited viewing capabilities of the kinetoscope, the Corbett-Courtney bout was the first film to make serious money, generating around $30,000. As a result, boxing is history's best recorded sport. What hindered film preservation was the fact that the nitrate films tended to deteriorate over time.

CHAPTER 17

Challenges Unfulfilled

James J. Corbett had boxed Peter Courtney during the time that negotiations were ongoing with Peter Jackson. In September 1894, there was further discussion of the Jackson-Corbett fight taking place in Iowa, but not until a date between May 15 or June 15 of 1895, yet another nine or ten months away. This was also in the face of clear opposition by the state's governor. As a result, a clause in the proposed contract also said that the fight might have to take place on a barge. The articles allowed each man $2,500 for training expenses, but also dictated that each make a $5,000 deposit to guarantee their appearance.

On behalf of Corbett, Bill Brady immediately signed the proposed articles. Jackson's manager Tom O'Rourke responded to Brady, "Say you're remarkably quick, ain't you? You must have had some previous understanding, because you're so anxious to put your name to the document." He was implying that the articles were drawn up by Brady and might actually be a bluff.

Peter Jackson questioned the authenticity of the Sioux City offer, especially in light of the unusually lengthy wait before the fight would come off. He did not want to wait that long to fight, nor did he want to fight on a barge and violate the law. There were other aspects of the potential agreement that gave him the impression that the offer was not on the up and up. He believed that Corbett and Brady were really behind it, using it as a way to feign interest in the fight, but that it was really just a sham. In his objection to the articles, Jackson stated,

> I'll not fight on any barge, and Corbett knows it. … In the first place, I would not wait eight or nine months to fight…. I have given up all my theatrical engagements in order to have this fight pulled off, and now the date is fixed for a time when Corbett's theatrical season will be closed. That shows you plainly enough that either Corbett, Brady, or both had a hand in drawing up these articles.
>
> In the second place I am not going to take the chance of being bandied about from one State to another like a shuttlecock, with a probability that in the end I will have to fight in the middle of the river. I will fight before a reputable club or not at all, and I must have the exact locality, even down to the club house, fixed. Then I must be guaranteed police protection. I am a law abiding citizen, and I am not going to break the law. Another objection is the clause about

compelling us to put up $5,000 each as guarantee, and then allowing us only half that sum for training expenses. Why, that is ridiculous.

I've been a secondary consideration in this business all along, and I am tired of it. On account of waiting for this business I have made no dates for my show. Now Corbett wants me to wait a year to fight him. I don't see why I should do so. If the public wants a fight they will get it. I am going to wash my hands of the whole matter. ...

I don't think the club is acting in good faith, and I don't believe it could bring off the fight, anyhow. It is pretty plain that all this is merely an advertising dodge of Corbett's. I am tired of being a party to it, and I quit right here.[689]

Jackson wanted to fight within three months on a positively named date and location, or before the National Club in London upon the same conditions. "You do not specify where the fight is to be held, and may compel me to fight in the woods or on a barge in some river." He felt the articles were not honest and were drawn up to satisfy Corbett. Jackson even questioned the existence of the Sioux City Athletic Club.[690]

The *New York Clipper* also reported Jackson's objections and feeling that the proposed fight such a long time off in the future was really a Corbett bluff/act to save face, not a legitimate offer and acceptance with a real intent to fight there.

[Corbett] knew well enough that he would not wait so long for a fight...and if he could not get it he would now give up trying, and would allow Corbett to continue unmolested in his theatrical business, which it was plain he preferred to fighting a man who in a previous unsatisfactory contest had proven his equal, although handicapped by an injured leg. He was determined to be no longer a party to the business of advertising the champion and Brady's show enterprises. Besides, he had little faith in the genuineness of the offer of the Sioux City people, or in their ability to deliver the goods.... While Corbett will have the best of the argument, in the minds of the general public, through having signed the articles, thinking people, who are aware that a champion has no right to set a date for a fight so far ahead, but that in all championship matches there are certain rules, long established, that cannot be ignored, even by so mighty a man as the champion himself, will withhold from him the credit of being at all anxious for another passage at arms with the dusky boxer who, on the occasion of their meeting on the Pacific coast, rendered quite as good an account of himself as did "Pompadour Jim" during the progress of their sixty round engagement. Evidently the champion has not

[689] *New York Sun*, September 9, 1894.
[690] *New York Sun*, September 12, 1894.

forgotten that meeting. From the present outlook it is not at all likely that Jim and Peter will ever meet, and, if they do not, the blame for the failure will not attach to the sable slugger any more than to the champion.[691]

However, unlike the *New York Clipper*, the *National Police Gazette* felt that if the fight did not take place, it would not be Corbett's fault. Ironically, it criticized Jackson's objection to fighting on a barge if the law would not allow the fight. Jackson said, "I am a law abiding citizen, and I am not going to break the law." The *Police Gazette* felt that Peter was unwilling to go the extra mile to make the fight happen, even in the North. After all, Sullivan and Corbett had fought on barges and contrary to the law. Violating the law was seen as part of the business.[692]

Corbett had won the title in September 1892, did not defend for one year and four months, and even then defended against a less than worthy contender in Charley Mitchell in late January 1894, avoiding Jackson. Early in the year, Jim said he needed three months to prepare for Jackson. By mid-1894, Corbett said he needed six months to prepare. Now, as of late August/early September, the fight was potentially going to be delayed for yet another nine or ten months. Thus, even if the offer was legitimate, Corbett was asking Jackson to wait over two and a half years since Jim won the title for Peter to have his rightful championship challenge. Certainly, to Jackson, it looked as if Corbett wanted to delay the fight as long as possible, until Peter was well past his prime, and so that Jim could continue making easy money on his theatrical tour while giving the impression that he intended to have the big fight so as not to be called a coward.

Corbett had fought Jackson 61 rounds to a draw and performed quite well. Jim had only gained valuable experience and strength since then and was in the prime of his life, and possibly could have defeated Jackson, who was not getting any younger. However, Corbett also knew that Jackson was no easy task and was at least a risk. Jackson was clever, larger, well conditioned, very experienced, and would likely make adjustments from their first fight, in addition to being better trained as a result of not having to deal with a hurt ankle. Corbett probably wanted easier paydays with less risk of losing the title.

Although he had to endure some criticism, Corbett also knew that not too many writers would give him hell over failing to make a championship match with a black man. He would be acting consistently with the time's social mores. Also, by stating that he would fight Jackson in the South and by signing the Sioux City articles, he at least gave some impression that he was interested in the fight, enough that he could avoid serious heat.

---

[691] *New York Clipper*, September 15, 1894.
[692] *National Police Gazette*, September 22, 1894.

Still, if Jackson had truly wanted the title, to put real pressure on Corbett to make the match, he could have agreed to fight in New Orleans, Florida, or Sioux City, and could have agreed to wait for the fight. He could have agreed to fight in the North in secret, outside the law. This would have left Corbett with no option but to fight him or appear ridiculously afraid. The South was the one place where the fight could possibly have been legally fought to a finish and the boxers paid what they required for such a huge match. By refusing to fight in the South or outside the bounds of the law, Jackson essentially left them with no immediately known place in America to fight.

It is possible that Jackson was no more interested in the fight than Corbett was. Jackson knew that defeating a prime and improved Corbett would be no easy task. Peter had already almost lost to him once, and Jim had only gained more experience and strength since then, while Peter was now 33 years old. Perhaps Jackson also felt that he had more to gain by the fight's failure to come off. He could go down in history as never having been defeated by Corbett.

However, it is also possible that Jackson believed based on his experience over the past couple of years that somehow the match would fall through and never materialize. He therefore decided to stop wasting his time. Jackson felt that the contract discussions were not in earnest and that it was all a Corbett "advertising dodge." Peter later said, "I am glad of one thing, and that is that I exposed his fake fighting club in Sioux City." He had a point. Corbett never did fight anyone in Iowa.[693]

Peter Jackson left America in mid-September 1894, saying, "He has had many chances to make this match, but for reasons best known to himself he has refrained from doing so. He can now go ahead with his theatrical tour. I will no longer annoy him, as I am convinced that he prefers the stage to the prize ring." He also said, "I am through with Corbett. He can say whatever he pleases... He is the champion of the world. I am plain Peter Jackson. Corbett has refused to be reasonable in making a match, and I have decided to let the matter drop. He has got all the advertising out of me he is going to get."

Still, some said that it was Jackson who was afraid to meet Corbett. A *National Police Gazette* writer later said, "It was Jackson who jumped out of the country, and whatever claim he had for a return match he forfeited with that masterly retreat. The chance to fight he then threw away."[694] Jackson subsequently became less and less active in competitive bouts, boxing mostly in short exhibitions, and was totally avoided by all the top fighters.

---

[693] *National Police Gazette*, September 22, 1894.
[694] *National Police Gazette*, September 29, 1894, June 1, 1895.

Corbett returned to performing in his *Gentleman Jack* tour, first stopping in Washington, D.C. in mid-September.[695]

Bob Fitzsimmons

Bob Fitzsimmons again challenged Corbett and made it known his belief that he could defeat him. However, Corbett said that he would not fight Bob unless he first defeated Steve O'Donnell. John L. Sullivan said that Fitzsimmons could defeat Jim and believed that Corbett did not want to fight anyone. Corbett felt that Fitzsimmons had to prove himself further as a heavyweight, that if he defeated Bob, it would be said that he was too small, and he would get no credit for the victory, as had been the case with Mitchell. Fitz countered that he had defeated heavyweight Peter Maher, and that Corbett had promised him a match if he defeated Joe Choynski and Dan Creedon, which he had done. Corbett denied that he had made such a promise. Fitz said, "I am not an actor; I am a fighter... If Corbett ignores

---

[695] *New York Clipper,* September 15, 1894.

me, I will go ahead and do the fighting and permit him to enjoy his ill-earned reputation by posing as an actor."

The Olympic Club offered a $25,000 purse for the Fitzsimmons-Corbett fight and said that if Corbett did not accept that it would recognize Fitzsimmons as the champion. Fitz posted his $1,000 deposit and wrote Corbett a letter stating that tradition dictated that if he did not accept the challenge that Jim would forfeit the championship. Corbett wrote back saying that he would only enter the ring once more and that he wanted it to be against the best man in the world, who he did not think was Fitzsimmons (but did not say who it was). "I care nothing for the past history of the ring or its obsolete rules."[696]

Things were starting to look bad for Corbett, especially given the course of the failed negotiations with Jackson. It appeared as if Jim did not want to fight any legitimate contender and that his ultimatum for Bob to fight O'Donnell was a bluff to avoid Fitzsimmons. The two parties met on October 11. Corbett began playing his negotiation games again, as he had done with Jackson, but they did not work this time. Jim insisted that his theatrical engagements prevented him from fighting until July 1895. Fitzsimmons agreed to wait, saying, "I'll give in. I'll waive everything so as to fight you. I'll make every concession."

> The champion was strangely averse to fighting in New Orleans as long as Bob seemed desirous of meeting him there, but when the Australian suddenly shifted and agreed to fight at Jacksonville Corbett had no alternative but to put up his money and fight. In short, Fitzsimmons has the satisfaction of knowing that he compelled Corbett to accept his challenge and that the O'Donnell bluff didn't go.

In order to save face, Corbett was essentially compelled to agree to fight Fitzsimmons. The two agreed to fight sometime after July 1, 1895 before the Florida Athletic Club, which made the highest purse bid of $41,000. The two also agreed to a stake/side bet of $10,000 each.[697]

For the rest of 1894, Corbett continued his theatrical engagements with *Gentleman Jack*, the real reason why he did not want to fight any time soon. He was making easy money in the theater.[698]

Corbett did not fight very often during his championship reign. To that point, since his September 1892 defeat of Sullivan, Corbett had only defended against Mitchell and Courtney in 1894, neither of whom were legitimate top contenders. It turned out that he would not defend at all in 1895, although as will be discussed, he was not entirely to blame. Legal and political complications would eventually cause the time and location of the

---

[696] *New York Sun*, September 28, 30, 1894; October 2, 1894.
[697] *New York Sun*, October 12, 1894.
[698] *Brooklyn Daily Eagle*, October 11, 1894; *National Police Gazette*, October 27, 1894.

Fitzsimmons match to be changed multiple times. It was postponed from July to October 1895, and then indefinitely.

In November 1894, Fitzsimmons killed Con Riordan in a sparring session. He would have to stand trial for manslaughter, which put the bout off for a while. Other legal issues intervened as well. In mid-December 1894, the Florida legislature passed a law making boxing a felony, so the fight could not take place there.[699]

Corbett continued boxing in many short exhibitions in 1895 with sparring partners such as Jim McVey and Steve O'Donnell, and later Jim Daly, amongst others, in addition to and usually as part of performances of the play *Gentleman Jack*. O'Donnell was an experienced Australian fighter who in the 1880s had sparred and trained with the likes of Peter Jackson, and possibly even Bob Fitzsimmons. In 1893, O'Donnell won a 4-round decision over Frank Craig and fought George Godfrey to a 6-round draw. He had also been a Charley Mitchell sparring partner.

Corbett was in New Orleans, Louisiana on January 4, 1895 with *Gentleman Jack*. The ticket prices ranged anywhere from $.15 to $1.00. The exhibition got a bit more serious than it was supposed to. According to the local paper, Corbett first sparred Australian Steve O'Donnell, but O'Donnell, "in doing the 'fake' knockout in the three-round bout, fell and sprained his ankle. Of course this necessitated another sparring partner, so big John McVey, the famous wrestler, was substituted." McVey was listed as being over 200 pounds.

McVey began by landing right and left swings. Corbett smiled and jabbed. McVey landed a hard right to the side. "The audience saw that the bout was out of the usual run of stage exhibitions, and when McVey landed one or two swings he was given a great cheer." After Corbett's face was reddened, he cut loose on McVey. He hit the nose with stiff left jabs, and the ribs with rights, keeping the pace fast. Corbett began driving him about the ring, and McVey swung back with both hands, landing several times. "McVey made a grand rush for the champion and tried to land swings with both hands. Corbett checked him with his left in the face and like a flash sent the right across the jaw. McVey fell in a heap." He was knocked out. The curtain fell and restoratives were applied, but it was some minutes before McVey came to.

McVey "remarked that he had not boxed with the champion in some time, and when he got into the ring he thought it was best to make matters warm." Corbett said,

> Poor Mac. It was accidental.... Now, as he is a big, strong fellow, you can imagine that his blows are rather hard. He knows nothing about boxing practically, and all he can do is to swing with both hands.... When he came in at me pretty stiff, I had to give it to him hard, for

---

[699] Fox at 61.

his blows would have knocked me against the ropes in a jiffy. I put it across his jaw, but I had no idea of knocking him out.

The local paper did not say how many rounds they had boxed. Most secondary source records indicate that it was a 3rd round knockout. It most certainly could have been the 1st round. Showing no hard feelings, they boxed again there again the following night, on January 5.[700]

Throughout January and February, Corbett and Steve O'Donnell gave sparring exhibitions, as O'Donnell was Corbett's main sparring partner at that time. Usually, their sparring was part of the touring play, *Gentleman Jack*.

STEVE O'DONNELL.

When interviewed in St. Paul, Minnesota in late January 1895, Corbett said that he was in the game for money and would quit while his credit was still good. Perhaps frustrated by the legal impediments to the sport, Jim said that pugilism had no future because the public was against it. Regarding his fight with Fitzsimmons and his motivation for remaining in the game, Corbett said,

> Is there anything in this fight for me but money? It is simply a business proposition with me. Some people say that I don't appreciate the glory there is in it. I tell you that the glory don't count. I settled that in my mind when I went into the ring with John L. Sullivan. When I put in an appearance there was a distinct hiss, and when the champion came in he was cheered to the echo. When I had him licked – and I knew he hadn't the least chance when he went into the ring – the people who had hissed me went wild with enthusiasm and cheered until they were hoarse. And what was there for Sullivan? – the hisses. Public favor is a great thing for a pugilist, but it only lasts while he is champion…. I can't last forever, and I don't intend that any one shall get hold of me when I am past my prime and beat me. I shall fight Fitz and then quit.[701]

---

[700] *Daily Picayune*, January 6, 1895; *Times-Democrat*, January 4, 5, 1895.
[701] *Minneapolis Tribune*, January 23, 1895.

Corbett was about the money more than the glory, and this probably explains his decisions while he was champion. Jim minimized risk by taking on what he thought were lesser challengers and scheduling matches out into the future as far as possible, so he could make money in plays during the interim.

Corbett spoke to a delegation of Minnesota legislators about the ethics of boxing. He said that boxing had greatly improved, that most boxing deaths were accidental, as a result of the head landing on the hard floor, not from the blows themselves. The remedy suggested was a padded ring. Brutality could also be done away with by requiring large gloves and expert referees who could stop bouts before the danger point was reached. The local writer opined,

> This would certainly destroy the brutality, but would it not also destroy interest in the prize fighting? The element of danger and bloodshed are the acute attractions. If ring contests are made mere "pillow fights," prize fighting would probably cease to be a profitable occupation…. Perhaps that would be a good way to abolish it.[702]

Regarding boxing's alleged brutality and the public's hypocrisy, late the previous year, Corbett had compared boxing with football.

> The college men play football for glory, and it looks to me as though the highest aim of some of the players is to maim an opponent. The spectacle of one fellow on the ground with half a dozen others jumping on his neck may be a pleasant one to some folks. I want none of it in mine.
>
> When it comes to brutality there is nothing that I know of…which compares with football…. Look over the record for this year alone and see the number of young men who have been permanently injured by being jumped on or kicked. Yet men and women who would hold up their hands in horror at the sight of a boxing glove pay fabulous prices to watch these brutal exhibitions and shout themselves hoarse before they get through.
>
> Boxing where professionals are concerned in it, is frowned upon by a majority of the people who patronize football games…. If I had sons, and they were in doubt as to whether they should become football players or professional boxers, I should advise them to take to the roped arena.[703]

Still, boxing remained illegal in most jurisdictions. Football was growing in popularity at the college level, and became a professional sport in 1895.

---

[702] *Minneapolis Tribune*, February 3, 1895.
[703] *Cincinnati Enquirer*, December 4, 1894.

While in St. Paul at the end of January and in early February, Corbett made money with *Gentleman Jack*. During the ring scene, the fans enjoyed his 9-ounce glove exhibition with Steve O'Donnell. Of his future plans, Corbett said, "Whatever the result of my meeting with Fitzsimmons...I shall quit prize fighting with the finish of that contest."[704] Corbett was tired of boxing.

There was some talk of Corbett fighting strong man Sandow, who was perhaps America's first body builder (and who had posed for Edison's films). Corbett said that he would bet anywhere from $2,500 to $10,000 that he would knock out Sandow in 1 round.[705] The fight did not happen.

Jim opened up a week's engagement in Philadelphia on February 18, 1895. His physical form appeared solid, as if he was in training. Showing respect for his next opponent, Corbett said that he did not think he would knock Fitzsimmons out very quickly, but felt confident that he would win within 20 rounds.[706]

While in Scranton, Pennsylvania on February 27, Corbett and O'Donnell sparred 3 rounds as part of *Gentleman Jack*.[707] They continued doing so in their travels from town to town.

While in Scranton, Corbett insisted that he did not and would not draw the color line, and also said that Peter Jackson was afraid to meet him, that when he was in England, Peter should have come over to fight him then. Of course, it was odd to say that, because Jim had previously said that he did not want to fight Jackson in England. Still, Corbett insisted,

> Some pugilists bar out men of color. Sullivan drew the color line. I will not. I will fight any man who puts up a forfeit and subscribes to reasonable conditions. Jackson has everything to gain by whipping me. It would mean thousands to me. ...
>
> I know that some people have said that I am afraid of Jackson, have even said that I am afraid of Fitzsimmons. That is simply because I have not adopted Sullivan's methods. I do not come out upon the stage and bluster. ... I am afraid of no man on this earth.

When asked what he thought of Fitzsimmons, Jim said, "Fitzsimmons, properly speaking, is a freak. He is a lightweight who is as large as I am, a man who has defeated all other light weights because he was much larger than they were. He is a heavyweight in everything except the weight, in that he is lacking." When asked whether Fitz was a very scientific fighter, Jim responded,

---

[704] *St. Paul Pioneer Press*, February 3, 1895.
[705] *Minneapolis Tribune*, February 5, 1895.
[706] *Philadelphia Inquirer*, February 19, 1895.
[707] *Scranton Times*, February 27, 1895.

Where has he demonstrated that? Surely not in the battles he has fought. In a recent glove contest Choynski nearly had him out, Fitzsimmons was groggy and I have defeated Choynski several times. I do not say that I can defeat him in three rounds, but I am confident that the fight will not last twenty.[708]

In March, 177-pound Steve O'Donnell boxed 220-pound Jake Kilrain to an 8-round draw, but Steve was considered to have had the best of it.[709]

By April 1895, Corbett declared that if Fitzsimmons did not come up with his end of the stake money for their fight that he would go to England and fight Peter Jackson, the very thing Corbett had said that he would not do when he had been negotiating a Jackson bout.[710] It had been rumored that Jackson was no longer in condition and was deteriorating as the result of a drinking habit. Thus, Corbett's reversal at that time left him open to some criticism. "By recognizing Jackson now, after scoring his pretensions so severely at the time the Australian had his money posted and was in condition to fight him, Corbett leaves himself open to criticism and a lot of things reflecting on his courage might be said by people who are inimical to him." Another report said,

> Corbett looks upon the black now as an easy proposition, and would like to force, cajole or coax him into a fight. To defeat him would clinch his claim to the title of champion of the world, upon which he could retire with a useful capital for the profession of acting, in which he aspires to be a shining light.[711]

Some felt that Jim was only willing to fight Jackson once he realized that Peter was no longer in fighting condition. Jackson was incredulous, saying, "It took you three years to make up your mind to fight me!" Corbett replied, "Yes, but now I've got you where I want you, and I'm your master!"[712]

Corbett was probably insincere about the proposed bout anyway, simply using the prospect of an alternative Jackson bout to put pressure on Fitzsimmons. He was not above using such tactics. However, some thought that Corbett was actually looking for a way out of the Fitzsimmons match, because he realized that Bob had a chance to win.[713] The out of shape and inactive Jackson at that point might have been an easier task. By 1895, the 33-year-old Jackson was living the good life and no longer active in the sport but for some short exhibitions, convinced that a Corbett bout would never occur. After 1895, he essentially retired.

---

[708] *Scranton Times*, February 28, 1895.
[709] *National Police Gazette*, March 30, 1895.
[710] *National Police Gazette*, April 27, 1895, May 11, 1895.
[711] *National Police Gazette*, May 25, 1895.
[712] *National Police Gazette*, June 1, 1895.
[713] *National Police Gazette*, June 1, 1895.

Some criticized Corbett, while others were glad that the Jackson match did not take place. In 1895, the editor of the *New York Sun* wrote,

> We are in the midst of a growing menace…a black rise against white supremacy. Just at present we are safe from the humiliation of having a black man world's champion, but we had a pretty narrow escape…. Less than a year ago, Peter Jackson could have whipped the world - Corbett, Fitzsimmons….but today he is a human wreck and thus the white race is saved from having at the head of pugilism a Negro.

It went on to say that although blacks had been made to feel that they belonged to "an inferior race," in recent years, with education and training, "the Negro has evinced as much courage in combat as the white man."[714]

Later in 1895, former champion John L. Sullivan said, "No man of principle…will fight in a ring with a colored man. No man can say I ever refused to fight when the time came for a fight, but I never would fight with a nigger."[715] He said this with pride.

The following year, in 1896, the Supreme Court of the United States decided *Plessy v. Ferguson*, holding that separate but equal accommodations for blacks did not violate the 14th amendment's equal protection clause. The decision meant that social discrimination was legally acceptable and enforceable. It allowed for the propagation and continuation of laws requiring separation of the races in all aspects of life. It was essentially an affirmation of the prevailing public opinion and scientific racism being espoused at the time.

The *Plessy* decision, because it lends insight into the status of race relations in America for decades to come, which affected how the sport of boxing was conducted, is worth partial reproduction herein. In *Plessy v. Ferguson*, 163 U.S. 537 (1896), a person who was 7/8 caucasian and only 1/8 black refused to move from a passenger train coach reserved for whites only into one reserved for blacks, as required by law. The court found that a law imposing separate but equal accommodations based upon race did not violate the 14th amendment, stating:

> The object of the amendment was undoubtedly to enforce the absolute equality of the two races before the law, but, in the nature of things, it could not have been intended to abolish distinctions based upon color, or to enforce social, as distinguished from political, equality, or a commingling of the two races upon terms unsatisfactory to either. Laws permitting, and even requiring, their separation, in places where they are liable to be brought into contact, do not necessarily imply the inferiority of either race to the other, and have been generally, if not universally, recognized as within the competency

[714] Nat Fleischer, *Black Dynamite* (U.S.: Nat Fleischer, 1938), volume 1, pages 6-8, quoting *The New York Sun*.

[715] *Brooklyn Daily Eagle*, December 10, 1895.

of the state legislatures in the exercise of their police power. The most common instance of this is connected with the establishment of separate schools for white and colored children, which have been held to be a valid exercise of the legislative power even by courts of states where the political rights of the colored race have been longest and most earnestly enforced....

[W]e think the enforced separation of the races, as applied to the internal commerce of the state, neither abridges the privileges or immunities of the colored man, deprives him of his property without due process of law, nor denies him the equal protection of the laws, within the meaning of the fourteenth amendment...

If the two races are to meet upon terms of social equality, it must be the result of natural affinities, a mutual appreciation of each other's merits, and a voluntary consent of individuals.

In his dissent, Justice Harlan stated:

The white race deems itself to be the dominant race in this country. And so it is, in prestige, in achievements, in education, in wealth, and in power. So, I doubt not, it will continue to be for all time, if it remains true to its great heritage, and holds fast to the principles of constitutional liberty. But in view of the constitution, in the eye of the law, there is in this country no superior, dominant, ruling class of citizens. There is no caste here. Our constitution is color-blind, and neither knows nor tolerates classes among citizens. In respect of civil rights, all citizens are equal before the law....

It is therefore to be regretted that this high tribunal, the final expositor of the fundamental law of the land, has reached the conclusion that it is competent for a state to regulate the enjoyment by citizens of their civil rights solely upon the basis of race....

In my opinion, the judgment this day rendered will, in time, prove to be quite as pernicious as the decision made by this tribunal in the Dred Scott Case.

It was adjudged in that case that the descendants of Africans who were imported into this country, and sold as slaves, were not included nor intended to be included under the word "citizens" in the constitution, and could not claim any of the rights and privileges which that instrument provided for and secured to citizens of the United States; that, at time of the adoption of the constitution, they were "considered as a subordinate and inferior class of beings, who had been subjugated by the dominant race, and, whether emancipated or not, yet remained subject to their authority, and had no rights or privileges but such as those who held the power and the government might choose to grant them." 17 How. 393, 404....

The destinies of the two races, in this country, are indissolubly linked together, and the interests of both require that the common government of all shall not permit the seeds of race hate to be planted under the sanction of law. What can more certainly arouse race hate, what more certainly create and perpetuate a feeling of distrust between these races, than state enactments which, in fact, proceed on the ground that colored citizens are so inferior and degraded that they cannot be allowed to sit in public coaches occupied by white citizens? That, as all will admit, is the real meaning of such legislation as was enacted in Louisiana.

Although there were some black champions in the lighter weight divisions, and some mixed race bouts in non-championship heavyweight matches, when it came to the most prestigious heavyweight championship, only white vs. white matches would be seen for quite some time. The Supreme Court's majority decision essentially reflected the views put forth by John L. Sullivan when he refused to fight Peter Jackson, and reflected the views of others who opposed mixed race matches. However, Corbett never admitted to drawing the color line. He argued that circumstances and Jackson himself had prevented the fight. If Corbett avoided Jackson, it probably had nothing to do with race, but economics: Jackson was a potential threat to his valuable championship status.

In early May 1895, in a rematch, Corbett sparring partner Steve O'Donnell scored a KO21 over former Sullivan challenger Jake Kilrain.

On June 8, 1895 at Madison Square Garden, Corbett and Fitzsimmons sparred in separate exhibitions at a benefit for Jack Dempsey. Corbett sparred John McVey, Fitzsimmons sparred Frank Bosworth, while Joe Choynski sparred Bob Armstrong, a black fighter, and John L. Sullivan sparred Dempsey.

At that point, both Corbett and Fitzsimmons had posted their $5,000 forfeit to guarantee their appearance in the ring for their now scheduled October 31 match in the bout's new location, Dallas, Texas (although still sponsored by the Florida Athletic Club).[716]

On June 27, 1895 in New York, 28-year-old Corbett and 36-year-old John L. Sullivan gave a sparring exhibition. Jim played with John, "tapping him where and when he pleased," sparring 3 "pretty but short rounds."[717]

In July 1895, a jury acquitted Bob Fitzsimmons after his trial for manslaughter in relation to the death of his sparring partner Con Riordan.[718]

On July 29, the Governor of Texas announced that he was refusing to allow the Corbett-Fitzsimmons fight to take place in Texas. Still, Corbett

---

[716] *New York Clipper*, June 15, 1895.
[717] *New York Herald*, June 28, 1895.
[718] *National Police Gazette*, July 20, 1895.

remained hopeful that the fight would take place in Dallas as scheduled, on October 31.[719]

On August 10, when both Corbett and Fitzsimmons were in Philadelphia, they got into a scuffle at a hotel, revealing that this match would be personal.[720] The hot-headed Corbett was severely criticized for pulling Bob's nose and then spitting in his face.[721] Corbett said of the incident,

> In pulling Fitzsimmons' nose I simply resented a long string of insults that he had heaped upon me. I did what any man would do under the circumstances.
>
> The fact that Fitzsimmons was in Philadelphia at another hotel 24 hours before I arrived makes it seem rather strange why he should come over to my hotel and register. I would also like to ask why he threw a decanter at my little brother instead of at me. Everybody held me, while nobody took hold of Fitzsimmons.
>
> Fitzsimmons is a coward, and he knows it himself. When I get him in the ring at Dallas I'll prove to the world what a quitter he is. Yes, I did spit in his face, but it was because I was held and I couldn't do anything else. Had I been free I would have given him one in the jaw…. Mitchell is more of a man than this fellow, because he said what he had to say to my face, and took his defeat later without a squeal.[722]

On August 12 in Scranton, Pennsylvania before a crowd of 6,000, Corbett played with the Scranton baseball team against Buffalo. Corbett received 40% of the gate receipts. He then headed to Buffalo.[723]

For ticket prices ranging from $.25 to $1, fans watched Corbett spar both Jim Daly and John McVey in Buffalo, New York on August 13, 1895. Apparently, the two Jims had made up and Daly once again joined Corbett's sparring team. Steve O'Donnell was listed as having been Corbett's sparring partner for the last year. It was reported that Corbett was willing to meet and stop anyone within 4 rounds or forfeit $100, but no one accepted.

Corbett first sparred Daly 3 rounds. Daly was mostly defensive, and "the last round closed with the inevitable uppercut that Daly knew so well to expect when he was Corbett's sparring partner in years gone by."

After an intervening exhibition, Corbett sparred McVey. In the 1st round, McVey lost his temper and Corbett laughed at him. In the 2nd round, Mac began slugging away in anger and landed some good blows before Corbett stopped him and said, "This here isn't a fight. Spar if you are going

[719] *Buffalo Courier,* July 30, 1895.
[720] *Buffalo Courier,* August 14, 1895.
[721] *National Police Gazette,* August 31, 1895.
[722] *Buffalo Courier,* August 16, 1895.
[723] *Buffalo Evening News,* August 13, 1895.

to but quit this." Corbett punished McVey in the 3rd round and gave him many good thumps that he would remember for a long time, but McVey was able to take it and mixed it up intensely, making it seem to be more of a fight. Corbett "delighted everyone with his general skill. He can duck and dodge, cut and counter, feint and follow, as well as ever and everyone believed he spoke the truth when…he said he would defeat Fitzsimmons."

While in Buffalo, Corbett said, "Jackson won't ever fight me; never. He won't fight anywhere else but London, and I would not fight him there because they won't have a fight to a finish." Speaking of Tom O'Rourke, George Dixon's backer and manager, who had also been advising Jackson, Corbett said, "Any man…who ties himself up to a couple of niggers tips himself off."[724]

A couple days later, on August 15, 1895 at Bath Beach, New York, Corbett again sparred 3 rounds with McVey. That day, Fitzsimmons and Corbett came within a few paces of each other at Manhattan Beach, but they simply glared at each other.[725]

On August 16 in Buffalo before a crowd of thousands, Corbett sparred 4 rounds with McVey, who "looked like a fattened cow ready for the butcher." "Corbett danced about and slapped him in the face whenever he wanted to."[726]

The next day in Buffalo, impressed spectators paid 50 cents each to watch Bob Fitzsimmons give a bag punching exhibition and spar 4 rounds with Tom Forrest.[727]

Interest in the Fitzsimmons fight was building, and in September, Corbett was said to be looking very good in his training sessions. One month before the scheduled fight, on the afternoon of September 30, 1895 at Madison Square Garden, Jim sparred, hit the bags, and demonstrated his condition. Corbett first threw the medicine ball with five men. He then worked with pulley weights and a wrist machine. Then he worked the bags. "At this game he has no superior. He jabbed and uppercut the ball with astonishing rapidity and precision."

Corbett also sparred single rounds with John Donaldson and Jim Daly, and then worked 3 rounds with Steve O'Donnell, who "was bleeding at the nose and badly winded when Corbett's trainers directed that the boxing stop." Summarizing Corbett's training and appearance, it was said, "He pranced and sparred and twisted and hopped like a school boy out for a good time, and if he does not defeat Fitzsimmons it will not be owing to lack of condition. His exhibitions of strength and endurance were remarkable."

---

[724] *Buffalo Courier*, August 13, 14, 1895; *Buffalo Evening News*, August 13, 1895; *National Police Gazette*, August 31, 1895.
[725] *Buffalo Courier*, August 16, 1895.
[726] *Buffalo Courier*, August 17, 1895; *Buffalo Evening News*, August 17, 1895.
[727] *Buffalo Courier*, August 18, 1895; *Buffalo Evening News*, August 17, 1895.

That same day, in the evening, Corbett again sparred. First he worked 3 rounds with Tom Forrest, who the previous month had sparred Fitzsimmons. "Corbett could have finished the Long Islander with a single blow, but he contented himself with giving him an occasional thump. ... Corbett and O'Donnell then sparred three clever rounds." Corbett seemed fresh at the end.[728] Clearly, he was taking Fitzsimmons seriously and was getting himself into shape well in advance of their fight. This was the type of condition that he had been in when approaching the Sullivan fight.

Unfortunately, legal difficulties put the Corbett-Fitzsimmons bout in jeopardy. Initially, Florida had wanted it, but a law was passed preventing it. Texas was then agreed upon, but political forces did not want to allow the fight there either. Texas governor Charles Culberson made an appeal to the state legislature, which then specially convened on October 2, 1895 and voted 27 to 1 in the Senate and 110 to 5 in the House to enact a law making boxing a felony punishable by imprisonment for not less than two nor more than five years. "Thus, within three hours did the Legislature put an end to prize fighting in Texas." Even the President of Mexico was opposed to allowing boxing in his country.[729]

On October 9, there was discussion of Hot Springs, Arkansas as a possible alternative location, for the fight to take place there as scheduled on October 31. The Hot Springs Railroad Company said that it would provide transportation to the fight grounds. The local mayor was in favor of hosting the fight.[730]

DAN A. STUART.

However, on October 10, a judge summoned the Hot Springs sheriff to inform him that a fight there would be in violation of the law and would outrage the dignity of the state. Prize fighting was a felony. The judge was backed by Arkansas Governor James Clark, who wrote a threatening letter to the pugilists and promoter Dan Stuart, warning them not to have a fight there.

On the 13th, in order to comply with the requirements of the law, the decision was made to amend the articles of

[728] *New York Herald*, October 1, 1895.
[729] *New York Clipper*, October 12, 1895; Fields at 93.
[730] On October 9, 1895, Corbett punched the bag and sparred a few rounds with Steve O'Donnell. *Arkansas Gazette*, October 10, 1895.

agreement to make the fight one of a limited number of rounds rather than to a finish, and to give the referee the power to stop the exhibition if it became too brutal.[731]

There was some indication that the bout might be in jeopardy when Fitzsimmons objected to it being scheduled for 25 rounds instead of a fight to the finish. However, the rounds limitation was necessary in order to satisfy the Arkansas court that it was not a "prize fight."[732] Corbett claimed that Bob was trying to wriggle out of the fight. This was somewhat ironic, given that the reason previously offered by Corbett as to why he would not fight Peter Jackson in England was that he would only defend the title in a fight to the finish, and that England would only allow a limited rounds contest. Clearly, Jim thought that he could stop Fitz within 20 or 25 rounds, but not Jackson.

On October 17, Corbett voluntarily submitted to arrest in order to test the Arkansas anti-prize fight law in the courts. His side argued that given that it was a limited rounds contest, it was not a prize fight in the true sense of the term. A judge found that no prize fight was contemplated, but a boxing contest with five-ounce gloves for a limited number of rounds, and that such was not illegal. The judge also said that boxing "is less dangerous than many of the other sports that are permitted in the State, such as baseball, horse racing and football." However, the Attorney General said that he would appeal the decision.[733]

On October 18, 1895 in Little Rock, Arkansas, Corbett sparred both Duncan McDonald and Jim McVey in an exhibition show. In his 3 rounds with McDonald, Corbett showed that he was "in fine fettle and as agile as ever." The bout with McVey was spirited and closed with an uppercut to McVey's jaw that "nearly knocked him out."[734]

Given that the ultimate legal decision was still in question, promoter Dan Stuart proposed to postpone the fight until November 11, after the state's Supreme Court could decide the issue. After some discussion, Corbett manager Brady agreed to the 11th. However, Fitz manager Martin Julian insisted that Bob would only fight on the 31st. The match was tentatively declared off.[735]

On October 23, the Arkansas Supreme Court decided that the 1891 law making prize fighting a misdemeanor was valid. At that point, the Florida Athletic Club said that it wanted nothing to do with the match, fearing that the governor would call out the militia to stop the fight.

However, the Hot Springs Athletic Club still wanted the match to be held on October 31, as contractually required. Since boxing was not a felony

[731] New York Clipper, October 19, 1895.
[732] National Police Gazette, November 2, 1895.
[733] New York Clipper, October 26, 1895.
[734] Arkansas Gazette (Little Rock), October 19, 1895.
[735] New York Clipper, October 26, 1895.

and was only a misdemeanor punishable by a fine from $1,000 to $2,500, the participants would not be subject to a prison sentence for the law violation. Therefore, it made economic sense to move forward with the fight. The Club wired Fitzsimmons in Texas and asked him to come to Hot Springs, assuring him that it would guarantee him $500 for lawyers and court expenses in case he was arrested for entering the state for unlawful purposes. Fitz said that he would leave for Hot Springs on the 28th. On the 28th, Arkansas legal authorities obtained warrants for the arrest of the participants, because it was believed that they intended to have the fight take place there anyway, in secret.[736]

Although the governor was against the bout, the local Hot Springs sheriff was happy to assist in making secret arrangements for it. On the 29th, just outside the Arkansas border, the sheriff entered the train that Fitz and his manager Martin Julian were on and handed them a letter which informed them that they should take another special train that would take them to the bout's location without stopping, and thus elude the service of the warrant. However, Fitz and his manager declined the offer, apparently because they thought it was some sort of trick. As a result, when the train crossed the Arkansas state line, they were arrested.

On November 2, the parties all went before a judge, who enjoined them from fighting under penalty of contempt for from two to five years in jail. This was said to have killed the fight, because instead of merely being subject to a fine for fighting, now, because Fitz was arrested and had to go before the judge, and therefore became subject to his injunction, they would face jail time if they fought.[737]

Corbett and some members of the press blamed Fitzsimmons for the bout's failure to take place. He had failed to take the special train ride that would have secretly transported him to the bout's Hot Springs location, instead using the regular train and submitting to arrest, knowing that legal difficulties would delay and/or end the bout. Corbett claimed that Fitz was a coward. The *National Police Gazette* wrote, "Every step he took seemed to indicate his fear…. Fitzsimmons' position is a most humiliating one. He went out of his way to badger Corbett into making the match…and then at the last moment quit, with all the characteristics of 'yaller dog.'" The fight was declared off, much to Corbett's apparent chagrin.[738]

The Florida Athletic Club paid Corbett $2,500, the forfeit money it was bound to pay in case the club failed to bring the fight off at the date and place arranged for. It authorized the payment because it considered that Corbett had always been ready to fight. It denied the same payment to

---

[736] *New York Clipper*, November 2, 1895.
[737] *New York Clipper*, November 9, 1895.
[738] *National Police Gazette*, November 2, 23, 1895; Corbett at 246-247.

Fitzsimmons, however, "on the plea that the Australian did everything to avoid a fight."[739]

Fitzsimmons' reputation had taken a blow. He had done all that he could in order to goad Corbett into the match, and then at the last moment took the course of action that would ensure that the fight would not take place. In his defense, Bob was not one to fight when there would be legal troubles as a result. He said, "I am a law abiding citizen," and "I will not break the law. I do not want to go to prison if I know myself."[740] It was a reasonable excuse. However, Corbett made a valid point in that they would have only been subject to a fine had they held the fight. Once a judge enjoined them from fighting, then the potential for jail time for contempt was in effect. That would not have been a possibility if Fitz had avoided arrest and fought. Jim believed that Fitz never really wanted the match. Still, Fitzsimmons might not have been fully cognizant of all the legal subtleties. He knew that the fight was illegal and that the state's governor was making efforts to prevent the bout, so he was obviously concerned.

Despite the attacks on Fitzsimmons, there were some who said even *before* the train incident that Corbett no longer wanted the fight. One wrote on October 26 that Corbett "has no desire to meet Lanky Bob. He is afraid he would be whipped.... The latest dispatches state that Corbett has declared himself through with pugilism."[741] Subsequent attempts to hold the fight in Mexico bore this out. Jim indeed declared that he was through with the fight game. Corbett was in great shape and prepared to fight, so it might have made more sense boxing-wise to have fought Fitzsimmons around this time.

Regardless of the genuineness of his disappointment regarding the fight's failure to come off, Corbett was more than content to return to the stage, which had been quite a lucrative business for him. He had saved face by demonstrating his willingness to fight, which then allowed his successful return to the stage without immediate public criticism. And, after all, Corbett said that money was his number one concern. He was making good money without actually having had to defend the title against a legitimate contender.

[739] *New York Clipper*, November 16, 1895.
[740] *Los Angeles Express*, November 1, 1895; *Brooklyn Daily Eagle*, November 1, 1895.
[741] *Los Angeles Express*, October 26, 1895.

CHAPTER 18

Another Hiatus,
Until the Sailor's Storm

Just after the Corbett-Fitzsimmons bout was officially declared off, on November 4, 1895 in Memphis, Tennessee, Corbett sparred 3 rounds with Steve O'Donnell between acts of a play called *The White Squadron*.[742]

On November 11, 1895 in Long Island, New York, 26-year-old Peter Maher knocked out Steve O'Donnell in the 1st round. Following the bout, James J. Corbett announced his retirement and gave his championship title to Maher. At that point, Corbett's heart was more aligned with the theater than the fight game.

Ironically, Peter Maher previously had been defeated by Peter Jackson (1889 LKOby2), Bob Fitzsimmons (March 1892 LKOby12) and Joe Goddard (December 1892 LKOby3), so he really was not deserving of the title. His only significant victories were an 1894 KO6 George Godfrey and KO3 Frank Craig, neither of which meant that much. A March 1895 bout between Maher and Jim Hall was stopped and declared a draw in the 6th round under the belief that the fight was a fake and neither giving an effort.[743] Bob Fitzsimmons held an 1893 KO4 over Hall.

Steve O'Donnell was a chief Corbett sparring partner and was essentially managed by him. The 177-180-pound O'Donnell had in the 1880s boxed with Peter Jackson (who was actually O'Donnell's teacher[744]). O'Donnell's bouts included: 1893 W4 Frank Craig and D6 George Godfrey; March 1895 D8 220 pound Jake Kilrain (O'Donnell better), and May 1895 KO21 Kilrain.[745]

Maher dropped O'Donnell down and out three times in the span of a minute for the 1st round knockout.[746] It was an impressive victory, but insufficient to make him champion.

Of his selection, Corbett later said,

> I bestowed the championship upon Maher because he is an Irishman, and because I prefer that he should bear and defend that title, rather than place it in the custody of either an Australian or an

---

[742] Fields at 93.
[743] *National Police Gazette,* March 9, 1895.
[744] *Philadelphia Press,* June 2, 1893.
[745] *National Police Gazette,* March 30, 1895, May 18, 1895.
[746] *National Police Gazette,* November 23, 1895.

Englishman.... I consider Peter Maher the peer of any man in the ring, and have no hesitancy in saying that he can whip Fitzsimmons.[747]

The public still considered Corbett the champion. The *Police Gazette* wrote of Maher, "He has been hailed as the champion, but conservative, reasonable, thinking people, appreciate the fact that the simple act of handing a title to a man on a gold plate is not the only thing that is requisite to make him a champion."[748] Corbett years later wrote of his handing over the title to Maher, "This, of course, I had really no right to do, for you cannot hand a championship to a man; he has to win that with his own hands in the ring."[749]

Even Maher did not consider himself champion. The *Clipper* said,

> Jim Corbett...took occasion to informally announce his retirement, and to declare Peter his successor to the championship. Of course, Corbett had no right to resign the championship in favor of Maher or any other man, and Peter, understanding this, afterwards said that he did not wish to get the title in any such way, even if he could have it, but that, if Corbett did not fight Fitzsimmons for it, he would issue a challenge to him therefore.[750]

Maher said that he would rather win the title in the ring than to accept it as a gift, showing a "disposition to repudiate Corbett's generosity in handing over the championship."[751] Maher had "declined to accept a title which Corbett, without authority, presumed to bestow upon him." He wanted to fight for the honor, feeling that he at least needed to defeat Fitzsimmons to deserve the title. So, to his credit, Peter Maher recognized that he was not the champion, and did not call himself champion.[752]

The day after Maher beat O'Donnell, on November 12, promoter Dan Stuart tried to arrange a Corbett-Fitzsimmons fight in Mexico for a $20,000 purse. Stuart said that he had acquired Fitz's signature on the contract. So, Fitzsimmons was willing to make the fight after all. Of course, Bob might have been motivated by the fact that some blamed him for the fight's failure to come off in Hot Springs, which had hurt his reputation.

Unfortunately, Corbett's manager William Brady telegraphed back to Stuart to say that Corbett had retired in favor of Maher. Stuart asked Brady where Jim got the authority to give away the championship, that the sporting law and usages had no such precedent. The *New York Clipper* opined, "If Jim ever did have a desire to fight Fitz, the way to demonstrate

---

[747] *National Police Gazette*, December 14, 1895.
[748] *National Police Gazette*, November 30, 1895.
[749] Corbett at 246-247.
[750] *New York Clipper*, November 16, 1895.
[751] *National Police Gazette*, December 7, 1895.
[752] *New York Clipper*, November 30, 1895.

the fact would seem to seize this opportunity."[753] For whatever reason, Corbett did not.

During subsequent weeks, Corbett insisted that he was retired and would not take the Fitzsimmons match. Former champion John L. Sullivan said that there was a question of supremacy between them, and that they "must come together eventually, and it might as well be now as at any other time."[754] He had a point. Corbett was in good shape, so it was probably a mistake not to take the fight immediately. Some felt that Corbett really did not want the fight. A year or so later, Corbett explained that the reason was economic.

> You remember Fitzsimmons and I were to meet for a $40,000 purse at Hot Springs. ... Afterward Stuart wanted me to chase around Mexico for a measly $10,000 purse. That offer I treated as it deserved. I said: "I am too good a business man to listen to such a proposition. I can make more than $10,000 on the road in three weeks."[755]

However, Stuart actually offered $20,000, no small number, and ironically, as it turned out; they would eventually fight for $15,000 in 1897.

On November 25, 1895 in Massachusetts, Corbett began acting in a play called *A Naval Cadet*, which would tour across the country.[756] He was making a lot of easy money on the road, without having to fight or train. During the play, Corbett would usually punch the bag and engage in a fight scene.

In early December, Bob Fitzsimmons scheduled a February 1896 rematch with Peter Maher for a $10,000 purse and the world championship.[757] At that time, Corbett left the comeback door open by saying that if Fitzsimmons were to beat Maher, "I'm right after him. I am not going to allow a flunker like Fitzsimmons to hold the championship. He flunked once with me and I am determined that he won't do it again.... I do not say that I will not fight again."[758] Thus, whether he really was retired could be called into question. It was a conditional retirement.

About a month before the Maher-Fitzsimmons fight, in late January 1896, Corbett again announced his intention to re-enter the ring and challenge the winner.[759] This essentially put him back on the scene after a brief two month retirement and made it more difficult for Maher or Fitzsimmons to be viewed as champions in the public eye, in part because they had not yet fought. Also, Maher was not deserving of the title and did not accept it anyway, and Fitzsimmons had failed to fight Corbett. Still,

---

[753] *New York Clipper*, November 23, 1895.
[754] *New York Clipper*, December 7, 1895.
[755] *San Francisco Chronicle*, February 12, 1897.
[756] Fields at 93.
[757] *New York Clipper*, December 14, 1895.
[758] *Brooklyn Daily Eagle*, December 8, 1895; *New York Clipper*, December 14, 1895.
[759] *National Police Gazette*, February 1, 1896.

there were some who considered that since Jim had retired and had not accepted the proposed Fitz fight in Mexico, the winner of the Fitzsimmons-Maher fight would be the recognized champion.

On February 5, 1896, the U.S. House of Representatives passed a bill making boxing in any federal territories (not the states) or in the District of Columbia a felony punishable by imprisonment from one to five years. The next day, the bill was passed in the Senate in three minutes. On February 7, U.S. President Grover Cleveland signed the bill into law. It was enacted specifically in an attempt to prevent the Fitzsimmons-Maher fight.[760] Although the law's territorial scope was limited, it was a sign of the prevailing legal trend. Boxing was illegal in most every state anyway.

To avoid the U.S. law, the bout was held in Mexico. On February 21, 1896, just across the Langtry, Texas border, (about 370 miles southeast of El Paso and 215 miles west of San Antonio), across the Rio Grande in Coahuila, Mexico, Bob Fitzsimmons knocked out Peter Maher in the 1st round. Immediately after the fight, Corbett wired him a challenge for the championship. Fitzsimmons replied, "I will not pay any attention to him." Thus, at this point, it was Fitzsimmons who was not interested in the fight.

Although few considered Fitzsimmons to be the champion, the *National Police Gazette* did, giving him its diamond belt. The *New York Clipper* also recognized Fitzsimmons, and criticized Corbett's "presumption to attempt to reclaim the title of champion of the world, basing his absurd claim upon the assertion that when he announced his retirement it was with the express understanding that in case the championship was won by a foreigner he would reclaim it."[761] Of course, the puzzling thing was that Maher, the man to whom he had bestowed the title, was a foreigner, being from Ireland. But, Corbett was of Irish descent, as was Maher and O'Donnell, so the Irish connection obviously and admittedly had something to do with his championship choice as well.

Because Corbett had repudiated his retirement before Maher had fought Fitzsimmons, and Maher had said that he did not want the title until he defeated Fitzsimmons (which he did not), the public generally disregarded any Fitz championship claim. The newspapers were another matter. For the time being, some called Fitzsimmons the champion.

While in Cincinnati, Ohio on March 25, Corbett's sparring partner for *A Naval Cadet*, John McVey, had to go to the hospital because of "a gathering in his ear, caused by the incessant pounding received in their nightly bouts." Mike Conley, "the Ithaca Giant," temporarily filled his place.[762] In 1883, Conley had been stopped in the 1st round by Frank Herald, who in turn went on to lose to Sullivan, Lannon, and Kilrain in 1886. In October 1888, Joe McAuliffe stopped Conley in the 2nd round.

---

[760] *New York Clipper,* February 15, 1896.
[761] *New York Clipper,* February 29, 1896.
[762] *New York Clipper,* April 11, 1896.

Mike Conley

A Naval Cadet opened a week's engagement in St. Louis, Missouri on the afternoon of April 5, 1896. There would be matinee and evening performances, with tickets selling anywhere from $.15 to $.50.

Corbett's relinquishment of the world championship had not affected his drawing powers, as standing room was at a premium in both the afternoon and evening showings on the 5th. "The most enjoyable act in the whole show is the bag-punching exhibition by the pugilist." At that point, Corbett was listed as weighing 192 pounds.

On the 6th, Corbett and Conley were not allowed to box in their usual 3-round sparring bout. The police chief sent word that it would have to be cut from the play, because the law prohibited even the friendliest public set-tos. Corbett was unable to persuade him otherwise. The local paper opined, "Pugilists will soon be avoiding St. Louis entirely, and there is a large and enthusiastic class in this city that admires boxing. This rule no doubt accounts, in a measure, for the large number of fights to a finish in private."

The following night, on April 7, 1896, Corbett and Conley decided to test the law, and disregarded the St. Louis police chief's order by sparring 3 short rounds as part of the last act of their play. "Corbett was at his best, and his quick ducking, side stepping and playful tapping of the sturdy Conley bewildered the Frenchman completely." After the show, both boxers were arrested and charged with violating the state law against boxing exhibitions. $200 bonds for their release were furnished.

The next day, the men appeared in court for their arraignment, but the prosecuting attorney dismissed the case. "He stated that he had examined into the evidence, and was convinced that the charge could not be sustained." He likely felt that it would be impossible to secure a conviction. For the rest of the week, big audiences watched Corbett and Conley perform in the play, sparring in the last act, as usual.[763]

[763] *St. Louis Daily Globe-Democrat*, April 5-9, 1896; *New York Clipper*, April 18, 1896; *St. Louis Republic*, April 5-9, 1896.

Although legal attacks on boxing were continuous, sometimes what appeared to be an attack actually helped foster the sport. On April 8, the New York Senate passed the Horton anti-sparring bill, which prohibited boxing anywhere in the state except in regularly incorporated clubs which own or lease for more than one year the house that they occupy.[764] This eventually led to more bouts being held in New York.

On April 15, 1896 in Chicago, Corbett took part in an interesting exhibition before a police trial board. "The set-to was for the purpose of testing armor recently invented which precludes the possibility of a knockout." The "armor" looked like a life preserver with a hood attachment padded inside with hair, or what we might call a headgear. Al Smythe and Boyd Fraser sparred 3 rounds. An electric register counted the number of blows landed. Although not saying which man he sparred with, the local *Chicago Times-Herald* said that Corbett registered 109 blows in 1 round at a private exhibition, "and his opponent was none the worse, except a few bruises around the eyes where no padding had been placed. ... Although using large gloves, the blows he administered would have put a man without the armor to sleep in short order." Jim said that he was ordering two sets for training purposes and that similar exhibitions would be given.[765]

On April 16, 1896 in San Francisco, 22-year-old "Sailor" Tom Sharkey, who for three years had been the undefeated Navy champion, took on Joe Choynski in an 8-round bout.[766] Sharkey was relatively new on the scene, but had impressed people with his natural fighting abilities. Tom was not a polished fighter, but in his previous battles had shown great strength, courage, and recuperative powers. Except for an early 1896 8-round draw against Alec Greggains, Sharkey had won all of his fights by knockout, including a July 1895 KO7 over Australian Billy Smith (against whom Corbett had won two 1889 6-round decisions – no knockouts being allowed). Sharkey was to become a prominent figure in boxing for many years to come.

Choynski was described as cool-headed and careful, having power in both hands sufficient to end a contest with one blow, and the ability to seize an opportunity to land a decisive blow.[767] Since being stopped in 5 rounds by Fitzsimmons in mid-1894, amongst his significant bouts, Choynski had fought an early 1895 6-round draw with Dan Creedon, and in January 1896 had won a KO13 over Jim Hall.

Choynski had contracted to put Sharkey out within 8 rounds or technically "lose" the contest. It was reported a day before the bout that Sharkey would weigh 177 ½ pounds, three more than Choynski.[768]

[764] *St. Louis Daily Globe-Democrat,* April 9, 1896.
[765] *Chicago Times-Herald,* April 16, 1896. Secondary sources say Corbett sparred Fraser. Cyberboxingzone.com.
[766] *Brooklyn Daily Eagle,* August 14, 1896.
[767] *San Francisco Examiner,* April 16, 1896.
[768] *San Francisco Chronicle,* April 15, 1896.

Sailor Tom Sharkey

At the start, the aggressive Choynski landed his hard left often. It initially looked as if Joe would stop him. Joe sent Sharkey against and through the ropes, falling into the crowd head first, almost landing on his head. When Sharkey re-entered the ring, Joe continued pounding on him. However, Sharkey hit Choynski with a low blow that immediately caused Joe to reel away, writhing in intense pain. Tom, as if realizing what he had done, looked on and did not advance. The round then ended. Choynski was in serious agony (there were no protective cups back then).

At first, the police lieutenant declared that the fight would not be allowed to continue. The crowd hissed. The suffering Choynski realized that the low blow was accidental, and after convincing the police, the bout was allowed to continue.

It was said that this low blow weakened Joe considerably and that afterwards he "did not display the same degree of vim." However, Choynski remained the aggressor throughout the bout and still administered a lot of punishment. The tough Sharkey took the punches well and fought back hard.

In the 4th round, Choynski landed his left either to the head or to the body, knocking Tom against the ropes and down. Sharkey rose and came back, but was hit with a succession of blows to the body and head. Joe threw him against the ropes and knocked Sharkey down a second time in the round with a left on the mouth. Tom rose and gamely fought back.

Both exchanged and landed inside blows in the 5th round, but Sharkey clinched often. Joe kept forcing matters in the 6th, moving Tom around the ring. Sharkey would duck and hug, but also exchanged with him. Choynski landed the hardest blows, but Sharkey took them well.

They fought hard in the 7th, and in a clinch Sharkey threw Joe against the ropes. When Joe led with his left, Tom ducked and countered, landing his left to the jaw or chest, staggering Joe back for a moment. They exchanged and Sharkey held his own until time was called.

The 8th round was fast and furious. Joe pelted him for the first half of the round. Sharkey when hurt would clinch to save himself, essentially using that as his defense. Still, he fought hard. Choynski knew that under the terms of the articles of agreement, if he did not stop Sharkey, he was to lose. Both landed lefts to the face, and Sharkey slipped and went down on his knees. He went down a second time, partly from a punch, partly from a push. Some protested and jeered, feeling that Sharkey was using survival tactics to kill time. However, the rest of the round was a continuous volley of left and right swings from both men, and Sharkey survived.[769]

The decision had to go to Sharkey because the agreement had called for Choynski to knock him out in order to win. Still, although Tom was game, Choynski had clearly done better. A couple days later, a local paper reported that it was believed that Choynski could have put him out but for the low blow that he had received.

Sharkey's gritty performance put his name on the map though. The local paper said that he "demonstrated that he is a perfect glutton for punishment and does not know when he is defeated. He is a fighter of the Goddard type." A couple months later, Sharkey would fight Corbett.[770]

During April, Corbett and Brady received a judgment against the Kinetoscope Exhibiting Company for $7,200 in unpaid royalties for the Corbett-Courtney film exhibition receipts and an unpaid $2,000 note. Boxing films were big business.

Also at that time, owing to the new embargo against boxing in Louisiana, the New Orleans Olympic Club was forced to close down. At its height of prosperity, the club had 2,000 members, and it paid out more prize money to fighters than any other organization.[771]

While in Chicago that month, Corbett posted $1,000 to bind a fight with Fitzsimmons, but the challenge was not accepted. Corbett believed that this

[769] *San Francisco Chronicle*, April 17, 1896.
[770] *San Francisco Chronicle*, April 18, 1896; *San Francisco Examiner*, April 17, 1896.
[771] *New York Clipper*, April 11, 25, 1896.

meant that Fitz forfeited his championship claim and that it reverted back to himself.[772] Fitzsimmons began taking some criticism for not accepting Corbett's challenges. The *New York Clipper* said that by refusing, he was taking a course which would lead to his forfeiture of the title and Corbett's reinstatement as champion.[773]

On April 25, promoter Dan Stuart made another attempt to match Corbett and Fitzsimmons. However, Fitz said that he would not accept until Corbett had defeated some other contenders, seemingly taunting Corbett with the same retort that Corbett had initially made towards him.

The press did not appreciate Fitzsimmons' rebuff. The *New York Clipper* said that Corbett would "now be justified, according to the custom in championship matters, in claiming the title which he voluntarily gave up, and which Fitzsimmons is unwilling to defend under the rules governing such matters." Custom dictated that champions had to accept bona fide challenges or forfeit the title.[774]

In late May, Fitzsimmons went to England to exhibit there. This lead to the belief "that he really dreads the result of a meeting in the ring with the Californian."[775] The newspapers once again recognized Corbett as champion, holding that Fitz's championship claims were forfeited by his failure to accept Jim's challenge.

On June 6, Jim Corbett and "Sailor" Tom Sharkey signed articles to meet in a 4-round contest at San Francisco's Mechanics Pavilion during the last week of that month. This did not give Jim much time to train, but then, it was only a 4-rounder. Still, Corbett needed to be in good shape, in part because of some challenging terms. "By the terms of the agreement, if Sharkey is on his feet at the end of the fourth round the match is to be declared a draw." This is an interesting fact because the post-fight reports and even Corbett and Sharkey's reaction to the eventual decision gave the impression that the fight was to be decided on its merits. It appeared though that it was one of those deals where Corbett was supposed to knock him out or it would be declared a draw.[776]

On June 24, 1896 in San Francisco, the 22-year-old (some say 24) Sharkey boxed against the once again recognized heavyweight champion, 29-year-old James J. Corbett. It was only scheduled for 4 rounds, so it is unclear as to whether this was considered a title defense. It was probably no less so than Sullivan's 4-round bouts. However, generally it was understood that for a championship to change hands it would be in a fight to the finish or at least for a much greater duration than 4 rounds. It was really more of an exhibition for a stipulated split of the gate, with Corbett imposing upon

[772] *San Francisco Bulletin,* June 26, 1896; Fields at 96-98.
[773] *New York Clipper,* April 18, 1896.
[774] *New York Clipper,* May 2, 1896.
[775] *New York Clipper,* May 23, 1896, June 6, 1896.
[776] *New York Sun,* June 8, 1896.

himself the task of stopping Sharkey or the bout simply being declared a draw.

Corbett had not fought in a serious fight since his September 1894 6-round bout against Peter Courtney, one year and nine months earlier, and even that match had very short rounds and lengthier rests than the usual one minute. Prior to that, Corbett had only met Mitchell in January 1894 and Sullivan in September 1892, both of whom had been inactive for quite some time and were well past their primes. Because the Fitzsimmons fight fell through and Jim had retired, as champion Corbett had not fought against a young and hungry legitimate contender at all. He had won the title in September 1892 and it was now June 1896. He was likely in less than good shape, given that all he had done recently was engage in mostly short, generally friendly exhibitions as part of plays. Corbett had not stopped performing in *A Naval Cadet* until May 2. He signed for the Sharkey fight on June 6 for a fight to take place on the 24th, allowing himself less than three weeks to train.[777]

On the other hand, Tom Sharkey had been quite active. Since beginning his career in the navy in 1893, he had at least 23 known bouts. Except for Choynski and Greggains, Tom had knocked out all of his opponents. Just a few weeks prior to the Corbett fight, on June 3, Sharkey scored a KO7 over Jim Williams. Thus, he was coming into the fight sharp. Before the bout, Sharkey said,

> I believe I will be as strong at the end of the four rounds as Corbett, if not stronger. ... He may be quicker, but he certainly is no stronger.
>
> Contrary to the general opinion, I am not entirely dependent on my strength. ... Because I may look awkward in the ring is not sufficient reason to warrant the supposition that I have no science to back me up.
>
> All these men who are supposed to be clever usually come out of the ring badly bruised, but the sporting world knows that I retire fresh and with little, if any, disfigurement. ...
>
> When I enter the ring it will be with the idea that I am there to make a desperate fight. ... If he don't come to me, I'll go fast to him. ... Because Corbett happens to be the champion it doesn't cut any figure with me. I am going across the ropes to fight him just as I would anyone else... I never took a beating from anyone in my life, and every time he hits me I'll come pretty near hitting him.
>
> After I get a rest of two or three months I will be ready to fight anybody in the world except a negro. There I draw the color. I prefer to meet Fitzsimmons.

---

[777] Fields at 237.

Sharkey was a man "famous for stamina, recuperative powers and courage," as well as "remarkable physical development as to make him proof against the assaults of all ordinary men." Tom was also an improving fighter, and "the higher class man he goes against the better he performs." Sharkey generally forced the pace with his windmill style.

The odds started at 10 to 7 that Corbett would not stop Sharkey in the 4 rounds, although they eventually switched around to Corbett's favor at 10 to 9. "Sharkey said he would not hug the carpet, though he might try repeated clinching." Thus, there was some evidence before the bout that Sharkey would clinch to survive, something which later became an issue of some controversy.

Corbett provided insight into his preparation and motivation for the match:

> [Spectators] will find me entering the ring in the best possible condition that the limited time which I have had to train would permit. While I may not have taken the pains that I would were I to contest in a finish battle for the championship, I am nevertheless well prepared to cope with my strong and large-muscled opponent. Financial gain, of course, cuts quite a figure in tonight's affair, but, as I have stated before, my main object in matching myself with Sharkey, is to furnish evidence to prove that I am fit to undertake another fight with my would-be rivals in the championship race.

Corbett also said that he would not seek a knockout unless the opportunity arose in a manner in which he could protect against injury to his hands. However, it was rumored that Corbett had privately bet $6,000 on himself to stop Sharkey.[778]

Oddly enough, the selected referee was Frank Carr, the brother of Jim Carr, one of Corbett's backers. It seems strange that such a conflict of interest would be allowed. It was not even discussed at the time. However, given that the referee's brother had money riding on Corbett and that Corbett might have had bets on himself, certainly this might have affected the referee's ultimate decision, which as will be seen, was considered controversial. For the fight, Corbett was seconded by *Jim Carr*, Bill Delaney, and George Green (a.k.a. Young Corbett).

Sharkey probably did not care who refereed, because all he had to do was last the 4 rounds in order to receive his pre-stipulated share. Also, the agreement was for the decision to be a draw if he lasted, although this fact was not really advertised by the local press, which may not have been aware of all the terms. The articles provided that Corbett receive 50% of the gross receipts regardless of the outcome, and for Sharkey to receive 35% of the

---

[778] *San Francisco Evening Post*, June 24, 1896; *San Francisco Bulletin*, June 24, 1896; *New York Sun*, June 25, 1896.

net receipts if he stayed the 4 rounds.[779] At that time, such a pre-stipulated share was not typical for a bout to be decided on its merits, and was a further indication that the fight was more of an exhibition.

The *San Francisco Chronicle* said that both boxers weighed about 180 pounds, and they fought with four-ounce gloves. Sharkey stood a stocky 5'8 ¾". The only indication of the weights from the *San Francisco Examiner* was an illustration that listed Jim as 192 pounds to the 5'8" Sharkey's 178 pounds. The *San Francisco Evening Post* the day before said that Jim was weighing nearly 20 pounds more than he had a few years earlier. According to the *New York Herald*, they were both 179 pounds. The *New York Sun* said that both weighed around 180 pounds. The *National Police Gazette* listed Sharkey as 190 pounds. According to Corbett's autobiography, he weighed 177 ½ pounds to the 5'8" 190-pound Sharkey (though Sharkey is usually listed as 178). They both likely weighed somewhere in the 180-190-pound range.

A huge crowd of 10,000 people witnessed the fight at San Francisco's Mechanics Pavilion under the sponsorship of the National Athletic Club. Both entered the ring at 9:30 p.m. wearing robes. Sharkey was announced as the undefeated champion of the navy and pacific coast.

The following account is based on reports from the *San Francisco Evening Post* (SFEP), *San Francisco Bulletin* (SFB), *San Francisco Examiner* (SFE), *San Francisco Chronicle* (SFC), *New York Sun* (NYS), *New York Clipper* (NYC), and Corbett's Autobiography (CA). Significant variations are noted.

1st round

Corbett started off well as the aggressor, pressing Sharkey. The careful Sharkey started off a little nervous and excited, and for a half-minute, no blows were struck. Tom pranced away and missed several wild blows in the air. Corbett had him guessing and laughed as Sharkey missed. Tom could only land on the neck, for Corbett was elusive with his head movement.

Jim landed a hard left but Tom did not wince. In a mix-up, Corbett landed heavily on the sailor's right eye, causing it to puff badly. One said that Jim had hit Tom's eye with a sharp left when Sharkey ducked. Another said that Corbett countered a Sharkey miss with a punch that almost closed Tom's right eye.

There were several clinches. In one clinch, Tom hit Jim in the back of the neck. Jim landed heavily on the heart and uppercut as they clinched again. More clinches followed. A Corbett right uppercut on the breakaway caused the crowd to hoot him. "The crowd showed its ignorance of the rules by hissing, when in fact it should have applauded Corbett for his speed." Under the Queensberry rules, hitting in clinches and on the break

---

[779] *New York Sun*, June 25, 1896.

was legal. Apparently, the crowd wanted clean breaks. Jim smashed Tom on the breakaways, particularly with the uppercut.

Corbett also landed several blows in between the many clinches. Jim forced the fight, landing rights to the ribs, and Tom clinched. A right to the nose made Tom bleed, and his face was looking bruised. Sharkey could not land a damaging blow. The referee had difficulty in getting them to break.

The smiling Corbett hit Sharkey almost at will, landing his deceptive left easily and often. It looked as if Sharkey would be finished. However, Jim's typical confident smile disappeared as he saw that he could not hurt Tom. Still, Sharkey got the worst of the round.

In Corbett's autobiography, Jim claimed that Sharkey could not hit him, was easy to hit, and had no skill. A hook raised a huge swelling over Sharkey's eye, and in the follow up, he almost put Sharkey out. However, in trying to finish him in the first 2 rounds, being in less than good condition, Corbett fatigued himself.

2nd round

Corbett hit Sharkey almost at will in the first two rounds. Jim went to work; feinting and making Tom throw short. A Corbett right landed on Tom's cheekbone and again they clinched. "Sharkey, to avoid punishment, throws his arms around Corbett repeatedly. Corbett lands on Sharkey's chest and face and hits him at will." Another Corbett right uppercut on a break made the crowd hiss Jim. Corbett hit Sharkey a number of times with his right on the breakaway, to the crowd's displeasure. As Sharkey was rushing, Corbett landed a left to the jaw that would have knocked out anyone but Sharkey, who did not flinch. At that moment, Corbett lost confidence. Although Corbett hit Sharkey with no problem, the punishment had no effect.

In the middle of the round, Sharkey "turned much after the manner of a cornered rat and began to fight." Sharkey "seemed to shut his eyes, throw his head down and swing wildly with both hands." Jim was actually a bit wild himself. Tom became the aggressor, fighting back wildly, clinching off of his attack, making it a wrestling match. There was plenty of infighting and clinching, Corbett uppercutting with his free hand when he could. Clinches were quite frequent, more frequent than punches, which were being smothered at this point. Corbett began to show signs of tiring, but was still landing on the break. Jim made a bluff at forcing the pace, but clinched a lot.

In the latter half of the round, Sharkey landed a number of chopping blows, but they were ineffective, for they landed on the top of the head or shoulders. Jim had Tom's neck under his left arm at the call of time.

3rd round

Corbett evaded a Sharkey rush to begin the round and hit him with a right to the temple before the usual clinch. Corbett landed some good half-arm blows, but that only spurred Sharkey on. Sharkey went at him like a bull.

Both clinched often. Jim did not use his usual footwork, but would mostly duck and clinch. Sharkey clinched off of his attack. In one clinch, Sharkey held on and dragged Corbett around. Later, Jim forced Tom over the ropes, hitting him on the ribs with his right. Tom threw his arms around Jim's neck, and Corbett complained. On a breakaway, Tom swung and hit the back of Jim's head, clinching again. Frequent clinches followed, and Jim continued landing a right on the break. Sharkey swung wildly and clinched. Jim was tired and complaining to the referee. They wrestled for fully thirty seconds, Corbett constantly speaking to the referee. Sharkey tried to break away, but Corbett held onto him like a barnacle. The referee unsuccessfully tried to break them. Finally, Tom threw Jim off. One source said that Tom threw him to the floor. Corbett was very tired.

The fatigued Corbett's punches were as wild as Tom's, and he hung onto Sharkey with all his weight, strangling him at the same time. Sharkey turned purple from the stranglehold, but managed to swing and land one or two that sent Corbett's head back. Corbett seemed groggy, distressed, and tired, but "showed demoniacal skill in worrying the sailor during the everlasting clinches." Jim held his head back in order to avoid Sharkey's vicious swings.

Near the end of the round, they exchanged rights, with Sharkey's landing better. The round ended in a clinch, where Tom shouldered and elbowed Jim, who seemed pitiful. "Confidence had vanished from his face as the realization had forced itself upon him that he was against a man who was his equal, if not his superior."

According to Corbett's autobiography, Sharkey made it more of an inside holding and wrestling match, Corbett feeling that it was a survival tactic on Tom's part. Sharkey resorted to excessive wrestling tactics, pulling, pushing, shoving and throwing Corbett all over. Jim continually appealed to the referee to no avail. The wrestling eventually fatigued Corbett, who then tied Sharkey up and held him around the neck, but was thrown down to the ground. Even the referee was thrown on top of Corbett.

4th round

The honors of the round went to Sharkey. Sharkey forced matters, while Corbett was on the defensive. Jim's blows had no effect on Tom, who was like a bull. Corbett resorted to closing in and clinching as Sharkey lead. Corbett clinched repeatedly and would not let go. The crowd urged him to let go and fight. "It was a wrestling match of the worst order here, with Corbett doing most of the hugging." Corbett would hit with the right on the break and in the clinch, while Sharkey would hold on and hit Jim in the face several times with his right. When the referee would break them, Corbett simply went right back to the clinch. Tom put his forearm against Jim's mouth and punched him with the other hand.

Jim kept talking to the referee all the time. Sharkey did most of the punching. Corbett got Tom's head under his arm in a strangle hold, "and almost cut his wind off through pressing his left arm on the sailor's neck." Sharkey eventually shook himself loose, and threw Corbett to the floor. Jim rose and clinched again. It appeared that Jim was even grabbing the referee. Sharkey got his arms around Corbett's neck, and the referee could not break them. They spun across the ring and went down.

Each local account gave its own version as to how matters ended:

SFEP: It appeared that Corbett "appealingly beckoned to Sergeant Wittman, and that official jumped on the platform and ordered the mill stopped." The angry Sharkey attempted to hit Corbett over the head of the officer. The referee called the battle a draw and declared all bets off. "In the minds of nearly every one present the victory should have been awarded to the 'champion of the American navy.'"

SFB: Corbett beckoned to the police, who rushed in and stopped the fight. Sharkey was far fresher and it looked as if Jim could not have fought another round. "Whether Corbett summoned the police or his seconds cannot be told but in either case he showed ten thousand people that he had had enough."

SFE: The referee was unable to separate them. The police captain entered the ring and pulled Sharkey away while Tom punched at Jim, across the policeman's arms. The bell rang just as the policeman advanced to separate them, but very few heard it.

SFC: The referee, seeing that his efforts to break them were useless, called for the police, and Corbett seconded the motion. The police had to force Tom to his corner. The referee said that he could not render any other decision but a draw, owing to the police interference before the round ended.

NYS: Sharkey's right eye was closed while Corbett was without a scratch. "After the call of time it required three policemen to keep Sharkey from Corbett."

NYC: The referee nodded to the police captain, who entered and pulled Sharkey away.

CA: Corbett said that he was exhausted despite the fact that he had not been hit. Tom continued his wrestling tactics and Jim continued holding. The police stopped the bout and the referee declared it a 4-round draw.[780]

The *San Francisco Evening Post* criticized the referee for his decision and for calling all bets off. It believed that the referee called for police assistance on the ground that the fight had concluded. However, the referee claimed that the fight was stopped before it was over, which typically caused a bout to be called a draw or no contest, justifying his decision to call the bets off. The *Post* opined, "Everybody who witnessed the battle was of the opinion

---

[780] *San Francisco Examiner, San Francisco Chronicle, San Francisco Evening Post, San Francisco Bulletin,* all June 25, 1896; *New York Sun,* June 25, 1896; *New York Clipper,* July 4, 1896; Corbett at 240-244.

that Sharkey was much the stronger man of the two at the finish and should have been awarded the decision."

The *San Francisco Examiner* agreed that the fight did come to its natural conclusion, as the timekeeper said that the bell had rung before the police entered, but that no one had heard it, therefore also disagreeing with the referee's decision to call all bets off. Apparently, the referee's decision was not on the merits, but a call of draw owing to his belief that the police had terminated the bout prematurely.

Thus, the question is whether the fight was supposed to be decided on its merits or pursuant to the pre-fight agreement to declare it a draw if Sharkey lasted the 4 rounds. The referee provided neither reason for his decision, arguing that the draw was called owing to the premature termination, and using that as a reason to call the bets off.

Surprisingly, the issue not raised at the time was the fact that the referee was the brother of Corbett's backer. If the Corbett faction had bet that Corbett would stop Tom before the 4 rounds expired, declaring the bets off would have saved them from financial losses. Claiming that the police interfered before the round officially ended provided a justification for calling the bets off. However, oddly enough, Corbett was not happy with the referee and argued that he should have done more to prevent Sharkey's wrestling tactics.

The closest one newspaper came to such a critical analysis was in November, when a writer for the *San Francisco Evening Post* said,

> There never was a more crooked decision given by a referee than the one rendered by Carr, when he called the bout a draw and declared off all bets. The inside history of the transaction has never been written, and it is better for the reputation of San Francisco for fair play that it should not be published, but if ever a man was swindled out of a decision and his backers buncoed out of their winnings Sharkey is the man.
>
> Referee Carr declared all bets off. Why? It looks very much as if he did it to protect those who had given odds on the proposition that Corbett would put the sailor out within four rounds.[781]

In the referee's defense, there is support in the local papers that there was so much noise that the referee might not have heard the bell, and so it is perfectly plausible that he believed that the police had entered the ring before the bell rang. Also, at least one local paper said that the police had entered the ring prior to the ringing of the bell.

After the fight was over, Jim said to Tom, "You're a pretty good wrestler, aren't you?" Sharkey replied, "Well, I can fight a little, too, can't I?" When stepping out of the ring, Sharkey took a cut at Corbett by

---

[781] *San Francisco Evening Post*, November 17, 1896.

shouting to Joe Choynski, "You are the best man in the world, Joe. You can whip that stiff any time." Tom was also was quoted as saying after fighting Corbett, "Choynski is the greatest fighter that I ever yet met."

The local *San Francisco Examiner* provided extensive coverage and views of the bout. One report noted that Sharkey swung often but generally only hit air. The fight developed into a wrestling match, with Corbett forgetting all about outside fighting, instead clinching and trying his new breakaway blow, which was basically hitting on the break, something perfectly legal under Queensberry rules. Corbett punched as long as he had one hand free, often sending in right uppercuts when breaking away. The crowd disapproved of this tactic, even though it was legal. Sharkey pressed his left hand over Corbett's mouth and chin in the clinches, and Jim answered by getting Tom's neck under his arm and squeezing it. Sharkey clinched and wrestled with him. Corbett was the weaker of the two by the 4th round, and Sharkey held with one arm and hit Jim with the free hand. It was a fight that suited Sharkey, and he scored as well as Corbett.

Another *Examiner* reporter said that under the rules, Corbett had every right to hit Sharkey on the break. This report said that Sharkey had fought foully, but the crowd did not hiss him. Corbett had made a mistake by fighting Sharkey's fight and trying to knock him out. Sharkey had brute strength, but his skills were criticized. It agreed that Sharkey hit him, but his blows had little effect because they were badly judged for distance and not straight. Corbett's fatigue was attributed to the wrestling and hugging.[782]

The *San Francisco Chronicle* complimented Sharkey's wrestling tactics. He tripped Corbett to the floor twice by using a leg lock. Of course, these moves were only legal under the London Prize Ring rules. Sharkey also rained blows on the champ and twice fought him to the ropes. It said that the surprising feature of the bout was not so much that Corbett failed to win, but the narrowness with which he escaped defeat. That said, it too agreed that the fight was a disappointing wrestling match.

A *Chronicle* woman reporter, seeing her first fight, noted that she found it odd that a statute made prize-fighting illegal, but that judges, politicians, doctors, lawyers, and trustees of prominent churches were in attendance. She observed,

> [Corbett] battered like a ram, but it was hitting a stone wall. It was give and take from both. Corbett clung to him and bullied the umpire and Sharkey, yelling, "Take the sailor off,"...when all the time it was his arm that was clinging and he appeared to be trying to choke his man.

She too noted that when the referee broke them at one point, Corbett fell with the referee on top of him. In the 4th, Corbett nodded an appeal to the

---

[782] *San Francisco Examiner*, June 25, 1896.

police, who entered and separated them. Sharkey thrust an officer aside, hit Jim with an uppercut, and offered to fight the police captain.[783]

The other two local papers were even harsher in their criticism of Corbett. The *Evening Post* said that Corbett had joined the ranks of good old "has beens."

> The fast pace at which he has traveled during the past few years has sapped his vitality, and he is today a mere wreck compared to what he was... In fact, he looked stale and weak.... Sharkey was magnificent by comparison. ... Whether or not Corbett will ever regain his old form is a question. Certainly he is a poor apology for a first-class performer at present. He is clever, but has not the sprightliness of old, and is physically weak and exhausted.... For the present, however, he is out of the game, and the sooner he appreciates his humiliating condition the better. He is far from the top now, and in order to regain his lost laurels will have to go through a course of self-denial.
>
> So far as Sharkey is concerned, the path to the championship looks clear. He has only Fitzsimmons to defeat. In that "phenom," however, he will find a hard nut to crack, as all have learned who have gone against the New Zealander.[784]

One man said that Corbett's championship days were about over. "Corbett committed many fouls. He should not have been permitted to strike Sharkey over the referee's shoulder during the break-away. Sharkey is the coming champion of the world. If Jim ever meets Fitzsimmons, the Australian will surely win."

The *San Francisco Bulletin* noted that the preponderance of ringside opinions were not good for Corbett. A doctor said,

> I don't think Corbett is the man he was a few years ago. ... Still, he was up against a hard man. It was like trying to handle a wild animal. ... He knocked Corbett and the referee down, fought the police and was ready to fight everybody and everything. I doubt if Corbett can keep him off in any kind of fight.

Another man said, "I don't think Corbett can lick that fellow. ... He can't keep away from that fellow. He is as strong as a bull and pretty lively, too. I was disappointed in Corbett, and I don't think he can lick Fitzsimmons."

A clerk for the U.S. Court of Appeals said, "Why that fellow would have licked Corbett if they had let him go on. He was as strong as an ox and he had blood in his eye. He actually had the best of it, and at the end Corbett

---

[783] *San Francisco Chronicle*, June 25, 1896.
[784] *San Francisco Evening Post*, June 25, 1896.

was glad enough it was over. It was a rattling mill. That fellow Sharkey is a wonder."

Another observer said that Corbett had deteriorated, that he had the worst of it and would have been licked had it gone on, and was "pretty anxious to quit." Still another said that Jim's blows had no effect at all. "Sullivan in his good days was the man to have fought Sharkey. He would have knocked his head off. It is true that Corbett signaled the police. I know that."

The chief of police thought that Corbett had received a gift, and that his men were ill-advised in obeying the call into the ring. "There was no disturbance there calling for their interference. The men were fighting, to be sure, just as they had been all along."

Most neutral observers believed that Corbett had called the police into the ring to stop it.

> Corbett was leaning over Sharkey, hanging on, when he beckoned, by throwing his head backward, for Captain Wittman to come on the platform. The champion's face then wore a look of distress, and Captain Wittman immediately mounted the platform and seized the sailor. Sharkey struck the captain and was ready to fight the balance of the world. But he was forced back into his chair.

There were some Corbett supporters. A secret service agent said that at first, it was Sharkey who held on to Jim.

> In the first two rounds Corbett hit him whenever he wanted to, and in the second round had him nearly out. The call of time saved him. Still, Sharkey is a stout fellow and wonderfully strong…. It is said that Corbett hugged him, but I was close to the ring and I could see that Sharkey did the clinging.

An Olympic Club member said that Corbett had simply not trained and lacked condition. The National Athletic Club president said, "I think Corbett outpointed the other fellow and did most of the leading. But I must say Sharkey astonished me, and I think he got the best of the fight, as it was fought."

Another *Bulletin* report said that Corbett made a bad decision when he elected to fight instead of box. "In a finish fight Corbett would perhaps fight differently. He is a great ring general, and would rely on his marvelous quickness to tap and get away, tap and get away, until he broke the sailor's heart."[785]

All sources agreed that Sharkey had a blackened, swollen right eye. The *Chronicle* said that Corbett only had a scratched face and a slightly swollen lip. According to the *Evening Post*, Jim showed no bruises from the battle and had not been hurt even a little bit.

---

[785] *San Francisco Bulletin,* June 25, 1896.

Corbett said, "I fully demonstrated my superiority over Sharkey in everything that appertains to square, straight-out pugilism." He wanted to fight Sharkey to a finish and claimed that it was Sharkey who had done the wrestling. "When I meet Sharkey again...I'll see to it that there is a referee who won't allow wrestling."

Corbett trainer Bill Delaney said that the fight was a surprise and that they had underestimated Sharkey. "Of course he is no match for Jim in science, but he held out wonderfully and proved that he could stand up to anyone in the world.... There is no bluff in him, for he is a fighter from the word go."

Sharkey said, "I found Corbett a much easier game than I anticipated. I know I can whip him.... I am as good, if not a little better than he is. Until he whips me I consider that I'm as much entitled to the championship as he is." He offered to fight for up to $10,000 a side for a fight of 10 rounds or one to a finish. Sharkey said that if Jim did not fight him, he was willing to box against any man, Fitzsimmons preferred.

The *Bulletin* said that Corbett was going to issue a challenge to all comers, Fitzsimmons preferred, and that if Bob did not accept within two weeks, he would fight Sharkey again for a side bet of $10,000. Jim said, "I don't imagine Fitz will take notice of any challenge. He has conclusively shown, time and time again, that he doesn't care to meet me." Corbett also said that he wanted to meet Sharkey in a finish fight and was through with limited-round bouts. "Sullivan and others may go about the country putting out dubs, but I do not care for it."

Regarding the breakaway punches, Sharkey claimed that he had an agreement with Corbett to break away nice, without punching on the break. However, in the very first clinch in the 1st round, Corbett got his left arm free and uppercut him, causing the eye injury. In the ring, Tom responded, "D'ye call that breaking away?" Corbett merely laughed at him. "He was laughing and sneering at me all the time then; but he didn't do it long."

Sharkey said that Corbett was the foulest fighter he had ever met. Jim played the clinching game, but he fought and beat Corbett at his own game.

> He saw I had the best of him, and he was getting tired. So he clinched me and laid his whole weight on me, trying to break me down. He choked me until I could hardly breathe, and he resorted to all the foul business he knew of. My seconds kept saying to me, "Break away from him; get away, and punch him." But I couldn't do it.... He simply didn't want to let go; he was scared, and he didn't mean fight.

Sharkey said that he had made Corbett quit, and deserved the decision. "In a finish fight I've no doubt I could best him. Why shouldn't I. I'm stronger than he is, I think, and I'm pretty near as clever."

Corbett responded,

I anticipated that he would come at me like an infuriated bull, and with about as much skill. He showed absolutely no generalship, and as for his punching me out, it is absurd to even entertain such a notion. ... He can't deliver an effective blow. I am sure fair-minded men who were present last night will bear me out when I say that he didn't strike me squarely once.

Corbett offered his unmarked body as proof. He only had bruises on his right leg and a slight abrasion on his face from being pushed onto the ropes.

Corbett admitted that he had made a mistake in grappling with Sharkey. If he were to fight him again,

I would not clinch with him. I would stay away and do only open pointing. It was his wrestling that tired me, and in the fourth round I was quite exhausted. I will frankly confess it. In throwing my science away and fighting Sharkey at his own game I weakened myself.

Jim said that by getting weak from wrestling, it had given some the impression that Sharkey was a great fighter, when in fact, "he does not know the first rudiments of boxing." Corbett claimed that he motioned to Delaney to claim the fight on a foul, not to call the police into the ring.

The next day, Sharkey told the *Examiner*,

[H]e tried to give the impression that I was hugging, but I was not. He had his left hand around the back of my head and would not let go. All the while he was saying to me, "Break away; why don't you break away and stop clinching." .... I had to wrestle to get away from him.[786]

In another paper, Sharkey complimented Corbett's power, saying,

You fellows...may think Corbett can't hit, but I tell you he can. Look at that eye. He hit me and he hit me hard. I have been in a good many fights, and I've been hit by some strong men, but I tell you nobody ever hit me like Corbett did. He is a hard hitter, and I guess I ought to know.[787]

Corbett said that he had made the worst fight of his career, that he was too anxious and overreached himself. He had never met a man so strong in the clinches, and had underestimated Tom's endurance. He still felt though that he deserved the decision. He believed that he had Tom going in the 2nd round, and said, "Sharkey did not hit me a blow that hurt, but he threw me around like a shuttlecock. He is a great wrestler, but I think very little of his fighting ability." Answering those who said that he was dead tired at the

---

[786] *San Francisco Examiner*, June 26, 1896.
[787] *San Francisco Bulletin*, June 26, 1896.

end, Corbett responded that he had paced himself for 4 rounds; that if it had been scheduled for longer, he would have fought differently.[788]

The *New York Herald* said that Corbett admitted that he had not properly trained and that Sharkey had surprised him with his endurance. "I knew at the end of the second round that I was not in condition to put him out.... At the end of the third round I realized I could not put him out in the next, but I also knew he could not hurt me, as he cannot hit." Corbett said it was the poorest fight of his life and that he was ashamed. Of Sharkey, he said that he was "a good wrestler, but he cannot fight. It takes time to fight a man like Sharkey, for he is wonderfully strong." Corbett was unscathed, while Sharkey had a black eye and a hurt shoulder.

Corbett felt that he should have won the decision because Tom had done nothing to bring about his weak condition. However, "Corbett's most generous friends admit that the champion was worsted, and that he could not have lasted another round." This report said that when the police entered, it took three of them to restrain Sharkey from rushing at Corbett, "who did not have enough breath left to continue his incessant protest to the referee. In brief, Corbett attempted to beat Sharkey at the latter's own game and received the worst of it."

This report also differed a bit from the report it gave the previous day.

> At first many supposed that Sharkey was doing the hugging, but it soon became evident that Corbett was skillfully resting upon his opponent's shoulders, at the same time working his jaw incessantly in a protest to the referee. This official labored heroically with the fighters, receiving many hard knocks in his attempts to separate them. At each break Corbett would uppercut Sharkey, while the sailor was seemingly nonplussed.[789]

The *Sun* also provided a reflective perspective from a San Francisco dispatch.

> Sailor Sharkey proved himself to be a new pugilistic wonder, who, if he can be...taught to strike straight from the shoulder, will be a match for any heavy weight champion in the ring. Much absurd matter was printed here this morning about what the fight showed. Eager admirers of Sharkey, who don't like Corbett, declare that the sailor demonstrated that he was a great fighter, worthy to meet any man.
>
> What the fight proved was this: First, that Corbett has lost greatly in vitality; second, that he cannot maintain his guard against wild rushes of a powerful man like Sharkey, who is not phased by heavy blows at short range. ... [Corbett] made no real effort to keep Sharkey off, but in the first round resorted to infighting. ... Part of this may have been

---

[788] *San Francisco Examiner*, June 26, 1896.
[789] *New York Herald*, June 26, 1896.

due to Corbett's desire to end the fight in two rounds, as he had considerable money on this limit.

There is no question that if Corbett's blows had had the steam in them that his blows had when he fought Jackson he would have dazed the sailor in the first round, for he smashed him in the eye and the throat, yet Sharkey was not seriously hurt. ...

The contest was full of foul fighting, which a strict referee would have stopped immediately, and Sharkey tried to injure Corbett by butting and Corbett retaliated by twisting the sailor's neck at every clinch. ... But what injured Corbett's prestige more than anything else was that he appealed to Police Captain Wittman to stop the fight.

As the fourth round was almost over, this was to save himself from punishing blows delivered by Sharkey and also to give ground for calling off all bets. These were made on the proposition that Corbett would stop Sharkey in four rounds. He not only didn't stop him, but Sharkey could have whipped Jim had the fight lasted two rounds longer.

Sharkey is an extraordinary man. ... He is as light on his feet as Sullivan was in his prime, but his blows are not so effective. Had he hit Corbett straight punches instead of the few swinging blows that landed, the ex-champion would have been out. ...

As for Corbett, he lacks stamina. He has wasted his splendid vitality, and as miracles do not occur, it seems impossible that he should ever again make his old showing in the ring. He secured $7,500 gate money last night, but lost a fortune in prestige.[790]

Two days after the fight, it was reported that Sharkey and Corbett had signed articles for a fight to the finish for a bet of $10,000 a side, and that each had put up a $2,500 forfeit. The fight was to take place within the next six months in the U.S. or Mexico, before the club offering the biggest purse.

Corbett claimed that Sharkey was the one who had done the wrestling and clinching in their fight, and insisted that a term be included in the articles of agreement wherein wrestling would be a foul which would cost the perpetrator the fight. Interestingly, Sharkey at first resisted, but then gave in. The fact that Sharkey initially objected to such a term lends some credence to Corbett's argument that it was Tom who was doing most of the wrestling. There had been reports before their fight that Sharkey intended to use clinching as a survival tactic. Furthermore, little discussed is the fact that Sharkey was originally a wrestler, doing so in the Navy before taking up boxing. "His chief sport was wrestling, at which he became quite proficient." Still, most reports agreed that after Corbett grew fatigued from

[790] New York Sun, June 26, 1896.

all the wrestling engaged in by Sharkey, it was Jim who resorted to plenty of clinching to save himself.[791]

The *National Police Gazette* months later said that there was "doubt as to the merit" of Sharkey's performance, but many nevertheless wanted to see him again.[792] Sharkey felt that he could defeat Corbett.

> I had him going in San Francisco and would have won easily if I didn't have to fight both Corbett and the referee, and later the police. Why, in the last two rounds Corbett was continually grabbing me by the arms and calling upon the police to come into the ring and stop the fight. They say I couldn't hit Corbett. Why, I smashed him worse than he did me, and he'd been a bad sight if the referee hadn't been with him. Each time we'd come together the referee wouldn't part us, but he'd come and put both hands to my stomach and shove me back, leaving Corbett to smash away.

He also again noted that Corbett suggested and agreed to break fair, but would then hit on the breaks, including the time he closed Tom's eye with a right.[793]

After such a lengthy period of inactivity against top boxers, Corbett was clearly not at his best. Many felt that he was slipping and no longer what he once was, even predicting that Fitzsimmons would defeat him. And still he had only gone 4 rounds. Corbett's stock dropped, while Sharkey had gained a reputation. Like Sullivan before him, Corbett had been more interested in the theater and the good life, and inactivity was apparently causing him to regress.

Tom Sharkey would eventually become famous, amongst other things, for giving future champion James J. Jeffries some of his toughest fights. He would go on to fight Bob Fitzsimmons twice and later have a rematch with Corbett, but the details of those fights will be discussed in subsequent volumes.

---

[791] *San Francisco Evening Post*, June 26, 1896; *New York Clipper*, July 4, 1896; *New York Sun*, July 5, 1896.
[792] *National Police Gazette*, September 5, 1896.
[793] *National Police Gazette*, September 12, 1896.

CHAPTER 19

State of Affairs and
the Long Awaited Defense

The Sharkey bout in June was Jim Corbett's only official 1896 fight. Two days after fighting Sharkey, on June 26, 1896, Corbett boxed an exhibition at the Olympic Club with the much smaller Robert McCord. "The ladies fairly went crazy over him." Corbett looked "superb," and was "as nimble as a rabbit; McCord couldn't touch him." Of course, the much smaller McCord was not a vicious rusher like Sharkey.[794]

According to a secondary source, Jim eventually left San Francisco and headed to New York, on his way giving exhibitions in Denver, Kansas City, and Chicago.[795]

On August 6, 1896 in Cripple Creek, Colorado (108 miles southwest of Denver), Jim sparred 4 tame and short friendly rounds with 200-pound Billy Woods, whose career included: 1891 LKOby34 Choynski; and 1895 LKOby15 Steve O'Donnell and LDQby9 George Godfrey. Woods had been a Bob Fitzsimmons and Jim Hall sparring partner, and would become one of Corbett's main sparring partners. Corbett and Woods' sparring was witnessed by 1,500 people and generated receipts of $2,000. Jim told the newsmen that he was ready to meet any heavyweight with sufficient backing to make a challenge.[796]

On September 12, 1896, the Corbett and Fitzsimmons parties met in New York to agree upon terms for a match between the two.

> [Fitz had] finally concluded that it was about time he stopped making himself appear either ridiculous or "afeard," just as people chose to look at it, by insisting upon the Californian doing something to "get a reputation" before he would agree to face him in the ring. The fact that Fitzsimmons had by his persistence in this respect, and his flat refusal to accept Corbett's challenge, forfeited the title of champion doubtless influenced him and his manager in taking this step.

The fight was scheduled to take place sixty days from the Corbett-Sharkey fight, provided that latter bout took place before the end of the year. If the Sharkey fight were declared off for any reason, Corbett bound

---

[794] *San Francisco Bulletin*, June 27, 1896.
[795] Fields at 98.
[796] *Denver Daily News*, August 7, 1896.

himself to box Fitz on or before March 1, 1897. The winner was to take the entire purse and stake money.[797]

Fitzsimmons was arrested on September 21 in New York on a warrant issued on an indictment charging him with conspiring to commit a crime by assisting in arranging a prize fight with Corbett, for whom a warrant had also been obtained. Corbett was arrested on the 23rd. They posted bail and were released.[798] New York was obviously sending the message not to have the prize fight there.

Corbett was supposed to have a December rematch with Sharkey. After all, Tom had hurt his reputation, and many were eager to see them in the ring together again. However, after Corbett signed to box Fitzsimmons, there were contradictory reports about the prospect of the Sharkey fight happening. One report said that the National Sporting Club had offered a purse of $20,000. It was subsequently said that the parties agreed to limit the bout to 10 rounds, and that it would take place at the Eureka Athletic Club. Initially, it seemed that the fight was on. On September 26, Sharkey left New York, heading for San Francisco, the fight site.

However, a September 28 dispatch out of San Francisco questioned whether the Sharkey fight was really genuinely intended or going to take place. It said that neither the National nor the Eureka clubs had deposited any guarantee money, and the fighters had not deposited any forfeit money.

> Corbett is conducting all negotiations for both himself and Sharkey, and this fact goes far to prove that the alleged match was a fake from its inception. No one has been able to discover a dollar of forfeit money deposited by either of the fighters or their backers, though each of the pugilists claims to have placed $5,000 in the hands of stakeholders.[799]

Corbett then said that since neither of the California clubs had deposited a purse and were not likely to do so, the Sharkey match was off, and he would devote his attention to the Fitzsimmons fight. When Sharkey learned of this, he "became very mad and announced that he would break Corbett's neck on sight." Sharkey's manager said that plenty of other clubs would be willing to offer a purse for the fight.[800]

Corbett later admitted to the *National Police Gazette* that the Sharkey rematch had been an advertising scheme, that once he had secured the desired Fitzsimmons bout he dropped the sailor at once. This demonstrated that he was not above such tactics, and had probably utilized them in the past. Sharkey was unaware that he was being used and was upset, confident

---

[797] *New York Clipper*, September 19, 1896.
[798] *New York Clipper*, September 26, 1896, October 3, 1896.
[799] *New York Clipper*, September 19, 1896, October 3, 1896.
[800] *New York Clipper*, October 10, 1896.

that he could whip Corbett.[801] Clearly, Corbett did not really intend to fight Sharkey.

Regardless, Corbett was in no rush to begin serious training for the Fitzsimmons fight either. On October 17, 1896 in Glen Falls, New York, Corbett resumed his tour of the country and Canada with his play, *A Naval Cadet.*[802]

Interestingly enough, Bob Fitzsimmons then decided to take on Tom Sharkey, perhaps realizing that defeating the man who had given Jim a tough go of it would further add to his reputation, seeking to one-up Corbett. He might have intended to fight Sharkey, impressively defeat him, and legitimize his subsequent avoidance of Corbett, who he could then say did not deserve a title shot because Jim had struggled with Tom. Even if he did still intend to fight Corbett, it was an additional intervening opportunity to pick up some very good money. An October 18 dispatch said that the National Athletic Sporting Club (which had promoted Corbett-Sharkey I), the same club which supposedly did not come up with a purse for the Corbett-Sharkey rematch, succeeded in inducing Fitzsimmons and Sharkey to fight 10 rounds in December for a $10,000 purse. Within a week, the club deposited $5,000.[803]

On December 2, 1896 in San Francisco, the power punching Bob Fitzsimmons administered a beating to the game Tom Sharkey, dropping him in the 1st and 5th rounds, until Sharkey was knocked out in the 8th round. However, Fitzsimmons was suspiciously disqualified by referee Wyatt Earp for a low blow that many believed never took place. It was a questionable call, and there were allegations, not unfounded, that the fight had been fixed in Sharkey's favor with the referee's cooperation. A legal battle ensued, and it appeared that Fitzsimmons would win, but a judge threw out the case on a technicality: boxing was illegal, so he could not enforce any contract regarding it, regardless of whether or not it was a fix. As a result of his "victory," Tom Sharkey began claiming that he was the champion. No one recognized him, particularly because most felt that Fitz had earlier forfeited his championship claim, and also because most felt that Bob had deserved to win the fight.

Fitzsimmons' reputation was unharmed by the Sharkey fight and he was still considered one of the two best fighters in the world. However, because Fitz had technically lost and had made no money from the winner-take-all fight, it may have served as additional motivation for him to go through with the Corbett fight.

From late 1896 to early 1897, Corbett continued touring with his play, traveling from city to city, occasionally giving sparring exhibitions, usually

---

[801] *National Police Gazette*, September 12, 1896, September 19, 1896, November 7, 1896.
[802] Fields at 99, 237.
[803] *New York Clipper,* October 24, 31, 1896.

with Jim McVey.[804] On December 14, 1896, before a crowd of 3,000 viewers at New York's Broadway Athletic Club, Corbett took part in a friendly exhibition benefit show. He received a warm reception, and, wearing a breech clout, boxed 3 lively rounds with Jim McVey, giving a "fine exhibition of science." Mostly though, Jim was enjoying acting.[805]

1896 had some activity amongst the top ranks. Joe Choynski scored a January KO13 over Jim Hall, essentially defeated Sharkey in an 8-round bout in April, and in August scored a KO4 over Joe McAuliffe. However, in November, 174-pound Peter Maher stopped the 165-pound Choynski in the 6th round. The power punching Maher was coming off a June 1896 KO4 over Frank Slavin.

Responding to the New York critics of the Choynski-Maher fight, the president of the police board, Commissioner Theodore Roosevelt, himself a glove practitioner and spectator of the contest said,

> When I was in Harvard and sparred for the championship, I suffered a heavier punishment than any man there did, and I have been knocked out at polo twice for a ten times longer period than Choynski was knocked out for. I don't care very much for professional sport of any kind, but I thoroughly believe in boxing, exactly as I believe in football and other manly games.[806]

Roosevelt eventually became President of the United States in 1901.

Also in 1896, Steve O'Donnell lost a 20-round decision to Gus Ruhlin in June, but in September scored his own KO4 over Frank Slavin. In a December 1896 rematch, 177 ½-pound Peter Maher again stopped a 181-pound Steve O'Donnell in the 1st round.[807] Thus, in knocking out Slavin, Choynski and O'Donnell, Maher finished up the year very well. However, as Fitzsimmons already had two victories over Maher, including a February 1896 KO1, as well as a prior knockout victory over Choynski, and had basically just stopped Sharkey, he was clearly the most deserving contender.

In November, in a rematch, Joe Goddard avenged his earlier loss to Ed Smith, knocking him out in the 4th round.

Two weeks after Fitzsimmons' disqualification loss to Sharkey, on December 17, 1896, Corbett and Fitzsimmons once again agreed to fight. It was for the heavyweight championship of the world and a $15,000 purse, the winner to take the entire purse. It was set for St. Patrick's Day, March 17, 1897.[808]

Corbett continued exhibiting with his play, although he did begin some additional training in anticipation of the upcoming Fitzsimmons bout. While in Kansas City, Missouri with his play on the last day of January 1897,

[804] Fields at 99.
[805] *New York Sun*, December 15, 1896.
[806] *New York Clipper*, December 5, 1896.
[807] *National Police Gazette*, February 1, 1896, November 28, 1896, January 9, 1897.
[808] *New York Clipper*, December 26, 1896.

he said, "I am in the finest condition and do not need any training at all. I am ready for the ring now. ... I never was in better condition in all my life." Corbett said that he did not anticipate any trouble with Fitzsimmons. He would finish out his theatrical performances in Kansas City over the next week, and then travel to San Francisco for a week or two to visit his parents. "I shall be training all the time, as I am now. After my visit, I shall go into the mountains of Nevada for four week's hard training." Nevada had legalized boxing on January 26, 1897, paving the way for the fight to be held there, at Carson City.[809]

Corbett gave his final performance of *A Naval Cadet* in Kansas City on February 6, heading west on the 7th. On the 8th in Denver, Corbett said, "Well, I never felt better in my life and never more confident of winning a fight. ... I have been training for the past six weeks."

Psychologically though, Corbett was less than enthusiastic about the fight game. When he was in Salt Lake on the 9th, one reporter observed, "Pugilism has become something of a bore to him. He considers it of secondary importance and showed this feeling in every line of his rather forced talk." Regardless, Jim said that he was 180 pounds and felt first rate. "I would be ready to go into the ring tomorrow if it were not for questions of endurance and wind. After returning from San Francisco to the battle ground in Nevada I shall go into systematic training as far as wind is concerned."

While in Salt Lake, Corbett gave a sparring exhibition with Billy Woods, before arriving back in San Francisco on February 11. Woods became a regular Corbett sparring partner in preparation for the Fitz fight, as was McVey.

Analyzing the upcoming fight, one paper said,

> Local sports consider that the big fight will depend solely upon Corbett's condition. They say that if he is right he will not let Fitzsimmons ever land that heavy punch, and that he will take advantage of the many openings Fitz leaves. On the other hand, according to the "wise" ones, if Corbett is not in condition Fitzsimmons is cunning enough to wear him out.[810]

It was said that in order to win, Corbett would have to avoid training on French dinners the way he had for Sharkey. Corbett responded to those who said that he had been dissipating, saying,

> I want to say that the public is all wrong about me. ... There seems to be a general impression that I have "gone back" by licensing my appetite. ... The fact is I was never in better condition prior to a fight

[809] *San Francisco Chronicle*, February 1, 1897; *Salt Lake Herald*, January 28, 31, 1897.
[810] *San Francisco Chronicle*, February 8, 1897; *Salt Lake Herald*, February 9, 10, 1897.

than I am right now. When I enter the ring it will be after a month's faithful training.[811]

Under normal circumstances, for an active fighter, a month's worth of hard boxing training after six weeks of light endurance training might be just right. However, only a month's worth of serious training after having been less than active for many years, and not having had a serious fight against a legitimate contender in five years, was probably not the best idea. And Carson City was at altitude, over 4,650 feet above sea level. The inactive Sullivan had prepared similarly for Corbett and came up title-less. True, Corbett did have a couple short bouts and some sparring exhibitions over the last few years, and had twice engaged in the training necessary for potentially longer fights against Mitchell and Fitzsimmons. However, when you consider that Sullivan and Mitchell were over the hill, the fact was that Corbett had not fought in a serious fight to the finish against a legitimately sharp and prime fighter since Peter Jackson in 1891, almost six years earlier. However, Corbett had not ballooned in weight the way Sullivan had, nor did he have a serious drinking problem.

The reports regarding Corbett's training were usually quite good. He trained very hard and was said to be looking in excellent form. He did some training in San Francisco on February 12, 1897, just over a month before the fight. He boxed and wrestled a few times there with McVey, before heading to Carson City, Nevada, beginning his training camp there on February 17.

It was clear from the subsequent reports that Corbett was training hard and diligently, sparring and wrestling many rounds almost daily with men such as Billy Woods, John McVey, his brother Joe Corbett, welterweight George Green (a.k.a. Young Corbett), Robert Edgren (the champion hammer thrower), and future heavyweight champion James J. Jeffries, then just a beginner, but a 200-plus-pound man already known for his strength and toughness. Corbett also took long walks and runs, punched the bag for lengthy periods of time, worked with weights, and played handball. The reporters generally liked Jim's appearance in the ring, for he was handling his sparring partners well, including the much larger Jeffries, and could box many rounds without fatiguing.

However, some felt that Corbett was overtraining, that if he kept up his pace of work, he would be stale by the time of the fight. Recall that a similar concern was expressed about John L. Sullivan before Sullivan fought Corbett. Many had said that because Sullivan had been so badly out of shape and inactive for so long, that he was training doubly hard to get himself into shape, but that overtraining was counterproductive. Certainly, after his poor performance against Sharkey, Corbett wanted to be in the best of shape against a man said to have excellent condition, big punching

---

[811] *San Francisco Chronicle,* February 12, 1897.

power, very good skills, and vast experience. Fitzsimmons' prior results made him a serious threat. Bob generally won by knockout, and in Sharkey had handled a man with whom Corbett had struggled. This made Jim train very hard. However, instead of gradually working himself into the best boxing shape over the course of many months, Corbett continued with his play and only did some running during that time, and then conducted intense boxing training for one month. Sullivan had trained similarly in preparation for the Corbett fight.

That said, most observers felt that both Corbett and Fitzsimmons were in excellent shape going into the fight and that victory or defeat would not depend on condition. Corbett looked very good in training, and the betting odds slightly favored Jim.

The long awaited Fitzsimmons–Corbett title fight finally happened on March 17, 1897 in Carson City, Nevada. The fight took place almost nine months after Corbett had boxed Sharkey. It was only Corbett's fourth fight since winning the crown in late 1892, having to that point averaged less than one serious bout per year. In his just over four year reign, he had not defended against a legitimate top contender in a lengthy bout. This was his first such defense.

It would be the last time that Corbett entered the ring as champion. During that fight, the generally cautious Corbett started well, cutting up Fitz's face and outpointing him, typically striking him with one or two outside punches and then moving away or clinching. Jim even dropped Bob with a right in the 6th round. However, the consistent and determined Fitzsimmons was a well-conditioned aggressor, stalking calmly and gradually pressing in, snapping quick and powerful punches. Jim could cut him up and momentarily stun him, but he could not take Bob out. In about the 9th round, Corbett began fatiguing, throwing fewer punches and slowing down. He had been working hard to keep away, but Fitz continued applying pressure and began landing more effectively. In the 14th round, after Corbett jabbed, Fitzsimmons dropped Jim with a quick counter left hook to the body. A stunned and breathless Corbett was unable to rise by the count of ten. At age 30, James J. Corbett's days as champion were over.[812]

---

[812] Substantial footage of this fight still exists. This fight will be discussed in greater detail in the Fitzsimmons volume.

CHAPTER 20

The Legacy

James J. Corbett is the first heavyweight champion of the gloved era to rely primarily on science as his strength. He was the forefather to slick fighters who relied primarily on defense, speed, footwork and intelligence to win their bouts. Corbett's defensive skills included head movement, blocking with the arms and shoulders, clinching, as well as graceful and shifty footwork. Jim was good at feinting his opponents in order to keep them worrying or to get them to throw at the wrong moment. His offensive arsenal included the full panoply of relaxed and speedy leads and counters to the body and head. Jim was a stiff puncher when he wanted to be, but was generally not regarded as a big knockout puncher. He was the first heavyweight champion to learn Queensberry rules boxing through instruction in a boxing club, and the first to have an amateur career.

The versatile Corbett could compete with both boxers and punchers. Before becoming champion, Jim demonstrated his superior skills against many veteran professionals. He proved his toughness, defense, and conditioning in his finish fight with the hard-punching Joe Choynski, stopping him in the 27th round. Furthermore, Corbett did what Sullivan was unwilling to do, and that was to break the color line by fighting the world's most respected and feared heavyweight contender, Peter Jackson. He took this risk in order to establish himself as a worthy contender for Sullivan's crown. Experts considered Jackson the most skillful fighter in the world, a veteran ring expert who was bigger than Corbett, and who generally broke his opponents down with pressure, good jabs and body shots. Jackson also had smooth defensive moves. Against him, Corbett demonstrated his superior skills, ability, and endurance. Most thought that Corbett had the better of their 61-round fight. This proved that Corbett at his best was an excellent ring general.

Corbett was also able to knock out the most talented heavyweight champion the world had ever known in the legendary John L. Sullivan. Although John L. had been inactive and was well past his prime, he was still an enormous puncher; considered the hardest puncher of all time up to that point, vastly experienced, and undefeated. Corbett easily outboxed and stopped him, demonstrating his wonderful science, speed, and endurance in doing it. Corbett was the only fighter ever to defeat Sullivan. At his best, Jim was quick, skilled, and very well conditioned. He was the hardest man in the world to hit cleanly.

So why has history never regarded Corbett as highly as John L. Sullivan (even the Irish)? Corbett defeated Sullivan, took on the most feared heavyweight in the world in Peter Jackson, fought in lengthy Queensberry rules fights to the finish, and even showed heart by fighting with broken hands against Choynski. Corbett and Sullivan were both Irish Americans and masters at their craft in their own ways.

Like many champions of the past, Corbett was the first to follow in the footsteps of an immensely talented champion who transcended his sport, who was so highly regarded that it was a daunting task to live up to a John L. Sullivan. Because Sullivan was well past his prime when they fought, like Tunney to Dempsey, Corbett has never received the kind of credit for his victory that he would have earned had the meeting taken place years earlier. Certainly though, that is not his fault.

Also, Corbett's style was simply not as awe-inspiring as Sullivan's was. Jim was very well respected and admired as a clever masterful boxer, which made him a lot of money, but he was not considered the phenomenon that the knockout artist Sullivan had been. This is the curse that most great outside boxers have faced. Traditionally, big punchers have captured the public's imagination and esteem more so than beautiful boxers. This was another factor that meant that Corbett would not be as highly regarded as Sullivan had been.

This is not to say that Corbett was not popular. People paid plenty of money to see him in plays, and although he was a decent actor, the real reason these plays did so well was because of his boxing status, as well as his good looks. Men and women enjoyed seeing the champion. This fact made Corbett a rich man, so rich that Jim did not see the need to fight very often. Corbett was in it for money, not glory. As champion, he only fought as much as he needed to in order to maintain his income as an actor.

Like Sullivan and many other subsequent heavyweight champions, as champion Corbett was less than willing to box against a black fighter. Boxing was the most socially progressive sport, breaking social barriers to some extent, distinguishing it from all other sports, but when it came to sport's most vaunted prize, heavyweight champions of that era generally followed the existing social norm of separation of the races. That said, Corbett claimed to be willing to box Peter Jackson. He was not entirely to blame for the failure of the Jackson fight to come off, as legal and social factors, as well as Jackson himself, were certainly strong impediments. However, Corbett certainly did not facilitate the fight either.

Because of his style and less than stellar championship career, Corbett's recognition has been somewhat begrudgingly bestowed. The former was not his fault, but the latter was. Corbett's rise was much more impressive than his championship career. As champion, Corbett was a cautious, risk-averse matchmaker who sought to make money from his championship status without having to risk his title in the ring. He was very calculating about who he fought, how he fought, and when he fought them. He was not anywhere near as much of a fighting champion as Sullivan had been.

Therefore, he never achieved the super lofty status of a John L. Sullivan. He essentially did what Sullivan did late in his career, but without having previously established his dominance and popularity over a decade the way Sullivan had.

Corbett's inactivity and cautious matchmaking decisions initially ensured that he would not lose his valuable status, which ironically helped him make a lot of money. People paid to see the champion. However, also ironically, by overprotecting his title and being less than active, he lost the boxing sharpness necessary to retain the title. Corbett was inactive as champion, did not take on a top contender in the first few years of his championship, and although it was not his fault that the Fitzsimmons fight failed to take place in 1895, his retirement and subsequent struggle with Sharkey, and eventual loss to former middleweight Fitzsimmons certainly hurts his legacy.

Because Corbett was more active on the stage than in the ring during his championship years, it likely damaged his substantial boxing prowess. Corbett was more interested in making money as an actor, capitalizing on the championship that he had worked so hard to achieve. Sullivan had done this in the final three years of his career, and it cost him. In taking a similar path, Corbett failed to maintain the interest and physical sharpness that was required in order to retain his title. Corbett was a brilliant boxer, but his inactivity may have had as much to do with his eventual losses as anything. Split allegiances are not good for a fighter. Champions are always at their best when they remain active and in condition. Sullivan's loss to Corbett had proven this, and Corbett, like many future champions, failed to benefit from that lesson.

Corbett always claimed that his loss to Fitzsimmons was a fluke, that he had been winning the fight up until the knockout. However, it was a fight to the finish, not a points bout. Fitzsimmons somehow usually managed to knock out most of his opponents, so his luck, if it can be called that, was likely more the result of his ability and studied design than chance. It may well have been that Corbett was in great shape for the Fitz fight, but because Fitzsimmons was such a great puncher, if you couldn't take him out, he would eventually find a way to land the big one, which he did against Jim. Unlike Fitzsimmons, Corbett was not a huge puncher, and he could not simply rely on Fitzsimmons' wearing himself out, because Bob was too clever and too well conditioned. In a finish fight, Corbett had to muster the power to knock him out, which apparently he could not do. Unfortunately, Fitz would not grant Jim a rematch, so Corbett was never able to prove his claim that Fitzsimmons could not duplicate his feat.

After losing the title, Corbett returned to the theater, which once again became his predominant profession. Failing to learn the lessons of inactivity, it would not be until one year and eight months later before Corbett would box again, in a November 1898 rematch with Tom Sharkey.

He once again struggled with Sharkey, even suffering a knockdown in the 2nd round, until he was disqualified in the 9th round when his cornerman Jim McVey entered the ring to complain about Tom's roughhouse tactics. Some suspected the entry was preconceived. The referee even called the bets off. Others felt that it was done to save Corbett from being knocked out. That fight ended Jim's chances for a rematch with Fitzsimmons. Fitz did not defend for two years, until 1899, when James J. Jeffries knocked him out in the 11th round. Jeffries was the former Corbett sparring partner who held a May 1898 20-round decision victory over Sharkey.

One year and five months after losing to Sharkey, in May 1900, a 33-year-old Corbett took on then champion James J. Jeffries. A motivated and re-dedicated Corbett trained for many months in preparation for the fight. Even past his prime, a 185-pound Corbett boxed brilliantly against a determined, well-conditioned 25-year-old champion who was much larger and stronger at 212 pounds. However, Jim was eventually worn down and knocked out in the 23rd round. Still, the performance served to prove Corbett's mettle to a lot of critics, and it gained him many admirers.

In late August 1900, Corbett scored a KO5 against Charles "Kid" McCoy. McCoy's career included: 1896 KO3 Jim Daly; 1897 KO1 George LaBlanche and KO2 Australian Billy Smith; 1898 W20 Gus Ruhlin and WDQ5 Joe Goddard; 1899 LKOby10 Tom Sharkey and W20 Joe Choynski; and 1900 KO5 Peter Maher and KO4 Joe Choynski. Although it was a significant victory for Jim, some suspected that the Corbett-McCoy fight was fixed in Corbett's favor. However, most neutral observers at the time felt that the fight was legitimate.

However, oddly enough, Corbett did not fight again for another three years. In August 1903, in his final fight, James Jeffries easily stopped a 36-year-old Corbett in the 10th round.[813]

Unfortunately, because Corbett's stiff tests against men like Fitzsimmons, Jeffries, and Sharkey came years past his prime, and more importantly, after he had been less than active, he likely did not have the same level of sharpness and conditioning that he had from 1889 to 1892. Like Sullivan against Corbett, it is difficult to know how Jim would have done with these men in his prime years.

The Corbett-Jeffries fight has been used in two different ways to assess Corbett. History has highly regarded Jeffries, so if a less than active, older, smaller, past his prime Corbett could do so well, one can speculate that he would have done much better when he was what he was in the late 1880s and early 1890s. However, on the other hand, although he was a great points fighter, Corbett was never much of a puncher, so in a fight to the finish, even a prime Corbett might never have been able to stop a Jeffries

---

[813] *In the Ring With Bob Fitzsimmons* and *In the Ring With James J. Jeffries* reveal the details of these stories.

type fighter, and might well have been worn down and taken out at some point.

Overall, it appears that men who were well conditioned, strong and active boxers, who could pressure consistently and take a punch (and not past their primes), would have given even a prime Corbett troubles. Sharkey, Fitzsimmons, and Jeffries proved that a well conditioned puncher who could take it from a less than his best Corbett, and persistently pressure him with power shots, would eventually catch up with him.

However, it is just as clear that at his best, Corbett could hit, elude and neutralize opponents almost at will, and keep it up indefinitely. A prime Corbett would have punched more, hit harder and faster, and have been able to move and punch more consistently and longer than did the Corbett who had been more focused on his acting career. He demonstrated this against Choynski, Jackson, and Sullivan. Therefore, it is not out of the question that the Corbett who existed during those years could have defeated those who eventually defeated him. In today's world of 12-round bouts, Corbett may well have gone undefeated. Ultimately, James J. Corbett should be remembered in his prime as the shiftiest, quickest, most skillful and intelligent boxer in the world, with the best pair of legs that the sport had ever seen on a big man.

Appendix:

James J. Corbett's Record

BORN : September 1 1866; San Francisco, California
DIED : February 18 1933; Bayside, Queens, New York at age 66.

1879 – 1884

Corbett boxed frequently in informal bouts in his father's stable, and around town in places such as the fire engine house and blacksmith shop. He was also not shy about engaging in street fights. By the time he was 16, he was known as being the best fighter amongst the local youths.

Date Unknown - Circa 1881

Fatty Carney	San Francisco, CA	W

This was an informal street fight.

Joe Robinson	San Francisco, CA	L

This was another informal street fight.

Date Unknown - Circa 1881 – 1882

Billy Kenealy	San Francisco, CA	W

Held in Corbett's father's stable.

Date Unknown - Circa 1883 - 1884

For about six months, Corbett took boxing lessons from Denny Dillon in his father's stable.

Dates Unknown – Circa 1884 - 1885

Joe Choynski	San Francisco, CA	KO 1
Joe Choynski	San Francisco, CA	KO 1 or 2
		Bareknuckle.
Choynski's brother	San Francisco, CA	KO
Joe Choynski	San Francisco, CA	KO 1

This fight may not have happened.

Most sources agree that Corbett and Choynski fought two to four times as youths in informal bouts and that Corbett won each time. The exact results are unconfirmed.

Possibly 1884

Corbett joins San Francisco's Olympic Club, a prestigious amateur athletic club where training and exhibitions in multiple sports took place. According to Corbett, he at first played baseball, but later sparred with and was shown-up by a German heavyweight boxing instructor. The next day, the club heavyweight champion, whom he called "Blackbeard", knocked out Corbett. It was not until almost a year later that Jim really began to formally learn boxing skills.

1885

Mar 30   Walter Watson arrives to teach boxing at the Olympic.

Apr   New Olympic Club opens.

| May 19 | William T. Welch/Welsh | San Francisco, CA | EX L 4 |

Corbett was listed as a heavyweight.

Corbett received boxing instruction from Professor Watson.

A secondary source claims that after almost a year of sparring and training with Professor Watson, and fellow students W.J. Kenealy, Bob McCord, and M.L. Requa, at the end of the year Corbett again boxed Welch and knocked him out in the 1st round. Another source said that after losing to Welch, Corbett trained with Watson for a few months and then met Welch again at the Acme Club in Oakland and nearly knocked him out in 1 round.

An 1889 source said that Corbett's first set-to at the Olympic was against Lem Fulda, whom Jim KO'd in four minutes. It took place sometime in 1885, possibly after the first Welch bout. However, Professor Watson said it was just a friendly sparring session.

Jul 24	Grosenberg	San Francisco, CA	EX W 4
Aug 28	Mike Cleary	San Francisco, CA	EX 2
			Cleary better.
Aug 28	Dave Eiseman/Eisman	San Francisco, CA	EX KO 2

Corbett was a heavyweight and much bigger than Eiseman. The rounds only lasted two minutes and Eiseman retired or was retired by Professor Watson during the 2nd.

May-Sep?	Jack Dempsey	San Francisco, CA	private sparring
Oct	Corbett possibly sparred Mike Cleary in private, for Cleary was training at the Olympic.
Oct 9	E.G. Slossen/Slosson	San Francisco, CA	EX W 3
Oct 23	James Hair	San Francisco, CA	EX 3
Nov 6	E.G. Slosson	San Francisco, CA	Walkover
Nov 6	Professor Watson	San Francisco, CA	Walkover

Corbett is recognized as the Olympic Club's heavyweight champion.

| Dec 3 | James Hair, E.P. Slosson, possibly Watson as well | San Francisco, CA | EX |

It is unclear as to who Jim sparred (possibly more than once) or for how long.

1886

| Jan 22 | James McCarthy | San Francisco, CA | EX |

According to a secondary source, Corbett scored a KO2 over Dick Matthews. It also claims that Corbett again boxed McCarthy in May 1886 and bested him. No primary source was offered regarding either claim.

Feb 12	Professor Walter Watson	San Francisco, CA	EX 3
May 14	Robert McCord	San Francisco, CA	EX
and/or	William Welch	San Francisco, CA	EX
Jul 3	Frank Smith	Salt Lake City, UT	WDQ 3 or 4

Professional fight to the finish. Smith disqualified for holding and wrestling. While in Salt Lake, Corbett posed as "Jim Dillon."

| Jul 14 | Duncan McDonald | Salt Lake City, UT | D 6 |

The general feeling was that McDonald had a slight advantage, but that the two were working together to keep it exciting and even, some calling it a "hippodrome."

| Jul 22 | Duncan McDonald | Salt Lake City, UT | EX 3 |

Corbett possibly gave some other exhibitions with McDonald.

| Nov 8 | P.T. Goodloe | San Francisco, CA | EX |
| Dec 2 | Jack Kitchen | Oakland, CA | EX |

1887

Sometime in late 1886 or early 1887, Corbett became a boxing professor.

Jan 25	Tom Johnson	Oakland, CA	EX W 3
Feb 2	Mike Brennan	San Francisco, CA	EX 3
?	James Daly	CA	KO 4, 1, or 2?
?	Martin "Buffalo" Costello	CA	W 3?
Mar 23	Joe Choynski	San Francisco, CA	EX W 5
Aug 27	Jack Burke	San Francisco, CA	ND 8

One local paper called it a draw, but two others said that Burke had the slight advantage and was the more scientific, mostly just playing and taking it easy with Jim. Corbett livened up and did better in the last 2 rounds. It was called a clever exhibition bearing little resemblance to a fight. Olympic Club members said that their man, Corbett, had won. It seems that the two were just working with one another in a scientific way.

Corbett subsequently said that he was retiring from boxing in favor of his job (his employers objected to his boxing) and as a result of a promise made to his father. He was not mentioned in the local press for the rest of 1887.

Corbett possibly trained and sparred with his pupil, Bill Kenealy, in preparation for Bill's bout with Joe Choynski, which Kenealy lost in late-November.

1888

| Jan 27 | William Kennealy/Kenneally | San Francisco, CA | EX |

Feb   After Walter Watson resigned, the Olympic Club hired Corbett to be its head boxing instructor.

| Mar 9 | William Kenealy | San Francisco, CA | EX 3 |

In April, Professor Corbett was hired by Joe McAuliffe to spar with him in preparation for McAuliffe's late May bout with Frank Glover. They began working together on April 8.

| Jun 29 | W.H. Quinn | San Francisco, CA | wrestling EX |

Each gained a fall.

| Jun 30 | Frank Glover | San Francisco, CA | EX 4 |

Corbett generally considered to have been better.

Jul 28	Joe Bowers	San Francisco, CA	EX W 4
Aug 21	Frank Bush	San Francisco, CA	EX 3
Nov 14	Robert McCord	San Francisco, CA	EX
Nov 24	Robert McCord	San Francisco, CA	EX 3

Corbett claimed to have sparred Joe McAuliffe late in the year, assisting Joe in preparations for his late December match with Peter Jackson.

1889

Corbett was continuing his coaching duties.

Sometime prior to May, although it was likely much earlier, Corbett won a 6-round bout against Professor William Miller. This bout may have happened sometime between November 1887 and November 1888.

| May 30 | Joe Choynski | San Anselmo, CA | NC 4 |

Fight stopped when sheriff arrived. Corbett was slightly better.

| Jun 5 | Joe Choynski | Carquinez Straits, CA | KO 27 |

| Jul 15 | Joe Choynski | San Francisco, CA | EX 4 |

Friendly exhibition, though Corbett better.

Jul and Aug   Professor Corbett sparred with Joe McAuliffe, helping Joe prepare for a bout with Pat Killen. At some point, Corbett may have defeated McAuliffe in a private 4-round bout for points in a barn.

| Sep | George Atkinson | San Francisco, CA | KO 1 |

Bout took place during the week prior to Sep 23.

| Sep 28 | John Donaldson | San Francisco, CA | EX W 4 |

| Oct 12 | J.B. Smith | San Francisco, CA | EX 4 |

| Dec 10 | Corbett resigned his professorship. |

| Dec 11 | Billy Smith | Portland, OR | W 6 |

No slugging or knockout allowed.

| Dec 12 | Billy Smith | Portland, OR | W 6 |

No slugging or knockout allowed.

| Dec 28 | Dave Campbell | Portland, OR | D 10 |

Likely a hippodrome. No slugging or knockout allowed.

1890

| Feb 17 | Jake Kilrain | New Orleans, LA | W 6 |

| Mar 17 | Corbett arrives in New York as the guest of Professor Mike Donovan. |

Over the next month, Corbett sparred Donovan multiple times in New York, and possibly in Boston, Brooklyn, Philadelphia, Baltimore, and Washington.

| Apr 14 | Dominick McCaffrey | Brooklyn, NY | EX KO 4/W 4 |

McCaffrey badly outclassed, and despite short rounds and long rests, he essentially quits before the expiration of the 4th round.

| May 1 | Corbett resumed his post as boxing professor at the Olympic Club. |

| Apr 30 | John Donaldson | Sacramento, CA | EX |

| Sep 3 | Robert McCord | San Francisco, CA | EX |

| Sep 3 | Jack Woolrich | San Francisco, CA | wrestling ex |

Woolrich was a young member of the juvenile class.

| Oct 8 | John Spreckles | San Francisco, CA | EX |

This was a private, friendly sparring bout, but Corbett broke his nose.

| Oct 9 | Robert McCord | Oakland, CA | EX 3 |

| Nov 7 | Jack Kitchen | San Francisco, CA | EX 3 or 4 |
| | | | Corbett better. |

| Dec 11 | A.G.D. Kerrill | San Francisco, CA | EX |

After arranging a match with Peter Jackson, on December 29, Corbett resigned his post as boxing professor.

Corbett subsequently went on a sparring tour in 1891, working with John Donaldson.

1891

Jan 15	John Donaldson	New Orleans, LA	EX

During the next few months, pursuant to a theatrical contract, Corbett and Donaldson toured around, sparring in exhibitions. They worked in New York City and Brooklyn during early February. They were in Chicago during the third week of February. Other places were probably visited.

Returning to San Francisco in late March, Corbett sparred for two months with Donaldson in preparation for the Jackson match.

Apr 19	Julian R. Brandon	Sausalito, CA	EX 4
May 21	Peter Jackson	San Francisco, CA	NC 61
			In reality a draw.
Jun 24	John L. Sullivan	San Francisco, CA	EX 3
Jul	Corbett exhibited with Joe Lannon in St. Paul, MN.		
Aug 5	Jim Hall	Chicago, IL	EX 4

Corbett better, though the exhibition was mostly friendly and short rounds were used for the first 3 rounds.

Aug 13   Corbett begins touring the country performing in the play, *After Dark*, during which he usually sparred 3 rounds with Jim Daly.

Oct 23	Billy Rocap	Philadelphia, PA	EX
Oct 23	Clarence Cramer	Philadelphia, PA	EX
Oct 25	Clarence Cramer	Philadelphia, PA	EX
Oct 25	H.W. Schlichter	Philadelphia, PA	EX
Oct 25	Lon Kitchen	Philadelphia, PA	wrestling bout Jim threw Kitchen.

Jim continues touring with *After Dark*.

Dec 26	Mike Donovan	New York, NY	EX 1
Dec 26	Bob Center	New York, NY	EX KO 1

1892

Jan 14	Jim Daly	Philadelphia, PA	EX
Jan 15	Billy Rocap	Philadelphia, PA	EX
Jan 18	Joe Donohue	Philadelphia, PA	EX KO 1
Jan 18	Jim Daly	Philadelphia, PA	EX 3
Jan 19	John McVey	Philadelphia, PA	EX 3
Jan 20	"Bubbles" Davis	Philadelphia, PA	EX 3
Jan 21	Bob Caffey	Philadelphia, PA	EX
Jan 22	Mike Donovan	Philadelphia, PA	EX
Jan 23	Bob Caffey/Caffrey	Philadelphia, PA	EX 3
Jan 23	John McVey	Philadelphia, PA	EX 3
Jan 25	Jim Daly	Boston, MA	EX 3

Corbett and Daly exhibited in Boston for about five days.

Feb 16	William Spilling(s)	New York, NY	KO 1
Feb 16	Bob Caffey/Caffrey/Coffey	New York, NY	KO 1

Feb 16	Joe Lannon	New York, NY	W 3
Mar 2	Jim Brady	Philadelphia, PA	EX (KO 2?)
Mar 3	Billy McLean	Philadelphia, PA	EX 3
Mar 4	Mike Monahan/Monaghan	Philadelphia, PA	EX KO 2
Mar 4	Jim Daly	Philadelphia, PA	EX 2

One March 12 non-local dispatch said that while in Philadelphia during the past two weeks, Corbett had also defeated Jack Langdon, Jack McVey, Sailor Brown, and a Port Richmond heavyweight, all of whom fell before him.

| Mar 21 | Jim Daly | New York, NY | EX |

In late March, Corbett and Daly sparred in New York, usually 3 rounds, concluding their engagement on April 2.

During the first week of April, Corbett and Daly gave exhibitions in places such as Hartford, Providence, New Haven, Syracuse and Buffalo.

Apr 4	Jim Daly	Providence, RI	EX 3
Apr 8	Jim Daly	Buffalo, NY	EX 3
Apr 9	Mike Donovan	New York, NY	EX 3
Apr 13	Jim Daly	Rochester, NY	EX
Apr 23	Jim Daly	Chicago, IL	EX 3

A secondary source indicates that Corbett and Daly's tour included sparring in Milwaukee, Minneapolis, Vancouver, Tacoma, and Portland, up until mid May, when they arrived and remained in San Francisco for ten days.

May 14	Manfred Olsen	San Francisco, CA	EX KO 1
May 14	Jim Daly	San Francisco, CA	EX 3
May 19	Jim Daly	San Francisco, CA	EX

The local paper said that over the next two weeks Corbett would give exhibitions in Los Angeles and San Diego, and throughout Arizona, New Mexico and Colorado, before going to Asbury Park, New Jersey, to train for the Sullivan fight. A secondary source said they also exhibited in Canton, Ohio.

Corbett and Daly sparred in New York for a week, beginning on June 6. On the 13th, they set up training quarters in Asbury Park, New Jersey, and sparred in preparation for the Sullivan fight. They exhibited on July 20 and 21 in New York. In early August, John McVey was added to the training camp.

| Aug 13 | John McVey | Trenton, NJ | EX |

Aug 19   At Asbury Park, NJ, Corbett wrestled with John McVey for 30 minutes, punched the bag, and ran some sprints.

| Aug 20 | John McVey | Newark, NJ | EX 2 - wrestling |
| Aug 20 | Jim Daly | Newark, NJ | EX 3 |

Aug 25   At Asbury Park, Corbett worked the wrist machine, pulled the weights, punched the bag, and wrestled with McVey, repeating this regimen again in the afternoon.

| Aug 26 | Jim Daly | Asbury Park, NJ | EX 3 |

Aug 28   At Loch Arbor, New Jersey, Corbett played handball, took a six-mile walk and ran back, and hit the bag for 30 minutes.

Aug 29   In New York at around noon, Jim worked at pulleys, played hand ball and punched the bag. At 2 p.m., Corbett worked the pulleys for 20 minutes, threw the 8-pound medicine ball with Delaney and Daly, and then wrestled with 220-pound McVey. Jim then played hand ball with John Lawler. Following that, he punched the bag for 20 minutes. Corbett then ran around a track for 10 minutes. That evening, Corbett sparred 3 rounds with John McVey and 3 rounds with Jim Daly.

Sep 2   In Asbury Park, in the morning, Jim hit the punching bag. In the afternoon, he spent 25 minutes on the pulley weights. He then won three games of handball. Subsequently, he wrestled 40 minutes with Daly and McVey, and then sparred McVey for over 30 minutes.

| Sep 4 | Jim Daly | Charlotte, NC | EX |

Corbett ran 1.5 miles, punched the bag for 30-40 minutes, and then wrestled and sparred Daly for an hour. Later, he ran 5 miles.

| Sep 5 | Jim Daly | Spartanburg, SC | EX |

Corbett punched the bag, wrestled and sparred with Daly, and tossed the medicine ball.

Sep 7	John L. Sullivan	New Orleans, LA	KO 21
Sep 9	Jim Daly	Birmingham, AL	EX
Sep 10	Jim Daly	Atlanta, GA	EX 3
Sep 12	Jim Daly	New York, NY	EX 3
Sep 13	Jim Daly	Baltimore, MD	EX
Sep 14	Jim Daly	Philadelphia, PA	EX 3
Sep 15	Jim Daly	Providence, RI	EX
Sep 16	Jim Daly	Boston, MA	EX
Sep 17	John L. Sullivan	New York, NY	EX 3

Corbett was scheduled to appear with Daly at Bridgeport on the 19th, Hartford on the 20th, New Haven on the 21st, Brooklyn on the 22nd, Danbury on the 23rd, and Troy on the 24th.

Sep 22	Jim Daly	Brooklyn, NY	EX 3
Sep 23	Jim Daly	Newburg, NY	EX
Sep 29	Jim Daly	Buffalo, NY	EX 3

On October 3 in New Jersey, Corbett began performing in the play *Gentleman Jack*, which over the next year toured across the country. During that play, he sparred with John Donaldson.

1893

July 3-18   Corbett exhibited at the Chicago World's Fair.

| Sep 4 | John Donaldson | New York, NY | EX |
| Nov 27 | John Donaldson | Buffalo, NY | EX 3 |

Corbett went into training in Mayport, FL for the Mitchell fight on or about December 14, sparring with John McVey, John Donaldson, Dan Creedon, Tom Tracey, and his brothers Joe and Tom Corbett.

1894

| Jan 25 | Charley Mitchell | Jacksonville, FL | KO 3 |
| Jan 27 | Dan Creedon | New York, NY | EX |

Corbett returned to performing in *Gentleman Jack*, sparring 3 or 4 rounds with John Donaldson. Places which were visited included Boston, Philadelphia, Pittsburgh, Harlem, and Washington D.C., amongst others.

| Feb 24 | Charley Mitchell | New York, NY | EX 4 |

Corbett returned to exhibiting with *Gentleman Jack*, performing in places like Cincinnati, St. Louis, Newark, Brooklyn, Louisville, and Philadelphia.

Corbett set sail for Europe on April 12, beginning to exhibit his play and spar with Donaldson there on April 21.

They exhibited in London and Paris, toured provinces of England, Ireland and Scotland. A mid-1890s Corbett biography said that he had visited London, Glasgow, Edinburgh, Liverpool, Manchester,

Birmingham, Newcastle-on-Tyne, Brighton, Southampton, Sheffield, Belfast, and Dublin. While in Paris for ten days, Corbett offered to spar French savate champion Charloment (sometimes called Charlomat) 3 rounds. Jim even said that he would allow him to kick if he wanted, but the Frenchman declined.

After setting sail on or about July 20, Corbett arrived back in America from Europe on August 1, 1894. Donaldson becomes semi-retired and Australian Steve O'Donnell takes over as Corbett's chief sparring partner.

| Sep 7 | Peter Courtney | Orange, NJ | KO 6 |

Short rounds and longer rests used, owing to the filming requirements.

Corbett returned to performing in *Gentleman Jack*.

1895

Jan 4	Steve O'Donnell	New Orleans, LA	EX 3
Jan 4	John McVey	New Orleans, LA	EX KO 1 or 3
Jan 5	John McVey	New Orleans, LA	EX

In the following months, Corbett and O'Donnell gave sparring exhibitions, usually as part of the play *Gentleman Jack*.

Jun 8	John McVey	New York, NY	EX
Jun 27	John L. Sullivan	New York, NY	EX 3
Aug 13	Jim Daly	Buffalo, NY	EX 3
Aug 13	John McVey	Buffalo, NY	EX 3
Aug 15	John McVey	Bath Beach, NY	EX 3
Aug 16	John McVey	Buffalo, NY	EX 4
Sep 30	John Donaldson	New York, NY	EX 1
Sep 30	Jim Daly	New York, NY	EX 1
Sep 30	Steve O'Donnell	New York, NY	EX 3

afternoon exhibition.

| Sep 30 | Tom Forrest | New York, NY | EX 3 |
| Sep 30 | Steve O'Donnell | New York, NY | EX 3 |

evening exhibition.

| Oct 9 | Steve O'Donnell | San Antonio, TX | EX 3 |

Corbett was in training for the Fitzsimmons fight.

Oct 18	Duncan McDonald	Little Rock, AR	EX 3
Oct 18	Jim McVey	Little Rock, AR	EX
Oct 31	Scheduled Fitzsimmons match called off.		
Nov 4	Steve O'Donnell	Memphis, TN	EX 3

Nov 11   Corbett announces his retirement and gives his title to Peter Maher, but repudiates his retirement and gift a couple months later. Maher never formally accepted the championship, saying that he felt he needed to win the title in the ring.

On Nov 25, Corbett began performing in the play, *A Naval Cadet*, touring the country.

1896

Feb   Corbett challenged Fitzsimmons after Bob defeated Peter Maher.

Mar   Corbett was sparring McVey in Cincinnati, OH, but McVey's ear was damaged and he went to the hospital on the 25th, so Mike Conley took his place.

Apr 7   In St. Louis, Corbett exhibited 3 rounds with Mike Conley as part of the last act of *A Naval Cadet*, and afterwards they were arrested. The prosecutor dismissed the charges, and the play completed its week-long engagement.

Apr 15   In Chicago, Corbett gave exhibitions with Al Smythe and/or Boyd Fraser, who wore padded armor to protect them from blows.

| Jun 24 | Tom Sharkey | San Francisco, CA | D 4 |

Referee calls all bets off.

| Jun 26 | Robert McCord | San Francisco, CA | EX |

Jim headed to New York, on his way giving exhibitions in Denver, Kansas City, and Chicago.

| Aug 6 | Billy Woods | Cripple Creek, CO | EX 4 |

On October 17, 1896, Corbett began touring again with *A Naval Cadet*, and would continue doing so until February 1897.

| Dec 14 | Jim McVey | New York, NY | EX 3 |

Corbett continued touring with his play, going from city to city, occasionally giving sparring exhibitions, usually with McVey.

1897

Corbett continued exhibiting with his play until February 6, 1897 in Kansas City, Missouri. He left there on the 7th. Jim stopped and gave a sparring exhibition with Billy Woods in Salt Lake on the 9th, before arriving back in San Francisco on the 11th.

| Feb 12 | Jim McVey | San Francisco, CA | EX |
| Feb 13 | Jim McVey | San Francisco, CA | EX |

Boxing and wrestling.

| Feb 14 | Jim McVey | San Francisco, CA | EX 3 |
| Feb 15 | Jim McVey | San Francisco, CA | EX 4 |

Feb 17   In Carson, Corbett boxed 17 minutes with Woods, wrestled with McVey for 35 minutes, and then sparred Woods again for 10 minutes. Another source said Corbett wrestled McVey 50 minutes, sparred Joe Corbett for a bit, and then sparred 15 rounds with Billy Woods.

Feb 18   Corbett boxed and wrestled Woods and McVey for over half an hour. Another source said he took turns boxing with Woods and Joe Corbett, and wrestling with McVey, for a total of one hour.

Feb 19   Jim sparred 10 minutes with Woods, wrestled and boxed with McVey, sparred with his brother Joe Corbett, and again sparred with Woods. Each session was ended when the other man said that he had enough. It was concluded after 54 minutes. Another source said Corbett worked with wrist weights, punched the bags, boxed 3-4 rounds with each sparring partner, ran and walked about 15 miles, and played handball for an hour or two.

Feb 20   Corbett sparred with Woods and McVey and played handball with Joe Corbett. McVey was given the rest of the week off. Another source said Corbett put in 52 minutes of sparring and wrestling.

Feb 21   Corbett dropped Woods in the 2nd round of their sparring.

Feb 22   Corbett played handball for 30 minutes, then boxed 4 rounds of 4 minutes each with Woods. Later, Jim hit the bag for an hour, played handball again, then boxed Joe Corbett 3 rounds, and then worked again for 10 minutes with Woods.

Feb 23   Corbett boxed with Joe Corbett and Billy Woods, and wrestled with Jim McVey. Another source said that Jim worked for 43 minutes without rest. Woods' face was getting worn out, so it was decided that he would wear protective body and head padding in the future.

Feb 24   Billy Delaney and James Jeffries arrived at the Carson camp. Corbett sparred Woods.

Feb 25   Corbett sparred Jeffries 12 minutes. Jim played handball, sparred with welterweight George Green (a.k.a. Young Corbett) for a short time, and then sparred 30 minutes with Woods. Jim also hit the punching bag and worked with the wrist machine.

Feb 26 Corbett sparred Jeffries and Woods for a half hour total, played handball, punched the bag, and worked the wrist machine.

Feb 27 Corbett allegedly dropped Jeffries and Woods in sparring. Jim also punched the bag and played handball.

Feb 28 Corbett sparred Woods and Joe Corbett for about an hour.

Mar 1 Corbett sparred 2 rounds each with Jeffries, Woods, McVey, Joe Corbett, and Bob Edgren (the California amateur champion hammer thrower and writer). Jim later played three games of handball and punched the bag for 15 minutes. One report said Jim sparred Jeffries for 3 rounds.

Mar 2 Corbett continued his daily training regimen.

Mar 3 Jim ran 12 miles instead of playing handball. No other training was done on the 3rd and 4th as Jim was visiting with his wife.

Mar 5 Jim ran about 8.5 miles, worked with the wrist machine, hit the punching bag 20 minutes, and then sparred 16 rounds without rest – alternating 1 round each in a circuit with Jeffries, Edgren, McVey, and Woods. Jim then sparred an additional round with his brother Joe.

Mar 6 Corbett worked with the wrist machine, hit the bag for 25 minutes, played a couple games of handball, and sparred with Jeffries, Woods, and McVey. In the afternoon, Jim wrestled with McVey.

Mar 7 Jim hit the bag for 20 minutes. McVey, Woods, Edgren and Jeffries sparred 3 rounds each. Two games of handball followed. Another source said Jim alternated 1 round each with Jeffries, Edgren, McVey (wrestling), and Woods, repeating the circuit four times. Handball followed. Jim worked for 2.5 hours total.

Mar 8 Jim played handball, hit the bag, and wrestled McVey. Corbett also sparred Jeffries, Woods, and Joe Corbett 4 rounds each. Another source said Jim alternated 1 round each between Jeffries, McVey (wrestling), Edgren, and Woods, repeating this four times for a total of 16 rounds.

Mar 9 Corbett climbed hills for 2.5-3 hours. In the afternoon, he hit the bags for 10–20 minutes, and also played handball and wrestled. Another source said that Jim also sparred in usual fashion with Jeffries, McVey, Edgren and Woods. One report said Corbett dropped Woods with a left swing to the jaw, and also allegedly knocked out Jeffries with a punch to the kidneys.

Mar 10 Corbett ran 3 miles, punched the bag, and worked the wrist machine. He also sparred 4 rounds each with Jeffries and Woods. He finished with 2 games of handball. Another source said Jim ran 10 miles and did the usual course of work in the afternoon that he had been doing for the past 10 days.

Mar 11 Jim jogged 8 miles, sprinting the last ¼ mile, played handball, punched the bag, and sparred. One report said Corbett sparred 3 rounds each with Jeffries, Woods, and Joe Corbett, and also wrestled with Jim McVey.

Mar 12 Corbett did 3 hours of road work, played handball, and sparred Woods and Edgren. Another report said Jim ran 10 miles, worked the wrist machine, hit the bag, played five games of handball, then wrestled 1 round with McVey, sparred 1 round each with Jeffries, Woods, Joe Corbett, and then repeated the circuit for a total of three times each, equaling 9 rounds sparring and 3 wrestling.

Mar 13 In the morning, Jim either ran 10 miles or walked 12 miles (depending on the source), worked with dumb bells and the wrist machine, punched the bag, and played three or five games of handball. In the afternoon, Jim sparred Woods, Jeffries, and Joe Corbett 4 rounds each. Another source said Jim worked with McVey (wrestling), Jeffries, Joe Corbett, and Billy Woods 4 rounds each in typical style, one round a piece and repeating the circuit four times.

Mar 14 Corbett took a 15-minute walk, worked the wrist machine 15 minutes, hit the bag for 20 minutes, and played three games of handball. One source said he boxed 1 round each with Woods, Joe Corbett, and Jeffries, and wrestled with McVey. Another said Jim wrestled with McVey for five minutes straight, then sparred 1 round each with Joe Corbett, Jeffries, and Woods and then repeated the circuit once more, each sparring partner going 2 rounds total for the day.

Mar 15 Corbett punched the bag, played handball, and sparred with Billy Woods and James Jeffries. Another said he worked with dumb bells and the wrist machine, punched the bag a little, sparred several light rounds, ran and walked a bit, then played three games of handball.

Mar 16 Jim played three games of handball and punched the bag. Another said that Corbett only played four games of handball and took a short walk.

| Mar 17 | Bob Fitzsimmons | Carson City, NV | LKO by 14 |

Corbett returned to performing in the theater with *A Naval Cadet*, and giving an occasional exhibition with McVey. Between subsequent fights, Corbett acted in plays and was part of vaudeville shows.

Significant post-championship bouts and exhibitions include:

1898

Corbett gave multiple July and August exhibitions with McVey, Tom Corbett, Tom Lansing, Steve O'Donnell and others.

| Nov 22 | Tom Sharkey | New York, NY | LDQ by 9 |

1900

Corbett sparred Gus Ruhlin in preparation for his bout with James J. Jeffries.

| May 11 | James J. Jeffries | Brooklyn, NY | LKO by 23 |
| Aug 30 | Charles "Kid" McCoy | New York, NY | KO 5 |

1902

May	Bob Fitzsimmons	New York	EX 3
Dec 9	Harry Nederlander	Detroit, MI	EX
Dec 9	Tommy Burns	Detroit, MI	EX 3

1903

Corbett sparred Yank Kenny, Sam Berger, and Tommy Ryan in preparation for the Jeffries bout.

| Aug 14 | James J. Jeffries | San Francisco, CA | LKO by 10 |

Photographic Acknowledgments

Clay Moyle, www.prizefightingbooks.com

Provided photos from:
Mike Donovan, *The Roosevelt That I Know* (New York: B.W. Dodge & Co., 1909).
Billy Edwards, *The Portrait Gallery of Pugilists of England, America, Australia* (Chicago: Athletic Publishing Co., 1894).
Richard K. Fox, *Life and Battles of John L. Sullivan Ex Champion Pugilist of the World* (New York: Richard K. Fox, 1891).

Clay is absolutely the best when it comes to old time photos and books. Be sure to check out his biographies on Billy Miske and Sam Langford.

Kevin Smith

He provided valuable advice and assistance in creating, formatting, and publishing this book. Be sure to check out Kevin's books on the history of the black prizefighter, *Black Genesis* and *The Sundowners*.

Alister Scott Ottesen

He kindly provided photos from his personal collection.

University of Iowa

Photos obtained from:
National Police Gazette
Richard K. Fox, *The Life and Battles of James J. Corbett, The Champion Pugilist of the World* (New York: Richard Fox, 1892, 1895).

Library of Congress, Prints & Photographs Division

Bibliography

Primary Sources

Arkansas Gazette (Little Rock), 1895.
Asbury Park Daily Press, 1892.
Birmingham Age-Herald, 1892.
Boston Daily Globe, 1889-1892.
Boston Herald, 1892.
Brooklyn Daily Eagle, 1890-1896.
Buffalo Courier, 1892-1895.
Buffalo Evening News, 1892-1895.
Chicago Herald, 1891-1894.
Chicago Times, 1892.
Chicago Times-Herald, 1896.
Chicago Tribune, 1891-1893.
Cincinnati Enquirer, 1894.
Cleveland Plain Dealer, 1895.
Colorado Miner (Georgetown), *1887.*
Daily Alta California, 1885-1891.
Daily Inter Ocean (Chicago), *1891.*
Daily Picayune (New Orleans), *1884-1895.*
Daily True American (New Jersey), 1891.
Denver Tribune-Republican, 1886.
Florida Times-Union, 1894.
Illustrated Sporting and Dramatic News, 1894.
Los Angeles Express, 1893-1895.
Los Angeles Times, 1907.
Morning Oregonian, 1889.
Milwaukee Evening Wisconsin, 1890.
Minneapolis Tribune, 1891-1895.
National Police Gazette (New York), *1884-1905.*
Newark Evening News, 1892-1894.
New York Clipper, 1884-1896.
New York Daily Tribune, 1892.
New York Herald, 1890-1896.
New York Sun, 1890-1896.
New York Times, 1892-1894.
Oakland Daily Evening Tribune, 1886-1887.
Oakland Enquirer, 1886.
Philadelphia Inquirer, 1891-1895.
Philadelphia Press, 1891-1894.
Philadelphia Public Ledger, 1892.

Portland Evening Telegram, 1889.
Providence Journal, 1892.
Referee (Sydney), *1887-1892.*
Rochester Union and Advertiser, 1892.
Rochester Democrat and Chronicle, 1892.
Rocky Mountain News (a.k.a. Denver Daily News), 1886-1897.
Sacramento Bee, 1890.
St. Louis Daily Globe-Democrat, 1894-1896.
St. Louis Republic, 1896.
Saint Paul and Minneapolis Pioneer Press, 1883-1895.
Salt Lake Daily Tribune, 1886.
Salt Lake Democrat, 1886.
Salt Lake Herald, 1886-1897.
San Francisco Morning Call, 1885-1890.
San Francisco Bulletin, 1896.
San Francisco Chronicle, 1885-1897.
San Francisco Daily Examiner, 1884-1896.
San Francisco Evening Post, 1885-1896.
Scranton Times, 1895.
Sydney Bulletin, 1884.
Sydney Daily Telegraph, 1886.
Times-Democrat (New Orleans), *1890-1895.*
Tucson Daily Citizen, 1890.

Additional Sources, Including Secondary Sources

William H. Adams, "New Orleans as the National Center of Boxing," *Louisiana Historical Quarterly* 39 (1956).

Australian Sporting Celebrities (Melbourne: A.H. Massina & Co., 1887).

Boxrec.com.

William Burns, *Incidents In The Life Of John L. Sullivan And Other Famous People of Fifty Years Ago,* (1928).

James J. Corbett, *The Roar of the Crowd* (N.Y.: G.P. Putnam's Sons, 1925).

James J. Corbett, *Scientific Boxing* (New York: Richard K. Fox Pub. Co., 1912).

Cyberboxingzone.com.

Mike Donovan, *The Roosevelt That I Know* (New York: B.W. Dodge & Co., 1909).

Armond Fields, *James J. Corbett: A Biography of the Heavyweight Boxing Champion and Popular Theater Headliner* (Jefferson, North Carolina: McFarland & Co., 2001).

Nat Fleischer, *Black Dynamite*, vol. 1 (N.Y.: Nat Fleischer, 1938).

Nat Fleisher, *The Heavyweight Championship* (N.Y.: G.P. Putnam's Sons, 1949, 1961).

Richard K. Fox, *The Life and Battles of James J. Corbett, The Champion Pugilist of the* World (New York: Richard Fox, 1892, 1895).

Harold Furniss, editor, *Famous Fights, Police Budget Edition*, Volume 7, No. 91 (London: Frank Shaw, publisher, 1901-1904).

The History of the Olympic Club (San Francisco: Art Publishing Co., 1893).

The Inflation Calculator, http://www.westegg.com/inflation.

Michael T. Isenberg, *John L. Sullivan and His America* (Chicago: University of Illinois Press, 1988).

Alexander Johnston, *Ten and Out!* (N.Y.: Ives Washburn, 1927).

Rex Lardner, *The Legendary Champions* (N.Y.: American Heritage Press, 1972).

Patrick Myler, *Gentleman Jim Corbett: The Truth Behind a Boxing Legend* (Great Britain: Robson Books Ltd., 1998).

Adam J. Pollack, *John L. Sullivan: The Career of the First Gloved Heavyweight Champion* (North Carolina: McFarland & Co., 2006).

John L. Sullivan, *I can lick any sonofabitch in the house!* (Carson City: Proteus Publishing Co., 1979), a reprint of the 1892 autobiography by Sullivan called *Life and Reminiscences of a Nineteenth Century Gladiator*.

Joseph R. Svinth, *Kronos: A Chronological History of the Martial Arts and Combative Sports* (Canada: National Library of Canada, 2004).

USA Boxing rulebook, U.S. Men's Champions.

Samuel H. Williamson, "What is the Relative Value?" Economic History Services, June 2005, http://www.eh.net/hmit/compare.

Acknowledgments

Randy Essing

Kevin Smith

Clay Moyle

The three of you deserve especially special thanks. Randy, Kevin, and Clay, without you, this book would not have been of the quality that it is. Your dedication, passion, and selflessness are inspiring.

Special thanks also to all those who have been wonderful in their assistance in researching, creating, reviewing and advertising this book, as well as the Sullivan biography:

Cheryl Huyck
Christine Klein
Emily Klinefelter
Alister Scott Ottesen
Pamela Barta-Kacena
Tracy Callis
Stephen Gordon
Todd Hodgson
Zachary Q. Daniels
Michael DeLisa
Armond Fields
Patrick Myler
Craig Davidson
David Goodner
Ron Marshall
Michael Hunnicutt
H.E. Grant
Thomas Gerbasi
Marty Mulcahey
Dan Cuoco
Tom Welsh
Jason Simmons
Matt McGrain
Barry Pollack
France Pollack
Prizefightingbooks.com
Cyberboxingzone.com

Boxrec.com
Boxing Digest
Eastsideboxing.com
Boxingscene.com
Our-ireland.com
Kocorner.com
Hotboxingnews.com
Womenboxing.com
Pugilistica.com
Ringsidereport.com
Boxinginsider.com
Thesweetscience.com
Saddoboxing.com
Doghouseboxing.com
Irishedition.com
Pugilibri
Antekprizering.com
Iowa City Press Citizen
Prairie Lights bookstore
The University of Iowa Interlibrary Loan Services
The University of Iowa Media Services
The University of Southern California

And all those who purchased this book or any of the others in my series.

Thank you.

Index

Ryan, Jim, 245

Ryan, Paddy, 37, 54, 59, 84, 101, 179, 195, 196

Ryan, Tommy, 37, 38, 54, 59, 84, 101, 179, 195, 196, 240, 245

Sailor Brown, 193, 341

Sandow, 289

Schlichter, H.W., 179, 340

Sharkey, Tom, 305-330, 333-335, 344, 346

Slade, Herbert, 35

Slavin, Bill, 92

Slavin, Frank, 43, 92, 124, 129-132, 139, 169, 171, 173, 176, 178, 179, 183, 193, 199, 200, 223, 241, 242, 246, 263, 327

Slosson/Slossen, E.G., 24, 25, 337

Smith, Billy, 92, 93, 95, 139, 305, 334, 339

Smith, Ed, 93, 114, 127, 129, 242, 259, 263, 268, 269, 327

Smith, Frank, 29, 31, 89, 93, 337

Smith, J.B., 90, 339

Smith, Jem, 102, 127, 130, 167, 199

Smythe, Al, 305, 344

Soto, Joe, 56

Spilling, William, 183, 184, 340

Spreckles, John, 123, 339

Starlight, 92, 172, 245

Stuart, Dan, 296, 297, 301, 302, 308

Sullivan, John L., 4, 6, 7, 8, 10, 13, 14, 17, 20, 23, 31, 35, 37-40, 44, 45, 50-52, 54, 57, 59, 62, 84, 85, 86, 88, 90, 91, 93, 97, 99-102, 107-109, 111-114, 118-122, 125, 127, 129, 130-132, 134, 135, 137, 141, 144, 163, 165, 167, 169-173, 176, 178-180, 183, 186-195, 197-232, 234-238, 240-242, 245-247, 249, 251, 255, 256, 258, 263, 268, 269, 271, 282, 284, 285, 287, 289, 291, 293, 296, 302, 303, 308, 309, 318, 319, 322, 323, 329, 331-335, 340-343, 347, 349-351, 365

Sullivan, Owen, 127, 172, 176

Taylor, Steve, 63, 88

Taylor, Tom, 63, 88

Tracey, Tom, 245, 342

Ungerman, Gus, 17

Van Court, De Witt, 16, 62

Van Court, Eugene, 17

Vanquelin, Felix, 102

Walcott, Joe, 264

Warner, Jack, 272

Warren, Tommy, 161

Watson, Walter, 15, 16, 18, 21, 26, 48, 51, 247, 336, 337, 338

Welch, William, 17, 28, 337

Williams, Jim, 309

Wilson, Billy, 113

Wittman, Captain, 314, 318, 322

Woods, Billy, 324, 328, 329, 344, 345

Woolrich, Jack, 123, 339

Young Corbett, 310, 329, 344

Adam J. Pollack is a staff writer for Cyberboxingzone.com, a member of the Boxing Writers Association of America, and an attorney practicing law in Iowa City, Iowa. Adam was a guest lecturer on the career of John L. Sullivan for the Whitehall lecture series at the Flagler Museum in Palm Beach, Florida, and also an interviewee in the documentary film on James J. Corbett, *The Gentleman Prizefighter*.

Books by Adam J. Pollack

John L. Sullivan: The Career of the First Gloved Heavyweight Champion

In the Ring With James J. Corbett

In the Ring With Bob Fitzsimmons

In the Ring With James J. Jeffries

In the Ring With Marvin Hart

In the Ring With Tommy Burns

Check them out at amazon.com, winbykopublications.com, or other online dealers.

Printed in the USA
CPSIA information can be obtained
at www.ICGtesting.com
LVHW041726170124
769199LV00002B/5